Revolutionizing Network Management: The Journey to AI-native Autonomy

RIVER PUBLISHERS SERIES IN COMMUNICATIONS AND NETWORKING

The "River Publishers Series in Communications and Networking" is a series of comprehensive academic and professional books which focus on communication and network systems. Topics range from the theory and use of systems involving all terminals, computers, and information processors to wired and wireless networks and network layouts, protocols, architectures, and implementations. Also covered are developments stemming from new market demands in systems, products, and technologies such as personal communications services, multimedia systems, enterprise networks, and optical communications.

The series includes research monographs, edited volumes, handbooks and textbooks, providing professionals, researchers, educators, and advanced students in the field with an invaluable insight into the latest research and developments.

Topics included in this series include:-

- Communication theory
- Multimedia systems
- Network architecture
- Optical communications
- Personal communication services
- Telecoms networks
- Wi-Fi network protocols

For a list of other books in this series, visit www.riverpublishers.com

Revolutionizing Network Management: The Journey to AI-native Autonomy

Csaba Vulkán
Nokia Bell Labs, Budapest

Péter Szilágyi
Nokia Bell Labs, Budapest

Nurit Sprecher
Nokia, Israel

River Publishers

Routledge
Taylor & Francis Group
NEW YORK AND LONDON

Published 2025 by River Publishers
River Publishers
Broagervej 10, 9260 Gistrup, Denmark
www.riverpublishers.com

Distributed exclusively by Routledge
605 Third Avenue, New York, NY 10017, USA
4 Park Square, Milton Park, Abingdon, Oxon OX14 4RN

Revolutionizing Network Management: The Journey to AI-native Autonomy / Csaba Vulkán, Péter Szilágyi, and Nurit Sprecher.

Routledge is an imprint of the Taylor & Francis Group, an informa business

ISBN 978-87-7022-863-3 (hardback)
ISBN 978-87-4380-789-6 (paperback)
ISBN 978-87-7004-117-1 (online)
ISBN 978-8-770-04147-8 (ebook master)
DOI: 10.1201/9788770041478

Contents

Preface **ix**

List of Figures **xiii**

List of Tables **xxi**

List of Abbreviations **xxiii**

1 Trends and Catalysts **1**
1.1 Introduction 1
1.2 Requirements of Automation in Mobile Networks 2
1.3 Wireless Communication Trends 7
1.4 Formative Megatrends. 10
1.5 Network and Service Management Evolution. 15
1.6 Summary 21
Bibliography. 22

2 Technology, Industry, and Standardization Landscape **27**
2.1 Introduction 27
2.2 Technology Enablers and Industry Landscape 29
2.3 Standardization Framework 34
2.4 Summary 42
Bibliography. 43

3 Data and Knowledge Management **45**
3.1 Introduction 45
3.2 General Concepts 47
3.3 Architecture Reference Model 48
3.4 Functional Components 51
3.4.1 Data collection and coordination function 51
3.4.2 Adaptors 52
3.4.3 Data forwarder. 52
3.4.4 Data descriptors 53

3.5 Deployment Options. 54
3.5.1 Chaining of data sources and data consumers. 54
3.5.2 Data lake integration. 55
3.5.3 Data anonymization 56
3.6 Data Collection in Machine Learning Pipelines. 62
3.6.1 Requirements of data collection in ML pipelines . . . 62
3.6.2 Data management reference architecture capabilities. 66
3.6.3 Self-measurement implementation and message flow 67
3.7 Summary 70
Bibliography. 71

4 Security, Trust, and Integrity **73**
4.1 Introduction 73
4.2 Element of Data and Model Security 74
4.3 Data Security and Truthfulness 77
4.4 Security and Trust Impact of the AI Technology 78
4.5 Trust in Machine Learning as a Service Deployments 82
4.6 Summary 92
Bibliography. 93

5 Native AI/ML and the Related Management Aspects **95**
5.1 Introduction 95
5.2 AI Native Networks 97
5.3 Management Aspects of AI 99
5.4 AI Model Embedding and Monitoring 99
5.5 Management of Federated Learning. 105
5.5.1 Model set management to protect against adversary attacks 107
5.5.2 Model integrity protection. 115
5.5.3 Local data protection 125
5.6 Summary 132
Bibliography. 133

6 Intent-based Network Management **135**
6.1 Introduction 135
6.2 Intent-based Network Automation 138
6.3 Dynamic Composition of Network Management Capabilities 142

6.4 Intent-based Network Management Architecture 145
6.5 AI Models for Intent-based Network Management 148
6.6 Summary 151
Bibliography 152

7 Closed Loop Automation **155**
7.1 Introduction 155
7.2 Closed Loops for Intent-based Network Management 157
7.3 Self-learning and Closed Loops 159
7.4 Benefits of Intent-based Closed-loop Management Automation 165
7.5 Summary 168
Bibliography 169

8 Human–Machine Interactions and Interfaces **171**
8.1 Introduction 171
8.2 Intent-based Human–Network Interactions 172
8.3 Network Application Embedding 175
8.4 Machine–Machine Interactions 181
8.5 Coexistence of Automatic and Manual Control 182
8.6 Summary 190
Bibliography 191

9 Intent Interface Evolution and the Role of Language Models **193**
9.1 Introduction 193
9.2 The Utility of Natural Language in the Intent Interface 194
9.3 The Role of LLMs for the Intent Interface 201
9.4 Summary 204
Bibliography 204

10 State Models **207**
10.1 Introduction 207
10.2 Comprehension of State Models 210
10.3 Network State Models for Anomaly Detection 212
10.4 State Modeling Techniques 214
10.4.1 Numerical state models 214
10.4.2 State models for log analytics 215
10.4.3 Self-annotating network states 218
10.5 Summary 219
Bibliography 220

11 Semantic Models and Semantic Composition **221**
11.1 Introduction 221
11.2 Full API Models: Syntax and Semantic 223
11.3 Semantic Composition of Software Modules 228
11.4 Mapping Natural Language Intents to Network Capabilities 236
11.5 Composition of Closed Loops for Autonomous Services . . 239
11.6 Summary 240
Bibliography 241

12 Decision Models **243**
12.1 Introduction 243
12.2 Automated Decisions Within Closed Loops 245
12.2.1 Active measurements 248
12.2.2 Consideration of environmental context 251
12.3 Conflict Resolution Across Closed Loops 259
12.3.1 Detection of conflicting intents 260
12.3.2 Conflict detection of quality of experience intents . 264
12.4 Summary 271
Bibliography 272

13 Network Digital Twin **275**
13.1 Introduction 275
13.2 Use Cases 280
13.2.1 NDT for network management 281
13.2.2 NDT for security 283
13.3 NDT Architecture 289
13.3.1 Service-based deployment architecture 293
13.4 Modeling and Composition 299
13.4.1 Composition and contextualization 304
13.4.2 Intent-based semantic NDT composition 306
13.5 Enterprise 310
13.6 Summary 313
Bibliography 315

14 Summary and Outlook **317**
Bibliography 318

Index **321**

About the Authors **323**

Preface

5G and 6G networks are expected to provide virtually-unlimited-gigabit and ultrareliable connections to people and objects, when and where it matters, supporting diverse use cases with an extremely demanding range of requirements (in terms of latency, throughput, reliability, coverage, and security, cost targets, etc.). However, building a network that supports a diverse set of new services, all of which can be set up, dynamically reconfigured, scaled, and torn down at a moment's notice, introduces several challenges.

The network's performance, coverage, and capacity should be constantly assured to satisfy the requirements of the active services. Any fault or degradation that might adversely impact the services should be resolved. Furthermore, unprecedented operational agility is required to allow services to be rapidly deployed, dynamically adapted, and continuously and seamlessly assured – similar to the way in which cloud providers offer on-demand, managed cloud services.

Each and every service spans multiple technological domains and is composed of cloud resources, connectivity, virtual and physical network functions, augmenting services, and application logic. The network includes hundreds of thousands of network functions and each function has multiple versions. In addition, 5G and 6G run on a virtualized infrastructure and are designed with a fully programmable approach to software and microservices, capable of supporting diverse use cases. This makes the network exponentially more complex to operate and manage. When we add distributed clouds, heterogenous networks, the 10X densification of RAN sites, meshing, and integrated multisupplier technologies to the mix, we introduce even more complexity, driving up the timescale and cost.

The accelerated worldwide deployment of 5G networks drives a radical change in the way networks and services are created, orchestrated, and managed. Evolving toward zero-touch and full end-to-end network and service automation have become an urgent necessity to manage this complexity and deliver services with agility and speed while adapting, assuring, and ensuring the economic sustainability of the highly diverse service portfolio. The ultimate target is to achieve the highest degree of automation while enabling fully autonomous operations driven by high-level business goals and policies. The autonomous networks will be able to self-manage and self-organize (configuration, healing, assurance, optimization, etc.) without human intervention beyond the initial transition of the business intents.

Realizing this vision requires a novel end-to-end architecture framework and enablers designed for self-management, near-real-time closed-loop automation, and optimized for data-driven analytics. Advanced machine learning (ML) algorithms and artificial intelligence (AI) will be essential tools to deal with the complexity and the diverse services.

End-to-end automation is a challenging objective and represents the industry's collective target for the technology evolution in years to come. The key components for increasing automation include the expression, as well as the translation, of high-level abstract business goals (e.g., intents) into efficient and impactful actions, deployment and interaction with closed loops, real-time data collection, extraction of meaningful insights from data, analytics and intelligence, and orchestration and resource control.

The practical implementation of an intent-based network requires substantial automation technology embedded in the network. The translation of the intent into efficient and impactful actions in each context requires self-evaluation and self-measurement capabilities. Many of these aspects still require further research work, learning, and sharing of best practices and guidelines in applying them in operational service providers' environments.

Autonomous networks rely on analytics and intelligence to learn, reason, produce causality analysis, predict, etc. The networks should be able to execute even in conditions of uncertainty and lack of knowledge or in cases of aleatory (randomness/variability). Analytics can learn from collected information, identify patterns, and generate models for various optimization and classification tasks. AI technologies may be used to empower the automation processes. While AI technologies are developing and expanding fast, some gaps must be overcome to fully leverage their potential.

AI and ML in service providers' networking are still in the early days. We only start to see how AI/ML can be usefully applied. Currently, AI-based solutions are driven by use cases and work in isolation, with limited systematic reuse. The view and use of the AI potential are limited, mainly with ML and deep learning at the descriptive and explanatory levels. AI is still resource-hungry and works on big dump data. The integration of AI in network and service automation still requires significant human involvement in all steps of the AI development and operation processes.

Automation is not only about technology. It requires changes in the processes and the mindset of people. Trust is a key barrier for adoption and building it will be a continuous learning process; as more automation and AI-empowered closed control loops are deployed and start to operate safely/efficiently, human trust will increase and the requirement for a level of supervision/visibility will diminish. The purpose is to apply transparent, reliable, and robust automation. To increase the comfort level of the human in automation, a level of supervision and transparency is needed. The ability to explain and trace the machine's decision-making process and the reasoning behind the decisions are key in supporting it.

The use of AI in network and service automation will evolve incrementally to the ultimate goals of realizing zero-touch intuitive AI and autonomous operations, leveraging machine reasoning and symbiotic human–AI interaction.

This book explores the megatrends and wireless evolution jointly influencing the development of network and management technologies. Chapters 1 and 2 will provide an overview of the technology, industrial, and standardization landscape to understand the need for automation, their technical means, and the main standard definition organizations producing relevant studies, reports, and normative specifications. Next, each of Chapters 3–13 provides a deeper view into one of the key technology enablers of network management automation and network autonomy, starting from fundamental and established ones, and building toward increasingly specialized and advanced topics. Chapter 14 provides a summary of the book and an outlook on the technology trends shaping the future of telecommunication systems.

List of Figures

Figure 1.1	Illustration of robot control use cases requiring time-sensitive communication.	5
Figure 1.2	Key cellular and Wi-Fi functionalities and expansion to adjacent areas.	9
Figure 1.3	Simplified network and service lifecycle model. . . .	16
Figure 1.4	Management domains and scopes from an e2e service perspective.	17
Figure 1.5	3GPP standard network and service management hierarchy.	17
Figure 1.6	The spiral of complexity in networks.	19
Figure 1.7	Open loop and closed loop automation.	20
Figure 1.8	Zero-touch network and service management.	21
Figure 2.1	Influence and adoption of technology across industries (time scale is not proportionate)..	30
Figure 2.2	A pyramid of technical enablers of autonomy in network and service management.	31
Figure 2.3	Standardization categories and key technical themes of the book.	33
Figure 2.4	Overview of the 3GPP standardization process. . . .	35
Figure 2.5	3GPP service-based management architecture.. . . .	36
Figure 2.6	Reference architecture of the ZSM e2e management framework. Reproduced from [10]..	37
Figure 2.7	Standardization of network data, exposure, and control enablers..	39
Figure 2.8	Standardization landscape of security and trust in the context of AI.	40
Figure 2.9	Standardization initiatives in native AI and automation.	41
Figure 2.10	Network digital twin standardization..	42
Figure 3.1	Full architecture decomposition of the data management reference architecture.	49
Figure 3.2	Chaining of data sources and data consumers.	55

Figure 3.3 Integration of the data management framework with data lakes. 56
Figure 3.4 Data anonymization, the first example. Illustration of two example requests, each with a request for the location of a specific UE, with a required anonymity of K = 5. Note that the returned area is not centered around the specific UE, making it impossible to infer the exact location of the requested UE. 57
Figure 3.5 Data anonymization, the second example. Illustration of a second example, requesting data of UEs from a given area with a deadline T, with required anonymity of K = 5. At the expiration of the deadline, there are still too few UE observations in the originally requested area, therefore the method minimally enlarges the area to be able to return data of K = 5 UEs. 58
Figure 3.6 The anonymization function in the context of the DMF. Blue arrows represent control messages, black bold lines show the actual data transfer. 59
Figure 3.7 Message sequence diagram showing the interactions with the anonymization function. 59
Figure 3.8 Flowchart of the steps of the anonymization method for a specific UE. 60
Figure 3.9 Flowchart of the steps of the anonymization method for multiple UEs. 61
Figure 3.10 Illustration of the multiflow data path optimization on a dynamic graph. 64
Figure 3.11 The self-measuring and optimization capabilities of the data management reference architecture. 67
Figure 3.12 Data request procedure extended with latency requirement on the transfer of data from data source to data consumer. 68
Figure 3.13 Measuring the latency and volume of data transfer from a data source to a data consumer. 69
Figure 3.14 Expose measurements to 3rd party orchestrators. . . 70
Figure 4.1 Zero trust e2e data security. 76
Figure 4.2 Data chunks in AI/ML operation. 77
Figure 4.3 MLaaS scenario, with multiple ML models in the MLaaS provider. 83

Figure 4.4 ML model certification, showing the MLCS and the roles of the interfaces.. 85
Figure 4.5 Benchmarking the MLP's ML model accuracy. . . . 86
Figure 4.6 Accuracy verification of an MLP's model M on an MLC's own data. 87
Figure 4.7 MLCS providing data and service proxy to the MLC. 91
Figure 5.1 AI native systems – a conceptual illustration. 98
Figure 5.2 AI native environment from the perspective of an AI/ML model. 98
Figure 5.3 Management tasks in AI native networks. 100
Figure 5.4 AI model embedding.. 101
Figure 5.5 The differences between SW modules with embedded AI and exposed AI. 102
Figure 5.6 Key integration points for SW modules with exposed AI (supervised/self-supervised model).. 104
Figure 5.7 Key integration points for SW modules with exposed AI (reinforcement learning). 105
Figure 5.8 The concept of federated learning. 106
Figure 5.9 The impact of adversarial local trainers in federated learning.. 108
Figure 5.10 Multiple models produced by the central trainer.. . . 109
Figure 5.11 The key functionality performed by thc central trained to create a model set. 110
Figure 5.12 Logical steps taken by the user of the model set to identify if an input data sample causes the models' output to separate along the division of mapping distributed trainers to models.. 113
Figure 5.13 Communication during model set management. . . . 115
Figure 5.14 Deployment options for integrating the general model set management mechanism into standard telecom architectures. 116
Figure 5.15 Model identity verification.. 117
Figure 5.16 Detailed steps for the basic proof (black-box ML model scenario).. 119
Figure 5.17 Detailed steps for the extended proof (white-box ML model scenario).. 121
Figure 5.18 Basic proof method complemented with input data verification. 123
Figure 5.19 MEE set interaction procedure.. 125

Figure 5.20 The problem of leaking local information through gradient updates. 126
Figure 5.21 Illustration of the three federated learning method modifications. 128
Figure 5.22 Steps of the selective gradient sharing. 129
Figure 5.23 Steps of the mixture of sensitive and nonsensitive data. 130
Figure 5.24 Steps of the local data transformation. 130
Figure 5.25 A combination of all three federated learning modifications. 131
Figure 5.26 The inference performed by the distributed trainer. . 132
Figure 6.1 Automation scope: Application, business/service, and networking. 139
Figure 6.2 High-level categorization of intents. 140
Figure 6.3 Illustration of the composition principle. 144
Figure 6.4 Functional architecture of intent-based network management. 145
Figure 6.5 Intent-based network management workflow. 146
Figure 6.6 AI models in an intent-driven closed loop. 149
Figure 6.7 AI models for intent-based network management. . . 151
Figure 7.1 General functional model of network management automation closed loops. 157
Figure 7.2 Main closed loops that build and exercise the capability of network management to dynamically handle intents.. 158
Figure 7.3 Example: the impact and efficiency of an automated action executed by a self-learning CL. 161
Figure 7.4 Micro-service-based self-learning CL decomposition. 162
Figure 7.5 Pairing of a measurement micro-service with an automation logic micro-service based on micro-service metadata. 164
Figure 7.6 Self-learning CL representation for deployment.. . . 165
Figure 7.7 Steps taken by the intent management entity during the deployment of a self-learning CL. 166
Figure 7.8 The benefits of intent-based network management. . 167
Figure 8.1 Summary of requirements for intent-driven H2M/M2H interfaces.. 174
Figure 8.2 Taxonomy of applications. 176
Figure 8.3 Definition and scope of network application embedding. 177

Figure 8.4 General network application embedding functional architecture. 178
Figure 8.5 Stage 1 – access to vendor and operator APIs. 179
Figure 8.6 Stage 2 – access to other NwApp APIs. 179
Figure 8.7 Stage 3 – orchestration of NwApps. 180
Figure 8.8 Stage 4 – NwApps used by the network functions and services. 180
Figure 8.9 Process to identify control interfaces that require manual control. 186
Figure 8.10 Control matrix data structure maintaining tristate control digit associations between any CL control instance and any controllable API, including the APIs of the CLs themselves. 187
Figure 8.11 Detection of potential conflict between CLs that control the same API. 188
Figure 8.12 Maintain the control matrix upon deploying a new CL. 189
Figure 9.1 Interaction with technology: digitalization, automation, and consumability.. 194
Figure 9.2 Expert knowledge and human-to-human expert interactions. 196
Figure 9.3 Delegation and automation of the methodological part of the human thought process. 197
Figure 9.4 Emulation of the expert knowledge. 198
Figure 9.5 Intent definition: dialogue using natural language. . . 199
Figure 9.6 NLP-based intent definition process: from objectives to intents. 201
Figure 9.7 Intent interface evolution: from NLP-based intent H2M to LLM-based M2H. 203
Figure 10.1 Network state modeling. 208
Figure 10.2 Network state models in a network and service management closed loop.. 209
Figure 10.3 Manual or semimanual annotation of network states. 211
Figure 10.4 Network state model capabilities leveraged by anomaly detection. 213
Figure 10.5 Log modeling with separate semantic (text) and numeric branches combined at the final modeling step to leverage the full content of log entries. 217
Figure 10.6 Artistic view of the output of a self-annotation state model.. 219

Figure 11.1 Intent-driven functional semantic closed loop composition. 223
Figure 11.2 Full API model with syntactical and semantical parts. 224
Figure 11.3 Software module discovery and API modeling. . . . 227
Figure 11.4 Graphical representation of the semantic API model of a method.. 231
Figure 11.5 Steps of the full method graph discovery and assembly (D&A) method.. 232
Figure 11.6 The key components and interactions of the intent-based semantic closed loop composition mechanism. 234
Figure 11.7 Identification and deployment of the SW modules required to fulfill an intent. 235
Figure 11.8 Semantic model of intent sharing the same latent vector space with the semantic API models. 237
Figure 11.9 Illustration of the module super-graph representing potential module interconnections, and a highlighted subgraph corresponding to a specific intent. 238
Figure 11.10 Dynamic semantic composition of intent-based made-to-order closed loops. 240
Figure 12.1 Illustration of the concept of considering the latency of actions in CL analytics and decision making. . . . 246
Figure 12.2 Self-evaluating and self-learning CL operation. . . . 247
Figure 12.3 Dynamic interaction with data sources.. 249
Figure 12.4 Closed loop with multiple analytics models, each requiring different (potentially overlapping) set of input data.. 250
Figure 12.5 Procedure flow for triggering active measurements from a closed loop. 250
Figure 12.6 Example of a datacenter cooling solution. 252
Figure 12.7 An example architecture integrating cooling awareness into a 3GPP system – cooling specific interfaces and capabilities are in shown red. 254
Figure 12.8 Procedures for cooling-aware orchestration. 256
Figure 12.9 The inputs and the outputs of the method, with example intent target database, state model, and measurement value relationships depicted as a graph. 261
Figure 12.10 The principal functional steps of the method. 261

Figure 12.11 The functional steps of the proposed method. 263
Figure 12.12 The interfaces used by the IM. 265
Figure 12.13 The main functionality of the IM. 266
Figure 12.14 The main functionality of the QM. 268
Figure 12.15 Resource pool info sent by the DCtrl/RC/NF to the QM. 268
Figure 12.16 S ervice to resource pool mapping. 269
Figure 12.17 Mapping to the O-RAN architecture.. 270
Figure 13.1 Digital twins are the key building blocks of the metaverse.. 276
Figure 13.2 NDT physical-virtual synchronization patterns. . . . 279
Figure 13.3 NDTs for open loops and closed loops.. 279
Figure 13.4 NDT use cases for network management automation. 282
Figure 13.5 The architecture using NDT-FNs to capture all user interactions on behalf of the twinned network components.. 285
Figure 13.6 System level integration of the NDT fake node concept. 287
Figure 13.7 Programmable network components leveraged by NDTs.. 290
Figure 13.8 Network management automation with network digital twin. 291
Figure 13.9 Network digital twin general architecture. 292
Figure 13.10 The different types of NDTs in the proposed taxonomy and their integration with the network, with each other and with external DTs.. 295
Figure 13.11 Exposure of multiple NDT-(M/C/U) services to external DTs via the NDT service layer. 299
Figure 13.12 Sources of NDT complexity. 300
Figure 13.13 Example modeling taxonomy for NDTs.. 301
Figure 13.14 Illustration of reusing data collection and models for building different NDTs. 303
Figure 13.15 Model reusability for efficient NDT engineering. . . 304
Figure 13.16 Composition and contextualization. 306
Figure 13.17 Composition and runtime contextualization within the NDT architecture.. 307
Figure 13.19 Intent-based NDT composition method (compose to create an NDT).. 308
Figure 13.18 Intent-based NDT composition architecture.. 308

Figure 13.20 Intent-based NDT composition method (compose by reusing an NDT). 309
Figure 13.21 Distributed deployment of an NDT composition. 310
Figure 13.22 System view: network of DTs and NDTs. 311
Figure 13.23 Interworking of NDT and DT. 313
Figure 13.24 NDT composition for enterprise DTs. 314

List of Tables

Table 1.1 Key attributes of the personal and commercial wireless use cases. 8

Table 4.1 Overview of attack on predictive AI. 80

Table 4.2 Comparison between engineering with traditional software versus AI. 82

Table 5.1 First example mapping of distributed trainers to model instances (x at a cell D_iM_j, i = 1, .., N, j = 1, .., N indicates that gradients from D_i are incorporated to model M_j). The mapping causes each model instance to be free of the gradients of two distributed trainers. 112

Table 5.2 Second example mapping of distributed trainers to model instances (x at a cell D_iM_j, i = 1, ..., N, j = 1, ..., N indicates that gradients from D_i are incorporated to model M_j). The mapping causes each model instance to be free of the gradients of three distributed trainers. 112

List of Abbreviations

3CA	3rd party consumer adaptor
3GPP	3rd generation partnership project
3PA	3rd party producer adaptor
5G-ACIA	5G Alliance for connected industries and automation
ACK	Acknowledgement
AGV	Autonomous guided vehicle
AI	Artificial intelligence
ANR	Automatic neighbor relations
AP	Access point
API	Application programming interface
APIC	API that is consumed
APIP	API that is provided
AQM	Active queue management
AR	Augmented reality
BBF	Broadband forum
BSS	Business support system
BW	Bandwidth
CD	Continuous development
CI	Continuous integration
CL	Closed loop
CLA	Closed-loop automation
CM	Configuration management
CN	Core network
CNF	Cloud-native functions
CPU	Central processing unit
CSP	Communication service provider
CU	Central unit
CWND	Congestion window
D&A	Discovery and assembly
DBSCAN	Density-based spatial clustering of applications with noise
DC	Data center
DCtrl	Domain controller

DCA	Data collector and adaptor
DCCF	Data collector coordination function
DF	Data forwarder
DL	Downlink
DMRA	Data management reference architecture
DNS	Domain name service
DPA	Data publisher and adaptor
DS	Data source
DSRC	Dedicated short range communication
DT	Digital twin
DU	Distributed unit
E2E	End-to-end
eNB	Evolved node B
ETSI	European Telecommunications Standards Institute
FM	Fault management
GAN	Generative adversarial network
GBR	Guaranteed bit rate
gNB	5G node B
GNG	Growing neural gas
GPU	Graphical processing unit
GSM	GSM Association
GSM	Global system for mobile communications
H2M	Human to machine
HE	Header enrichment
HTTP	Hyper-text transfer protocol
HTTPS	Hyper-text transfer protocol secure
HW	Hardware
I/O	Input/output
IEEE	Institute of Electrical and Electronics Engineers
IETF	Internet Engineering Task Force
IM	Intent manager
IME	Intent management entity
IMT	International Mobile Telecommunications
IP	Internet protocol
IRTF	Internet Research Task Force
ISM	Industrial, scientific, medical
IT	Information technology
ITDB	Intent target database
ITU	International Telecommunication Union
KPI	Key performance indicator

KVI	Key value indicators
LLM	Large language model
LTE	Long term evolution
M2H	Machine to human
M2M	Machine to machine
MaaS	Model as a service
MAC	Media access control
MAPE-K	Monitor-analyze-plan-execute with knowledge
MBH	Mobile backhaul
MEC	Multiaccess edge computing
MEE	Model execution entity
ML	Machine learning
MLaaS	Machine learning as a service
MLB	Mobility load balancing
MLC	Machine learning as a service consumer
MLCS	Machine learning certification server
MLP	Machine learning as a service provider
MLVS	Machine learning certification server
MnS	Management services
MRO	Mobility robustness optimization
MSE	Model supervisor entity
MSS	Maximum segment size
NACK	Negative acknowledgment
NDT	Network digital twin
NE	Network element
NEF	Network exposure function
NF	Network function
NFV	Network function virtualization
NLP	Natural language processing
NR	New radio
NWDAF	Network data analytics function
OAM	Operations, administration, and maintenance
OFDMA	Orthogonal frequency division multiple access
OODA	Observe-orient-decide-act
O-RAN	Open radio access network alliance
OSS	Operations support system
OT	Operational technology
OTT	Over-the-top
PCC	Policy and charging control
PDU	Protocol data unit

PKI	Public key infrastructure
PM	Performance management
PNF	Physical network function
QCI	Quality class indicator
QM	QoE manager
QoE	Quality of experience
QoS	Quality of service
QUIC	Quick user datagram protocol internet connections
RAA	Radio analytics application
RAM	Random access memory
RAN	Radio access network
RC	Resource controller
ReLU	Rectified linear unit
REST	Representational state transfer
RIC	Ran intelligent controller
RRM	Radio resource management
RTO	Retransmission timeout
RTT	Round-trip time
SBA	Service-based architecture
SBMA	Service-based management architecture
SDN	Software defined network
SDO	Standard definition organizations
SLA	Service level agreement
SMCD	State model-based conflict detection
SMO	Service management and orchestration
SON	Self-organizing network
SW	Software
TCO	Total cost of ownership
TCP	Transmission control protocol
TG	Throughput guidance
TLS	Transport layer security
TMF	TM forum
TSC	Time-sensitive communication
TWT	Target wake time
UDP	User datagram protocol
UE	User equipment
UL	Uplink
URL	Uniform resource locator
V2X	Vehicle to everything
VM	Virtual machine

VNF	Virtual network function
VR	Virtual reality
WAP	Wireless application protocol
WFQ	Weighted fair queuing
ZSM	Zero touch network and service management

1

Trends and Catalysts

The first generation of digital cellular mobile networks was designed to support voice communication on the move at large nationwide commercial scales. Since then, the technology and system architecture of mobile networks have evolved along the developing requirements toward increasingly diverse services including packet based data services, low latency communications, high speed mobility, private networks, and many more. The requirements and the corresponding technological advances partly originate from trends within the wireless industry itself (including both cellular and other technologies) and partly from megatrends started by adjacent verticals (industry, digital twins, enterprise automation) or by innovations at a global scale (metaverse, cloud, AI). The technical evolution of the mobile networks has not only impacted the services but also the operational workflows and experience of the communication service providers. The most influential factor has been the gradual adoption of automation technologies (up to and including native AI) and the resulting increase of network autonomy. The integration of such technologies into network and service management have created not only new capabilities but also additional complexity that needs to be handled by the technology itself.

1.1 Introduction

The current fifth generation of mobile cellular networks and the corresponding network and service management techniques are products of evolution along several technological paths, some of which have spanned multiple decades. The evolution is influenced by many factors. On the one hand, systematic evolution within the telecommunication industry has defined increasingly ambitious functional and nonfunctional requirements for mobile systems to cope with the growing traffic demand of end users and applications. Each network generation had to fulfill the design objectives by advancing the

DOI: 10.1201/9788770041478-1

technologies of the radio and core network domains, also coevolving the network and service management capabilities to provide service providers with the means of governance and operations. On the other hand, cellular networks have been evolving in parallel with other technologies including other (sometimes competing) wireless technologies, networking in general, information technology (IT), computation hardware, clouds and data centers, data science and algorithms, and AI/ML. Adopting solutions from parallel technology tracks answering the needs of common megatrends has been another means to extend the capabilities of cellular systems, with the speed benefit of shortening the path from design to implementation through proven and established technologies.

This chapter will provide an overview of the requirements from various networking roles that are shaping the telecommunication design goals, tracking the impact of expectations by the end users, network operators, and more recently, adjacent vertical industries. A more detailed discussion will be devoted to the analysis of trends in the closest confines of cellular networks, that is, the group of wireless communication technologies, positioning cellular networks as trendsetters in specific technologies related to spectrum allocation. Next, the chapter will discuss megatrends influencing the evolution of telecommunication and cellular networks from outside of their own domain. This is followed by a closer look into the evolution of network and service management, showing how the initial attempts at automation per use case had to be replaced by a more systematic methodology resulting in the concept of intent-based automation.

1.2 Requirements of Automation in Mobile Networks

Mobile networks are used, owned, and operated by different individuals or entities, having different roles and objectives, and therefore imposing different requirements and demands on the system. This section will first provide an overview of the entities and roles, followed by an analysis of their requirements, with the aim to collect drivers behind the trends forming the evolution of the networks especially from the management perspective.

In the context of using, owning, and operating mobile networks, three major roles may be identified: first, individual end users (so-called subscribers); second, the traditional network operators or communication service providers, operating the network infrastructure to provide services to subscribers; and third, vertical industries integrating telecommunication technologies and services to enable or enhance their own systems and solutions.

Subscribes use terminal devices to interact with networked applications that use telecommunication services (e.g., accessing content from the internet via mobile networks). Their primary use case and expectation is to access their devices and applications anytime, anywhere with good quality and no technical issues. Any obstacle to having an instant experience through their devices, regardless of its origin, immediately creates frustration [1]. This requires full coverage and availability from the network side, with a quality of service that provides a good end-user experience while interacting with digital applications and content, and this has to be available regardless of location, time, and mobility.

Network operators own and control all technical assets (spectrum, network equipment, services infrastructure) required to provide telecommunications services to their subscribers. They purchase network equipment, software, and solutions from usually multiple vendors, and sell telecommunications services to end users and business customers. Operator expectations and responsibilities include capacity, quality of service, availability, and reliability, as well as cost, efficiency, and manageability. Capacity means that the network technology scales to support high user and device densities. Quality of service means controlling service performance parameters such as bandwidth, throughput, latency, and jitter, which are partly required to satisfy end-user expectations but also motivated by regularity requirements. Similarly, availability (percentage of time in which an entity is operable) and reliability (mean time between failures of an entity) are also due partly to end-user requirements, and partly to regulatory and operational requirements.

Cost, efficiency, and manageability are clearly operational expectations to be supported by network and network management technology and by the operator's own internal processes. Cost and efficiency mean the cost associated with providing a specific level of service or functionality. Cost is usually a multidimensional measure consisting of HW/SW cost, resource cost (frequency, bandwidth, compute), human staff, etc. High efficiency and low cost are optimization goals, for example, to achieve the same level of service with less cost. Manageability refers to the ability (with associated effort and cost) to deploy, configure, operate, monitor, troubleshoot, and evolve a network and its services according to the operator's business goals. It is impacted by reliability (due to the potential need for manual intervention at failures), level of automation (self-configuration and self-management), and system flexibility (effort needed to change policies and operational goals or introduce new services). Manageability can be significantly improved through technologies that enable network automation and reduce the complexity that requires manual workflows to handle.

The third role is assumed by the vertical industry, that is, industries or sectors with their own technologies and businesses (e.g., production, manufacturing, and logistics) where networking (especially wireless) is not the primary product or main technology component of the overall solution. Rather, industries integrate telecommunications as one of many technologies into their technical assets to build solutions that deliver their own business goals. The expectations from vertical industries are thus formulated from the perspective of the industry rather than through direct telecommunication service specifications. The industrial expectations must be actively transformed into telecommunication requirements that can be fulfilled by the network. This creates a semantic gap between the industrial application of telecommunication compared to traditional CSP business where the end-user subscription packages directly map to telco services.

Vertical industries might have extreme requirements in terms of traditional quality of service, including availability and reliability, as well as impose new requirements such as time-sensitive communication (TSC) and deterministic services that are not regularly required by mobile broadband use cases. Industrial use cases that may need high availability and TSC include industrial automation, production quality control, preventive maintenance, and cyber-physical control applications that may involve communication between industrial digital twins and their physical counterpart (Figure 1.1).

Availability is measured in a number of nines, such as five nines meaning 99.999% availability of the time. Availability not only means accessibility of the system (such as the operator being able to log in or query status information through a management interface) but also the network's capacity to fully function according to the end-to-end service requirements, such as being able to enable services with predefined SLAs. Five nines of availability translate to no more than 6 minutes of downtime yearly. This is the availability requirement for standard voice and data services [2], and it already assumes a robust system with built-in redundancy and automatic resiliency mechanisms on protocol layers and resource/domain controllers. With the vertical industry integrating telcos into their critical operational technologies, telecommunication systems are challenged on two fronts. First, the complexity of the services increases, due to the diversity of machine control loops and physical–virtual interactions extended over the network, resulting in a variety of more stringent delay, time-sensitive, and deterministic services. Second, orthogonal to the expansion of services, the system's availability needs to increase to six nines, or 99.9999%, meaning less than 30 seconds of yearly downtime for critical machine types of communication [2]. Clearly, at such

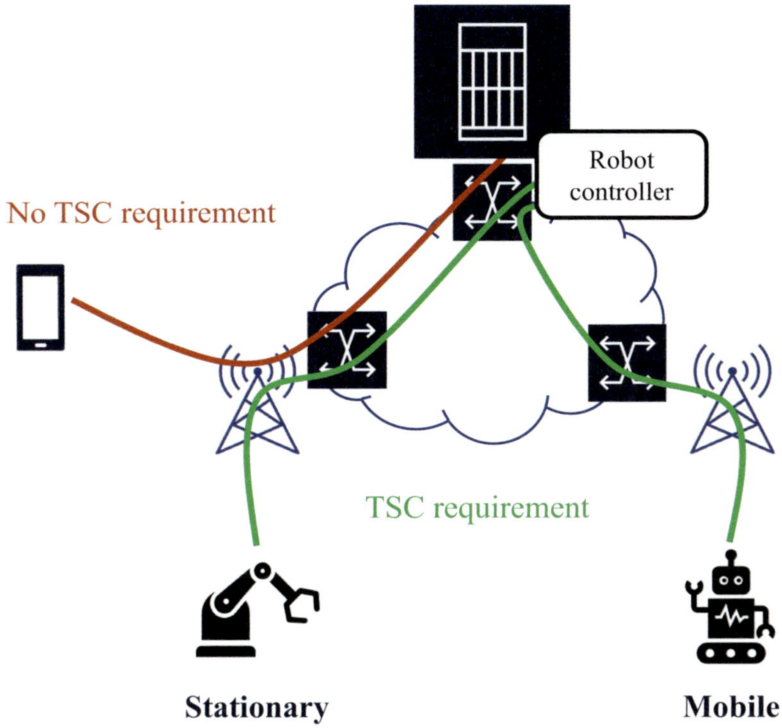

Figure 1.1 Illustration of robot control use cases requiring time-sensitive communication.

a level of requirement, there is no room for any manual intervention and any degradations of resource, network, or service level must be prevented rather than resolved. This can only be achieved with highly automated network and service management mechanisms supported by technologies that enable the network to autonomously predict and prevent any potential issue from escalating to service degradation or downtime.

Integrating telco technology into the vertical industry's solutions imposes new security and integration requirements to the network in addition to what was already discussed with the services. Security considerations that are specific to industrial environments include:

- Security of devices (often legacy ones) that have no built-in protection against IT attacks (e.g., sensors and cameras) are physically more accessible (and thus prone to tampering), and have constrained HW resources that prevent the integration of extensive on-device security mechanisms.

- Separation between network traffic for operations (e.g., product line automation) and general IT/communications (e.g., access to web or timesheet management) over the same network infrastructure.
- As the network becomes a part of the critical infrastructure, it also has to contribute to the industry's established functional and nonfunctional safety principles, including the safety of physical assets, and above all, the safety of human staff. This requires a risk assessment and the development of protection measures to prevent network problems that may propagate to machine failures that might even endanger operator personnel.
- Data security and ownership, especially if using cloud technology, may be critical to remain at the industry's physical premise or at least within the organization's intranet. This limits or completely blocks the possibility of using public cloud services or sharing infrastructure (e.g., via slicing) with commercial networks, promoting the use case of industrial private networks.

Unlike CSPs, vertical industry engineers and operators are traditionally not telecommunication domain experts. They already operate a mixture of technologies that are the industry's core assets. Gaining expertise in yet another one, such as 5G, would need significant investment, whereas 5G would not become their business selling point but a supporting technology. Integrating 5G into the industrial system, processes, and workflows would be more compelling if the 5G itself supported seamless integration into the operational technology and end-to-end business solution (e.g., production, manufacturing, and logistics). This again imposes a set of requirements on industrial 5G deployments and in general on telecommunication systems supporting industrial communications, such as

- Capability of autonomously creating the communication services necessary to support the industrial processes, without having to create detailed telco service profiles using the complexity of telco domain language and configuration.
- Dynamically adapt the network's behavior to the changing conditions on the industry floor such as moving robots or AGVs, or virtual industrial assets such as DTs, to always operate according to the industrial use case requirements (e.g., availability, robustness, resiliency, determinism, and e2e performance).

The above requirements assume both a high degree of autonomy in the system and high-level technology-agnostic management interfaces for governing the telco networks. Automation and ease of operation are also priorities of the CSPs; but while CSPs try to optimize the cost and efficiency of owning and operating networks that have by and large been deployed and functional as a primary source of revenue, for vertical industries automation and ease of integration and operation of networks is essential already for the adoption of the technology in the first place.

1.3 Wireless Communication Trends

Although cellular mobile networks are at the forefront of global telecommunication systems and large wireless communication, it is not the only widely used wireless technology and it is not evolving in isolation. Wireless communication standards and technologies have evolved to address different core use cases and requirements. As technology evolution increased their capability beyond their initial scope, some use cases and deployment scenarios have become supported by multiple alternative technologies, creating the potential of integrating multiple accesses within the same system. This not only increases the technological diversity but also the adoption of once-distinct use cases and deployment scenarios across technologies.

As a starting point, two fundamental communication use cases could be identified:

1. Wireless networks for local and personal low-cost, best-effort, plug-and-play deployments, for example, personal area networks, communication at home, and private broadband internet access, usually at a physical location that is privately owned by the user.
2. Large-scale commercial telecommunication services with regulated requirements on availability, reliability, and service quality, providing always-on services at a global scale over coverage areas of geographical proportions.

Table 1.1 provides a comparative overview of the key attributes of the two different wireless communication use cases.

The most prominent representative of personal wireless networks is Wi-Fi, whereas commercial networks are globally dominated by 3GPP cellular technology from 2G to 5G (with research and standardization already ongoing toward 6G). Therefore, in the rest of the discussion, the Wi-Fi

Table 1.1 Key attributes of the personal and commercial wireless use cases.

Attribute	Personal	Commercial
Technology	Wi-Fi, Bluetooth	Cellular mobile
Spectrum allocation	Shared access (unlicensed)	Exclusive access (licensed)
Channel access	Distributed channel access mechanisms with accepted negative consequences on TX delay and spectral efficiency	High spectral efficiency with central TX scheduling, scales to a large number of active devices, guaranteed transmission opportunities
Mobility	Mostly indoor, static, or nomadic mobility, acceptable interruption while on the move	Indoor and large-scale outdoor, seamless roaming across large areas, no acceptable interruption due to mobility

family and the cellular mobile networks (especially the 5th generation) will be used as examples to illustrate wireless technology trends, depicted in Figure 1.2.

The technical differences between Wi-Fi and cellular are due to primarily addressing separate demands and use cases, which influenced their architecture design and carry over to impact their operation, services, scalability, and reliability. In the era of 2G, the core cellular design targeted voice service with seamless mobility over large-scale coverage, which was secured by becoming the first global international standard for cellular mobile. From this core service domain, which the subsequence generations up to 5G, it has expanded to packet-switched data services, first best effort than gaining quality of service capabilities; high-speed mobility; expansion to small cells and indoor, as well as to high altitude platforms and nonterrestrial satellite networks; from large scale commercial deployments to industrial private networks. Wi-Fi, on the other hand, started as a technology for short-range data connections with stationary or nomadic mobility profiles; and private usage (even just with a single access point) where the user is also the owner and operator of the equipment (access point); and over nonlicensed spectrum that requires no coordination or regulation among users (apart from basic spectrum access rules and transmission power limits). Since its beginning, Wi-Fi has evolved to support high data rates comparable to LTE and even 5G (up to multiple Gb/s), better spectrum coordination to resolve scalability issues due to its initial contention-based MAC (now supporting OFDMA in Wi-Fi 6 [3], the same spectrum access used by 3GPP radio access since LTE), and more advanced scheduling schemes such as target wake time (TWT) [4] that enables access points to deterministically schedule transmission

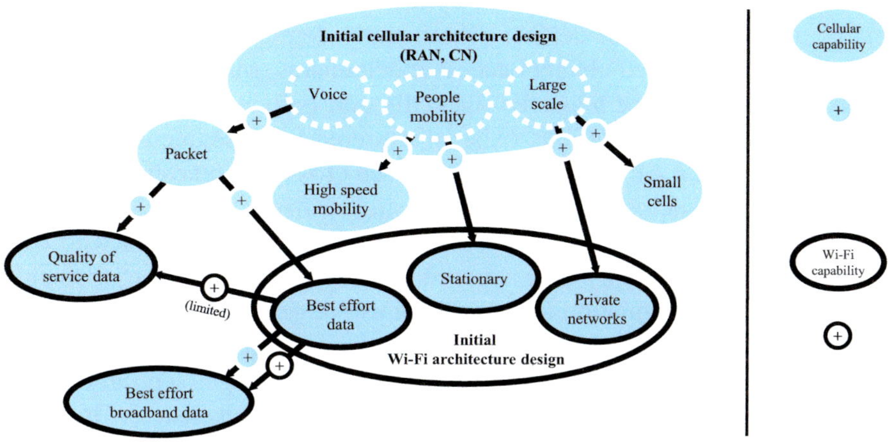

Figure 1.2 Key cellular and Wi-Fi functionalities and expansion to adjacent areas.

opportunities to selected devices. Wi-Fi was even the first to penetrate new markets such as connected cars, with the Wi-Fi derivative Dedicated Short Range Communication [5, 6] being the first technology enabling direct car-to-car communication to implement V2X use cases [7]. However, 3GPP responded with the creation of the Cellular V2X standards [8, 9, 10, 11], catching up with its device-to-device direct communication support that has not been a focus of any previous generations due to the heritage of the prevalent UE-to-base-station communication originating from the earliest cellular network design principles. This shows that trends in wireless communication impact all wireless standards, at least in use cases where both technologies have comparable offerings or stakeholders of the technology see a potential market share.

The alternative evolutionary path of Wi-Fi and cellular networks has led to key differences in network ownership and operation, services, scalability, and reliability. Regarding Wi-Fi, anyone can own, install, and operate devices certified to be used in the ISM bands (where requirements of channel conformance, such as TX power limitations, and listen-before-talk mechanisms are implemented and enforced by the device itself). Wi-Fi networks comprise individual access points providing IP connectivity with traditionally no guarantee (best effort) on availability, reliability, bandwidth, latency, etc. Some mechanisms have been proposed to improve QoS through Wi-Fi multimedia support [12] and more deterministic spectrum access through OFDMA and TWT in Wi-Fi 6 [3, 4], however, they do not match the spectral efficiency, device density, and QoS guarantees cellular networks can provide. Without support for those mechanisms both by the Wi-Fi access point and the terminals, a high number of devices significantly degrade Wi-Fi performance due to contention-based channel access mechanisms. Most consumer Wi-Fi access points need to be managed manually and individually, however, proprietary management solutions exist in the enterprise segment supporting cloud-based central AP management and even cross-AP interference control mechanisms, but such capabilities are not standardized.

Cellular networks are deployed and managed by operators who own licensed spectrum that only their network equipment and devices of their subscribers may use. Regulations on spectrum use (e.g., max. TX power) apply to the network equipment and UEs. The operator may provide dedicated guaranteed services to users (due to exclusive spectrum usage, centrally scheduled radio interface, and dedicated quality of service mechanisms). Operators own disjoint spectrum; no interference is possible between different networks. Cellular technology scales to nationwide networks with 10–100 thousand base stations under the same operator's management. Performance is maintained even with high UE density. Mechanisms exist for interbase station coordination, load balancing, and real-time optimization in a standardized manner.

1.4 Formative Megatrends

Technology megatrends are trends influencing the technical evolution (research, standardization, development, and productization) of multiple industries roughly at the same time and in similar directions. Megatrends are driven by fundamental technologies that become relevant for adoption by multiple industries, or pushed by demands and requirements from users, operators, or other stakeholder groups that share an interest or are targets of multiple industries. This section will discuss recent influential megatrends that impact the evolution of the telecommunication sector.

Virtualization, cloudification, and softwarization: This trend developed at the data centers of web scales, producing technologies such as containers (e.g., Docker [13]) and container management platforms (e.g., Kubernetes [14]). The adoption of virtualization and containerization in cellular networks started with the 5G, the first cellular generation with service-based core network functions [15] that fit the model of micro-services and dynamic orchestration enabled by this technology trend. During the first wave of adopting the virtualization concept, containerized network functions have become the norm of deployment and operation in 5G core networks. A second wave of adoption is ongoing to bring the same technology to the access network, creating cloud RAN and virtualized RAN solutions. O-RAN [16] is one of the advocates of disaggregated RAN architecture and produces RAN standards that fit this paradigm (see also Chapter 2). As a consequence of this trend, dictated by the all-software-based implementation of network functions or the "softwarization" of telco, is to increasingly adopt software methods and mechanisms such as REST APIs in how the network functions interact with each other and how their capabilities are exposed. This enables network capabilities to be consumed through service APIs and makes network integration technologically similar to software integration. However, this alone does not solve the need for deep technical telco knowledge to perform the integration as APIs, although technically fitting regular SW APIs like [15, 17, 18], may be still very telco specific.

Increasing utilization of AI and "Native AI": AI/ML is a technology that has a very long history with theoretical concepts such as the neuron being decades old [19]. However, practical implementations providing results that outperform classical algorithms, manual feature engineering, or statistical analysis have only been achieved in the last decade [20]. Deep learning training algorithms require both a large amount of training data and a sufficiently large neural network, which must be matched with compute power that was not available at the time of conceptualizing the foundations. Leveraging the increase and concentration of compute power at data centers (partly as a byproduct of the previous trend discussed above) and the development of accelerator HW including GPUs, the AI/ML landscape rapidly developed into a variety of techniques and use cases.

The flagship deep learning use cases were targeting tasks that mimic human perception: handwriting and text recognition, speech-to-text, machine translation, computer vision (including object detection such subcases like face recognition), and various games such as chess, Go or computer games [20, 21, 22, 23, 24]. By targeting the machine replication of human capabilities such as reading, speaking, manipulating language, or playing popular games, the performance of AI solutions could be interpreted easily and intuitively, which is a great benefit for algorithm evaluation and development. Additionally, AI reaching human-level capability in selected tasks could be published in popular media to the general public [25], establishing AI's reputation as one of the biggest contemporary technology trends impacting not only industries but also everyday life. On the technical side, training AI models where human perception is the benchmark also makes it easier (or even possible at all) to produce labeled datasets. These attributes have driven the research of AI techniques toward supervised learning and a variety of models that specialize in categories of use cases such as convolutional neural networks [26] for image recognition and object detection [21], recurrent neural networks [27] for sequence analysis including machine translation and natural language processing (NLP) [28, 29], or new training methods such as reinforcement learning for computer games [30].

Meanwhile, the digitalization and softwarization of industries including telecommunications have led to large datasets that have become impossible to analyze, operationalize, or monetize using manual or traditional statistical methods. With AI already becoming a promising technology for data processing and a catalyst for successful new machine capabilities that were previously impossible, the trend of applying AI to industrial data emerged. Industrial data, unlike human perception type of data (e.g., text and images), is comprised of numerical data series, software logs, configuration files, or other structured data that were meant to be interpreted programmatically. Approaching such computer-oriented datasets with an AI technology that was largely driven by human perception tasks on labeled datasets has multiple long-lasting impacts that are setting the telco industry trends on applying AI still to this day:

1. The lack of labeled training data in this field makes many AI architectures and pipelines well-performing on human-centric tasks underperform on industrial datasets. This has motivated to research and invest in unsupervised or self-supervised training algorithms. For such algorithms, however, it is challenging to define a clear benchmark that sets the limits of achievable performance, or to even have clear expectations on the outcome of the algorithm itself.

2. The output of AI algorithms on industrial data is not intuitive and hard to interpret (given that the input was already like that). This has led to new explainability and trust issues related to accepting and using the results of AI, some of which are still open today (see Chapter 4). In contrast, explainability was not a question when the AI model directly produced a result that belongs to the native human perception and comprehension, such as classifying or annotating an image. The only question was how to debug the model if the result is not correct but not the evaluation of the result itself. The correctness problem still persists today, including the universal security case of adversary attacks, which will be explored in Chapter 4.

3. The private ownership and sensitivity of industrial datasets (mostly by the producing organization and containing confidential data) have

driven the adoption of federated training algorithms, that do not require all training data to be centrally available and processed on a large compute resource. Apart from the privacy-preserving benefits of federated learning, it also makes training scalable on deployments where compute resources are traditionally distributed across many physical sites and locations, such as telecommunication edge clouds or even the RAN itself [16]. Even when using on-demand cloud computing platforms, distributed learning brings economic benefits as it is more expensive to rent a single virtual machine with large computing power than to have the same cumulative power distributed across more but less powerful machines [31].

In addition to the above trends in the evolution of AI techniques and the application of AI, an orthogonal trend is for the telco system to become "AI native." While AI native is not a standardized attribute, it is usually interpreted as having a network architecture that explicitly supports the use of AI models for implementing network functionalities and management capabilities, as well as systemic support for managing the AI models and related workflows such as training data collection, model training, deployment or performance monitoring [32]. AI native network not only uses AI for its own operation but also has to operate the AI technology, leading to new management scopes, which are discussed in Chapter 5.

Generative models and large language models: Generative models are AI models that produce an extensive amount of output that may be similar to their training data or input domain. Generative models have been used even before they became popular, for example, recurrent neural networks producing machine translation of an input text are also generative models. Yet, the term generative has been popularized with the generative adversarial network (GAN) architecture that was successful in use cases such as image generation [33] or neural style transfer [34]. Still, the most famous generative networks are the large language models (LLM) that are technically based on the transformers [35] neural network architecture. Generative networks and LLMs in particular have a role in providing new types of human–machine interactions, enabling less syntax and technology-driven interfaces in favor of conversational interfaces [36]. The telecommunication impacts of LLMs and human–network interfaces are discussed specifically in Chapter 9.

Intent-based autonomous networks: While technically could be considered two trends, intents and autonomous networks have already converged into intent-based network automation, service automation, and network autonomy [37]. Intents have become part of the major interests of multiple network and telecommunication standardization bodies [38, 37, 39, 40, 41], becoming the de facto approach to network management interfaces. Intents represent a paradigm shift in the abstraction level of the interfaces between networks and operators or even private network owners, generally providing intuitive, ease-of-use interactions. Adopting the intent paradigm is by far not only an interface concern. Although intents require new means of interaction with the network, innovating on the human–machine front (see Chapter 8), they also require a high level of network autonomy (see Chapters 6 and 7). Governing networks through declarative goals assume that the underlying system is not only capable of interpreting and validating the intents but also of composing and organizing its own closed loops to deliver the required outcomes without being presented with an executable fulfillment and assurance workflow. The need for network autonomy is driving the network's modeling capabilities, including state models, semantic models, and decision models (Chapters 10–12) to compose fully autonomous intent-driven closed loops.

Metaverse: Although no standard definition exists for the Metaverse, according to a systematic literature review [42], a Metaverse may be regarded as an online virtual space supporting real-time collaboration among concurrent users and digital assets. The implication of Metaverse telecommunication networks is the dynamics and distribution of service demand generated by Metaverse use cases such as simulation, gaming, health care, education, or other collaborative scenarios accessed through immersive devices using augmented or virtual reality (AR/VR). Metaverse interactions may create a large-scale on-demand distribution of collaborative low-latency flows with joint compute and network demands requiring flexible resource allocation and fast service provisioning. Therefore, agility of service creation, dynamic and autonomous adaptation of resources, real-time service management, and intent (use case) based service fulfillment all play a role in enabling Metaverse-like demands. The need to access scalable cloud computing with low latency (e.g., for personalized scene rendering) is a driver for converging the infrastructure to a cloud-network continuum [43] where distributed computing resources are interconnected by a distributed network. Metaverse demand is different from distributed but isolated individual streaming services or access to cloud-based content, as collaborative users must replicate their interactions through the virtual scene with each other in real time. The incorporation of haptic feedback further tightens the latency requirements of the communication channels and even brings deterministic and time-sensitive needs similar to what was discussed for industrial use cases in Section 1.2.

Network digital twin (NDT): NDT is a recent trend that transfers the concept of industrial digital twins to the network and telecommunication domain [44, 45, 46, 47]. An NDT is a virtual representation of a real operational network, or a part of it, using modeling and abstraction techniques to simplify the complexity of the physical network. The virtual NDT replica provides extended capabilities such as what-if analysis, configuration validation, event prediction, and simulation and emulation, which produce analytical outcomes or optimized actions directly relevant and applicable to the real network. NDTs implement use cases such as network and service management automation (e.g., supporting the evaluation of hypothetical scenarios to calculate and validate the optimal configuration for the real network before they are applied), closed-loop automation (especially the analytics and decision stages that require evaluation and planning of potential next actions in the current context of the network and the operational or service level targets), or even providing extra functionalities on behalf of a network function to augment a network's baseline capabilities without disrupting its regular operation. The NDTs leverage many of the other technological trends, including cloudification, AI/ML integration (including generative models), and provide a potential means of based network autonomy. Connecting with the original DT concept, NDTs may be useful actors in industrial networks where network abstractions provided by NDT(s) and operational abstractions provided by industrial DTs collaborate in order to create an end-to-end solution. A detailed discussion of NDTs is presented in Chapter 13.

1.5 Network and Service Management Evolution

In a CSP context, network management is a collection of tasks and supporting tools or applications that enable a network operator to administrate, configure, monitor, and maintain a network infrastructure with the purpose of providing communication services. On the top of an operational network, service management performs the tasks and workflows associated with the provisioning, fulfillment, assurance, and security of communication services according to SLAs. Figure 1.3 shows a simplified lifecycle of a network and its services from an operator's perspective, assuming, as a thought experiment, the deployment of a new network. The first stage is the planning and dimensioning of the network according to its location, coverage, and the expected demand for the targeted services. The second stage is the deployment of the network, including installation (for physical resources) and orchestration (for software assets), followed by initial configuration to make the network operational. Based on the experience collected during the

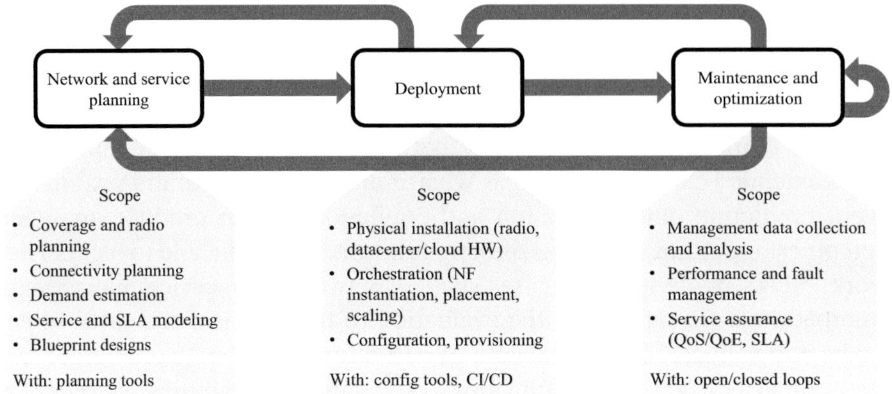

Figure 1.3 Simplified network and service lifecycle model.

deployment, the planning may be iteratively refined. The third stage is the maintenance and optimization of the network, both to increase the efficiency of the infrastructure serving the demand to and adapt the network configuration to the shift in the service demand or other environmental conditions. Short-term adaptations to the dynamics of the services (e.g., to maintain the QoS of the service against the changing mobility, radio, and load conditions) are handled through service assurance capabilities that are usually autonomous closed loops acting according to the insight collected from network and service level. Long-term adaptations to permanent changes in the network operation or significant changes in the demand pattern or user behavior may trigger iterations at previous stages including changes to the deployment (e.g., increasing the size of resource pools) or even planning (e.g., through physical extension or relocation of the network's footprint). These actions may impact the capital or operational expenditure of the network that requires accounting considerations.

An end user usually experiences the network capabilities by consuming services such as end-to-end communication through applications (considering both client and server-side apps) and devices. Therefore, the service management aspects have a direct impact on the end-user experience. Service management, however, depends on the network infrastructure and functions enabled through the network domains, including cloud, core, mobile backhaul (MBH), RAN, and device, each having its associated configuration, performance, fault, and security management scopes. The interaction between the management domains and scopes from an end-to-end service perspective is shown in Figure 1.4.

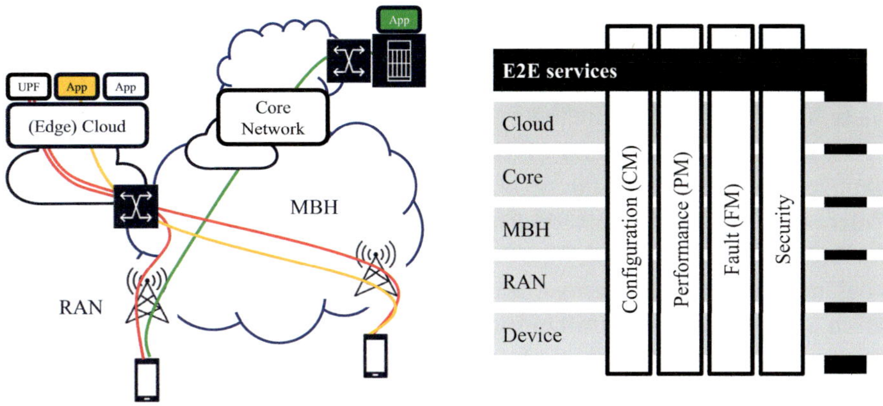

Figure 1.4 Management domains and scopes from an e2e service perspective.

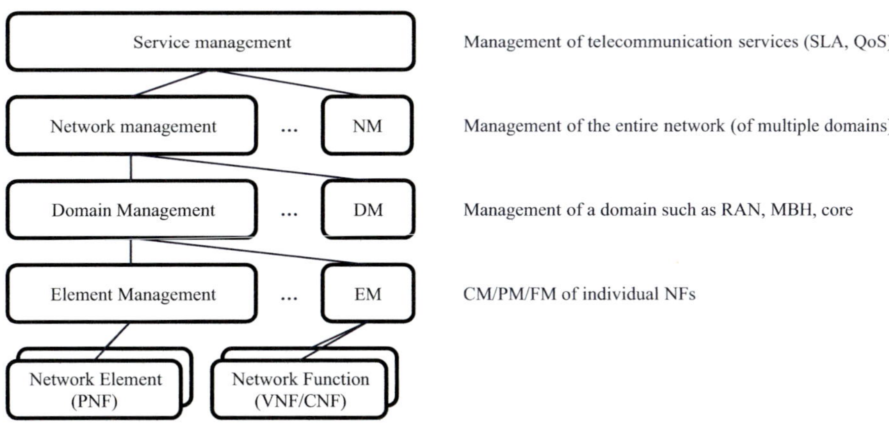

Figure 1.5 3GPP standard network and service management hierarchy.

Traditionally, network management architectures followed the granularity of the network elements, functions, or domains (Figure 1.5). Up to and including the long-term evolution (LTE) generation of cellular networks, the lowest management granularity was on the network element (NE) level. A network element is a physical network function (PNF) such as a radio base station. Before the virtualization trend was adopted by telecommunication, core network elements such as packet gateways or control plane entities were also physical elements. Starting with 5G, the core network is increasingly implemented through cloud-native functions (CNF), a transformation that is detailed in Chapter 2. Nevertheless, the lowest network management granularity remains at the function level and interacts with the network elements of functions directly, for any of the scopes (CM, FM, and PM) outlined in Figure 1.4. The next management granularity level is on the domain level, where a domain usually means a technology domain such as the RAN, core, MBH, or (with the adoption of virtualization) also the cloud infrastructure. Management at this level interacts with domain controllers such as RAN controllers (for the access network) or SDN controllers (for MBH), or through element managers. On top of the domain level is network management, which is balancing and harmonizing e2e network objectives including resource allocation and optimization, utilization, efficiency, quality, or cost aspects across domains. Network management actions may take effect through interactions with domain managers, element managers, or the infrastructure hosting the network functions.

In 5G, the above management stack has been modernized to adopt a service-based principle similar to the service-based architecture (SBA) that was introduced in the core network domain [15]. The new architecture is referred to as the service-based management architecture (SBMA) [48], where the management capabilities are not organized into management functions (as implementation units). Instead, only abstract management services (MnS) are defined exposing their capabilities through APIs. This modernization of the management architecture fits the second wave of the softwarization trend as discussed in Section 1.4. Yet, the logical management scopes and domains remain as discussed in Figures 1.4 and 1.5.

The management capabilities are implemented by software systems that usually collect management services or functions with a specific scope. Traditional management systems are divided into business support system (BSS) and operations support system (OSS) [49]. BSS is concerned with customer care, self-care, billing, and product management; whereas OSS handles network and service aspects including planning and rollout, provisioning workflows, network, and asset management. Additional operations, administration, and maintenance (OAM), or in O-RAN [16] terminology, service management, and orchestration (SMO) [39] capabilities include the CM, PM, and FM management scopes in all management domains including the services (QoS, SLA), network, domain, and element or function level. Due to the megatrends of virtualization, softwarization, and native AI, new management scopes appeared such as SW management, orchestration, the management of AI models, and the security impact of AI technology. These aspects are discussed in detail in Chapter 5.

The abundance of management scopes, domains, and granularities, all modulated by the multivendor environment resulting in vendor-specific

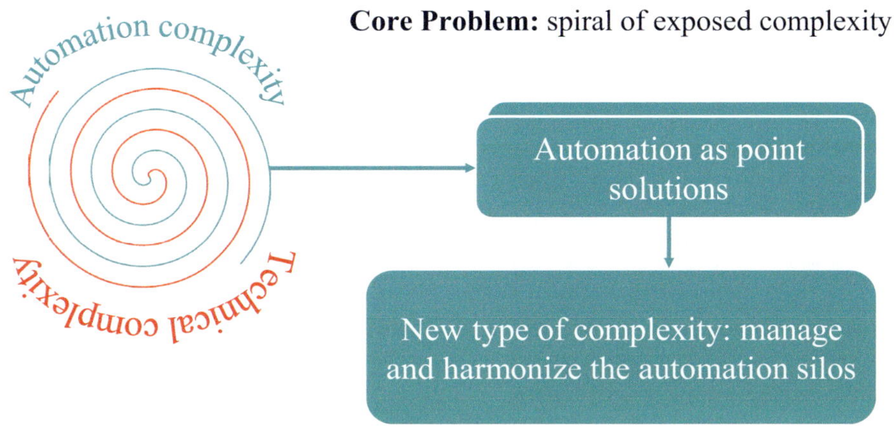

Figure 1.6 The spiral of complexity in networks.

tools, has led to high management complexity and fragmentation of management interfaces exposed to the operator. Vendor-specific management tools (such as element managers or RAN controllers) are often further extended with operator-developed in-house tools, scripts, or workflow automation, furthering the complexity and management overhead with the need to keep all the tools synchronized and adapted to the changes in upstream releases. The management complexity is underpinned by the technological complexity of the network, its geographical scale of deployment, the density of services, and the dynamic demand and behavior of the users. When all of it is exposed to the network operators, it requires an ever-increasing technical skillset and operational knowledge to create and maintain new services.

Technical and management complexity has only been one type of complexity faced by the operators. In attempts to simplify network management, operators have been pushing for network and service automation (Section 1.2). As something paradoxical, automation itself created further complexity due to the new technologies and parameters introduced to govern and program the automation techniques themselves. While adding new types of complexity, automation still has not eliminated all the previous technical complexity. This results in a spiral of complexity in which both traditional technical complexity, as well as new automation-related complexity are present (Figure 1.6). One of the reasons why automation has not eliminated the technical complexity was the approach to automation as individual domain-specific point solutions driven by bottom-up key issues and use cases, rather than building a systematic approach of defining automation scopes with a clear governance

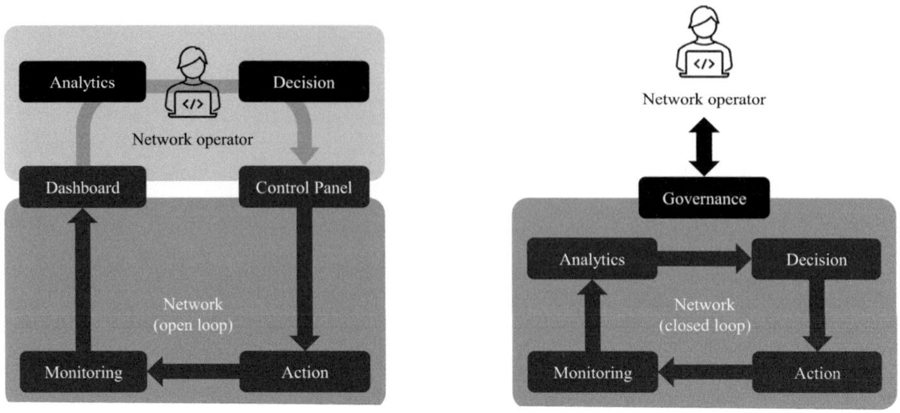

Figure 1.7 Open loop and closed loop automation.

and coordination structure. A representative example of point solutions is the self-organizing networks (SON) [50] concept introduced with the LTE generation. The scope of SON was to embed automated loops (closed loops acting without human intervention) in the network operation, as opposed to the then traditional open loop approach that required manual actions even to change any of the configuration parameters (Figure 1.7). The general concept of SON materialized in a few separate use cases such as automatic neighbor relations (ANR) [51], mobility load balancing (MLB), and mobility robustness optimization (MRO) [52]. These use cases were specified individually, without any harmonization or coordination, to the extent that when enabled simultaneously in the system, they could have been acting on the same set of cellular radio parameters. The result could lead to oscillations in the RAN due to parameter fighting, for example, between MLB and MRO [53]. Also, as SON use cases were initially specified strictly for the RAN domain, the individual algorithms were formulated without any consideration of the end-to-end services or even adjacent domains such as the MBH, causing suboptimal or even counter effects in e2e [54]. Therefore, despite the goal of simplification, automation attempts like this have rather increased complexity, contradicting the expectations of network operators and vertical industry in terms of manageability and ease of integration with other solutions.

Nevertheless, closed-loop automation as depicted in Figure 1.7 has been further researched with more systematic methodologies [55, 56, 57], advancing the understanding of network and service automation, and merging the evolution path of intents and network autonomy into a single influential megatrend. Intent-based autonomous networks have become a common

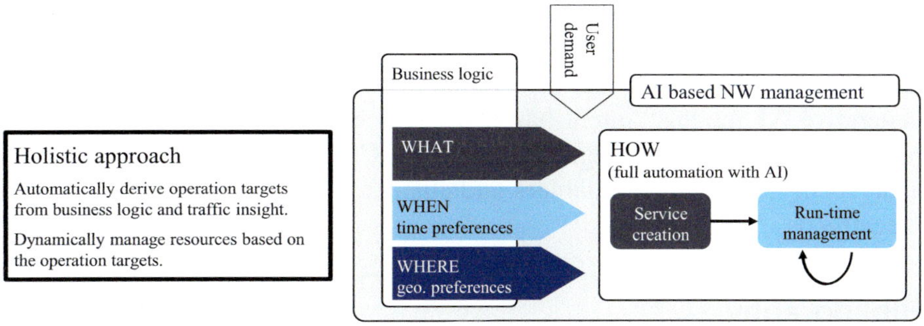

Figure 1.8 Zero-touch network and service management.

denominator across the approach of multiple SDOs [37, 39, 40], working toward the common vision of zero-touch network and service management. Zero-touch, illustrated in Figure 1.8, means a concept where the network considers the full spectrum of input requirements (business intents and user demand), the available resources, the system state, and internal capabilities to derive its internal operational targets in harmony with the business objectives and bring them to fulfillment through AI-based service automation. It remains to explore strategic questions like how to interact with networks; how to manifest the network to the operator and user; or how to govern autonomous networks. Some of these questions and topics will be opened and further discussed in Chapters 6–8.

1.6 Summary

This chapter provided a brief overview of the trends and catalysis that have shaped the evolution of mobile networks and network management in particular into their current form. On the one hand, requirements and expectations from network operators have set a trend to explore enablers of automation to counter the complexity of the technological diversity and scale of the networks and services. The extension of the scope of the network to industry verticals has created even more stringent requirements not only in terms of new QoS such as time sensitiveness and critical reliability but also a need to integrate networks into industrial solutions without having telco knowledge.

The network and automation evolution has not happened and is not happening in isolation. Networking has been impacted by various megatrends that spread common technologies into different industries. Among the most influential trends are the full range of virtualization solutions up to and including the latest container technologies creating cloud-native network functions and management services across all network domains and in e2e; the increasing utilization and integration of AI to create AI native networks; generative AI models; intent-based network autonomy; Metaverse; and a recent uptake of network digital twins. Next, Chapter 2 will provide a deeper analysis of the technical enablers and standardization impact driven by the megatrends.

Bibliography

[1] Ericsson ConsumerLab, "Experience shapes customer loyalty", Report, 2016, https://www.ericsson.com/en/reports-and-papers/consumerlab/reports/experience-shapes-mobile-customer-loyalty

[2] 3GPP TS 22.261 Service requirements for the 5G system

[3] "IEEE Standard for Information Technology – Telecommunications and Information Exchange between Systems Local and Metropolitan Area Networks--Specific Requirements Part 11: Wireless LAN Medium Access Control (MAC) and Physical Layer (PHY) Specifications Amendment 1: Enhancements for High-Efficiency WLAN," in IEEE Std 802.11ax-2021 (Amendment to IEEE Std 802.11-2020), pp.1–767, May 2021. Available at: https://doi.org/10.1109/IEEESTD.2021.9363693

[4] S. K. Venkateswaran, C-L. Tai, R. Garnayak, Y. Ben-Yehezkel, Y. Alpert, R. Sivakumar, "IEEE 802.11ax Target Wake Time: Design and Performance Analysis in ns-3", in 2024 Workshop on ns-3 (WNS3 2024), June 05--06, 2024, Barcelona, Spain. ACM, New York, NY, USA 9 Pages. https://doi.org/10.1145/3659111.3659115

[5] D. Jiang, and L. Delgrossi, "IEEE 802.11p: Towards an International Standard for Wireless Access in Vehicular Environments", Vehicular Technology Conference, May 2008. VTC Spring 2008. IEEE, page 2036–2040. DOI: 10.1109/VETECS.2008.458

[6] B. Y. Yacheur, T. Ahmed, M. Mosbah, "Analysis and Comparison of IEEE 802.11p and IEEE 802.11bd", Communication Technologies for Vehicles: 15th International Workshop, Nets4Cars/Nets4Trains/Nets4Aircraft 2020, Bordeaux, France, November 16–17, 2020, proceedings pp. 55–65, https://doi.org/10.1007/978-3-030-66030-7_5

[7] 5G Automotive Association, "Working Group Standards and Spectrum Study of spectrum needs for safety related intelligent transportation systems - day1 and advanced use cases", 5GAA TRS-200137, June 2020, Version 1.0, https://5gaa.org/content/uploads/2020/06/5GAA_S-200137_Day1_and_adv_Use_Cases_Spectrum-Needs-Study_V2.0-cover.pdf

[8] 3GPP TS 23.285, Architecture enhancements for V2X services
[9] 3GPP TR 37.985, Overall description of Radio Access Network (RAN) aspects for Vehicle-to-everything (V2X) based on LTE and NR
[10] ETSI EN 303 613, "Intelligent Transport Systems (ITS); LTE-V2X Access layer specification for Intelligent Transport Systems operating in the 5 GHz frequency band" V1.1.1 (2020-01)
[11] ETSI TR 101 607, "Intelligent Transport Systems (ITS); Cooperative ITS (C-ITS); Release 1" V1.2.1 (2020-02)
[12] H. Wu, X. Wang, Q. Zhang and X. Shen, "IEEE 802.11e Enhanced Distributed Channel Access (EDCA) Throughput Analysis," 2006 IEEE International Conference on Communications, Istanbul, Turkey, 2006, pp. 223–228, DOI: 10.1109/ICC.2006.254731.
[13] D. Merkel, "Docker: lightweight Linux containers for consistent development and deployment", Linux Journal, 2014(239), p. 2
[14] Kubernetes, "What is Kubernetes?", https://kubernetes.io/docs/concepts/overview/
[15] 3GPP TS 23.501 System architecture for the 5G System (5GS)
[16] O-RAN Alliance, Online, https://www.o-ran.org/
[17] OpenAPI Initiative. Available online: https://www.openapis.org/
[18] GitLab repository of 3GPP OpenAPIs, https://forge.3gpp.org/rep/all/5G_APIs
[19] H. Law, "Bell Labs and the 'neural' network, 1986–1996", 2023, BJHS Themes. 8. 1–12. 10.1017/bjt.2023.1.
[20] G. Van Houdt, C. Mosquera, G. Nápoles, "A Review on the Long Short-Term Memory Model", 2020, Artificial Intelligence Review. vol 53. 10.1007/s10462-020-09838-1.
[21] J. Redmon, S. Divvala, R. Girshick, A. Farhadi, "You Only Look Once: Unified, Real-Time Object Detection", 2015, cite arxiv:1506.02640.
[22] Y. Dong and D. Li, "Automatic Speech Recognition: A Deep Learning Approach", 2016, 1st ed., Springer Publishing Company, Incorporated, ISBN:978-1-4471-6967-3
[23] E. David, N. Netanyahu, L. Wolf, "DeepChess: End-to-End Deep Neural Network for Automatic Learning in Chess", 2016, p. 88–96. 10.1007/978-3-319-44781-0_11.
[24] D. Silver, A. Huang, C. Maddison et al., "Mastering the game of Go with deep neural networks and tree search", Nature 529, 484–489 (2016). https://doi.org/10.1038/
[25] D. A. Blum, "Kasparov versus Deep Blue: the showdown between human and computer", 2001, PC AI, vol. 15, no. 1 (Jan./Feb., 2001), pp. 49–51., Knowledge Technology, Inc., ISSN 0894-0711

[26] K. O'Shea, R. Nash, "An Introduction to Convolutional Neural Networks", 2015, CoRR abs/1511.08458
[27] L. C. Jain, L. R. Medsker, "Recurrent Neural Networks: Design and Applications", 1999, 1st ed., CRC Press, Inc., USA
[28] Tomas Mikolov, Kai Chen, Greg Corrado, Jeffrey Dean, "Efficient Estimation of Word Representations in Vector Space", arXiv:1301.3781 [cs.CL], 7 Sep 2013
[29] Jacob Devlin, Ming-Wei Chang, Kenton Lee, Kristina Toutanova, "BERT: Pre-training of Deep Bidirectional Transformers for Language Understanding", arXiv:1810.04805 [cs.CL], 24 May 2019
[30] K. Shao, Z. Tang, Y. Zhu, N. Li, D. Zhao, "A Survey of Deep Reinforcement Learning in Video Games", 2019, arXiv:1912.1094
[31] S. Zhou, B. Yuan, K. Xu, M. Zhang, W. Zheng, "The Impact Of Pricing Schemes On Cloud Computing And Distributed Systems", 2024, Journal of Knowledge Learning and Science Technology ISSN: 2959-6386 (online), 3(3), 193–205. https://doi.org/10.60087/jklst.v3.n3.p206–224
[32] O-RAN next Generation Research Group (nGRG), "Research Report on Native and Cross-domain AI: State of the art and future outlook", Report ID: RR-2023-03, September 2023, https://mediastorage.o-ran.org/ngrg-rr/nGRG-RR-2023-03-Research-Report-on-Native-and-Cross-domain-AI-v1_1.pdf
[33] Y. Kataoka, T. Matsubara and K. Uehara, "Image generation using generative adversarial networks and attention mechanism," 2016 IEEE/ACIS 15th International Conference on Computer and Information Science (ICIS), Okayama, Japan, 2016, pp. 1–6, doi: 10.1109/ICIS.2016.7550880.
[34] L. A. Gatys, A. S. Ecker, M. Bethge, "A Neural Algorithm of Artistic Style", Journal of Vision, DOI:10.1167/16.12.326, August 2015
[35] A. Vaswani, N. Shazeer, N. Parmar, J. Uszkoreit, L. Jones, A. N. Gomez, Ł. Kaiser, I. Polosukhin, "Attention is All you Need", 31st Conference on Neural Information Processing Systems (NIPS 2017), Long Beach, CA, USA, 2017
[36] B. K. Saha, L. Haab, Ł. Podleski, "Intent-based Industrial Network Management Using Natural Language Instructions", 2022 IEEE International Conference on Electronics, Computing and Communication Technologies (CONECCT), Bangalore, India, 2022, pp. 1–6, doi: 10.1109/CONECCT55679.2022.9865738
[37] ETSI GR ZSM 011, "Zero-touch network and Service Management (ZSM); Intent-driven autonomous networks; Generic aspects" V1.1.1 (2023-02)

[38] 3GPP TS 28.312 Management and orchestration; Intent driven management services for mobile networks
[39] O-RAN Alliance, "O-RAN SMO Intents-driven Management 3.0", WG1.TR.SMO-INT-R004-v03.00, October 2024
[40] TM Forum, "Intent in Autonomous Networks", IG1253, Version 1.3.0, August 2022
[41] Alexander Clemm, Laurent Ciavaglia, Lisandro Zambenedetti Granville, Jeff Tantsura, "Intent-Based Networking - Concepts and Definitions", October 2022, https://www.rfc-editor.org/info/rfc9315
[42] G. D. Ritterbusch and M. R. Teichmann, "Defining the Metaverse: A Systematic Literature Review," in IEEE Access, vol. 11, pp. 12368–12377, 2023, doi: 10.1109/ACCESS.2023.3241809
[43] A. Carrega and M. Repetto, "A network-centric architecture for building the cloud continuum", 2017 International Conference on Computing, Networking and Communications (ICNC), Silicon Valley, CA, USA, 2017, pp. 701–705, doi: 10.1109/ICCNC.2017.7876215
[44] C. Zhou et al., "Digital Twin Network: Concepts and Reference Architecture," draft-irtf-nmrg-network-digital-twin-arch-05, 4 March 2024, https://www.ietf.org/archive/id/draft-irtf-nmrg-network-digital-twin-arch-05.txt
[45] ETSI GR ZSM 015, "Zero-touch network and Service Management (ZSM); Network Digital Twin" V1.1.1 (2024-02)
[46] 3GPP TR 28.915 Study on management aspect of Network Digital Twin
[47] ETSI GS ZSM 018, "Zero-touch network and Service Management (ZSM); Network Digital Twin for enhanced zero-touch network and service management", V1.1.1 (2024-12)
[48] 3GPP TS 28.533 Management and orchestration; Architecture framework
[49] TM Forum, "Agile OSS/BSS Toolkit", Online, https://www.tmforum.org/resources/toolkit/agile-ossbss-toolkit/
[50] 3GPP TS 32.500 Telecommunication management; Self-Organizing Networks (SON); Concepts and requirements
[51] 3GPP TS 32.511 Telecommunication management; Automatic Neighbour Relation (ANR) management; Concepts and requirements
[52] 3GPP TS 38.300 NR; NR and NG-RAN Overall description; Stage-2
[53] N. Zia, S. S. Mwanje and A. Mitschele-Thiel, "A policy based conflict resolution mechanism for MLB and MRO in LTE self-optimizing networks", 2014 IEEE Symposium on Computers and Communications (ISCC), Funchal, Portugal, 2014, pp. 1–6, doi: 10.1109/ISCC.2014.6912543

[54] P. Szilágyi, Z. Vincze and C. Vulkán, "Enhanced Mobility Load Balancing Optimisation in LTE", 2012 IEEE 23rd International Symposium on Personal, Indoor and Mobile Radio Communications - (PIMRC), Sydney, NSW, Australia, 2012, pp. 997–1003, doi: 10.1109/PIMRC.2012.6362930

[55] ETSI GS ZSM 009-1, "Zero-touch network and Service Management (ZSM); Closed-Loop Automation; Part 1: Enablers", V1.1.1 (2021-06)

[56] ETSI GS ZSM 009-2, "Zero-touch network and Service Management (ZSM); Closed-Loop Automation; Part 2: Solutions for automation of E2E service and network management use cases", V1.1.1 (2022-06)

[57] ETSI GR ZSM 009-3, "Zero-touch network and Service Management (ZSM); Closed-Loop Automation; Part 3: Advanced topics", V1.1.1 (2023-08)6]

2

Technology, Industry, and Standardization Landscape

Increasing autonomy in network and service management is a result of integrating multiple solutions, which either originate from within the networking and related management technologies or are adopted from information technology (IT) and operational technology (OT) developments that influence the evolution of telco through megatrends. The focus on automation and autonomy unquestionably puts the emphasis on artificial intelligence (AI) based mechanisms and solutions, such as AI-driven management of networks, services, resources, and even the AI components themselves. Putting AI at the base of the technologies also brings extra requirements such as AI efficiency and security, which need to be solved systematically to ensure reliable and trustable autonomy of networks. Standardization is a must to ensure interworking and interoperability in heterogeneous environments that occur due to the fragmentation of telecommunication technologies, vendors (of both HW and SW), operational deployments, and stakeholders. The key standardization areas include network data, exposure and control; native AI and automation; security and trust in the context of AI; and network digital twins. The key SDOs include the 3rd Generation Partnership Project (3GPP), TM Forum (TMF), Internet Engineering Task Force (IETF), European Telecommunications Standards Institute (ETSI), Zero-touch network and Service Management (ZSM), and Open Radio Access Network (O-RAN) Alliance.

2.1 Introduction

Mobile networks are complex systems of systems integrating many different technologies (e.g., radio, core, transport, virtualization, management, and AI/ML), implemented by multiple vendors (e.g., equipment, device, and software), owned and operated by heterogeneous stakeholders (e.g., CSPs and

DOI: 10.1201/9788770041478-2

industrial partners), at a large variety of scale (e.g., private networks to nationwide commercial deployments) and different purposes (e.g., for telecommunication services, or supporting end-to-end solutions in industrial operational technology use cases). Creating not only working but resilient, highly available "telco-grade" systems at such a scale of diversity and complexity would be impossible without building on the foundation of international standards. Complex systems must be practically segmented into interworking subsystems or components with a clear separation of technological and administrative concerns to allow for distributed activities in research, development, deployment, operation, and maintenance. The resulting system should, however, fulfill both functional and non-functional requirements such as key performance indicators (KPI), key value indicators (KVI), and economical requirements of maintainability, operability, ownership, and governance [1, 2, 3]. The practical need for segmenting the system into subsystems and components drives the need for controlled and validated means for integration and interworking across the components. Due to the multistakeholder and multivendor environment, integration inevitably occurs across vendor and organization boundaries, requiring multilateral agreements on technological (e.g., interfaces and procedures) and administrative (e.g., management) integration points, governed by international standards.

The scope of standardization is to enable interoperability in the technical realization of a system with predefined functionalities and capabilities while adhering to a set of nonfunctional requirements. Standards may also cover operational processes and governance models related to the system. In this book, the focus will be on the technological aspects, as those are the ones that define the fundamental architecture, functionalities, interfaces, and capabilities of the system and drive the design choices that will end up in agreements and normative standards.

The rest of this chapter is organized as follows. Section 2.2 provides an overview of mega-trends that define the technology areas where both research and development and the accompanying standardization work define the key technology areas in network and management automation. The section enumerates the fundamental technical enablers such as data and knowledge management, security, closed-loop automation, human–machine interfaces and intents, AI/ML, various modeling aspects, and digital twinning. Section 2.3 reflects on these technologies by landscaping the corresponding work of the most prominent standard definition organizations (SDO). The technical areas are classified into a few high-level themes to make it easier to characterize their intersection with the standards, which themselves have also overlapping scopes. Section 2.4 provides the summary of the technical and standardization overview, bridging the work toward Chapters 3–13 that will unpack the detailed technical deep dives into each technology area including their individual standardization impact.

2.2 Technology Enablers and Industry Landscape

The evolution of mobile networks is conducted in a rich ecosystem with many technologies that influence, interact with, and enable others. As mobile networks have been developing, other fundamental technologies and industries have also been evolving rapidly, such as chips and the semiconductor industry, leading to cloud computing and AI/ML at scale; the internet and web technologies; network infrastructure such as wired and other (non-3GPP) wireless systems like Wi-Fi; consumer devices such as smartphones, IoT, and AR/VR devices; operational technologies involving autonomous robotics; aviation and space; and many others. In such a diverse technological evolution, generations of the mobile network (especially LTE and 5G) have not only evolved on top of their telecommunications legacy but also adopted the technologies of their era. Reasons for adopting technologies in a system rather than remaining in isolation may be economical (e.g., gain new capabilities or improve operational efficiency through field-proven technologies rather than investing in research and development of different ones), but also strategic (e.g., improve compatibility with existing systems and thus scale to new markers easier with reduced integration effort). Key technical trends that were influencing telecommunication evolution originate from the IT, including classical computer networks and the internet (TCP/IP and other protocols), web (HTTP, WAP, and HTTP/2), and cloud (virtualization, containerization, micro-service architecture, and orchestration). Recently, AI/ML and digital twins were also adopted from adjacent industries such as data sciences, analytics, and operational technologies as enablers of automation in telecommunication networks and network management. These trends and their impact on the telecommunication evolution are illustrated in Figure 2.1.

Adopting and internalizing technologies originating from IT, OT, or AI not only creates new capabilities in the network functions (such as the service-based architecture and network data analytics in the 5G core network, or AI/ML in radio resource management) but also has an impact on the network and service management. First, these technologies are also available for the management as potential capabilities; and it is indeed being exploited through AI/ML-based closed-loop automation and network digital twins. Second, these technologies also provide new management tasks and potential optimization opportunities that the management services need to consider,

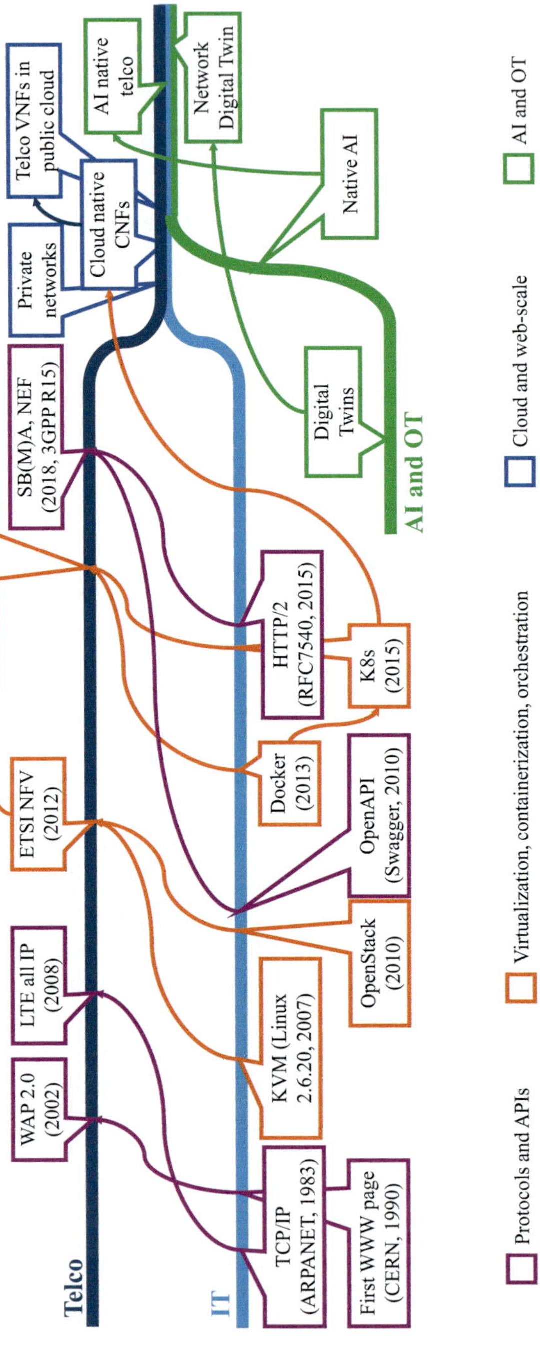

Figure 2.1 Influence and adoption of technology across industries (time scale is not proportionate).

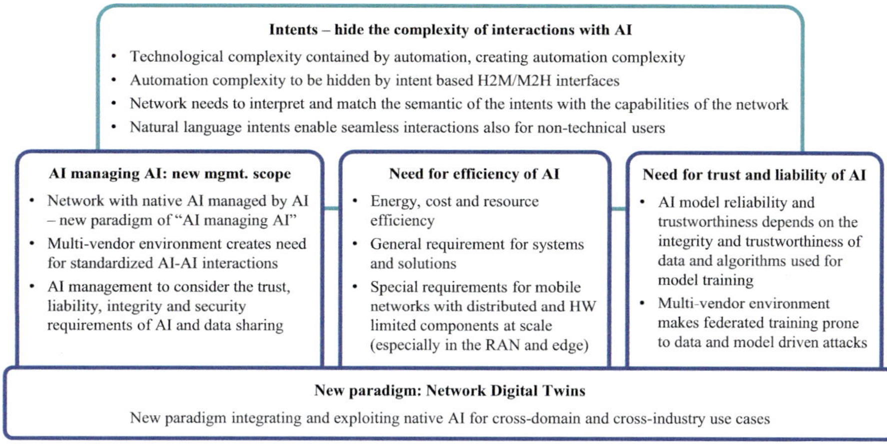

Figure 2.2 A pyramid of technical enablers of autonomy in network and service management.

handle, or leverage; for example, virtualization and cloud-native functions have created the need for network function orchestration; whereas integrating AI/ML natively into the network have created new management tasks related to the AI model training, deployment, performance and operation.

This book will discuss technologies mostly in the first category, that is, technologies that are available for the purposes of network and service management, especially with the scope of increasing network autonomy, and related standardization work. The key technologies are visualized in Figure 2.2. At the top, intents provide a mechanism to handle the complexity of the various technologies including the ones providing the means of automation itself. The next layer displays the "native AI" concept, that is, the immersive role of AI is visible both from the perspective of new capabilities provided by AI, as well as from the new management and security aspects generated by AI itself. At the foundation is the network digital twin concept, which leverages AI and modeling across domains and even industries to bring automation to the level of end-to-end solutions.

Considering the breadth and depth of the technologies, they are further broken down into smaller themes that will be explored in this book. Altogether, the following 11 technical themes will comprise the next Chapters 3–13:

Chapter 3: Data and Knowledge Management: Requirements and logical framework for efficient, flexible, and extendable data collection, distribution, and analytics with aspects of controlled quality and privacy of data delivery.

Chapter 4: Security, Trust, and Integrity: Data security with applications to AI federated training scenarios, and security and trust impact of AI technology focusing on ML as service deployments.

Chapter 5: Native AI/ML and the Related Management Aspects: New management tasks emerging due to the integration of AI into native system functionalities focusing on distributed scenarios and federated learning.

Chapter 6: Intent-based Network Management: The paradigm of system governance through declarative intents and the necessary autonomous system capabilities enabled by AI models.

Chapter 7: Closed-loop Automation: Closed loops in the context of intent-based management, providing advanced autonomy through adaptive self-learning closed loops.

Chapter 8: Human–Machine Interactions and Interfaces: The impact of intents on the interactions between humans (operators, private network owners, industry experts) and the network.

Chapter 9: Intent Interface Evolution and the Role of Language Models: The technical enablers and mechanisms for using natural language as a form of expressing intents and obtaining feedback from the system.

Chapter 10: State Models: A fundamental enabler of system-level autonomy providing the network with self-awareness of the current and future context of its own operation.

Chapter 11: Semantic Models and Semantic Composition: Another enabler of autonomy by modeling the system's own capabilities and providing intent-based dynamic composition of closed loops, delivering intent assurance without predefined blueprints.

Chapter 12: Decision Models: Technology enablers of data fusion and self-learning context-based AI decision models mapping insight (state models) and system capabilities (semantic models) to actions delivering impact on the system.

Chapter 13: Network Digital Twin: The new paradigm in network and service management automation, providing extended capabilities through a virtual replica and advanced AI modeling of the network.

The selection and order of the above technical themes follow an approach in which more generic topics are discussed first, followed by increasingly specific and advanced ones. Reflections and references to standardization

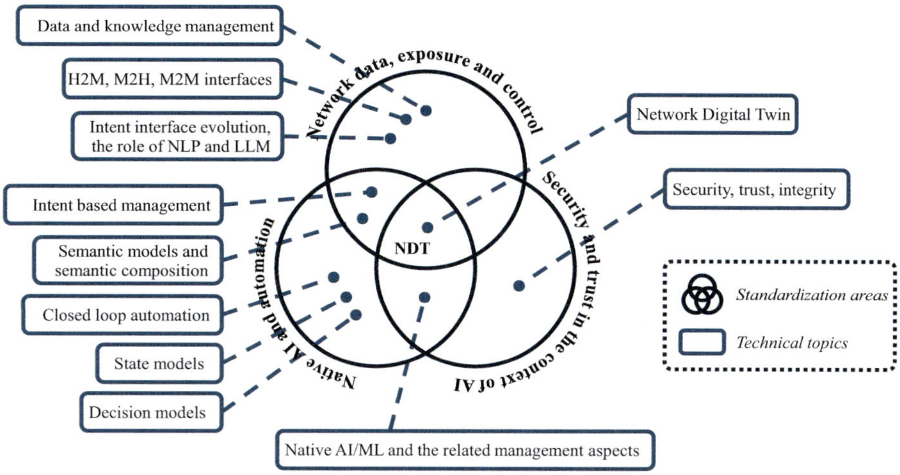

Figure 2.3 Standardization categories and key technical themes of the book.

are provided in each chapter driven by the discussion logic of the theme. However, in practice, standardization work is governed by various standards developing organizations (SDO), each organizing their work into a high number of study and work items, which have their own limited scope and lifecycle. Before going into the details of standardization activities (see Section 2.3), a more comprehensive overview of the common standardization areas is provided. The following four standardization areas represent a grouping across the agenda of prominent SDOs from recent years related to the megatrends and technical themes of the book:

- Network data, exposure, and control
- Security and trust in the context of AI
- Native AI and automation
- Network digital twin

Figure 2.3 illustrates the linkage between the book's technical themes and the standardization areas. As shown by the Venn diagram in Figure 2.3, there are intersections between most of the standardization areas, with the special case that network digital twin is at the intersection of all other areas as it integrates those concepts and technologies into a coherent solution. The 11 technical themes are mapped to the Venn diagram according to their relation to one or multiple of the standardization areas.

Both the mappings of the technical themes and the intersections of the standardization areas indicate a high level of interdependency among the technologies. This can be attributed to the iterative nature of technology evolution and innovation; evolving a use case or requirement with a new set of technologies that have become available since the last revision will create new solutions adopting what is useful from the new technologies, and as a by-product, producing the corresponding standardization work to make the solution multivendor, interoperable and scalable.

2.3 Standardization Framework

In most of the SDOs, standardization work is categorized either as a study or a specification. Studies are exploratory works, reporting key issues or technical challenges to which potential solutions are collected and discussed. Studies are part of the approved material produced by the SDO, but they are informative, that is, they do not mandate any implementation or adoption for standards compliance. Specifications, on the other hand, provide the normative standards that become the definitive guideline on how to design and implement a system that is interoperable with other systems following the same standard. The process of standardization is an iterative, collaborative workflow that involves technical discussions, interim agreements, and negotiations among the full spectrum of the ecosystem players from chipset and device vendors through telecommunication equipment and solution vendors to network operators and even vertical industries. Figure 2.4 illustrates the workflow of the 3rd Generation Partnership Project (3GPP) [4] which is one of the key and oldest established SDOs that has a great impact both on the technical approach and work methods of other more recent SDOs. In this book, both normative specifications and informative reports are considered, as novel topics often spend multiple years in the study phase, already collecting a great amount of knowledge and reflecting the thinking and vision of the SDO about the direction of future normative specification work. Given that many technical themes of this book belong to exploratory areas at least when applied in the telecommunication and network management field, limiting the standardization aspects to approved specifications only would have yielded a limited and biased scope.

The most prominent SDOs related to the key technological themes of the book are the already mentioned 3GPP, the ETSI Zero touch network and Service Management (ZSM), the TM Forum (TMF), the Open Radio Access Network Alliance (O-RAN), and in selected topics the Internet Engineering Task Force (IETF) or the Internet Research Task Force (IRTF).

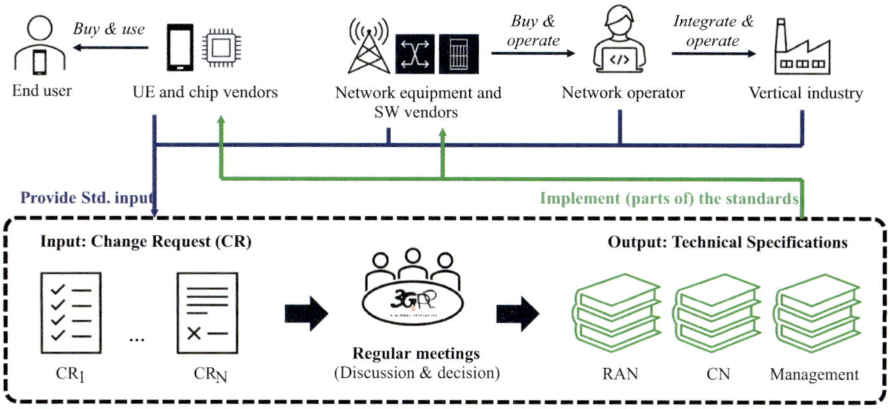

Figure 2.4 Overview of the 3GPP standardization process.

The 3GPP [4] defines the standards for generations of cellular mobile networks and the corresponding management technology. Existing mobile networks since GSM through LTE and 5G (and in the future, 6G) are all based on the 3GPP standards defining the detailed system architecture, data-plane protocols, signaling, management and security aspects of radio, core network, various subsystems, and terminals. While 3GPP is the definitive SDO for the fundamental cellular radio and mobile communication technology, is also studying the impact of data-driven analytics and AI/ML on the system. In Release-15 frozen in January 2018, 3GPP has defined service-based architecture (SBA) for most of the core network control plane function interactions [5]. The need for SBA is driven by technology evolution (networked APIs of micro-services) and pushback from the complexity (specification, design, and implementation) of telco reference point-based architectures. 5G is the first telco generation to natively specify its CN C-plane as SBA. RAN and U-plane remain reference point-based (but the number of such interfaces is limited). This is a transition from previous point-to-point interfaces (integration reference points) and greatly reduces the complexity of introducing new capabilities and services into the mobile core network.

In the 3GPP core network, 5G brought two important novelties relevant to data, analytics, and eventually automation. First, the Network Data Analytics Function (NWDAF) [6] is a new 5G core network function that was made possible by the transition to the SBA itself. The scope of NWDAF is to collect and analyze network data using the services of other NFs and the OAM and to provide analytics outputs as a service to other NFs and to network management. Second, the Network Exposure Function (NEF) [7] is

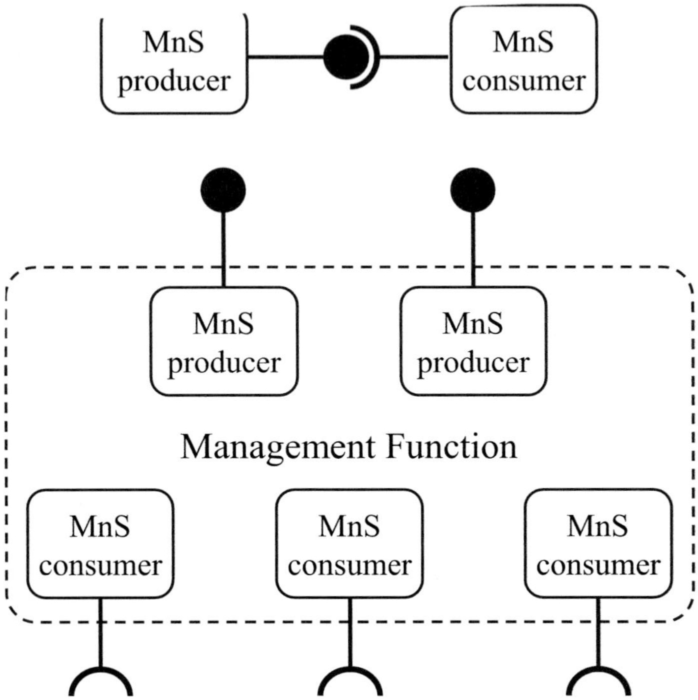

Figure 2.5 3GPP service-based management architecture.

a new network function and concept to expose the 5G system's capability to external entities (application functions) enabling network programmability and the integration of 5G into other technology domains.

Similarly to the core network SBA, the 3GPP management architecture also experienced a transition for services (Management Services, MnS) instead of functionalities, yielding the service-based management architecture (SBMA) [8], which shares a similar design but not to be confused with SBA. The MnS-based management architecture creates a clean service-based design, where only services are defined. Services are provided by MnS producers, and consumed by MnS consumers, which are logical roles that could be assigned to any functionality. For this reason, management functions are no longer defined by the standard, leaving them to implementation; a management function may be any collection of MnS producer and consumer roles, in addition to other business logic that is outside of the scope of 3GPP specification (Figure 2.5). This gives a high degree of freedom in network management and enables software and service orchestration concepts (applied together with virtualization, containerization, and their management) to be leveraged in the implementation of a network management system.

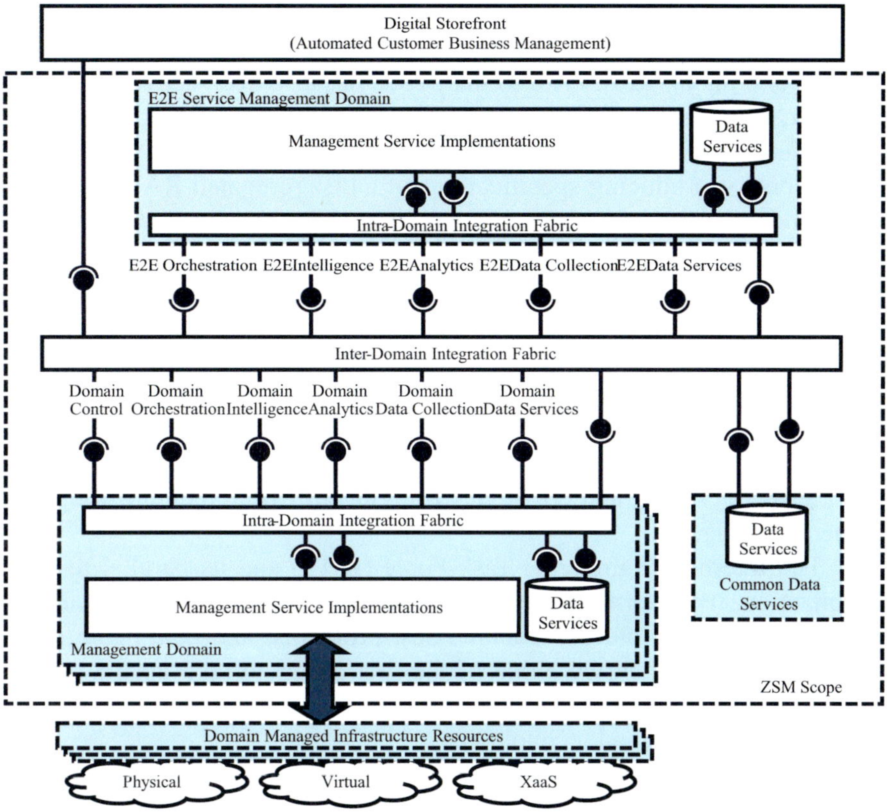

Figure 2.6 Reference architecture of the ZSM e2e management framework. Reproduced from [10].

The ETSI ZSM [9] was launched at the end of 2017 with the initiative to define the requirements, reference architecture, and mechanisms for end-to-end network and service management automation. From day one, ZSM adopted a service-based architecture with management domains cooperating through an integration fabric [10]. The 3GPP MnS architecture and ZSM reference architecture display a common theme: management capabilities are represented by services, which can be advertised, discovered, produced, and consumed according to software-defined service concepts well known from the IT evolution. The reference architecture for the end-to-end ZSM framework is shown in Figure 2.6. Later reports and specifications of ZSM used this reference architecture as a basis to introduce automation, such as closed loops [11, 12, 13], intents [14, 15], and network digital twins [16, 17].

The TM Forum (TMF) has a long history of producing studies and recommendations addressing network operation and management issues and hosting collaborative events for players in the telecom industry. The TMF has been active and one of the frontrunners advocating network autonomy [18, 19] and intents [20]. Prior to that, TMF has also been active in AI management, APIs, and operations [21, 22].

The Open RAN Alliance (O-RAN) was formed in 2018 with the primary scope of producing specifications of a disaggregated RAN with open multivendor interfaces (partly 3GPP, partly O-RAN driven). O-RAN also defined the architecture and platform for near-real-time and nonreal-time ran intelligent controller (RIC) to host closed-loop control mechanisms using AI/ML applications in the RAN. In the RIC architecture, applications are integrated into the RAN via bidirectional interfaces, that is, not only accessing network insight but also manipulating the network's behavior, especially through RRM programming. O-RAN is relevant in defining use cases and framework for management automation in the RAN, adopting intent principles [23], and effectively bringing AI/ML and cloud computing to the radio edge.

The Internet Engineering Task Force (IETF) and its parallel research organization, the Internet Research Task Force (IRTF) are traditionally the definitive SDO for Internet technologies, protocols, and data-plane mechanisms. However, they were one of the first SDOs to take up the concept of network digital twins [24], produce a reference architecture, and collect related requirements and technologies.

Although each SDO has its own scope and focus, each has one or more of the big trends and standardization areas depicted in Figure 2.3 on its agenda. The last part of this section will aim to chart selected works from the major SDOs that were introduced above, categorized along the standardization areas. Note that the selection is not comprehensive, as its intent is merely to demonstrate the variety of activities and give a hint of how well each area has been established (or, rather, being a more recent domain) through a slice from the history of standards.

The charts display a rough time axis to illustrate the time when the studies or specifications first appeared and potentially the time span through which they have been actively developed. Note that some of the listed standards are works in progress, therefore, their development window may have been extended, or new works could have been spin-off since the time of writing. Therefore, these charts are meant to be illustrative and not comprehensive or an ultimate source of mapping all SDO activities.

The first standardization area is network data, exposure, and control enablers, depicted in Figure 2.7. As producing network measurements and operational data is intertwined with the network technologies, inarguably

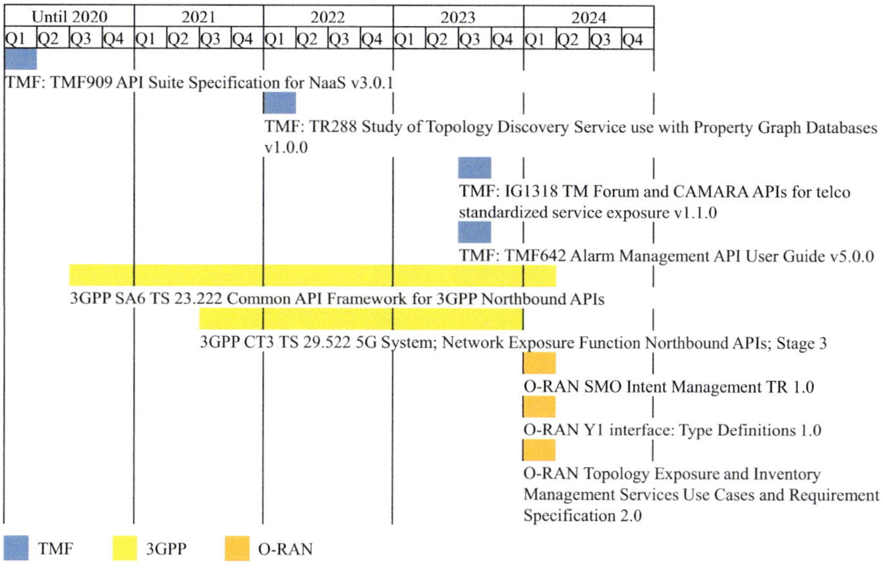

Figure 2.7 Standardization of network data, exposure, and control enablers.

there are more fundamental standards that go back to the days of defining configuration, performance, and fault management. However, the scope of this book is to look out for the enablers of automation and in this case observability and programmability, hence the selection of the shortlisted standards. TMF has been an established player in producing APIs for network as a service and exposure of topology and services; 3GPP is definitely providing the enablers through APIs and NEF; whereas O-RAN has also been active in defining enablers of RIC service management and orchestration.

The next standardization area is security and trust in the context of AI, shown in Figure 2.8. The AI context is deliberately mixed into the scope as security by itself is a huge topic, however in this book, the focus will be on the aspects of AI both in terms of data security applied to AI training (such as in federated learning) or the security issues created by the AI technology itself. Still, the intersection of AI and security is a topic that has stirred the interest of most SDOs, and doing that quite recently shows that the topic is trending and there is more to be expected. Works were published already from ETSI ZSM, 3GPP, and TMF, all addressing security concerns of AI in their respective systems. O-RAN also established a work group dedicated to security aspects of O-RAN. The relevance of AI and security is expected to increase with the adoption of AI and native AI (that is an expanding topic on its own – see the next standardization area).

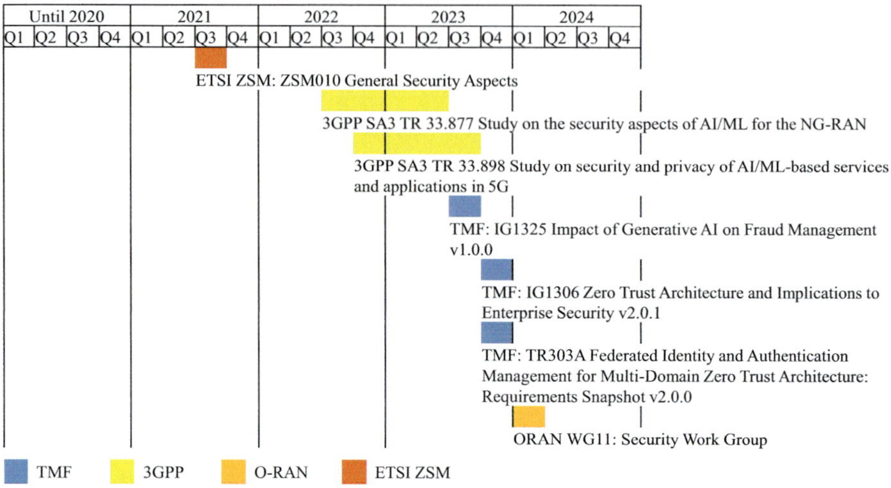

Figure 2.8 Standardization landscape of security and trust in the context of AI.

Therefore, the current chart may be just the initial head of a rapidly growing body of standards.

The third standardization area is native AI and automation, depicted in Figure 2.9. Despite being a very advanced and broad technology area, there are a significant number of standard documents that have been produced since 2020. TMF is clearly leading by the number of assets released, creating an abundance of sources to learn about the fundamental concepts of AI management and operations, autonomous networks, and intents. ZSM produced fewer but significant works starting from a systematic survey of the means of automation, then focusing on closed loops (going as far as advanced self-learning closed loops) and intent-driven network autonomy. The ZSM studies on intents and autonomy are also well aligned with the TMF works, even sharing the basic taxonomy of owning and handling intents in the network management domain. O-RAN was also active in mapping AI/ML operations (one that is similar to TMF's AIOps) onto the RIC architecture. 3GPP has also worked on the management of AI and intent-driven management services, integrating these concepts into the SBMA. It is expected that these topics continue with more study and specification work as AI and related automation technologies develop and mature.

The fourth standardization area is the network digital twin, illustrated in Figure 2.10. This is the youngest of the identified standardization areas, due to the network digital twin concept being rather fresh itself. The front runners, IRTF and ZSM, are running in parallel and at the current time of

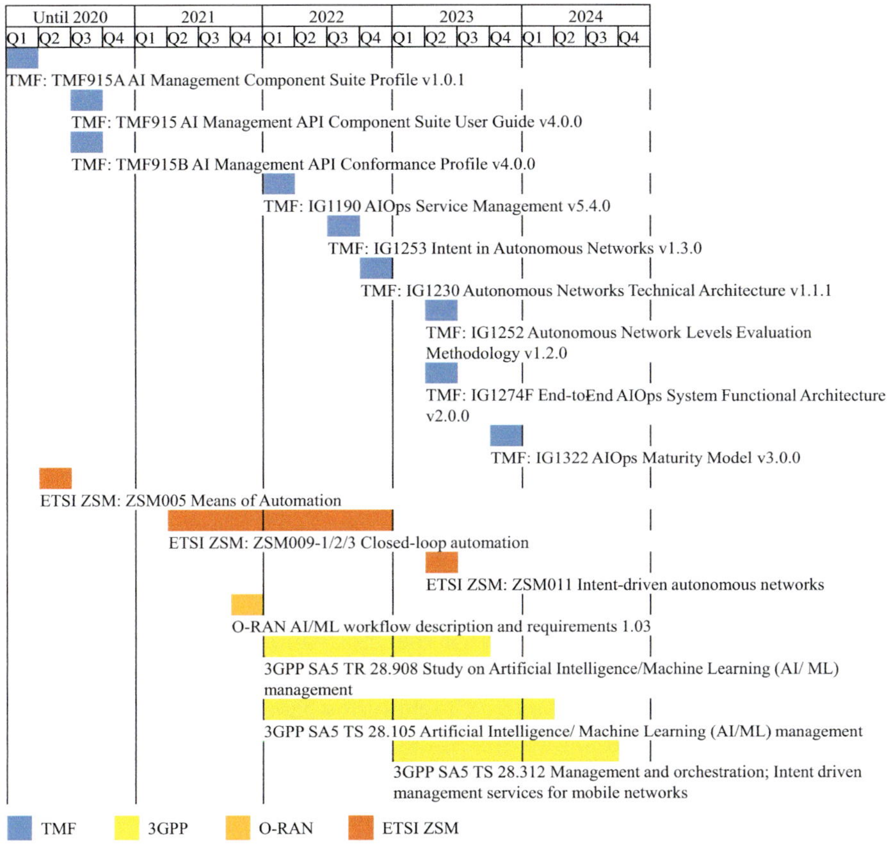

Figure 2.9 Standardization initiatives in native AI and automation.

development already reference to each other. TMF has also picked up the topic although with the specific scope of decision intelligence, whereas IRTF and especially ZSM are targeting network management automation use cases with NDT. Although this standardization area may seem to be understaffed, it has been elected as a standalone topic for two reasons. First, its momentum is clearly gaining, with increasing contributions to the standards and also from nonstandard material such as white papers, industry blogs, and press releases. Second, and even more importantly, NDTs are at the intersection of all technologies that are in the other three standardization areas: they are a novel combination and organization of data exposure, a multitude of AI modeling, automation mechanisms, and security (both as a concern and as potential use cases). This positions NDTs into the intersection of all three other identified standardization areas and justifies it is on the spot on the

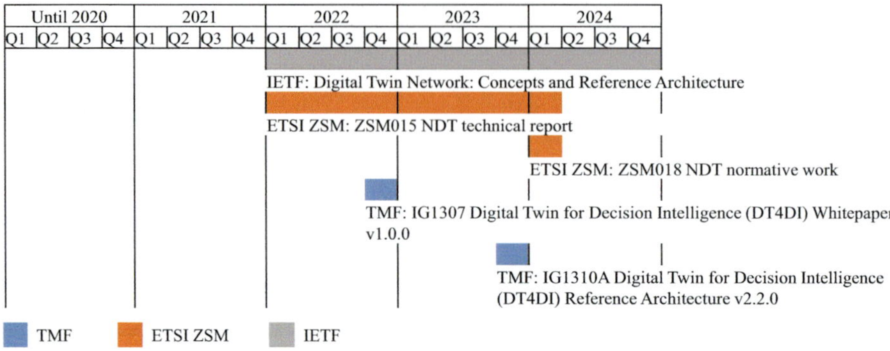

Figure 2.10 Network digital twin standardization.

chart. The entire Chapter 13 is dedicated to discussing the rich technological spectrum of NDTs for the same reasons.

2.4 Summary

This chapter provided an overview of the motivations for normative standards in the specification, operation, and maintenance of complex system of systems such as mobile networks. A technology landscape across IT, telco and OT/AI industries has shown that today's telecom systems have adopted many technologies from other industries especially ones that provide strong enablers of automation. As those technologies bring their own management requirements and potential security issues to the telecom world, now they need to be handled natively in the telecom systems and ultimately governed through telecom standards.

The chapter introduced the book's technical themes covering the enablers for automation, starting from data collection and knowledge management, through security, native AI, closed-loop automation, intents, and NDTs. These themes correspond to the mega-trends of the technical evolution that include the evolution of requirements toward network and service management, with many of the actual technologies being adopted from other industries. The technical themes also mapped out the relevant standardization aspects.

Due to the large extent of standardization work produced for networking and specifically mobile systems, four standardization areas were identified, which contain selected reports and specifications produced by the prominent SDOs. At this point, the technical themes of the book were also mapped to these areas, creating a one-glance view of the themes and the standards, including potential overlaps and intersections between the standard areas.

The next part of the book, consisting of Chapters 3–13, will traverse through the technical themes and explore them one by one. Each chapter may be read on its own, but the order of the chapters was chosen to enable a linear read. To maintain bidirectional cohesion across the themes, cross references appear not only backward but also forward to highlight later topics, indicating that some topics may have an extension or an adjacent related material under a different theme.

Bibliography

[1] International Telecommunication Union, Radiocommunication Sector, "Detailed specifications of the terrestrial radio interfaces of International Mobile Telecommunications-2020 (IMT-2020)", Recommendation ITU-R M.2150-2, December 2023

[2] Next Generation Mobile Networks Alliance, "5G White Paper", Version 1.0, February 2015

[3] 6G Smart Networks and Services Industry Association (6G-IA), "What societal values will 6G address?", Version 1.0, May 2022, DOI 10.5281/zenodo.6557534

[4] 3rd Generation Partnership Project (3GPP), Online, https://www.3gpp.org/

[5] 3GPP TS 23.501 System architecture for the 5G System (5GS)

[6] 3GPP TS 23.288 Architecture enhancements for 5G System (5GS) to support network data analytics services

[7] 3GPP TS 29.522 5G System; Network Data Analytics signalling flows; Stage 3

[8] 3GPP TS 28.533 Management and orchestration; Architecture framework

[9] European Telecommunications Standards Institute (ETSI), "ZSM Zero touch network & Service Management (ZSM)", Online, https://www.etsi.org/technologies/zero-touch-network-service-management

[10] ETSI GS ZSM 002, "Zero-touch network and Service Management (ZSM); Reference Architecture", V1.1.1 (2019-08)

[11] ETSI GS ZSM 009-1, "Zero-touch network and Service Management (ZSM); Closed-Loop Automation; Part 1: Enablers", V1.1.1 (2021-06)

[12] ETSI GS ZSM 009-2, "Zero-touch network and Service Management (ZSM); Closed-Loop Automation; Part 2: Solutions for automation of E2E service and network management use cases", V1.1.1 (2022-06)

[13] ETSI GR ZSM 009-3, "Zero-touch network and Service Management (ZSM); Closed-Loop Automation; Part 3: Advanced topics", V1.1.1 (2023-08)
[14] ETSI GR ZSM 011, "Zero-touch network and Service Management (ZSM); Intent-driven autonomous networks; Generic aspects" V1.1.1 (2023-02)
[15] ETSI GS ZSM 016, "Zero-touch network and Service Management (ZSM); Intent-driven Closed Loops" V1.1.1 (2024-10)
[16] ETSI GR ZSM 015, "Zero-touch network and Service Management (ZSM); Network Digital Twin" V1.1.1 (2024-02)
[17] ETSI GS ZSM 018, "Zero-touch network and Service Management (ZSM); Network Digital Twin for enhanced zero-touch network and service management", V1.1.1 (2024-12)
[18] TM Forum, "Autonomous Networks Technical Architecture", IG1230, Version 1.1.1, December 2022
[19] TM Forum, "Autonomous Network Levels Evaluation Methodology", IG1252, Version 1.2.0, June 2023
[20] TM Forum, "Intent in Autonomous Networks", IG1253, Version 1.3.0, August 2022
[21] TM Forum, "AI Management API Component Suite User Guide", TMF915, Version 4.0.0
[22] TM Forum, "AIOps Service Management", IG1190, Version 5.4.0
[23] O-RAN Alliance, "O-RAN SMO Intents-driven Management 3.0
[24] C. Zhou et al., "Digital Twin Network: Concepts and Reference Architecture," draft-irtf-nmrg-network-digital-twin-arch-05, 4 March 2024, https://www.ietf.org/archive/id/draft-irtf-nmrg-network-digital-twin-arch-05.txt

3

Data and Knowledge Management

Network data is a diverse set of information provided by all components of an operational mobile system, including configuration files, traditional telecommunication performance and fault management indicators, up to infrastructure and network function or application software logs. Collecting, correlating, analyzing, and operationalizing this information is a challenge due to the distributed data sources, the overhead of data production, transition, storage, and processing, as well as the semantic challenge of how to find, understand, and extract actionable insights from the abundance of digital information, especially when the goal is to drive closed-loop autonomous network management and operation. A data and knowledge management framework is necessary to deal with the complexity and size of network data efficiently, ensuring both low resource overhead and high data utility. Modularity, extendibility, and support for a multitude of data sources and consumers (even ephemeral ones) are key requirements, just, as well as the highest standards of security, such as confidentiality, authenticity, integrity, and anonymity. Considering AI data patterns such as model (re)training, inference, reinforcement, and distributed or federated learning scenarios is also necessary.

3.1 Introduction

Mobile networks generate a large amount of data from different types (e.g., PM, FM, logs, traces, probes, and telemetry), for various purposes (e.g., internal C-plane procedures, optimization, monitoring, and management), on a wide range of time scales (from real-time on-the-spot consumption to long-term persistency), from multiple technology domains (e.g., RAN, transport, and core) and layers (U/C-plane interfaces, transport and application protocol stacks, and devices), at wide geographical/topological distributions (from thousands of RAN sites to a few centralized core data centers). Some of the

DOI: 10.1201/9788770041478-3

data is specific to the telecommunication technology, equipment, services, and their management, while others are a product of implementation technology such as software solutions, virtualization, and containerization, and hosted cloud infrastructure. The OSS/BSS involved in the management of the networks also produce operational data.

Producing, transferring, consuming, and potentially storing data all have their overheads, both in terms of resources (such as computing, network, and storage) and in terms of operational effort (e.g., to properly configure data sources, collection, storage, and exposure to consumers). Usually, not all data that could potentially be produced by a mobile network (or even by a single equipment or VNF/CNF in a network) is actually produced; likewise, not all data that is produced is actually consumed or stored; and finally, not all data that is stored for the long term will be eventually utilized. Therefore, there is potential to improve data availability, however, it is desirable that the associated costs and overhead are kept limited and justified by the capabilities enabled by the data.

Network data is essential for any planning, operational, optimization, and management use case, especially if those are (at least partly) to be automated or to be driven by real insights and awareness of the state of the network, including its services, resources, and demand. The key technology enabler for data-driven analytics and automation is to integrate AI/ML models both in the NFs and within the network management services and tools supporting network operation. The uptake of AI/ML has a dual impact on the utility of network data. First, AI/ML has the potential to analyze such high quantities of data that have been previously impossible, making the collection of such quantities of data justified in the first place. Second, AI/ML enables to implement capabilities (analytics, decision, automation) that used to be out of reach of a manual or scripted network operation, increasing the potential value of the produced (collected) data.

The current state of data availability within various deployed networks is mixed. The quantity of data produced may be already very high, sometimes even causing practical problems in storing or collecting it (especially in distributed and resource-limited parts of the network such as the RAN). At the same time, the usability (and consequently the potential value) of the data may be limited. A prominent reason for this is the disparate and uncorrelated production of data at different parts of the network (topologically, geographically, and domain- and technology-wise). However, for management automation purposes (especially for e2e service management but also for e2e performance modeling), it is important that network data produced at different locations remains in correlation with respect to their e2e scope. For example,

PM data collected separately from the RAN and core network related to the same PDU session only enables to reconstruct the e2e performance of the PDU session if the RAN and core data both carry a shared identity associated with the PDU session (either as metadata, or in-line with the data itself). Many of the 3GPP-defined data types are traditionally domain-specific (RAN vs. core) and thus lack network-wide identities that would enable e2e correlation. Some of this limitation is built into the technology specification, for example, by defining RAN-specific identities in RAN procedures and measurements that are not known at the core network (and vice versa), requiring out-of-band methods (such as correlation of RAN/core IDs via different domain and network management systems and logs) to find out matching measurements. Other limitations are due to implementations that do maintain the necessary mapping between domains and IDs but only internally, within their runtime state (e.g., C-plane NFs participating in e2e signaling procedures) and do not expose them to an external consumer. The lack of methods and interfaces to expose even what is available as correlated information has given rise to external probe systems that try to reconstruct e2e information by listening to the network traffic on multiple interfaces (both U-plane and C-plane). Had the network standards and implementations enabled the exposure of correlated information, the probes as they were would not have been necessary.

The richness and abundance of network data, combined with the potential value of applying AI/ML technology, and the lessons learned from the history of probing (i.e., reasons and consequences of lacking native enablers for collecting correlated insight), motivate a more holistic approach to the production, collection, consumption, and storage of network data. The rest of this chapter introduces and discusses a data management reference architecture, with the essential role of becoming a key infrastructure element in enabling network management automation. The reference architecture is based on abstract roles such as data source, data consumer, and entities involved in the transit or storage of data. In any specific implementation of the reference architecture, these abstract roles may be associated with existing network components, such as NFs, or management functions, or delegated to new entities. The purpose of the reference architecture is to enable the discussion of data management-specific requirements and solutions in a neutral way, without being framed by any specific network standard or taxonomy.

3.2 General Concepts

The key design aspects of the data management reference architecture (DMRA) are related to the concepts that ensure commonality, extendibility, programmability, efficiency, and feasibility. Overall, these concepts ensure the applicability and flexibility of the DM and its capability to interwork/ support future technologies and management paradigms. The concept terms refer to the following attributes and capabilities:

Commonality: The reference architecture enables the collection of any data (trace, PM, logs, analytics result, etc., both standardized and custom) from any data source. That is, the reference architecture can just as well incorporate and distribute data from existing data sources having an already well-defined data production interface as from any future data source, without the need to redesign the reference architecture itself.

Extendibility: New data types, data sources, and data consumers can be added without architecture or standardization impact.

Programmability: Data consumers can discover available data, and consumers can dynamically specify (and modify) when and what data they want to receive. Selecting all input data for a consumer implementation (e.g., an analytics service) does not have to be a design and deployment time decision, enabling consumers to discover and request data by adapting to data availability and other dynamic contexts. Programmability is enabled by an up-to-date view of the available data (from available data sources), so that data consumers may issue a query for available data and data sources, and request for actual data on a need basis. An additional enabler for programmability is the use of metadata to describe data, which enables data consumers to locate a known and required type of data, or filter through the available data and decide whether one or the other would be useful for their operation.

Efficiency: Data sources do not need to produce data that is not consumed at all, and data sources do not need to replicate data due to multiple consumers. Data routing may be optimized by leveraging common paths between a data source toward multiple consumers, with late replication to minimize duplicate transfers.

Feasibility: When the reference architecture is implemented in a specific technology domain or standard area, strive for maximum reuse of existing interfaces and functional blocks rather than creating additional architecture layers and components.

3.3 Architecture Reference Model

The data management reference architecture is introduced through a view showing a full architecture decomposition of logical components and their

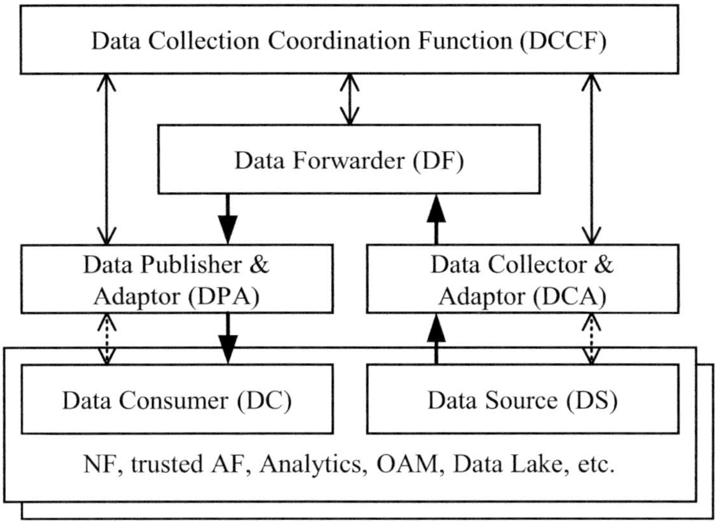

Figure 3.1 Full architecture decomposition of the data management reference architecture.

interfaces (Figure 3.1). This view enables a clear-cut understanding of how the key concepts are realized and where the potential touchpoints and commonalities with state-of-the-art systems.

In summary, the backbone of the reference architecture is defined by the data flows, which originate at data sources, go through the data forwarder (handling data replication and routing), and terminate at data consumers. The data flows are programmed by a logical controller entity referred to as the data collector coordination function (DCCF). There are additional adaptors that attach the data sources and data consumers to the data forwarder, responsible for translation between existing interface specifications and the data forwarder technology.

In more detail, the roles and functionalities of the logical components are listed below:

Data source (DS): Producer of data; maybe a network function from any domain (e.g., gNB CU-CP, UPF, and SMF), OAM, analytics function, application function, and the like. Anything that produces data that may be of interest to another entity may be considered a DS from the reference architecture's perspective.

Data collector and adaptor (DCA): A logical functionality that integrates one or more data sources to the reference architecture. The primary scope of the adaptor is protocol translation from the data source's native data production interface to a potentially different data input service access point exposed by the data forwarder. The adaptor decouples the technology or standard evolution of the data source interface and the data forwarder interface. The adaptor enables to integrate an existing (and potentially standardized, productized, immutable) data source to the architecture without having to modify the data source. A second scope of the adaptor is to translate between the DCCF and the data source during registration procedures (i.e., making the data source and its potentially producible data known to the DCCF) and during data requests (i.e., request from the DCCF to the data source to start producing data).

Data forwarder (DF): A scalable and programmable messaging framework responsible for the transfer of data from the data sources to their data consumers. The functionality of the DF includes data replication (i.e., when multiple DCs request the same data – removing the replication burden from the producing DS), and implementing the efficiency design goal.

Data publisher and adaptor (DPA): The data consumer side of the adaptor, with a functionality analogous to the DCA but for DCs. That is, the DPA integrates one or more DCs to the reference architecture, translating between the DC's interfaces and the DF (for the data transfer) and the DCCF (for DC registration and data requests).

Data consumer (DC): Consumer of data; like a data source, a data consumer can also be a network function from any domain (e.g., gNB CU-CP, UPF, and SMF), OAM, analytics function, application function, or anything that consumes data produced by others for any reason.

Data collection coordination function (DCCF): The DCCF is the controller layer of the data management reference architecture – it handles data source and consumer registrations (to enable authorization and maintain an up-to-date registry of what data is available from where); handles requests to receive data (by triggering data production and the relevant data sources, and programming the DF to convey the data to the right data consumers). Note that the DCCF does not transfer data itself, it only knows about data (types, locations, sources, consumers) and orchestrates the production and delivery of the data through the DS-DCA-DF-DPA-DC chains.

The presented functionalities denote only logical roles within the DMF. An actual implementation may consider merging multiple functionalities into a single entity (e.g., into a micro-service implementation). Notable examples of merged functionalities are:

- A real function may be both a data source and a data consumer as per its roles within the DMF. That is, a function may be a consumer of multiple input data; perform processing on them (e.g., analytics or any other business logic – not within the scope of the DMF); and finally provide one or more output to other functions to consume.
- A data source may be collapsed with its data collector and adaptor, and likewise a data consumer may be collapsed with its data publisher and adaptor. This practically means that a data source or consumer can directly interact with the DCCF and with the DF.

Persistency of the data may be handled by attaching data lakes or any other database to the DMF. Such integration logically means having data consumers with storage capability, which may also act as data sources serving their stored data to other consumers.

3.4 Functional Components

3.4.1 Data collection and coordination function

As the master entity orchestrating the data flow from data sources to data consumers, the DCCF has multiple roles.

First, the DCCF acts as a registry, keeping track of the following information:

- The list of data sources
- The list of data consumers
- All data that could be produced by each data source
- The data that is currently produced by each data source
- Active data requests: the data that is requested by each data consumer (that is, if the data is produced by a data source, the DMF has an obligation to deliver it to the designated Data consumer).

The second role of the DCCF is to provide an interface to the data source and data consumers that enables them to register themselves, describe their data source capabilities (by data sources), or supply requests for data (by data consumers). Such interactions cause changes in the registry maintained by the DCCF and enable the DCCF to provide notifications to interested parties (e.g., if a data source announces to the DCCF that it has become capable of producing a new type of data, e.g., due to a software update, the DCCF may notify data consumers about it), or to trigger data production at data sources (e.g., if a data consumer requests a data).

The third role of the DCCF is to interact with the data forwarder, which is the messaging framework responsible for the actual delivery of data from data sources to data consumers. The optimization of the data flow (e.g., routing and optimal data replication leveraging if multiple data consumers request the same data) is the responsibility shifted to the DF and does not concern the DCCF.

3.4.2 Adaptors

The role of the adaptors between the data sources and the DCCF (data collector and adaptor) and between the DCCF and the data consumers (data publisher and adaptor) is to translate between the interface/API of the DCCF and that of the data sources/consumers. Such adaptors are needed in case an existing data source/consumer with its own unchangeable API has to be connected to the DMF. Examples of such cases include data lakes (see also Section 3.6.2), standardized network functions such as SA2 NWDAF [1] or SA5 management services [2, 3], or connecting ZSM domain management functions through the domain integration fabric or the cross-domain integration fabric [4]. In such cases, the adaptors would correspond to actual implementations (e.g., as micro-services per each API they need to connect to the DCCF/DF). In other cases, when a new data source or data consumer is implemented, they could directly interface with the DMF without adaptors. In those cases, the internal implementation of the data source/consumer may still consist of a functional entity (e.g., a data API micro-service) that implements the role of the adaptor, but as a component internal to the data source/consumer.

3.4.3 Data forwarder

The role of the data forwarder is to transfer the data from data sources to data consumers in an efficient manner. The DF ensures that each data source needs to produce a single piece of data at most once regardless of the number of data consumers that have requested that data. On the data consumer side, the DF ensures that every data consumer gets its own copy of the data, and it gets no other data than what it has requested. Therefore, every data consumer may operate in full isolation from every other data consumer as do not need to implement filtering on the incoming data (as opposed to a shared message bus where they could receive data that others have requested). Another benefit of this isolation is that every data consumer may be authenticated and authorized to receive only a restricted set of data, which can only be enforced if the final delivery of data is handled separately per data consumer.

Internally the DF may implement optimization techniques such as lazy data replication, meaning that two data consumers requesting the same data cause the data to travel in a single copy as long as possible, up to the last point where the data paths toward the two data consumers branch. This requires appropriate transport topology and data-aware forwarding nodes within the DF. Such optimization capabilities are considered implementation-specific to the DF as they do not change the observed behavior of the DF from the DCCF or data source/consumer perspective.

3.4.4 Data descriptors

The data descriptor's role is to provide a machine-readable summary of the syntax, semantics, and production/consumption conditions of a piece of data. The syntax of the data enables programmatic interpretation of the data in operations such as serialization, parsing, and storing. The semantics of the data captures the meaning and utility of the information encoded by the data. The semantics of the data should also be machine interpretable which enables programmatic comparison of two distinct pieces of data (through their descriptors) to test for their semantic equivalence or similarity. Computable semantic equivalence enables to automate queries and searches for available data with specific semantics, which is a key requirement for the data management reference architecture and its DCCF logical component (see Section 3.4.1).

In addition to the syntax and semantics of the data, the descriptor should also contain information that can allow SLA management and arbitrate between data providers and consumers while access to data is provided. This is needed especially to handle cases when there are competing requests for the same data or there are resource limitations associated with producing or serving data from a producer to a consumer. Information may be associated both at the production side of the data (i.e., describing the capabilities of a data source) or the requirements/expectations at the consumption side (i.e., describing the conditions of how a data consumer would like to get the data). Information may include (without limitation) the following aspects:

- Maximum latency from producing the data (at the data source) and receiving it (by the data consumer). This limit may be used by the DCCF or the DF to ensure proper QoS for the data in transit, and also potentially by the data source to prioritize the production of data with more urgency.

- Frequency of the calls (data source side: indicates the capability to produce the data at a given frequency; data consumer side: describes the requirement to receive the data at a given frequency). Even if the right data (considering its syntax/semantic) is available at a data source, if it is not able to produce it with the expected frequency, it may be unusable for a data consumer who needs it more frequently.
- Availability and reliability: Data consumers may express requirements on tolerated outages of the data. For example, an analytics algorithm that is sensitive to the order of subsequent data points may fail or deliver false output if certain intermittent data points are missing from a sequence.
- Quality of information: Data consumers may express requirements on missing or wrong data points, which may disqualify certain data sources from serving such consumers (even if the syntax/semantic of the produced data would be acceptable).

In addition to machine-readable information, data descriptors should also contain human-readable text descriptions to help engineers and designers work with the data. Moreover, text descriptions are also potential sources of additional semantic layers extracted through NLP artificial intelligence mechanisms, as discussed in more detail later in Chapter 9.

3.5 Deployment Options

3.5.1 Chaining of data sources and data consumers

Usually, analytics functions are not only consumers (of multiple input data) but are also producers (providing insight or algorithm output). Therefore, the DMF supports that the same logical entity acts both as data source and data consumer (Figure 3.2). Within the same entity, as data source, any number and type of data may be supported; likewise, as data consumer, there is no limit on the diversity of the data to be consumed. Such flexibility enables to break down a complex multistage analytics pipeline into reusable components (each implemented as cloud-native micro-services) and combined into a working solution by chaining the data flow among the necessary modules together via the DMF. The output of the components may also be stored persistently by integrating the reference architecture with one or more data lakes.

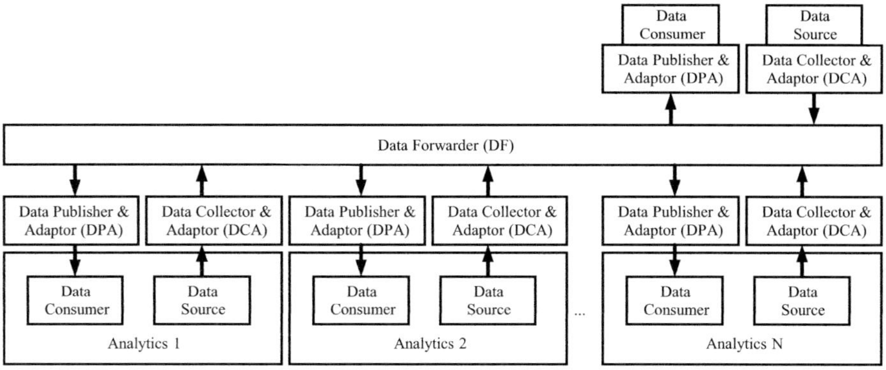

Figure 3.2 Chaining of data sources and data consumers.

3.5.2 Data lake integration

Data generation at a source and processing at a consumer with a purpose may be two activities separated in time; for example, postprocessing historical data to train machine learning models or unsupervised anomaly detection are use cases that need to access large amounts of data past their production. Naturally, data lakes may be integrated with the DMF to store data for long-term usage. In some cases, a piece of data that is produced has both real-time and long-term consumers (e.g., an entity consumes the data immediately for a real-time operation, and another entity will process the data later). In some other cases, data is only to be stored for long-term usage without any immediate use. Therefore, persistent storage of data should be supported regardless of the existence of real-time consumers.

According to the above considerations and the functional architecture of the DMF, the most generic integration of data lakes is achieved by turning data lakes into data consumers (Figure 3.3). This means that the data lakes may individually (i.e., independently from other real-time data consumers) act as entities that should receive certain types of data – only in their cases, the immediate usage of the data is persistency. However, since the DMF is not interested in the business logic of the data consumers (i.e., what happens to the data once it is delivered to them), from the DMF's perspective data lake integration is transparent. From an implementation point of view, existing data lakes should be extended with data publisher and adaptor frontend between the data forwarder and the data lake itself, to outsource protocol translation from either the DF or the data lake. This is a good example of the value of the DPA.

Access to persistent data (i.e., data from the data lake) may be implemented by direct access to the data lake by data consumers. Such interaction

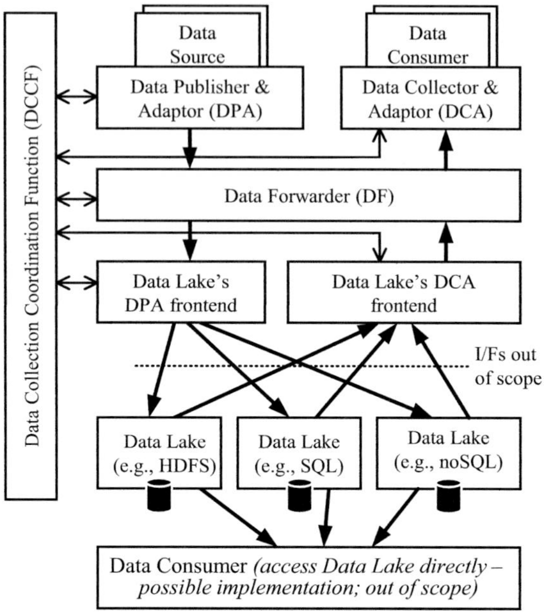

Figure 3.3 Integration of the data management framework with data lakes.

is outside of the scope of the DMF as it uses APIs and mechanisms specific to the data lake. This approach may be best in the case of big data analytics, where the data, once stored in the data lake, should be analyzed on a platform that is integrated with the data lake itself (e.g., Hadoop and Spark). Alternatively, data lakes may be turned into data sources (as per the DMF perspective) by attaching a Data Collector and Adaptor to the data lakes (similarly to DPA). This would bridge the data lake's own mechanisms offered to retrieve data with the DCCF/DF type of interfaces.

3.5.3 Data anonymization

The data framework may provide capabilities such as data anonymization to enable the leverage of data that is useful but cannot be shared as-is due to its sensitive nature. data sources that provide access to sensitive data may opt to have their data published only through a method that ensures the anonymity of individual data points by obfuscating identifiable features while retaining the maximum amount of useful information.

The following example studies the use case of sharing UE data through the DMF, describing a method that generalizes data provided about any

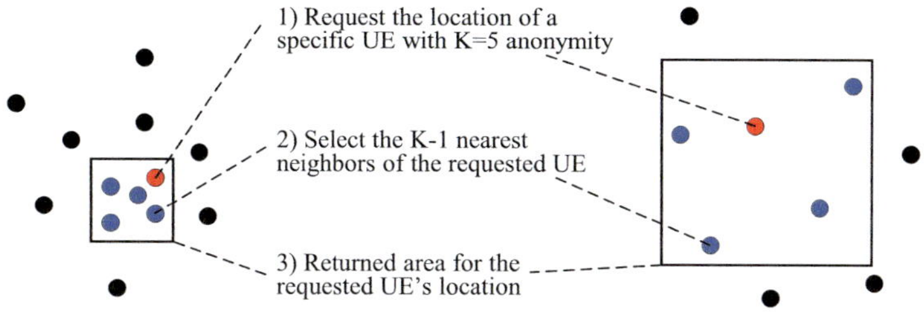

Figure 3.4 Data anonymization, the first example. Illustration of two example requests, each with a request for the location of a specific UE, with a required anonymity of K = 5. Note that the returned area is not centered around the specific UE, making it impossible to infer the exact location of the requested UE.

single UE so that the same data could have been also valid for at least a given number of additional UEs, providing k-anonymity [5]. During generalization, data is kept as detailed as possible to maximize its utility while ensuring that the data does not reveal information that is specific to any of the UEs. The DMF collects and keeps UE data in detail; the generalization only happens during the presentation of the data. Different users of the data collection framework may be entitled to access UE data through different levels of generalization (e.g., trusted/internal functions could have access to the original detailed data, while externally hosted applications could have access only to significantly generalized data).

In one example (illustrated in Figure 3.4), the DMF responds to a query that requests data about a single UE whose identity is supplied to the DMF. In this case, the goal of the framework is not to conceal the identity of the UE (as it is known to the requestor) but to ensure that the additional data returned for the UE is not unique to the UE. That is, given a preconfigured threshold number K, the framework alters the presented data so that the same data could also be returned as a response to at least K-1 other UE identities. Such generalization ensures that a requestor, who knows the UE (device) identity but perhaps not the human (personal) identity of the device's owner, is not able to correlate the data obtained from the DMF with the behavior of the person observed through other channels. By way of example, the observed behavior may include a location at a given time, pattern of application usage, device type, or any other data that reflects personal taste, preferences, or actions.

In another example (illustrated in Figure 3.5), the DMF responds to a query that requests data about multiple UEs (without knowing or caring about their identity) that fulfill a given condition (e.g., about UEs that are in a given geo-area, UEs that use a given service during a given time of

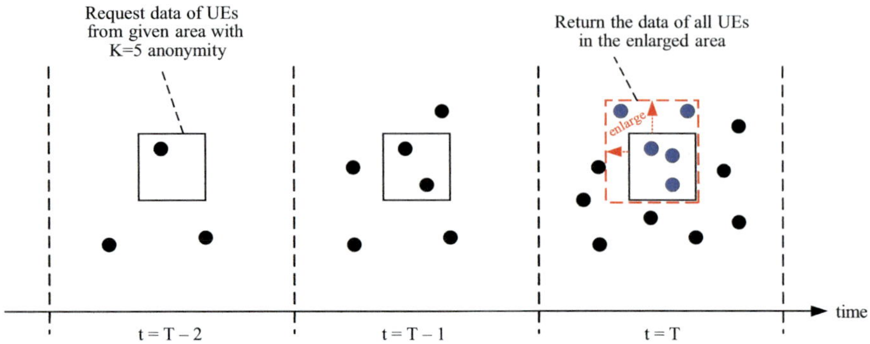

Figure 3.5 Data anonymization, the second example. Illustration of a second example, requesting data of UEs from a given area with a deadline T, with required anonymity of K = 5. At the expiration of the deadline, there are still too few UE observations in the originally requested area, therefore the method minimally enlarges the area to be able to return data of K = 5 UEs.

day, UEs of specific terminal type, UEs using specific applications, and UEs within a given network slice). The purpose of such a request may be to collect training data for machine learning. The requestor may also specify a deadline for getting the response. In this case, the goal of the framework is to return data about at least K UEs in a single response, if this is possible until the specified deadline. Otherwise, at the end of the deadline, the DMF relaxes the conditions given by the requestor so that at least K UEs would satisfy the relaxed conditions. The relaxation is done along those conditions that require the least amount of change to supply data from K number of UEs. From the data of at least K number of UEs returned by the DMF, it is not possible to correlate the data of individual UEs with data that was collected outside of the DMF or obtained by observing the UE or the owner/user of the UE in person.

In the context of the DMF, the anonymization functionality may be implemented as a dedicated anonymization function, which is a combined data source and data consumer: as a data consumer, it consumes detailed UE-specific data from UE data sources; as a data source, it produces anonymized data. The functional architecture is shown in Figure 3.6.

The interaction with the anonymization function within the DMF is shown in Figure 3.7. In step 1, the data consumer (who wants to collect anonymized UE) places a data request to the DCCF. The data request carries the UE ID (in case of the first embodiment) or the conditions to be fulfilled by the UEs subject to data collection (in case of the second embodiment), the data fields that are required from the UE(s), and the anonymity level K,

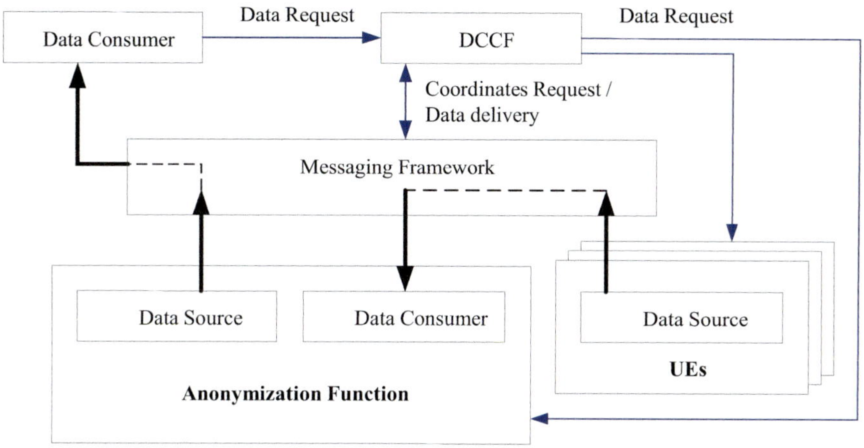

Figure 3.6 The anonymization function in the context of the DMF. Blue arrows represent control messages, black bold lines show the actual data transfer.

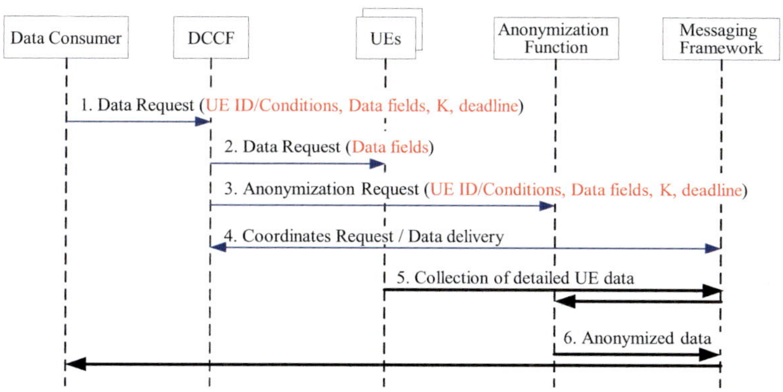

Figure 3.7 Message sequence diagram showing the interactions with the anonymization function.

and an optional deadline in case of the second embodiment. Alternatively, the anonymity level may be defined as a policy in the DMF (in DCCF) and assigned to the data consumer. The DCCF may evaluate whether the data consumer is eligible (according to the policy) to receive the requested data fields with the requested anonymity level. If the requested K is lower (less strict) than the eligible K, the DCCF may either fall back to the stricter eligible K value or reject the request. In step 2, the DCCF activates UE side data sources to produce data. Note that even in the first example, it is not enough to collect data from the dedicated UE (with UE ID) as data from additional UEs are also needed for anonymization to maintain the realism

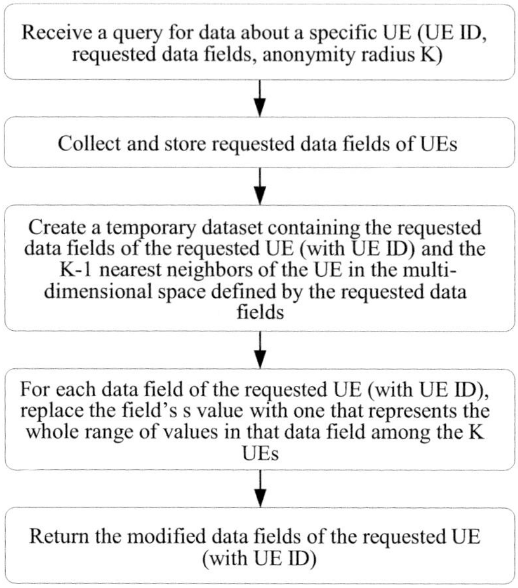

Figure 3.8 Flowchart of the steps of the anonymization method for a specific UE.

of the eventually produced generalized data. In step 3, the DCCF configures the anonymization function by providing the parameters in the data request. In step 4, the DCCF configures the DF, creating a data pipeline from the UEs through the anonymization function to the data consumer. In step 5, the UE data is collected from the UEs (through the DF) at the anonymization function. The anonymization function produces the anonymized data. In step 6, the anonymized data is transferred (through the DF) to the data consumer.

The internal steps of the anonymization method targeting a single UE are shown in Figure 3.8. The method is initiated by receiving the request for data fields of a specific UE (with a UE ID), along with the method parameter K specifying the anonymity level. UE-specific data fields may include but are not limited to, the UE's location, time of presence/activity, terminal type, data consumption, application usage, mobility (handovers), etc. The method collects and stores the requested data fields of UEs (including the one with the requested UE ID). Once the data has been collected (which may already be available from previous data collections or from historical databases), the method performs generalization of the requested UE's data field. The method collects the K-1 nearest neighbors of the requested UE (with UE ID) into a temporary dataset. The K-1 nearest neighbors of the requested UE are those UEs whose data points are closest in the multidimensional space of

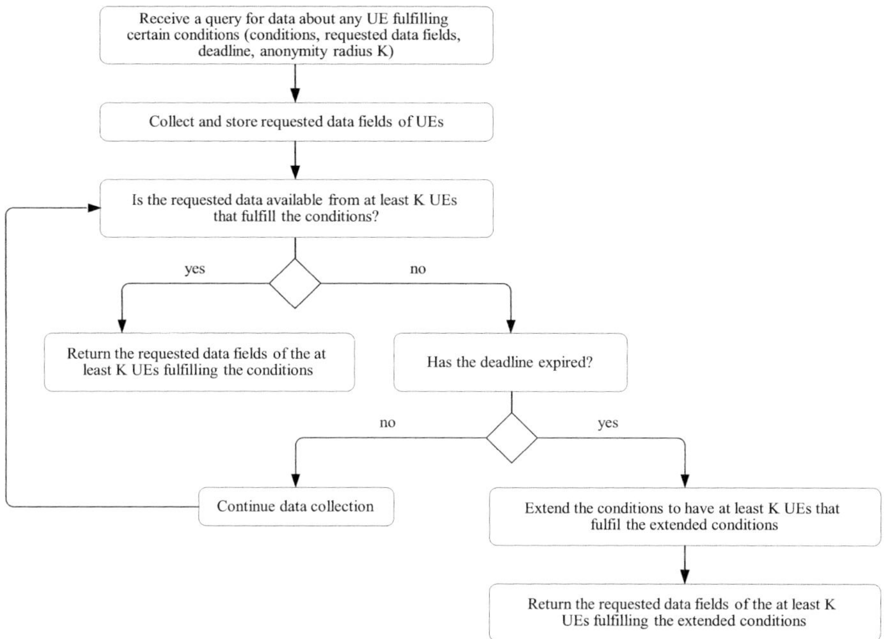

Figure 3.9 Flowchart of the steps of the anonymization method for multiple UEs.

the requested data fields in terms of the Euclidean distance metric. Instead of Euclidean distance metric, any other metric (or function) or their combinations could be used to form the K-1 nearest neighbor UE group (e.g., using L1 norm also known as Manhattan distance and using Hamming distance or Jaccard distance for categorical data fields). After identifying the K-1 nearest neighbors of the requested UE, the method creates a generalized value for each data field of the requested UE. The generalized data field represents the whole range of values produced by the total K UEs (including the requested UE) without providing a clue about where the requested UE's data lies. That is, the generalization ensures that the requested UE's original data value is not deterministically placed within the range (e.g., at the center). The method outputs the generalized data fields for the requested UE.

The steps of the anonymization method targeting all UEs given a set of conditions are shown in Figure 3.9. The method is initiated by receiving a request for data fields of any UEs that satisfy certain conditions, along with the method parameter K specifying the anonymity level. The data fields of the UE may be those that were listed in the first embodiment. The conditions may be specified on one or more of the data fields. A data field on which a condition is specified may not be part of the requested data fields (e.g., a request may ask for a UE's location given that the UE was active within a given time window). The request may also contain a deadline by which the data collection should be completed. The method internally collects and stores the requested data fields of UEs, but not only from those UEs that satisfy the given conditions (as the conditions may need to be relaxed later). Note that data may already be available from previous data collections or from historical databases. If data from at least K UEs fulfilling the conditions is available before the deadline expires, the data is returned to the requestor. Otherwise, data collection continues until the expiration of the deadline. If the deadline expires without having K UEs fulfill the conditions, the method relaxes the conditions (as little as possible) so that at least K UEs fulfill the relaxed conditions. The data fields of the at least K UEs that satisfy the relaxed conditions are returned to the requestor.

The relaxation or extension of the conditions should follow a minimum-touch approach. That is, the method selects the condition (or set of conditions) that require the least amount of change (in absolute amount, or relative amount compared to the values provided in the conditions).

There may be additional limits specified for the conditions that guide (or constrain) the method in the condition extension process. For example, the requestor of the UE data fields may specify that one of the conditions is nonnegotiable, in which case the method is not allowed to extend that condition to reach the anonymity requirement. In another example (potentially in combination with the previous one), the requestor may specify a priority list for the conditions in which order the extension should be attempted. The requestor may also provide numerical limits (e.g., absolute plus/minus tolerance values, relative percentage values, or any other means) for conditions to specify the amount of extension that is tolerated.

3.6 Data Collection in Machine Learning Pipelines

3.6.1 Requirements of data collection in ML pipelines

An ML model may require obtaining and processing large amounts of data, not only for training the model but also during runtime, after deploying one or more instances of the model for inference. The data sources processed by the model may be diverse, requiring data from multiple types of network nodes (e.g., RAN, CN, and OSS) distributed at many locations (RAN sites, various near/far edge clouds, central clouds, etc.). Selecting the deployment location of an ML model instance (i.e., the model placement task) is an optimization problem that has to consider multiple aspects:

- Potential model execution hosts based on HW/SW environment capabilities (e.g., need for HW accelerators for running the model instance efficiently and support for compatible virtualization or container framework). The HW/SW environment may not only be prohibitive or permissive for a model instance, but it could impact its execution speed (e.g., a model instance may run on both CPU and GPU, but be faster if GPU is available – such speed gain, if known, could enable fine grained optimization).
- The data volume consumed by the model instance, and the cost of producing, collecting, and transporting data from their respective sources to the model instance's input. Placing a model instance closer to a high-volume data source (e.g., into the same edge cloud or close to a RAN node) may be more optimal than hosting the model instance in a core cloud. However, given the potentially diverse location of the data sources, all potential locations may be compromised.
- The data volume produced by the model instance toward the consumers of its output (if any). In analytics pipelines, it is common to break down the e2e implementation into a chain of micro-services, each producing an intermediate output toward the next one until the final output is published. The micro-services in the chain may be implemented as standalone ML model instances, therefore a model instance may act as a data source for other model instances.
- In analytics pipelines, the end-to-end latency from data sources through all model instances (note: maybe just one) to the final output. In closed-loop automation, model instances automate analytics and decision stages that trigger controllers to carry out actions. The actions cause changes in the network behavior that are feeding back to the data sources and model instance inputs, creating a continuous loop of data collection, analytics, decision, and action. Such closed loops may have latency requirements on the overall time from data ingestion to action (e.g., may need to fit into a predefined time periodicity). The time spent with data collection impacts how much time is left for a model instance to process the data; putting the model on a faster compute node may help fit into that limit. On the other way around, if the model execution takes a nonnegotiable amount of time, the model may need to be placed closer to the data source, shortening the data collection time, to spare time for its execution.

The above model instance placement optimization considerations may be formulated as a multiflow optimization problem on a dynamic graph

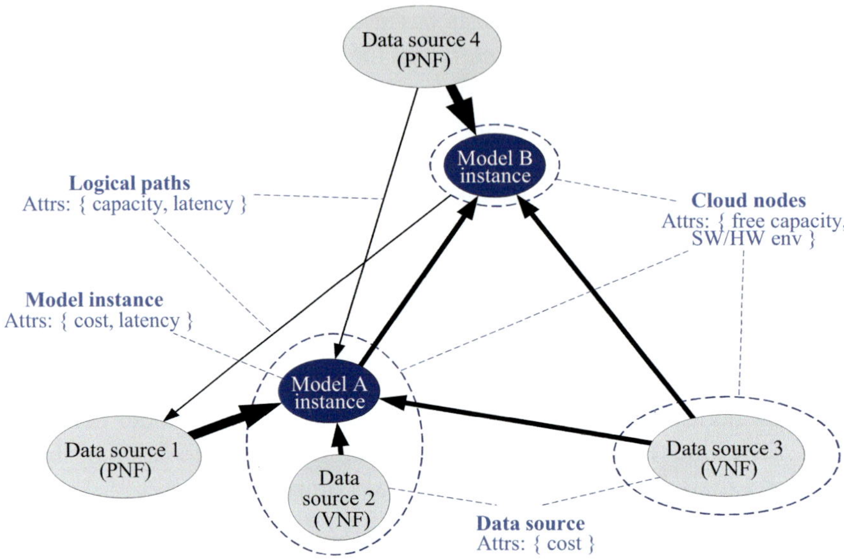

Figure 3.10 Illustration of the multiflow data path optimization on a dynamic graph.

(Figure 3.10). A graph G = (V, E) may be defined with V and E denoting the graph nodes and edges as follows.

The node set V of G includes:

- PNFs may be data sources for a model instance, or data consumers of a model instance's output. The PNFs are not considered to be model execution hosts for the dynamic model instance placement problem. That is, a model instance cannot be colocated with a PNF.
- Cloud nodes as potential model instance locations and VNF locations, with semistatic attributes such as HW/SW environment capability and dynamic attributes such as free compute capacity (RAM, CPU/GPU).
- VNF instances, which run on cloud nodes and may be data sources/ consumers.
- Model instances, which may run on cloud nodes and may be data sources/consumers. A model instance may be colocated with a VNF if the cloud node hosting the VNF has HW/SW capabilities compatible with the model instance. However, a model instance cannot be colocated with a PNF.

It is important to note that there is a hierarchy in the nodes in the sense that VNF instances and model instances have to be embedded in cloud nodes (as opposed to PNF nodes, which do not have any intersection with cloud nodes).

Dynamic attributes are associated with model instances (e.g., latency of producing an output from an input and associated compute cost) and with all types (PNF, VNF, model instance) of data sources (e.g., the cost of producing the data, which may be measured by compute cost or collateral reduction of core functionality due to the additional load of data production – such as an eNB or gNB DU not being able to reach its peak U-plane throughput if it has to produce large amount of measurement data).

The edge set E of G includes logical paths between V node pairs u and v where node u is a data source for node v. Logical paths have dynamic attributes such as capacity and latency, or any other cost metric or finite resource associated with the transfer of data from node u to v.

A data flow is defined as a chain of V nodes via E edges in the graph. A data flow has e2e requirements (e.g., latency between the first and last node), and additionally, requirements may be broken down into specific segments or logical paths (e.g., latency from the source node to first model instance and from a model instance to the next model instance).

The dynamic model instance placement optimization task is the following. Given the set of nodes (PNFs, VNFs, clouds, and model instances) and their attributes, the logical paths between potential V node pairs and their attributes, and the set of data flows and their requirements, provide a placement of model instance nodes on cloud nodes so that the data flow requirements (e2e or per segment) are satisfied and the node and logical path costs (total sum of all cost, a weighted total cost metric, etc.) are minimized. In this formulation, the location of PNFs, clouds, and the placement of VNFs on clouds are taken as input. An extended problem statement would be to enable the joint optimization of the placement of VNFs and model instances.

If all dynamic attributes of the nodes and edges were known and static, the above optimization problem could be solved by an algorithm at deployment time. However, there are both unknowns in the attributes (e.g., how fast would a model run if deployed on a specific node? How much data in Megabytes is actually transported to the model instance from a given data source?), and there is dynamicity or context dependency in some of the attributes (e.g., changing latency between a data source and the model instance based on the presence of other traffic; varying amount of data produced by a source VNF depending on its load). Currently, however, calculating the optimal placement of a model once during deployment is not possible (due to unknowns in the attributes), and even during runtime, a once "optimal" location may become suboptimal (due to shifts in the dynamic attributes).

3.6.2 Data management reference architecture capabilities

The data management reference architecture may play a critical role in optimizing the placement of ML model instances with respect to the model's requirements toward data flows. The DCF may measure, collect, and publish the dynamic attributes of data sources, model instances, execution nodes (clouds) and data flows. The DCF may be extended with four functionalities:

1. Collect requirements on the data transfer of data consumers (e.g., latency from data source to data consumer).
2. Measure data volumes and latencies between data sources and data consumers (which may be model instances). Also, collect the compute resource use of data sources and data consumers.
3. Maintain a history of the above measurements and expose them to 3rd party analytics functions (e.g., VNF and ML model orchestrators outside of the data management reference architecture) to enable the optimization of model instance placement (including initial deployment placement and dynamic relocation).
4. Optimize the internal data transfer within the reference architecture based on (1) the requirements collected from data consumers and (2) the measurements collected from 3rd party producer adaptors (3PA) and 3rd party consumer adaptors (3CA). This enables to prioritize data that is more urgently requested over data having a larger latency budget.

The self-measuring and optimization capabilities of the data management reference architecture are shown in Figure 3.11. They consist of the interface capabilities (depicted by the arrows and caption) and the internal capability of the data management reference architecture to perform dynamic data transfer measurements. The NFV/ML Orchestrator is a consumer of the data management reference architecture but not part of the DMRA.

The collection of data transfer requirements from data consumers requires to extend the interface between the data consumer and the DCCF.

The 3PA and 3CA adaptors are extended with data volume metering and data latency measurement capabilities. The 3PA and 3CA interact with their respective data source and data consumer to collect cost metrics associated with producing or consuming the data. This interaction requires standardization (preferably by extending existing 3GPP interfaces that are used by the adaptors to collect/provide data, such as C-plane notification used on SBA).

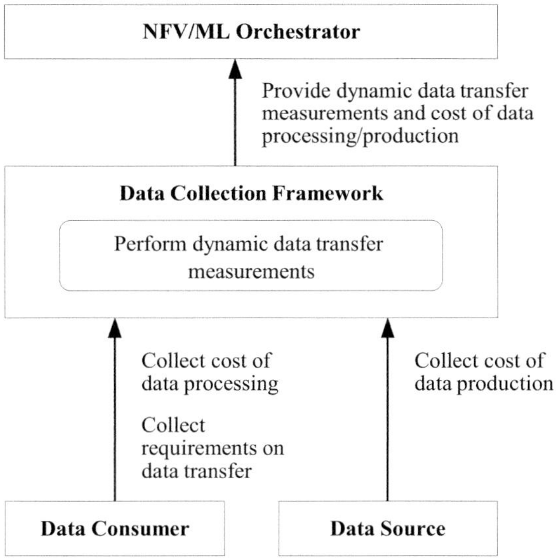

Figure 3.11 The self-measuring and optimization capabilities of the data management reference architecture.

The measurement history and internal data transfer optimization are implementation aspects. However, the capability of the data management reference architecture to expose measurements to 3rd party analytics or orchestrator functions requires an additional standardized N-bound interface for the DCCF.

The functionalities provide an implementation framework for realizing the ZSM Integration Fabric [4], which enables the collection and distribution of real time and historical measurements within and across domains, for example, from measurement entities to domain controllers. Through the distribution of information (data and knowledge), the framework is also a good fit for closed loops [6] that require accurate and timely data flow across the various closed loop stages such as monitoring, decision, and action [6].

3.6.3 Self-measurement implementation and message flow

The message sequences between the entities of the data management reference architecture or the DCCF and external entities corresponding to the functionalities described in the previous section:

1. Collect the data transfer requirements of data consumers
2. Measure data volumes and latencies between data sources and data consumers

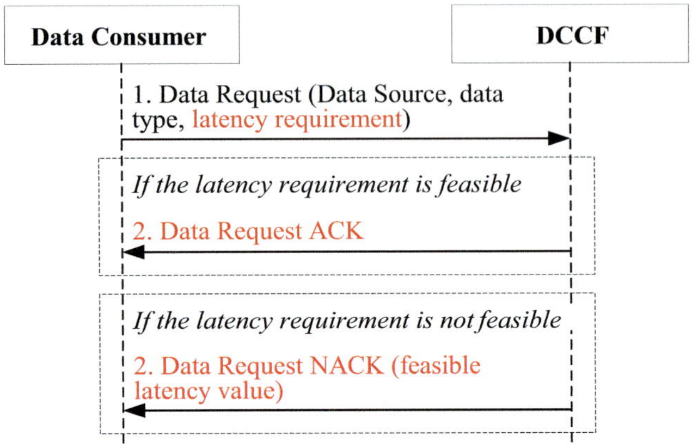

Figure 3.12 Data request procedure extended with latency requirement on the transfer of data from data source to data consumer.

3. Maintain and expose the measurements
4. Optimize the internal data transfer

The *Collect the data transfer requirements of data consumers* message sequence uses the information elements of the data request procedure to encode the data collection requirements.

The data request message is sent by the data consumer to the DCCF (Figure 3.12). The requirements may be indicated separately for each data source or type of data requested from a data source. The requirement may include a latency target defining the maximum time between the data source providing a piece of data and the data consumer receiving the data from the data management reference architecture.

The DCCF may evaluate the feasibility of the data consumer's latency requirement and return an acknowledgment (positive – ACK, or negative – NACK). ACK may be sent when the DCCF, according to the historical data transfer measurements it has collected from the 3PAs/3CAs, estimates that the requested latency can be achieved. Otherwise, a negative acknowledgment is returned. The NACK may indicate what latency the DCCF finds feasible on the data that the data consumer has requested. The data consumer may use the returned feasible latency value to check if that would be acceptable for its intended use of the data and reissue the data request with a new latency requirement relaxed according to the DCCF's hint.

In the *measure data volumes and latencies between data sources and data consumers* sequence, each pair of 3PA and 3CA provides two potential

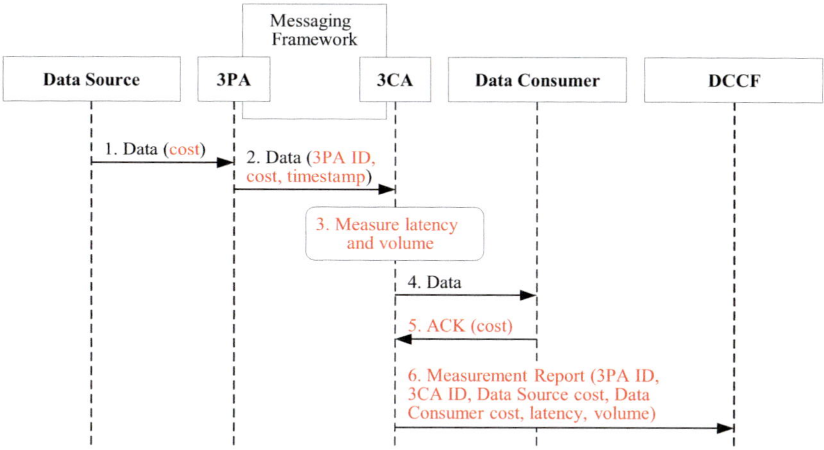

Figure 3.13 Measuring the latency and volume of data transfer from a data source to a data consumer.

measurement points for flows that transfer data from a data source behind the 3PA to a data consumer behind the 3CA.

The 3PA and 3CA may interact with the data and with each other via in-band signaling to measure the latency of conveying data from the 3PA to the 3CA (Figure 3.13). Such interaction is possible regardless of the implementation of the messaging framework and the data source and data consumer capabilities. The in-band interaction between 3PA and 3CA means that the 3PA attaches metadata to the data it collects from the data source. The metadata contains its own 3PA identity, a timestamp, and the cost of producing the data by the data source (which needs to be collected from the data source using a data source specific procedure). The metadata is conveyed from the 3PA to the 3CA along with the data itself. The 3CA produces a latency measurement by calculating the time difference between receiving the metadata and the 3PA's timestamp in the metadata. The 3CA also meters the volume of the data. The 3CA may interact with the data consumer to collect the cost associated with processing the data. The cost may include the compute resources used by the data consumer (e.g., a model instance) to process the data and produce its own output. The 3CA transfers the latency and volume measurements and the costs associated with data production and consumption to the DCCF. The measurements are associated with the identity of the 3PA and 3CA, which indicate an end-to-end data flow within the data management reference architecture.

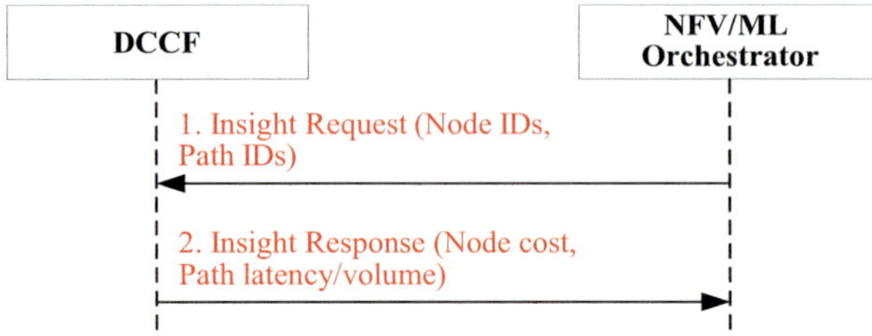

Figure 3.14 Expose measurements to 3rd party orchestrators.

Through the *maintain and expose the measurement sequence*, the DCCF may maintain a per-path (from 3PA to 3CA) and per node (3PA/data source, 3CA/data consumer) view of the dynamic attributes (current measurements) and also maintain a historical database of past measurements. Based on historical and current measurements, the DCCF may provide insight into a model placement optimization and orchestration function (Figure 3.14) that decides on the initial placement of a model instance or relocates a model instance due to changes in the dynamic attributes of data collection.

The request from the orchestrator may contain the identity of nodes (data sources, data consumers) or paths (between pairs of data source/consumer). The response may contain costs associated with the nodes (data production/consumer cost) or delay/volume measurement associated with the path.

Transferring data from the 3CA to 3PA is the responsibility of the messaging framework, the optimize internal data transfer sequence. The messaging framework may implement concepts of data priority or have control over network resource management or configuration (such as transport network QoS or packet schedulers). Those mechanisms, that is, the *optimize internal data* transfer sequence, may be used by the messaging framework implementation to ensure that data requested with shorter latency requirements is expedited over data that is less urgent.

3.7 Summary

The abundance of network data provides both a challenge in terms of its collection, storage, and distribution, and a fundamental enabler of any level of automation through obtaining insight into the network, devices, functions, traffic, and services in terms of operational state, performance and any event of interest including but not limited to exceptions, failures, or anomalies. Data not only provides the first level of raw insight into the network, services, and their state, but it is also the input to all kinds of modeling, behavior abstraction, event detection, and prediction that any automation requires to carry out operations in closed loops.

The scope of data and knowledge management in networks is to support the discovery, collection, transfer, and storage of any data among data producers (data sources) and consumers. This chapter discussed the general concepts and requirements of data and knowledge management using a logical reference architecture for illustrating the concepts in a tangible manner. The data collection framework needs to support data in transit (real time, streaming), as well as the storage and recollection of historical data; it needs to scale to transfer high amounts of raw data with a deadline on the delivery; it needs to be efficient both on the data producer and on the transfer (minimize overhead); and it has to provide a set of nonfunctional requirements in terms of latency, quality, and security. The reference architecture was mapped to the 3GPP and ZSM to illustrate how the concepts are integrated into the prominent standards defining cellular networks, and the ETSI network and service management automation framework.

Special issues and potential solutions related to security, anonymity, and efficiency are also addressed. It was analyzed how to integrate measurements and monitoring into the data collection itself to have insight into its own performance while serving the data operations initiated by sources and consumers. This capability is an enabler to fulfill specific nonfunctional requirements (e.g., delay) requirements related to the delivery of data. Security (such as authentication and integrity) and trustworthiness are also inevitable aspects of data and knowledge management especially if the insights are driving autonomous actions. Therefore, the next chapter is entirely dedicated to discussing security and trust matters in the context of data collection and network automation.

Bibliography

[1] 3GPP TS 23.288 Architecture enhancements for 5G System (5GS) to support network data analytics services

[2] 3GPP TR 28.866 Study on Management Data Analytics (MDA) – Phase 3

[3] 3GPP TR 28.873 Study on data management, subscriptions and reporting

[4] ETSI GS ZSM 002, "Zero-touch network and Service Management (ZSM); Reference Architecture", V1.1.1 (2019-08)

[5] Samarati, Pierangela; Sweeney, Latanya (1998). "Protecting privacy when disclosing information: k-anonymity and its enforcement through

generalization and suppression". Harvard Data Privacy Lab. Available online: https://dataprivacylab.org/dataprivacy/projects/kanonymity/paper3.pdf
[6] ETSI GS ZSM 009-1, "Zero-touch network and Service Management (ZSM); Closed-Loop Automation; Part 1: Enablers", V1.1.1 (2021-06)

4

Security, Trust, and Integrity

Autonomous networks must not only be secure in the classical sense of cryptography (implementing key properties of authenticity, confidentiality, and integrity) but also in terms of operational integrity and trustworthiness with regard to their autonomous decisions and actions. Technically, diligent usage of cryptography for data security is an absolute must, which needs to be extended to cover AI-based interactions and AI models themselves, considering that AI models are both data themselves (and quite sensitive ones) and at the same time the largest data mobilizers. Data flowing to and from AI models, either during model training, reinforcement learning, or inference, creates not only new data flows to be secured but also new control flows (consider AI-based closed loop operation) that need to be trusted to maintain the integrity of the system and ensure the right outcomes in terms of operational targets. Trustworthiness needs to provide enablers for validating and verifying the integrity of AI models and their response to input even if the models are accessed over a networked interface.

4.1 Introduction

Security requirements in the context of network management automation need to target the security capabilities of individual system components; their interactions with each other in autonomous relations (e.g., in closed loops); and the interactions between operators and the management system, both in terms of governance of the system by the operator, and feedback/insights by the system to the operator. As such, security aspects should be integrated into all levels of the system as native capabilities, rather than being outsourced to a separate entity. Native security means that each system component (e.g., management function) implements the necessary means to contribute to the overall security of the system as much as it is possible from within the scope of the component (e.g., considering the data and intelligence available for the

DOI: 10.1201/9788770041478-4

component; the means and interfaces of its communication with other components; and the potential risk of the used technologies, their vulnerabilities and the impact of exploitation on the component and the overall system).

Autonomous systems use AI models to automate analytics, inference, and decision capabilities. In one system, and even in one component within, numerous AI models may coexist, with different AI architectures (e.g., multilayered neural network, sequential models, and language models), training history (e.g., having been trained on disparate datasets), lifecycle (e.g., offline training vs. online reinforcement learning). The AI models present a stochastic computation paradigm where the model's output is not only a function of its internal architecture and the input, but also of the training dataset and hyperparameters used during its training. As neither the quantity nor quality of the training data is comprehensible by humans, the resulting AI model and its operation (while being defined by the final model parameters) are also not transparent. This creates problems specific to AI models, such as explainability (i.e., how to understand the process that led the AI model to produce a given output) and trustworthiness (i.e., how can the output of an AI model be trusted to drive subsequent autonomous steps in a system such as executing a management action, without jeopardizing the integrity, correctness, efficiency, and SLAs to be maintained by the system). As AI is a fundamental technology to implement automation and autonomy in management systems, the security aspects brought in by AI should also be handled.

Since the inception of AI models starts with the collection and curation of training data, the security requirements of AI also include areas of data security, such as identity, integrity, authenticity, and confidentiality. In addition, AI models themselves are also data when they are stored and transferred, therefore, data security has a direct impact on the security of AI models.

The rest of the security section discusses applying zero trust in information security, aspects of AI security and trustworthiness, and the importance to assure the truthfulness of information in addition to conserving the integrity of information.

4.2 Element of Data and Model Security

Data and model security means to ensure the authenticity, integrity, and confidentiality of all data (including AI models) that is produced, transferred, stored, or consumed within the system. Authenticity means the ability to validate the producer of a piece of data. Providing authenticity prevents impersonation attacks when a malicious actor injects data into the system on behalf of another entity. Integrity means to ensure the accuracy and completeness of the data, either in transit or when it is stored and recalled. Providing integrity prevents tampering with the data while it is stored or moved. Confidentiality means to ensure that data is accessible to authorized entities only. Providing confidentiality prevents eavesdropping or acquiring information without permission.

A challenge to ensure authenticity, integrity, and confidentiality properties in a distributed system is that data can be replicated and modified without impacting the original copy – yet all three properties should be ensured throughout all copies of a piece of data. Key technical enablers of implementing all properties simultaneously in a system may be provided as follows:

1. Data is produced in chunks that are uniquely identifiable pieces of data within the system.
2. Data chunks are immutable: There are no versions of data chunks – if it changes, it is a new chunk of data. Identical copies of the same chunk are allowed to be stored and used within the system for efficiency.
3. Producing a chunk of data is an act that irrevocably creates the identity and authenticity of the data chunk, which are inseparably attached to the data chunk.
4. Data chunks are always signed by their producer and encrypted toward the target consumer – both during transfer and in storage.
5. The identity, authenticity, and integrity of a data chunk should be verifiable by any data consumer.

In any transaction of a data chunk, whether that is a direct production consumption between two entities or a persistent storage of the data chunk for multiple future consumers, the authenticity of both the producer and the consumer is mutually verified. This creates a zero-trust framework where no data is exchanged and accepted based on a trust relation that was established previously between entities based on past activities.

Allowing for a zero-trust operation is an important enabler of security hardening as trust relationships are traditionally posing potential security issues. According to [1], the trust relationship between management domains is a key security risk, especially as the set of management services or management functions may change within the domains. An overview of the potential deliberate data security threats targeting network management systems is also provided in [1]. The main sources of threats include:

- Deception, impersonation, identity spoof: Leveraging a pre-existing trust relationship between an entity and the impersonated target, or adversary modification between content exchanged between two trusted

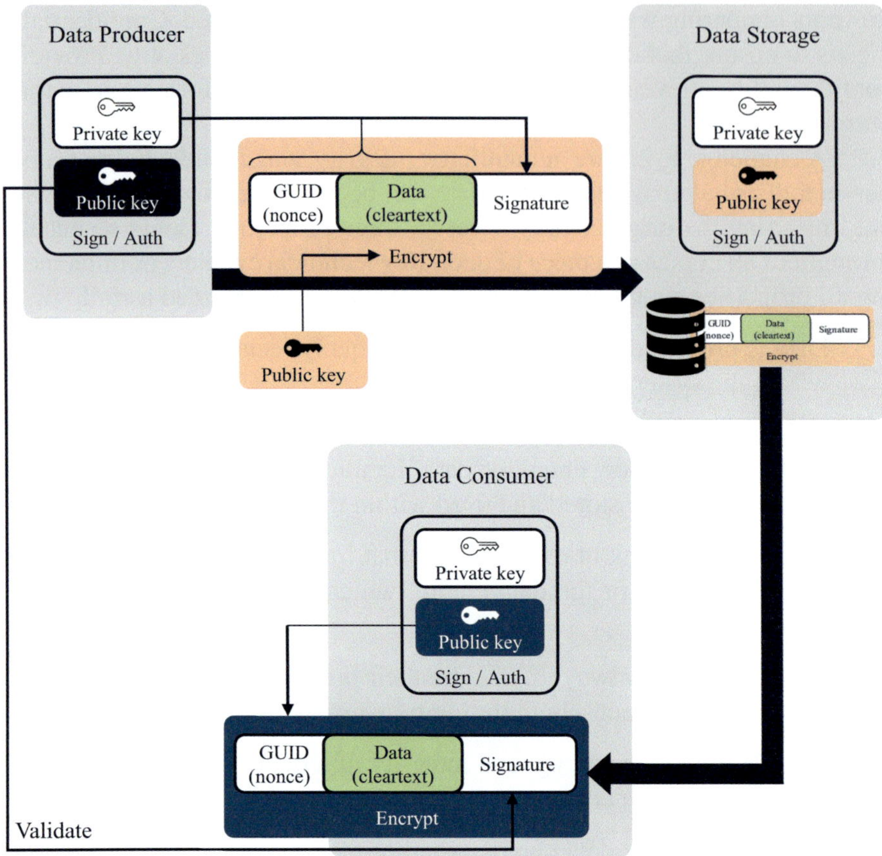

Figure 4.1 Zero trust e2e data security.

entities. This threat also motivates to move toward a zero-trust security framework to avoid the misuse of trust relations.

- A trusted insider of a system may leak information outside where it is collected and analyzed: this also motivates employing zero trust to eliminate the possibility of opening channels from inside of a system to outside entities without ensuring their identity and authenticity.

A potential logical e2e data pipeline with elements of zero trust is shown in Figure 4.1. Note that within the pipeline data storage may be bypassed if no intermediate persistency is needed, and data can be transitioned directly to a consumer (e.g., volatile data between steps of a data pipeline).

The zero trust e2e data security naturally applies to AI as well, considering how AI operations may adopt information exchange through data chunks

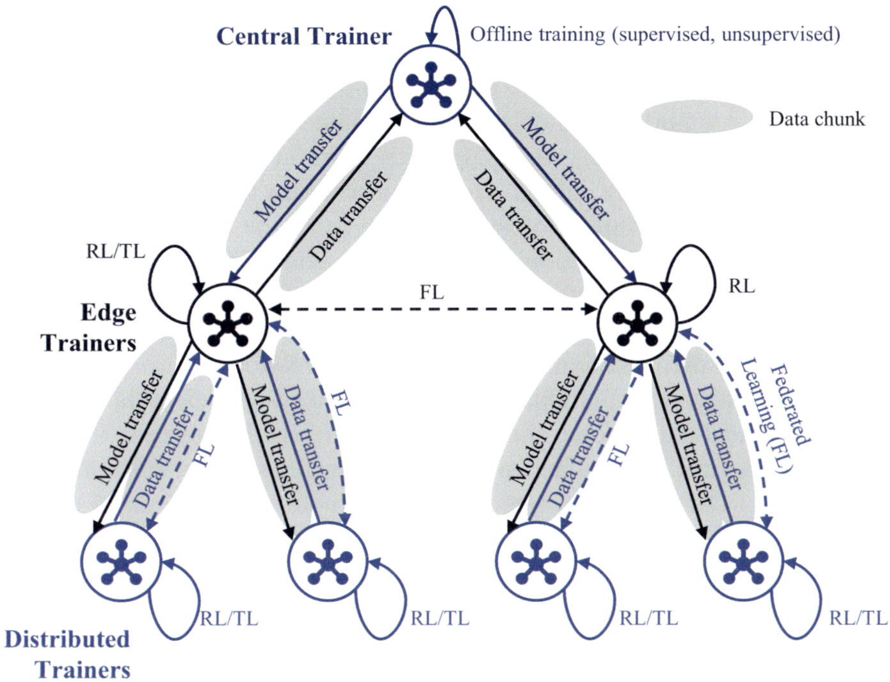

Figure 4.2 Data chunks in AI/ML operation.

(Figure 4.2). AI models are data structures, and as such may be regarded as a data chunk each. For example, AI models may be untrained models (e.g., NN model architecture with random initial weights), but also trained models (e.g., NN with weights set via training algorithm over a training dataset). In the operations of distributed/federated AI training, gradients transferred from the local trainer to the central trainer (each training iteration produces a new data chunk), and also data shared across trainers may be regarded as data chunks. In reinforcement learning, new iterations of a model trained within an entity become new data chunks whenever they are released/transferred to other entities. In summary, while AI training and operation creates a complex data pattern, any piece of data in transit or any version of a model in training could be captured as a data chunk, therefore, assuring the properties of authenticity, integrity, and confidentiality within AI operations.

4.3 Data Security and Truthfulness

The analysis of the key management security issues [1] also identified a deliberate threat through the manipulation of data structures and system resources (including files, configuration, and applications). This attack essentially means to alter information that is later trusted or acted upon autonomously by the system due to its trusted source (e.g., a well-known configuration database that "should" contain only valid data). Utilizing compromised configuration data may yield suboptimal, wrong, or even harmful outcomes, even if the access of the (maliciously altered) configuration or the transfer of the configuration information is fully protected later on using the full power of information security (authentication, integrity, and confidentiality). Therefore, there is a need to separate information/data security from the concept of what could be called the "truthfulness" of the data. The two important aspects of e2e security and their relationship are discussed as follows.

Data security is a functional requirement of a system, essentially meaning to implement and enforce zero-trust principles (authentication, integrity, confidentiality) in e2e on all data production, transfer, storage, and consumption relations. Data security assures that the producer of a piece of data is verified; data integrity and confidentiality are ensured both in transit and in persistency; and access is restricted to authorized consumers only. Therefore, once a piece of information is produced, it can be traced throughout the system and its immutability can be assured.

Truthfulness is a nonfunctional requirement of a system, meaning the ability to verify that the data itself is valid, it is true to its intended or communicated identity, and semantic (e.g., if it is a measurement with a given unit, the value should be really the truly measured quantity and it should be encoded in the indicated unit). Truthfulness relates to the production/consumption of data (or models, considering that they are also handled as data when stored or in transit). If the data was maliciously or erroneously produced, or an AI model is changed by the consumer, data security cannot help prevent the impacts, hence the additional need to investigate enablers of truthfulness. The challenges to verify the truthfulness of data include, for example, ensuring transparency into the data that is used to train an AI model (which has an impact on the truthfulness of the resulting model itself) or ensuring that an AI model transferred to an inference point (with all data security ensured) is not altered later by the consumer (i.e., user) of the model to produce an output that would be different from that of the original model.

4.4 Security and Trust Impact of the AI Technology

Training and using AI models in a system brings in aspects of security and trust that are inherent to the AI technology, although they do not necessarily require a mitigation tactic that is specific to AI. AI-related security issues could be classified into two large categories:

1. Increased attack surface with potential threats that have become possible due to the nature of the AI technology, including training data management, model training, model operation, and management. This assumes a deliberate malicious attacker that tries to exploit vulnerabilities opened by the system through its use of AI.
2. Lack of transparency (i.e., explainability challenges) of the AI technology and functions or capabilities implemented using AI. These do not assume any malicious activity but simply consider the impact of operating and trusting systems incorporating AI especially if the AI is driving closed-loop automation with potential actions on the system.

Regarding AI-specific attacks, NIST has released a comprehensive survey and classification of adversarial attacks and potential mitigation techniques [2]. Although many of the attacks are deeply scientific in the vulnerability and mathematical constructs of the models, or delivering attacker impact through careful training data manipulation, the conclusion of the work itself [2] is that the most plausible (and thus also most impactful, when successful) attacker capability is to have access to the interfaces of the model (i.e., can send input data to the model, and receive output) but not to the model itself. This is the well-established ML as a Service (MLaaS) or Model as a Service (MaaS) principle [2, 3], which fits well into a web-scale service model where consumers can access capabilities through network APIs without having access to the actual infrastructure and software serving the requests. Therefore, it is interesting to analyze which identified attacks do require AI-specific measures (i.e., steps incorporated into how training data is organized and how training is performed) whereas which are the ones that could be reduced to standard IT security measures such as controlling and authenticating access to critical infrastructure that produces and hosts AI models. The survey identifies two high-level AI classes: predictive AI and generative AI and analyzes attacks and mitigation per each class. For the sake of this methodology, only the predictive AI part will be considered, however, the same method could be applied to generative AI as well (and providing a very similar outcome).

Table 4.1 summarizes the attack tactics in the context of potential attacker objectives and attacker capabilities according to [2]. The attacker objectives may be availability breakdown (try to render the ML service unavailable), integrity violation (make the ML service produce incorrect output), and privacy compromise (obtain information about the model or potential training

Table 4.1 Overview of attack on predictive AI.

	Attacker objectives		
Attacker capabilities	**Availability breakdown**	**Integrity violation**	**Privacy compromise**
Training data control	Data poisoning	Targeted poisoning Backdoor poisoning	
Secure code control		Backdoor poisoning	
Test data control		Backdoor poisoning Evasion	
Model control	Model poisoning	Model poisoning	
Label limit	Clean-label poisoning	Clean-label poisoning Clean-label backdoor	
Query access	Energy-latency	Black-box evasion	Model extraction Reconstruction Membership inference Property inference

data samples used to train the model). The attacker capabilities range from having various levels of leverage on the training data, training process, and the model to the point where only query access is given, which corresponds to the MLaaS model. Therefore, analyzing the impact of real-world attacks may focus on the query access line. Additionally, considering the availability and integrity of the system as a primary concern (as they cause service breakdown), there are only a few attack tactics that remain relevant, namely energy latency and black-box evasion. Energy latency is a tactic that tries to compute adversarial samples that cause the ML model to take an unusually long time to complete, increasing the latency of the model's response, and thus causing delayed decisions that depend on the model's output. Black-box evasion is a tactic that tries to make the ML model produce wrong output such as incorrect predictions or classification through inputting adversarial samples. The mitigation tactics for both attacks recommended by [2] are adversarial training (including adversarial samples in the training data) and randomized smoothing (training under Gaussian noise perturbation). These are mitigations that require AI-specific measures to be integrated into the training process of the AI model. For all other attacks that require access to sensitive training data or the model itself, AI technology-specific mitigations still exist [2], however, securing the machine learning deployment via means of conventional IT security would already deprive the attacker from the required capacity to execute the tactic [4]. The privacy compromise attacks also require data and model-specific mitigation, with the scope to provide data anonymity through differential privacy [2] or approaches discussed in Section 3.6.3.

Regarding lack of transparency, trustworthiness issues emerge due to the opacity in the AI model's operation, resulting in end-to-end unpredictability in terms of the model's performance and output for hypothetical input samples. Although model unpredictability may lead to indeterministic system functionality when implemented with AI, it is important to differentiate between observed indeterminism on the system level and the underlying unpredictability of the models. An AI model may deterministically provide the same response to repeated processing of the same input, yet no prediction can be made for a group of input (or even for a single input sample) to which boundaries the output will fall without actually applying the model on the input. As in real systems, it is rare that the exact same scenario repeats, in practice the AI models will process different input even in situations that are "similar" to a high-level observer, leading to the impression of indeterministic end-to-end system behavior. The unpredictable property of AI models is in contrast to classical algorithms or even computer programs where algorithm analysis and verification can provide proof of performance and correctness without having to execute the algorithm on all potential inputs. This unpredictability is the driver to seek alternative means of trust in the model, especially if the model is going to be included in closed loop operation where the risk of any failure can escalate proportionally to the impact of the action it triggers.

In practice, an AI model may be regarded as a set of common operations defining a computation graph that is executed by a program code on specific input data [5]. Therefore, comparing traditional software to software with AI from a practicing software developer's perspective in Table 4.2 provides further insight into the reasons why AI may seem indeterministic.

According to the attributes of AI-based software, AI should be considered as a statistical tool for engineering due to the following observations:

1. The lack of inherent transparency and intuitive explainability of AI models and their outputs on individual input data samples renders AI models a tool of mass and statistics. Interpreting AI quality metrics such as accuracy, precision or recall already requires many experiments that are statistically evaluated, and they provide no guarantee whether the next individual experiment will result in a true or false outcome.

2. With statistical behavior, there comes the probability of failure, risk, and the need to manage trust in the AI model's output.

Table 4.2 Comparison between engineering with traditional software versus AI.

Capability	Traditional software	AI software
Components	**Source code**	**Source code and model**
Transparency	Yes. By studying the code, the functionality and behavior of a traditional SW are logically defined and comprehensible by a human engineer.	No. Although the model part is also fully defined by the training data, the training algorithm, and the resulting model parameters, it is not comprehensible by a human engineer because (1) the training data is either not human readable or its sheer volume prohibits anyone to have complete knowledge over it; (2) the trainable model parameters are not comprehensible with formal logic. Insight to an AI can only be obtained by running experiments (executing the model on concrete input data), which give only partial or statistical description. No formal reasoning is possible on "what would happen" given a future input sample – the only means to know is to apply the model to the data.
Debugging potential	Bugs can be tracked back to the source code, therefore, they can be fixed	Wrong output from AI (e.g., misclassification on an input data sample) cannot be traced back to model parameters – no actionable insight is obtained by analyzing which model parameters could be changed to correct the output of the model for that single input, and even if a change is made, the consequences to all other input data samples are unknown.

3. Additionally, there are adversary attack vectors opened by the data channel of the AI (in addition to its source code/SW channel), which requires security mechanisms developed for AI.

Overall, importing AI into a system means importing the above trust and security requirements as well.

4.5 Trust in Machine Learning as a Service Deployments

Machine learning (ML) as a service (MLaaS) is a service model where an MLaaS provider (MLP) encapsulates ML models to implement use cases

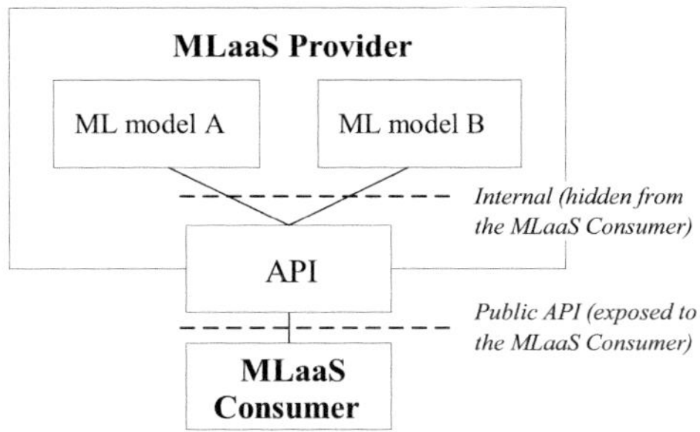

Figure 4.3 MLaaS scenario, with multiple ML models in the MLaaS provider.

that are accessible to MLaaS consumers (MLC) through an interface (e.g., a REST API). MLaaS is already popular among public cloud and analytics providers (providing, e.g., speech-to-text API and image analysis API). The importance of this AI/ML deployment also stems from being native to service-based network and service management architectures [6], therefore, service-based encapsulation of AI/ML capabilities is directly relevant to telecommunication systems. As telco networks are multivendor systems, with potentially different providers of each AI/ML-based service, having a mechanism that can create technical proof both for the provider and the consumer on the genuineness of a model used for the service may help build and maintain trust between the partners.

In practice, the MLP may have multiple models trained for the same ML use case (Figure 4.3). Different models may solve the same task with different accuracy (e.g., 90%, 95%, and 99%). The TCO of a more accurate model is usually higher than that of a less accurate one due to more data and compute-intensive training process, larger model size and more compute resources needed for executing the trained model for inference. The TCO may be reflected in the MLP's charging model: the MLP may charge the MLC per API calls or by the amount of processed data, and vary the price based on the requested accuracy level.

A general problem in the context of MLaaS is how to ensure that the ML model behind the MLaaS API is accurate, for example, according to a public statement of the MLP on its own model accuracy, or according to the accuracy selected by the MLC via the API or for which the MLC is eligible via its subscription. The ML models are trained, hosted, and executed by the MLP privately (i.e., the ML models cannot be accessed and studied by the MLC or any other entity). When an MLC submits its data to the MLP for analysis, the MLC receives the result of the model execution, which bears no trace of the identity or any other attribute of the ML model that was processing the data.

By using the MLaaS, there is no proof for the MLC that its data has been analyzed by an ML model with the agreed accuracy. The MLC cannot obtain such proof on its own, for two reasons:

1. The amount of an MLC's data may be simply too low for statistically relevant benchmarking. For example, by submitting 10 samples for an ML model, and benchmarking the model's accuracy by evaluating the number of samples for which the model gave good response, the error of benchmark accuracy is ±10% (a single sample output being right/wrong causes 1/10 = 10% difference). Additionally, model benchmarking on 10 samples is not statistically significant; even for ML models that are generally highly accurate, one could find particular data samples on which the model does not perform well – but that does not mean the model as such is poor.
2. The MLC usually cannot validate the MLaaS result's correctness even on a single data sample, as that capability would require the MLC to independently solve the ML use case it is delegating to the MLP. If the MLC could solve the ML task itself, there would be no reason to use MLaaS in the first place. Therefore, the MLC needs to trust the MLP on the accuracy of the results, with no formal or experimental proof.

Another related technical problem is on the MLP side: how can the MLP prove, without exposing its ML model publicly, that an MLC's data was indeed processed by an accurate ML model? For example, a malicious MLC may deliberately submit low-quality input data to the MLP and complain that the results are poor (below the agreed accuracy) whereas in fact, the data was simply not fit for the model.

A potential solution to the above problems may be to create technology that (1) enables to certify the accuracy of an ML model accessed through an MLaaS interface; (2) enables MLaaS consumers (MLC) to obtain proof that their data were processed by a ML model with certified accuracy; (3) enables the MLaaS provider (MLP) to prove that it has processed an MLaaS consumer's data with a certified ML model. During this process, the ML models remain secret to the MLP. The process should be applicable to existing MLPs (e.g., in public clouds) without any change to their current interface; also, the method should not require cooperation from the MLP or any additional service beyond what it already provides to the MLC as part of its own business.

The general solution is illustrated through an example to render the idea more tangible. The example process assumes the existence of a special function, the ML Certification Server (MLCS), as shown in Figure 4.4. The

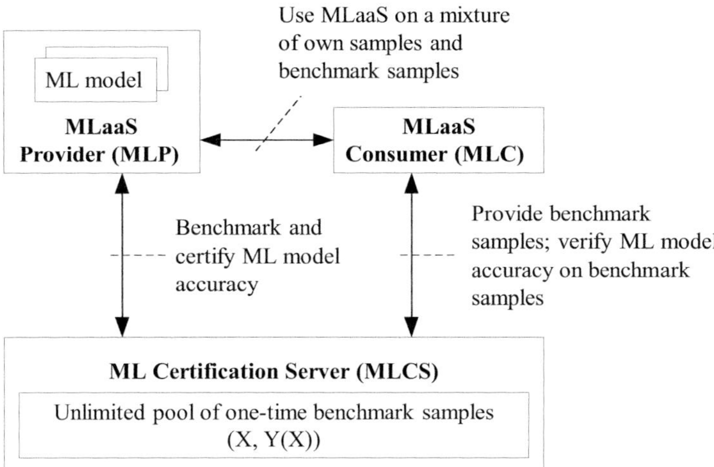

Figure 4.4 ML model certification, showing the MLCS and the roles of the interfaces.

MLCS can generate an unlimited number of data samples (X, Y(X)) where X is an input data suitable to be processed by an MLP's ML model and Y(X) is the expected result when inputting X to the ML model. The data samples need to be syntactically and semantically fit to be processed by an ML model. Therefore, the MLCS generates (X, Y(X)) data samples per ML model. The MLCS generated (X, Y(X)) data samples are one-time samples, that is, they are never recycled or used more than once, ever. Any entity getting to know an (X, Y(X)) data sample is not able to use it to fake an ML model's expected operation by simply returning Y(X) for X because the same X will never be encountered as input to the ML model again.

The MLCS can benchmark and verify the accuracy of an MLP's ML model M by acting as an MLC, subscribing to its model M, and generating (X, Y(X)) samples fit to be processed by model M. The method is illustrated in Figure 4.5. The MLCS sends the X part of the data samples to the MLP; the Y(X) part is kept secret by the MLCS. The MLP processes X with ML model M; however, the processing step is hidden inside the MLP. The MLP only returns a y(X) response as a result of input X. The MLCS compares Y(X) with y(X) to measure how accurately the MLP was able to produce the expected output Y(X) for input X. The MLCS may release a public certificate stating that the MLP's ML model M has a certain accuracy.

The MLCS can verify that the data samples of an MLC (other than the MLCS itself) were also processed by an ML model M of the MLP with the same accuracy level as certified by the MLCS for the MLP's model M. This method is illustrated in Figure 4.6. The MLC has its own data A that it would

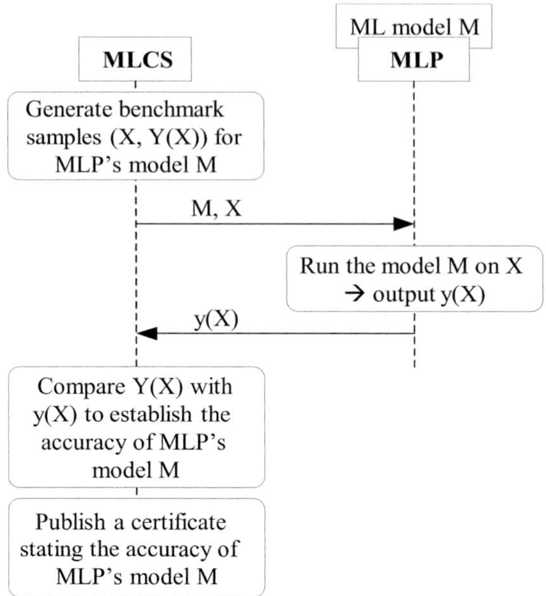

Figure 4.5 Benchmarking the MLP's ML model accuracy.

like to submit to MLP to be analyzed by model M. The MLC does not know the expected output Y(A) for its data A, and neither does the MLCS. The MLC requests the MLCS to provide one-time benchmark samples fit to be processed by the same ML model M of MLP. The MLCS generates new one-time benchmark samples (B, Y(B)) and provides part B to the MLC but keeps Y(B) as a secret to itself. The MLP mixes its own data A with the one-time benchmark sample B obtained from MLCS and sends the A + B mixture to MLP for processing. The MLP runs the ML model M on A + B and returns the output y(A) + y(B) to the MLC. The MLC forwards the y(B) to the MLCS for verification. The MLCS, knowing Y(B), calculates the accuracy of model M on the one-time benchmark data B and compares it to the accuracy established during a previous certification. If the current accuracy matches the certified accuracy, the benchmark data B was very likely processed with model M at MLP. Since the MLP had to process the mixture of A + B, performing well on part B implicitly proves that the same model M was running on data part A too. The MLCS sends this positive verification to the MLC. If the two accuracies do not match, the MLCS sends a negative indication to the MLC. Therefore, by using the service of MLCS, the MLC obtains proof of whether or not its own data was analyzed by a proper model of the MLP.

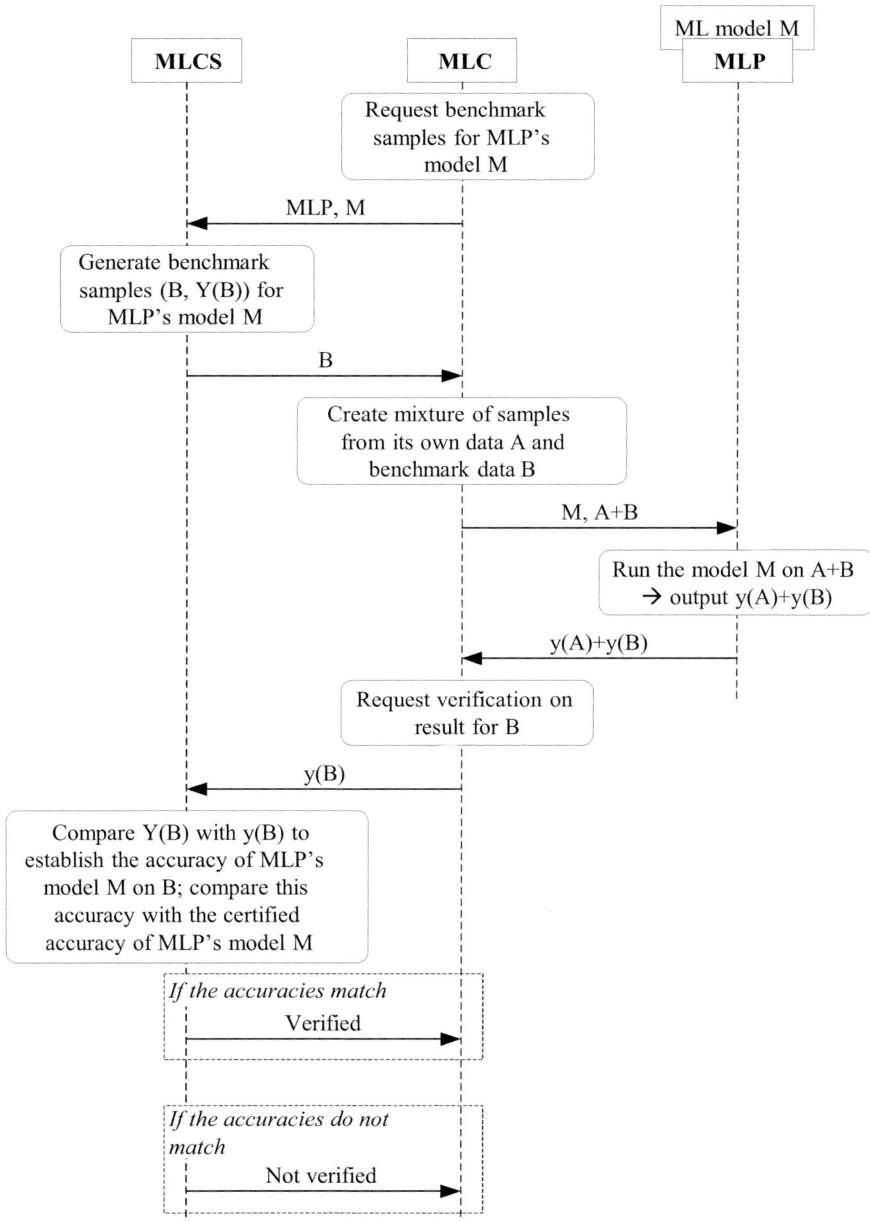

Figure 4.6 Accuracy verification of an MLP's model M on an MLC's own data.

The method's strength does not depend on whether the MLP knows exactly that it is under benchmark or is totally ignorant of the entire MLCS presence. Theoretically, it could be possible that the MLP cleverly separates the A + B data to parts A and B, runs a good model on part B, and a poor model on part A. However, such tinkering is very risky as the MLP may guess which part is A and B wrongly, in which case the MLCS would detect the issue and red flag the MLP, causing serious reputation and business loss for the MLP. Additionally, since even a cleverly cheating MLP has to process part B with a good model, simply ensuring that the amount of data in part B is at least in the same order of magnitude as data in part A amortizes the MLP's potential saving of computation power by processing part A with an inferior model. In practice, often the MLC's own data (part A) may be much less in quantity than what is needed for the benchmarking process to be statistically significant, that is, the amount of part B may even be an order of magnitude higher. Therefore, there is really no cost incentive for the MLP to try to separate the mixture of data and process the parts separately, whereas there is a large reputation loss at stake if even a single mistake is made in the separation ever.

In general, the MLCS could keep the Y(X) part of the one-time benchmark data (X, Y(X)) secret. However, in certain situations (e.g., dispute, legal proof, and court order) the MLCS may be required to publish its benchmark data to prove that the data was suitable for benchmarking a given ML model and Y(X) is indeed a correct output for X. Due to the one-time use of any (X, Y(X)) data sample, the benchmark data may become public without weakening the already issued MLCS certificates. Additionally, the MLCS may even voluntarily publish samples from its benchmark data to increase trust in itself.

The MLCS not only proves to the MLC that its data was processed by an ML model previously benchmarked to provide the agreed accuracy, but at the same time, it also provides proof to the MLP in case an MLC debates this fact. In an extreme case, an MLC's data may be semantically unfit for the ML model for which the data was submitted for processing, therefore, resulting in poor accuracy on the MLC's data. Yet providing good accuracy on the one-time benchmark data of MLCS proves that the agreed ML model was used, annulling the false claims of MLC for any refund. That is, the MLCS is an unbiased source of truth regarding the fact whether input data was processed by a preagreed ML model. Note that, since the MLCS (and none of the other entities) has actual access to the ML model, technically the MLCS proves that the MLC's data was processed by an equivalent of the previously benchmarked ML model. In reality, it could be a slightly improved (e.g., retrained and updated) version of the ML model. Still, as what matters is the quality of the model's output, this proof is sufficient in practice.

The MLCS generates one-time benchmark data samples using simulations driven by a high entropy random source. Different types of simulations are needed for different ML tasks. For example, for image recognition, image rendering is needed; for speech-to-text transcription, speech generation is needed, and for network state modeling, network data generation is needed. The exact method by which the MLCS generates the benchmark samples is implementation-specific.

The MLCS may use ML itself for the generation of data. For example, the MLC may share its own data samples (or part of it) with the MLCS when asking for one-time benchmark samples. The MLC's own data samples may serve as a clue to the MLCS about exactly what kind of data the MLC will use. The MLCS may use generative ML models seeded by the MLC's own data to produce further data that resembles the MLC's data but for which the MLCS knows the expected output from the MLP. For example, for images, neural style transfer may be used to produce images with predefined content (e.g., known location of objects) but in the style of the images provided by the MLC. Such style transfer makes the one-time benchmark samples generated by the MLCS to blend in with the MLC's own data even more.

The MLC may mix the one-time benchmark samples obtained from the MLCS on different levels. The most trivial (and often sufficient) mixture is to simply concatenate its own samples after the benchmark samples, potentially randomly shuffling the ordering of the samples (whenever the order of samples does not matter for the analysis). A deeper mixture is also possible, by merging a benchmark sample and one of its own samples together into a single atomic sample. For example, for images, a benchmark image and one of the MLC's own images may be copied side-by-side to make a larger image and use that larger image as a sample submitted to the MLP. This makes it even more complex for the MLP to try to split the data into benchmark and original parts and improves the likelihood that the MLP runs the same model on all data.

The certificate generated by the MLCS should at least contain the identity of the MLP, the identity of the MLP's ML model that is certified, and the certified model accuracy. Additionally, the certificate may contain statistics or further information on the data that was used for the benchmarking. Ultimately, samples from the benchmark data may also be published or linked to the certificate.

The benefit of this approach is that it does not require any change on the MLP's interface/API (neither when interacting with the MLCS nor with the

MLC). Any currently available MLP can be certified as-is, and MLCs may use the MLCS to obtain proof of the accuracy of the MLP's model processing their own data. The benefit for the MLP is also realized without any change on their side.

The key interactions through the interface between the MLCS and the MLC:

- *MLC→MLCS: request for one-time benchmark samples.* This request should include the identity of the MLP and the identity of the ML model of the MLP. In practice, this could be a URL pointing to the REST API resource where the MLP offers the service corresponding to a given model (including the accuracy of the model). Additionally, the MLC may provide further clues about the kind of data it will send to the MLP so that the MLCS can generate one-time benchmark samples that are very similar to the MLC's own data. For example, if the ML task is image analytics, the MLP may describe the resolution and quality of its own images to the MLCS, and the MLCS may initialize its random image generator so that it will create images of the same resolution and quality.
- *MLCS→MLC: provide one-time benchmark samples.* This response should carry a container with the data that can be mixed by the MLC with its own data.
- *MLC→MLCS: the response obtained from the MLP on the one-time benchmark data.* This notification should contain only what the MLP has returned for the one-time benchmark data, and not the response for the MLC's own data. The MLC has to demultiplex the response of the MLP by reversing the mixing process it has done earlier.
- *MLCS→MLC: verification of the accuracy of the MLP model.* This response is essentially an acknowledgment or negative acknowledgment indicating whether the accuracy of the MLP's model was found to match the same model's previous benchmark accuracy. The response may also contain the quantified accuracy for this particular model run, and the previously certificated accuracy.

As an additional service, the MLCS may implement a data and service proxy functionality for the MLC (Figure 4.7). In this setup, the MLC does not interact with the MLP directly but only with the MLCS. The MLC submits its own data to the MLCS, naming the MLP and the ML model/service by which the data needs to be analyzed. The MLCS generates one-time benchmark data samples and performs the mixing of the MLC's data with the one-time

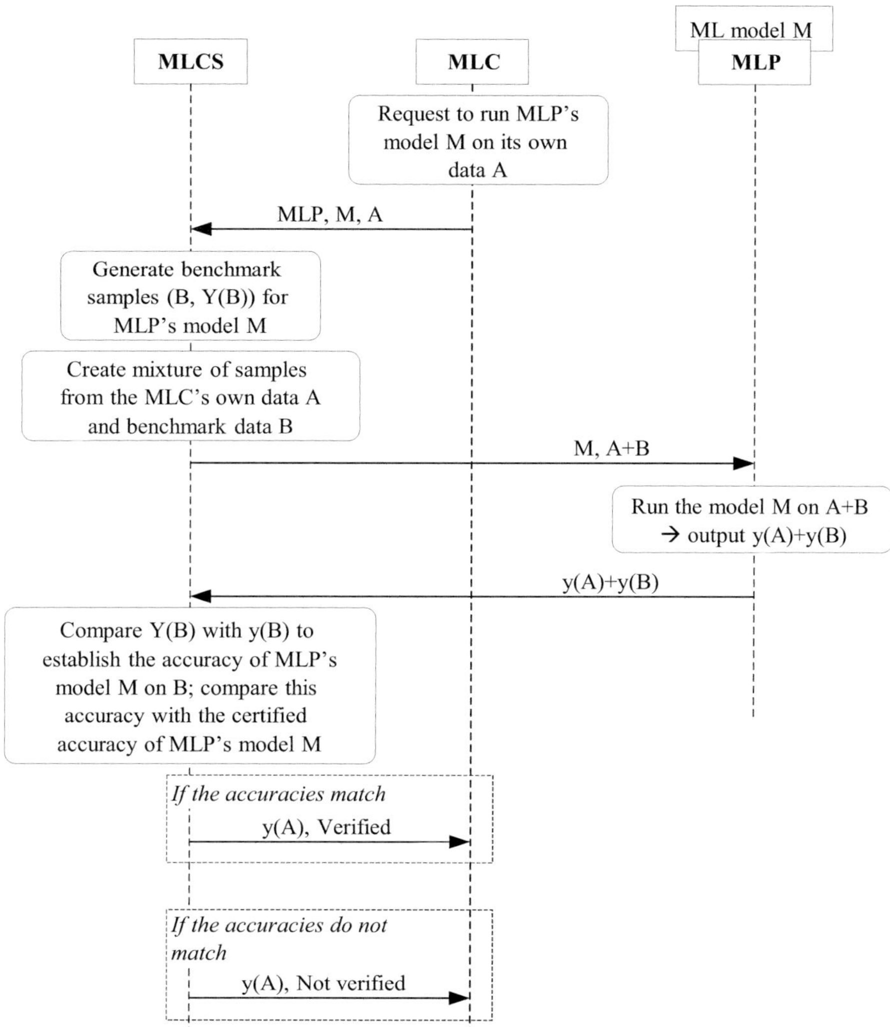

Figure 4.7 MLCS providing data and service proxy to the MLC.

benchmark data. The MLCS sends the mixture of the data to the MLP using its own subscription to the MLP APIs (which is anyway needed for the MLCS to perform the certification). The MLP returns the result on the mixture of data to the MLCS. The MLCS extracts the MLP's response corresponding to the one-time benchmark data and verifies the accuracy of the MLP model. Finally, the MLCS returns the MLP's response corresponding to the MLC's own data along with the accuracy verification result to the MLC.

This service has multiple benefits for the MLC:

The MLC does not need to deal with the complexity of mixing the one-time benchmark samples with its own data – this could be provided by the MLCS as a service to the MLC. As a side effect, the MLCS may take advantage of the insight into the full MLC data to generate compelling one-time benchmark samples resembling the MLC data.

- The MLC does not need to maintain a subscription to the MLP, which may have its own cost.
- The MLC is not charged directly by the MLP for the additional one-time benchmark samples. The MLCS pays for using the MLP's service for both the MLC data and the one-time benchmark samples. Since the MLCS may have a bulk institutional subscription with better price negotiation ability, the per-sample cost may be lower if all samples are submitted by the MLCS. The cost of the MLP service can be shared back to the MLC by the MLCS, as well as the additional cost of the MLCS's own services (data mixture, accuracy verification, etc.).

In this case, the MLC trusts the MLCS with its own data. This is the choice of the MLC and it is a nontechnical decision. However, the MLC already trusts the MLP with its data, therefore the quantum leap of providing data to external entities has been anyway made by the MLC when it started to use MLaaS.

4.6 Summary

In autonomous networks, data and AI models are not only highly integrated (as data is input to models, whereas models produce data that could be further input to other models, etc.) but also converged in the sense that models are also data by themselves. Therefore, models as data are subject to similar operations as conventional data, including persistent storage and transmission through interfaces. The intersection of models and data was a central motif of this chapter to discuss about elements of data and model security together rather than putting data and model security on separate tracks.

A major part of data security falls into the scope of classical cryptography, such as authentication, integrity, and confidentiality. These should be generally applicable to both data in transit and data at rest. This chapter presented a PKI-based generic data security framework that is applicable to these requirements, and also to scenarios when data represents full or partial AI models (e.g., in the case of federated learning).

AI modeling brings in additional aspects of security. First, AI-specific security issues may be addressed within the confines of the core AI technology and related operations such as security-aware training mechanisms. Second, trustworthiness issues, which originate from theoretical attributes of the AI technology and therefore require mitigation strategy outside of the AI technology itself.

In terms of AI security, there needs to be awareness of the additional surface opened toward a range of new adversarial attacks. There is ongoing research producing mitigation tactics against various types of AI attacks. With AI as a service, many of the attack categories become theoretical ones as they require access to sensitive model parts or operations that are not available in properly managed environments (i.e., AI security falls back to traditional and well-practiced IT security). Still, it remains a challenge to obtain proof of correctness or even proof of work by a specific AI model that may be a contracted requirement between a service consumer and an MLaaS service provider. This chapter provided a detailed description of a potential mechanism to collect (statistical) proof of processing input samples with a specific preagreed model with the plausible assumptions of exercising control over the model's input and receiving the model's output. The next chapter will continue the theme of AI/ML models with a deeper dive into how to internalize the models (as opposed to keeping them separate from a system) to improve the efficiency of the data-model pipeline and retain full ownership over AI-based capabilities.

Bibliography

[1] ETSI GR ZSM 010, "Zero-touch network and Service Management (ZSM); General Security Aspects", V1.1.1 (2021-07)

[2] National Institute of Standards and Technology, "Adversarial Machine Learning, A Taxonomy and Terminology of Attacks and Mitigations", NIST Trustworthy and Responsible AI, NIST AI 100-2e2023, https://doi.org/10.6028/NIST.AI.100-2e2023

[3] W. Gan, S. Wan and P. S. Yu, "Model-as-a-Service (MaaS): A Survey," 2023 IEEE International Conference on Big Data (BigData), Sorrento, Italy, 2023, pp. 4636-4645, doi: 10.1109/BigData59044.2023.10386351.

[4] National Institute of Standards and Technology. Artifcial Intelligence Risk Management Framework (AI RMF 1.0). https://doi.org/10.6028/NIST.AI.100-1, 2023.

[5] Open Neural Network Exchange, "The open standard for machine learning interoperability", Available online: https://onnx.ai/

[6] ETSI GS ZSM 002, "Zero-touch network and Service Management (ZSM); Reference Architecture", V1.1.1 (2019-08)

5

Native AI/ML and the Related Management Aspects

AI is a key technology enabler of network and service management automation. As to core technology of AI is developed externally to mobile networks, applying it to workflows and functions within the network requires a level of integration between existing networking architecture, processes and solutions, and the infrastructure and mode of operation imposed by the AI technology. AI native networks bring integration to the level of owning and defining all elements (resources, processes, interactions) of and with AI inside the system architecture rather than attaching to AI-based capabilities through carefully separated data and control exposure interfaces. Native AI removes dependency from external platforms and services in favor of exercising full control over the AI technology becoming part of the networks, including the training, validation, deployment, and operation of the AI models. AI native networks also need to handle all challenges related to security, trust, and efficiency created by the integration of AI technology itself, especially considering the heterogeneous, large-scale, distributed, and sometimes, resource-constrained environments of networks, which are in contrast to the data center driven upstream AI deployments.

5.1 Introduction

The complexity of telecommunication technology and mobile network deployments has steadily been increasing with new generations of mobile systems. Some of the sources of complexity include the abundance of applications, the domain-specific technologies coexisting with each other; virtualization, software technology, and clouds adopted by telco solutions, creating new abstraction layers and management requirements; and the proliferation of management domains and the associated vendor- and technology-specific

DOI: 10.1201/9788770041478-5

tools and processes. In a traditional network management and operation environment, this multifactor complexity is exposed to the operator and creates an integration and operation burden. A typical technological response to complexity is the attempt to increase the level of automation throughout the system. Automation capabilities targeting the reduction of management complexity have been part of the mobile networks since LTE, coining the self-organizing network [1] concept. SON has defined standardized use cases and corresponding mechanisms to delegate the configuration or optimization of selected parameters to the network. Still, the SON use cases provide only point solutions for specific configuration or optimization tasks by design, even if their implementations have undergone intermittent upgrades to state-of-the-art technologies including the use of machine learning [2].

Over the years, the scope of network automation has been extended to e2e network and service management [3]. Automation evolved not only in terms of abstraction from single equipment through the domain to the e2e level [4] but also in terms of the applied technology from predefined simple algorithms [1] to the adoption of AI/ML [5, 6]. As of today, AI/ML technologies increasingly penetrate all domains and layers of telecommunication networks. AI/ML has a wide range of applications including the realization of network functionalities or capabilities, improving network efficiency through learning and optimization, increasing the autonomy of networks through closed-loop management services, or providing predictive modeling capabilities for network digital twins [4, 7, 8]. With the increase of generic compute capacity available to telco networks through the cloudification of the infrastructure [9], AI/ML-enabled to target real-time distributed optimization such as radio beamforming or complex scenarios such as QoS or energy efficiency [10].

Even though AI/ML has been adopted as a de-facto technology to help network automation, current networks have not been designed with AI/ML in mind. Rather, AI/ML has been engineered on top of already standardized, productized, and deployed network architectures bearing little resource headroom and flexibility to accommodate the infrastructure, development, and operational differences of new technologies. This has left AI/ML to work on a separate infrastructure (including resources not owned by the operator such as public clouds), bringing along its own operation and management tools and frameworks, and having the operator develop ad-hoc mechanisms to integrate AI/ML with the traditional network functions and management solutions. The separation between AI/ML and the telco systems has multiple sources, including independent or even disparate technology evolution, misalignment in the technology cycles, pace of development, and independent timing of new releases and capabilities [11]. The lifecycle of solutions created with AI/ML is also fundamentally different from traditional CI/CD in HW/SW engineering, which has multiple reasons. One is the new engineering roles and technological requirements created by the data-driven nature of AI/ML (both in training and operation), resulting in new human skills (such as data engineer) and new infrastructural capabilities (created by the need for data collection and mediation, cleaning, labeling, training, model management, etc.) that need to be integrated in the operation of a network with AI/ML. Another reason for the separation of AI/ML and the rest of the network is the inherent semantic gap (i.e., lack of explainability) between the latent space of the AI/ML models and the real-world concepts and tasks to which the AI/ML models are applied, making the integration of AI/ML models with established operational workflows a practically hard problem.

5.2 AI Native Networks

In an AI-native network, the assets and impacts of the AI/ML technology are a visible part of the network architecture, infrastructure, and operational/management processes, fully owned and executed by the network itself [11]. Similarly to how the impacts of radio propagation are represented throughout the design of the radio interface (e.g., in the use of physical and logical channels, adaptive modulation schemes, and all the associated measurements and RRC signaling between the UE and the gNB), the impacts of AI/ML modeling should be represented in the design of the AI native network. Therefore, AI nativeness is not marked by a single new network functionality but rather a systematic integration of AI/ML technology in all levels of the network functions, data management, and operation automation that should all support the requirements imposed by the AI/ML technology. The concept is illustrated in Figure 5.1.

The AI-specific characteristics of an AI native network thus may be discussed by describing it as an environment from the perspective of an AI/ML model (Figure 5.2):

- Design and development phase: The lifecycle of AI/ML models (including the collection and availability of training data, training execution, inventory, and availability of trained models) is well-defined and automated, similar to the CI/CD of traditional cloud native SW modules.
- Deployment phase: The AI/ML models are shipped with all necessary software environment that enables instantiation, configuration, execution, and integration with other system components as part of an

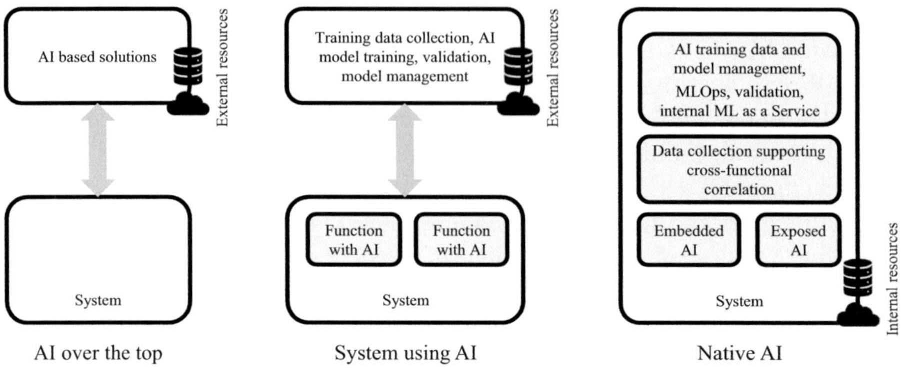

Figure 5.1 AI native systems – a conceptual illustration.

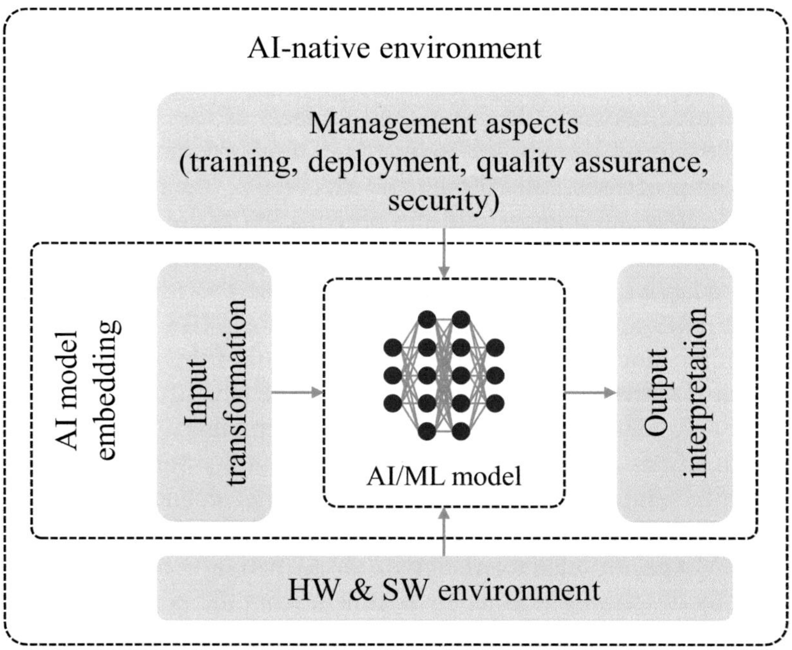

Figure 5.2 AI native environment from the perspective of an AI/ML model.

automated orchestration process, similar to the deployment of traditional SW modules.

- Operational phase: The data availability (and transformation, if necessary) for AI/ML model input, and the interpretation of the AI/ML model output should be a close loop operation provided automatically as part of the deployed SW environment of the AI/ML model.

- AI/ML model management: Throughout all the above phases, AI/ML model quality monitoring and assurance, fallback mechanisms, and security aspects should be provided.

The subsequent sections provide more details on potential approaches that help realize the above requirements, focusing on the new management aspects created by the adoption of AI/ML technology in networks.

5.3 Management Aspects of AI

The overall management tasks in AI native networks are summarized in Figure 5.3 covering the lifecycle of SW modules with AI. The lifecycle starts with creating the SW module image, which is the product of developing the SW (usually a SW asset produced by a CI/CD pipeline). The SW module is instantiated, scaled, and terminated by the orchestrator, which performs traditional infrastructure/SW management tasks. The implemented functionality of the SW module itself, if it is a network function, is also managed in terms of traditional CM/PM/FM type of network management. In addition to these traditional management scopes, if the SW module has exposed AI, the new AI management responsibilities are provided by the AI management service of the AI native network. AI management could be regarded as a new management domain [2] with concerns such as model training/retraining, AI model performance monitoring, model arbitration/switch-over (including failover to non-AI implementation), model and data protection, federation between multiple AIs, security and trust, and explainability.

5.4 AI Model Embedding and Monitoring

In network management using AI and within native AI networks, operational AI models are not standalone assets, but they are part of or encapsulated in a deployable and manageable SW module (such as a container image). However, the development and validation of AI models often happen in incubation (e.g., in a sandbox or using offline resources) rather than in the final environment where the resulting trained model would effectively operate. Therefore, it is important to make a distinction between AI models and a SW module wrapped around or integrating an AI model, as illustrated in Figure 5.4.

AI model: A data structure representing a single instance of an untrained or trained AI model, as it is produced by the software library used to define (and/or train) the model. An AI model can be stored, transferred, and loaded

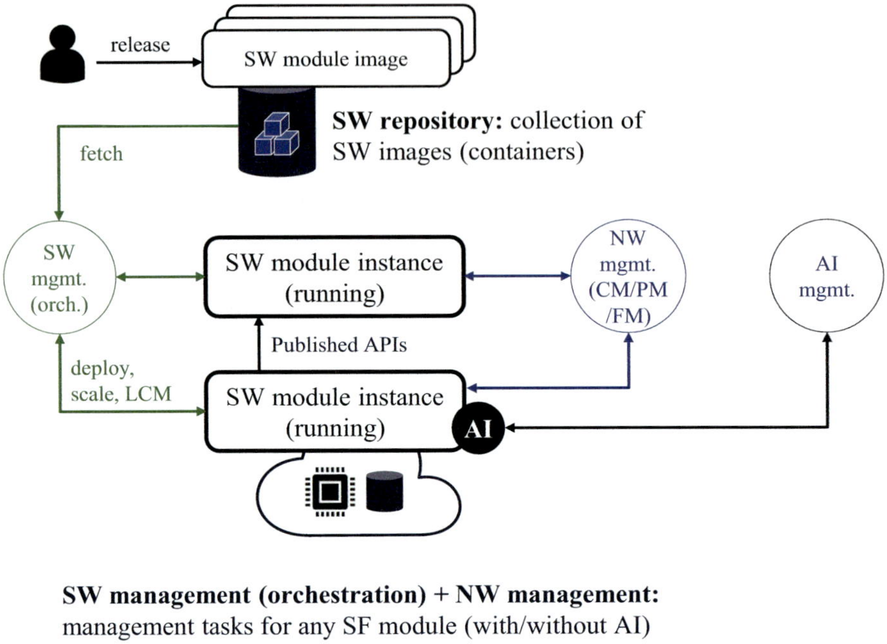

Figure 5.3 Management tasks in AI native networks.

as any other data structure (albeit a potentially large data structure), but in order to operate the model (e.g., apply it to input data and generate output), additional SW executable is needed (which may use the same, or in case of standardized model formats [12], even different software library that was used to produce the model). As the AI model itself is only operational with SW to animate it, any AI-based capability of functionality needs to be implemented as a combination of the AI model and SW.

Software module with AI: Trained (but potentially still retrainable or fine-tunable) AI model(s) integrated into a deployable SW module with clearly defined purpose and APIs. One purpose of the SW around the model is to provide the executable environment for the AI model that enables to make computations with the AI model, for example, by fitting the model to input data and capturing its output. Another purpose of the SW wrapping the model is to improve the flexibility of the model, for example, by offering integration with different types or formats of input data and internally transforming them to the one that is natively expected by the AI model's input ingestion point. Further capabilities may also be integrated into the SW module, such as producing recommendations or even making decisions based on the AI model's

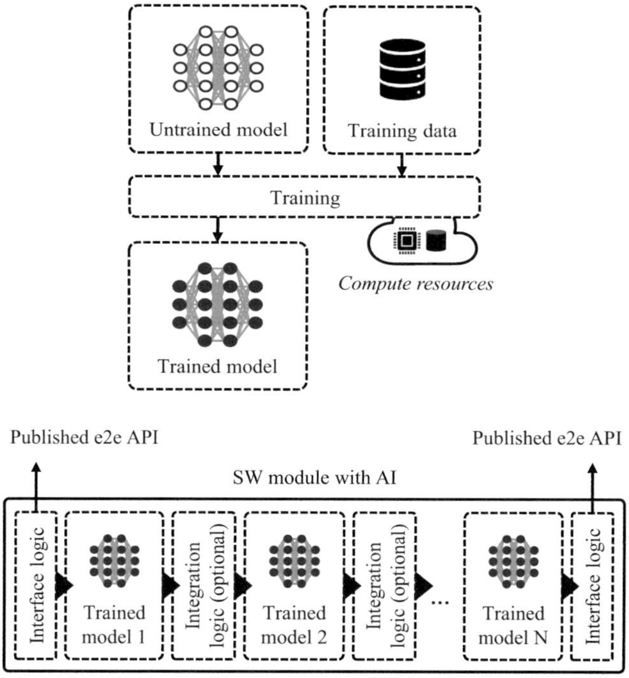

Figure 5.4 AI model embedding.

output. Such capabilities may be offered to consumers through the API of the SW module. If multiple AI models are embedded in the same SW module, it is possible to use them alternatively (e.g., by selecting a model based on the input data received by the SW module) or by implementing an incremental pipeline of serial AI models where a model's output is directed into the input of a subsequent model. However, all this potential internal complexity may be fully hidden from the consumer of the SW module's API, which is another benefit of wrapping AI models in SW modules.

The AI-specific management aspects of AI native networks cover the entire lifecycle of AI models, and consequently, the lifecycle of the SW modules (NFs, management services, etc.) that are embedding the AI models themselves. Trained models are integrated into SW modules to become a deployable unit ingesting data and providing services or capabilities via APIs. The integration may be at two levels, resulting in SW modules with two types of AI: embedded AI and exposed AI. The architecture of the two types of SW modules is illustrated in Figure 5.5.

In the case of the embedded AI, the AI aspects of the SW module are not visible outside the SW module itself. That is, neither the platform executing

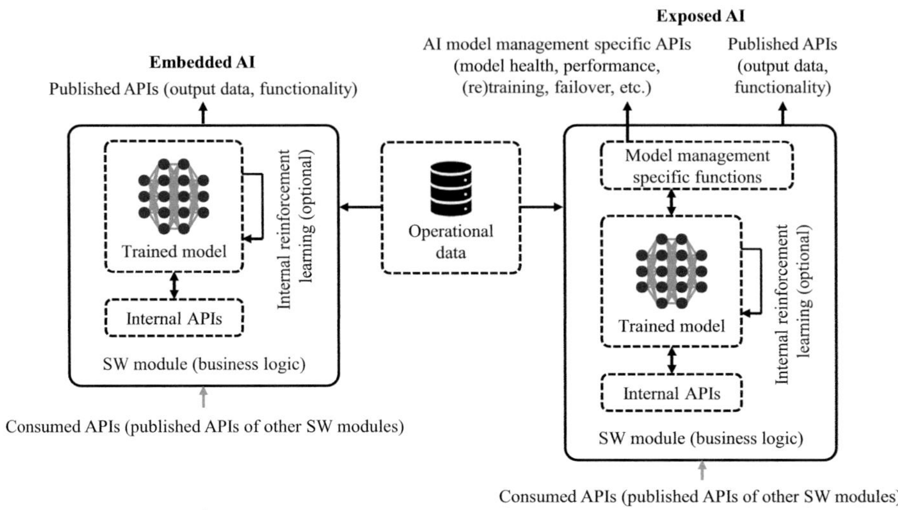

Figure 5.5 The differences between SW modules with embedded AI and exposed AI.

the SW module, nor the other SW modules integrating with it (e.g., by providing data or consuming the SW module's published APIs) are aware of even the fact that the SW module has an AI model inside. In this case, the full responsibility of managing the AI model is on the SW module (and its vendor), including the training, monitoring, and updating of the AI model. Such embedding is feasible for SW modules that implement well-defined interfaces and have a narrow and static scope that can be covered by an AI model. Still, it does not exclude even advanced AI capabilities such as continuously training the AI module (e.g., using reinforcement learning mechanisms) within the SW module itself, but all such mechanisms must be provided as part of the SW module's internal logic. That said, SW modules with embedded AI do not generate any additional management responsibilities compared to traditional network or management functions, and the management of the AI model will happen through regular software updates.

In the case of the exposed AI, the SW module not only publishes APIs that are related to its functionality or service but also related to the management of the AI model that is utilized by the internal business logic of the SW module. This is the case when the AI native network has additional AI management responsibilities, such as monitoring the status, performance and health of the model, trigger or manage (re)training or fine-tuning of the model (which also includes data management tasks such as collecting and selecting the right training data for the model), and handling model failures and fail-overs. The SW module exposing AI also has responsibilities in supporting the management of its model, for example, by calculating and producing metrics about the model's performance, implementing mechanisms to arbitrate between multiple versions of the model, or implementing a fail-over mechanism to a non-AI-based backup implementation in case of insurmountable modeling issues.

Examples of the need for exposed AI may include:

- Models within RAN L1-2-3, NWDAF, or other NFs require the detection of concept drift to be resolved by model reselection/retraining and/or intermediate fallback to non-AI mechanisms. Including such mechanisms per each network function (where the primary scope of the function is non-AI related) would generate unnecessary overhead and fragmented implementation for those network functions. Instead, the functions could provide AI telemetry that is analyzed and handled by an AI model management service that has a single but detailed implementation to catch concept drifting.
- Any SW module (including management services themselves – c.f. managing AI with AI models) could benefit by outsourcing adversary attack detection, alerting, and mitigation to a component that is continuously updated with the latest results of this challenging and fast-changing area.

Traditionally, AI models are trained and utilized in separate phases of their lifecycle, creating a clear transition point in between. In the training phase, the model is updated to learn from its training data, and its output is not utilized outside of the context of the training itself. In the operational phase, the model receives input data and generates output that is utilized for the use case of the model, whereas the model itself is not modified anymore. Such a clear split makes it possible to conduct the training and operational phases in entirely different environments, which has benefits in terms of potential availability and access to a higher amount of computing power and specialized accelerator hardware during the training phase (and potential overhead in terms of central data collection and retention). Yet a separate training process may afford to process higher amounts of data, usually yielding more accurate, more general, or even larger models that would not be conceivable on the limited resources of the operational premise. The trained model may be even scaled-down using techniques such as quantization to fit operational environments with significantly lesser resources and still provide acceptable performance.

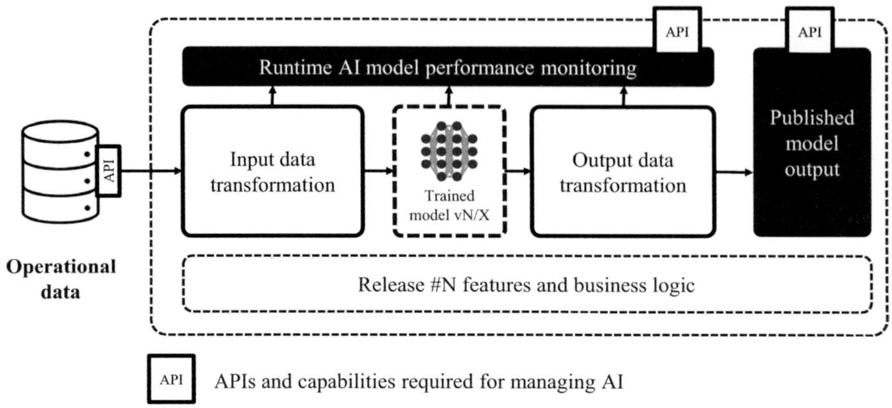

Figure 5.6 Key integration points for SW modules with exposed AI (supervised/self-supervised model).

The definite separation between training and operation is not necessary and does not follow any AI technological constraint. Therefore, given the right resources and computing capabilities, models may continue training while already producing useful output. This paradigm may be fulfilled by various AI training methods, such as reinforcement learning or incremental learning, however, the biggest benefit in terms of autonomy (and thus, fulfilling the concepts of AI nativeness) is realized when the training is self-supervised requiring no manual data preparation, model hyperparameter tuning or any other external input that would prompt for human intervention. Models that may harvest all information necessary to continue their training in their operational environment may be regarded as self-learning models. Self-learning AI models may follow changes in their modeled data domain to incorporate new patterns into their model structure, capable of evolving along with their context. More details on the concept of self-learning will be provided in Section 7.3.

The key APIs and integration points for SW models with exposed AI are shown in Figure 5.6. Apart from the APIs that are exposed to provide the declared functionality of the SW module (referred to as the published model output), there are runtime AI model performance monitoring APIs that are consumed by the AI model management service of the AI native network. If the AI models are continuously trained while in operation, such as using reinforcement learning techniques, the internals of the SW module including the AI model itself may change (see Figure 5.7) and consequently the APIs for runtime AI model performance monitoring may also need to

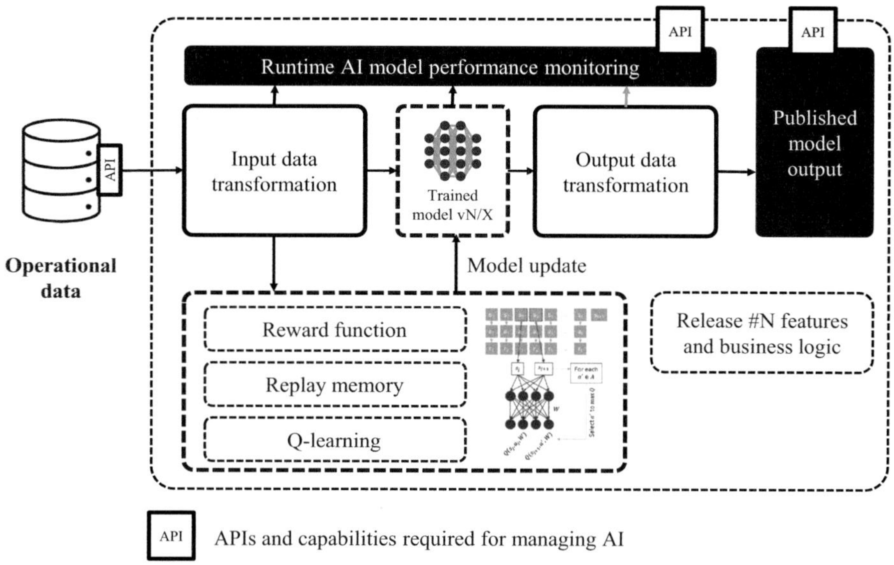

Figure 5.7 Key integration points for SW modules with exposed AI (reinforcement learning).

include notification emitted by the SW module about updates instrumented to the AI model so that the AI model management service is aware of the changes.

5.5 Management of Federated Learning

Federated learning is a kind of distributed machine learning where multiple distributed trainers and a central trainer collaboratively build a model [13]. The distributed trainers each have their own local data sources, which can only be accessed by their associated distributed trainer. Federated learning starts with the central trainer initializing a new (untrained) model and sending a copy of it to each distributed trainer. Each distributed trainer performs a model training step (e.g., gradient descent) based on the model and its own local data. After the training step, each distributed trainer sends back its updated model (or the updates to the model, such as the gradients obtained in the training step) to the central trainer. The central trainer then combines the updated models (or model updates) into a new version of the central model. The updated central model is shared back to each distributed trainer and the training cycle is repeated until the central model has converged to a stable state (usually after each distributed trainer has used all of its own local training data, maybe through multiple epochs, during

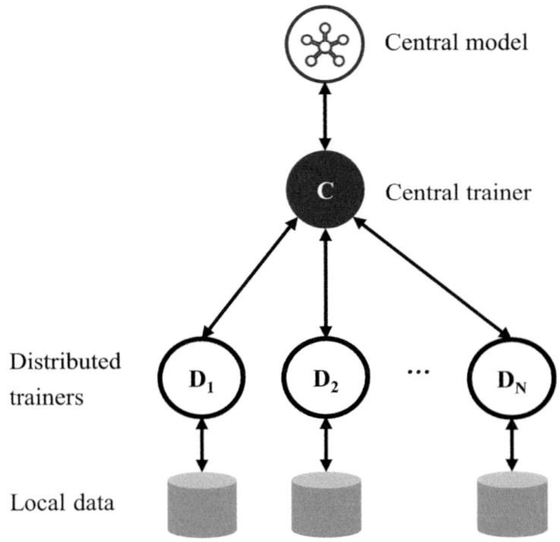

Figure 5.8 The concept of federated learning.

the distributed training). The concept of federated training is illustrated in Figure 5.8.

Federated learning is a relevant technology in all systems that are natively distributed, such as a mobile network with highly distributed and disaggregated radio access networks. Federated learning is also the go-to technology to bridge the gap between multiple stakeholders having private data but a common goal to build a shared model, incentivized by the accuracy and performance of a shared model that is trained on their collective data. In telco terms, a collection of networks or domains (e.g., governed by an entity offering managed services) is a typical scenario where models trained on insights collected from multiple networks may benefit the managed service provider by outperforming individual network-specific models in terms of generalization to new data and robustness against adversary attacks. However, mixing data across networks may not be possible due to privacy reasons. In another scenario pushing distribution to the extreme, each UE may be considered to be a separate stakeholder with its own private data, with the network playing the role of a central entity. Such a scenario fits into the direction of AI/ML for the NR air interface, where the AI model is assumed to be running at the UEs (or at both the UE and gNB) [6]. One possible way to train such a model without centralizing data collection in the network is to apply federated learning. In summary, federated learning is inevitably part of AI native systems and AI native networks, which pulls in the related model and data management requirements and technologies.

There are multiple model management challenges related to creating and using models through federated learning, which is attributed to the asymmetric relationship between local trainers and the central trainer, as well as the security and trust aspects of the local data and local trainers. Challenges may be grouped into two main categories based on which of the key federated learning assets is impacted: the shared model (i.e., the product of the federated learning); or the privacy of the local data (i.e., the promise to be kept by the federated learning). Challenges related to the model may be further split into training versus usage phases. During the training, the main concern is the validity, correctness, and robustness of the resulting model (provided that no single entity controls or even knows all the training data). During the usage of the model, which often happens by the same distributed entities that participated in creating it as local trainers [6], a concern is the integrity of the model (due to potential changes introduced by distributed users) and trusting that collaborating entities using the same model. As for the privacy of the local data, which is a fundamental promise of federated learning, concerns are focused on the training phase to ensure that local data remains private not only in terms of cleartext access (which could be prevented by state-of-the-art crypto) but also in terms of preventing any indirect leak of information such as inference of attributes or distribution of the data through local training material (e.g., gradient updates) that is inevitably shared during the federated model training.

In the next subsections, a selection of the above model management aspects is discussed in more detail. The selection covers prominent aspects of concerns related to the protection of the two most important aspects: model security and robustness; and local data privacy.

5.5.1 Model set management to protect against adversary attacks

There is a trust asymmetry between the distributed trainers and the central trainer in the federated learning process, that is, distributed trainers never expose their data, however, they have full access to the model that is being constructed in the federated learning process. This makes the created central model vulnerable to maliciously distributed trainers because they could provide gradients to the central trainer that weaken the model toward specific adversary attacks. For example, inspecting the model's architecture (neural network layers, activation functions, connections between the layers, etc.), a distributed trainer with malicious intent could exploit the mathematical

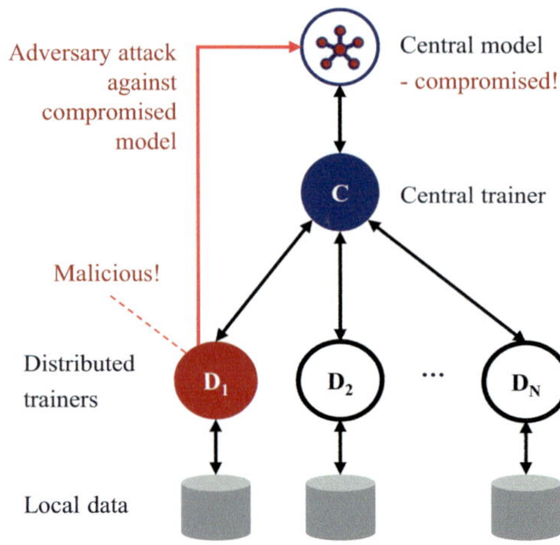

Figure 5.9 The impact of adversarial local trainers in federated learning.

vulnerabilities of a ReLU activation function [14] and provide gradients toward the central trainer that amplify this vulnerability. The malicious distributed trainer could even construct a set of adversary data samples, for which the vulnerability is specifically triggered, planning to exploit this vulnerability after the central model is finished. The exploitation of the vulnerability may be done by itself, acting later as a data source for the trained central model, or it could monetize the attack by selling adversary data samples to other malicious actors. This is very similar to software backdoors planned by a contributor and then exploited directly or through other malicious hackers (in fact, as ML models are software themselves, this analogy is directly applicable). The problem is illustrated in Figure 5.9.

As the distributed trainers share only gradients with the central trainer, it cannot detect whether the distributed trainer's gradients would cause the model to become vulnerable to a specific adversary attack, because only the malicious distributed trainer is aware of those data samples that would trigger the attack. The compromised model could then be deployed to many execution points (e.g., in each RAN node to perform scheduling, physical layer, or other RRM procedures), potentially creating a large attach surface (the entire RAN) toward malicious attacks.

With a suitable federated learning model set management framework, the impact of adversary distributed trainers on the centrally trained model could be limited. The central trainer may produce not only a single central model that contains the reported gradients of all distributed trainers, but it may train a set of multiple models, where each model selectively lacks input

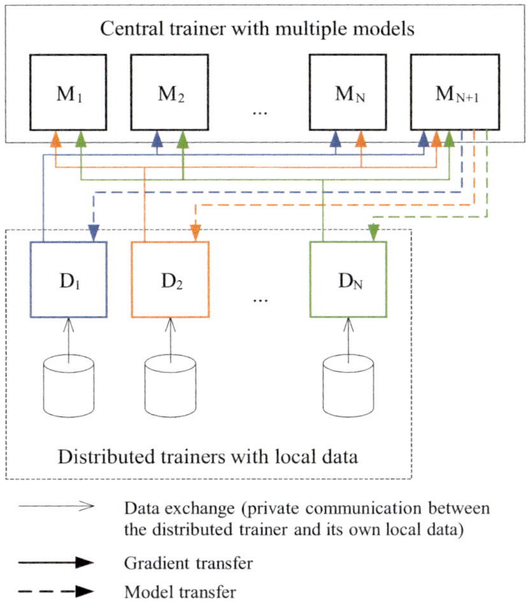

Figure 5.10 Multiple models produced by the central trainer.

from specific distributed trainers. In this way, the impact of any distributed trainer (however malicious that is) is localized to a subset of all trained models. The set of trained models can later be used (deployed, executed) together. Using a model management method, the user of the model set may detect if the models receive input data that likely tries to exploit a vulnerability that could have been injected by one of the distributed trainers during the federated learning process. The method also enables to identify the models that are impacted by the attack, and model management actions could be taken, such as revoking models from the set and blacklisting distributed trainers.

In the example shown in Figure 5.10, there are N distributed trainers, referred to as D_1 to D_N, each with their own local data that never leaves their premise. There is a central trainer that, during the federated learning process, builds N + 1 models. The models are denoted M_1 to M_{N+1}. The models are built by receiving and combining gradients from each distributed trainer in a specific pattern. For models M_i, i = 1 to N, each model M_i incorporates gradients sent by each distributed trainer except D_i. That is, each model M_i represents all distributed local data except that of D_i, and therefore, model M_i is free from any potential adversary gradient injection D_i would try to get through. In the last model, M_{N+1}, all gradients are incorporated, that is, this model represents all data of all distributed trainers. The role of this model

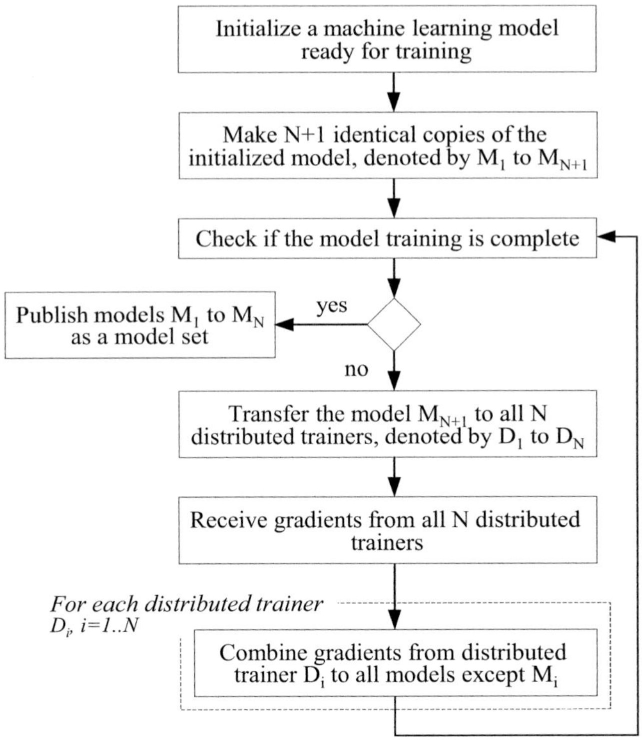

Figure 5.11 The key functionality performed by the central trained to create a model set.

is that during the federated learning process, it is shared back to every distributed trainer to perform their next learning step. This corresponds to the classic federated learning cycle and ensures that the distributed trainers are not aware that there are additional models M_1 to M_N trained on selective gradients to form a model set rather than a single model – that is, adversarial distributed trainers cannot adapt to the central trainer's different model training strategy.

The key functionality performed by the central trainer during the training of the model set is shown in Figure 5.11. The method starts with initializing a machine learning model ready to be trained. This initial (yet untrained) model instance is replicated in N + 1 instances, which will form the starting point of models M_1 to M_{N+1}. Then a training cycle starts, which ends when the training is completed (e.g., gradient updates received from the N distributed trainers are below a predetermined threshold). Until that happens, in each cycle, the central trainer transfers model M_{N+1} to each distributed trainer, collects their gradients (that the distributed trainers generated by updates to model M_{N+1} on their own local data), and combines the gradients to corresponding models. In the combination, gradients collected from D_i are incorporated in all models except M_i (I = 1, ..., N). The cycle is repeated by checking for the stopping condition and transferring the updated model M_{N+1} to every distributed trainer if further training is necessary.

The result of the training process is a set of models, M_1 to M_N where each model is free of the gradient updates of one of the distributed trainers. The model set could be used in a combination to perform inference (i.e., apply the trained models to new data). During the inference, each model would ingest the same input data and produce slightly different outputs. In case one of the distributed trainers produced compromising gradients to the central trainer, and the input data used for inference is an adversarial attach sample that is supposed to trigger the model's adversarial behavior, it will be observed by a significant difference between the output of one model (the one free of the compromised gradients) versus all others (that all contain the compromised gradients). If such differences are observed systematically with the same model, the user of the model set may conclude that models affected by the adversary gradients should be discarded.

The central trainer has created N+1 models as a result of the modified federated learning process where there are N number of distributed trainers. Each model M_i, i = 0,...,N incorporated gradients from all distributed trainers except D_i, whereas model M_{N+1} incorporated gradients from all distributed trainers. This mapping between gradients to models creates a model set of M_1 to M_N where each model is free of the gradients of exactly one distributed trainer. This scheme can be arbitrated so that each model is free of the gradients of two, three, etc. number of distributed trainers, which enables the user of the model set to have a higher confidence in detecting if gradients coming from a distributed trainer (and the models incorporating them) are likely to be adversary. Tables 5.1 and 5.2 show two examples of distributed trainer to model instance mapping, which cause each model instance to be free of the gradients of two or three distributed trainers, respectively.

As the mapping between distributed trainers and model instances ensures that each model instance is free of the gradients of at least one distributed trainer, an entity performing inference by ingesting a data sample to each model in the model set can detect if one or more of the models where likely compromised during the training and that the data sample constitutes an adversary data sample. The steps performed by the user of the model set (e.g., one of the distributed trainers) are described in Figure 5.12. The user of the models receives a data sample on which the machine learning models are to be executed. As the user of the models

Table 5.1 First example mapping of distributed trainers to model instances (x at a cell D_iM_j, i = 1, .., N, j = 1, .., N indicates that gradients from D_i are incorporated to model M_j). The mapping causes each model instance to be free of the gradients of two distributed trainers.

	M_1	M_2	M_3	M_4	M_5	M_6
D_1	x	x	x	x		
D_2		x	x	x	x	
D_3			x	x	x	x
D_4	x			x	x	x
D_5	x	x			x	x
D_6	x	x	x			x

Table 5.2 Second example mapping of distributed trainers to model instances (x at a cell D_iM_j, i = 1, ..., N, j = 1, ..., N indicates that gradients from D_i are incorporated to model M_j). The mapping causes each model instance to be free of the gradients of three distributed trainers.

	M_1	M_2	M_3	M_4	M_5	M_6
D_1	x	x	x			
D_2		x	x	x		
D_3			x	x	x	
D_4				x	x	x
D_5	x				x	x
D_6	x	x				x

has a model set (instead of a single model), it ingests the data sample to all models. The output from the models is then clustered to see if they significantly differ from each other, and how many characteristic outputs are. Clustering can use a common clustering algorithm known in the state of the art, including k-means, DBSCAN [18], or others. If there are at least two clusters (i.e., the outputs of the models are not uniform), the user of the models investigates if the pattern of clusters matches the pattern of mapping distributed trainers' gradients to models (such as one illustrated in Tables 5.1 or 5.2). There is a matching if the models to which a specific distributed trainer's gradients are incorporated are separated (based on their output) in entirely different clusters than those models that are free from the same distributed trainer's gradients. In other words, for a given distributed trainer, there is no match if there is a cluster that contains a mixture of models including at least one model that has incorporated gradients from said distributed trainer and at least one other model that has not incorporated gradients from the same distributed trainer. In case there is a match for a distributed trainer, the identity of the distributed trainer is reported to the central trainer.

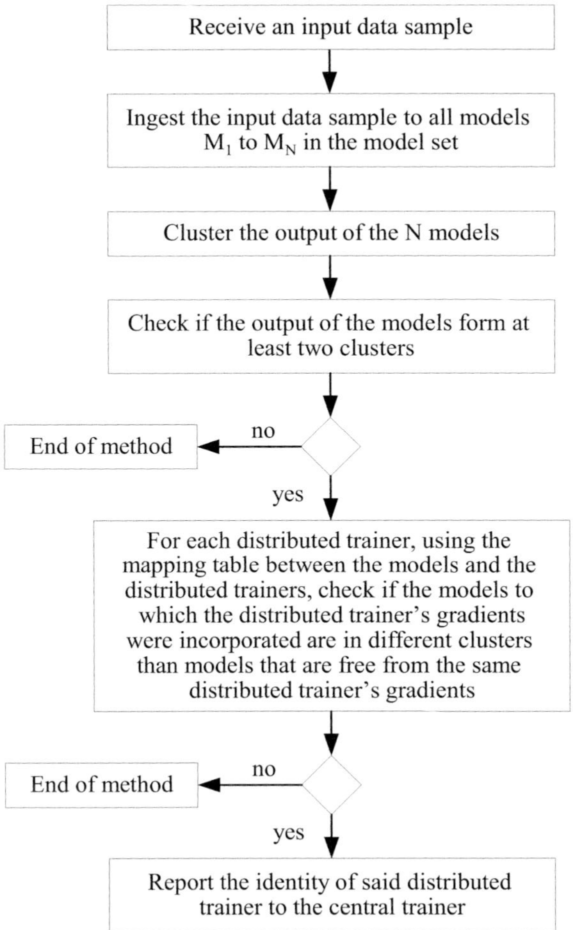

Figure 5.12 Logical steps taken by the user of the model set to identify if an input data sample causes the models' output to separate along the division of mapping distributed trainers to models.

The model set management-related communication taking place between the central trainer and the users of the model is depicted in Figure 5.13. The description assumes that the users of the models are the distributed trainers themselves, which is a common federated learning scenario. However, the method equally applies to scenarios when the users of the models are partly or fully distinct from the distributed trainers. The method starts when the central trainer has finished the training of the model set.

- In the first message M1, the central trainer transfers two information elements: (1) the model set, and (2) a mapping table to each user of the model. The model set consists of the trained machine-learning models. The mapping table, of which examples were given in Tables 5.1 and 5.2, consists of pairs of distributed trainer identities and model identities indicating which distributed trainer's gradients were incorporated in which model. The distributed trainers' identities may be symbolic or obfuscated identities concealing their real identity.

- Next, the users of the model keep executing the steps described in Figure 5.12. As part of this method, the users may detect attempts of adversary attacks toward models that incorporate the gradients of a distributed trainer, and report the identity of said distributed trainer's identity to the central trainer. The report is shown as message M2 and it contains one or more distributed trainer identities as it was indicated in the mapping table received in M1.
- The central trainer decides whether one or more models should be considered as compromised by correlating reports from multiple distributed trainers. The correlation mechanism may be to identify if at least a predefined number of distributed trainers have reported the same distributed trainer identity, or whether such reports were received within a time interval. In such cases, the models that incorporate the gradients of the reported distributed trainers could be considered compromised. Other means to decide whether models have been compromised are possible as valid implementation alternatives.
- Upon deciding that one or more models are compromised, the central model signals the identities of the compromised models to all users of the model set as message M3. The users of the model set may then stop ingesting input data to the compromised model. Additionally, the central trainer may decide to initiate a new federated learning process, potentially excluding those distributed trainers that were reported in the context of the model set, and potentially inviting other, previously unused distributed trainers.

The model set management mechanism discussed so far is applicable to any federated learning scenario as it only assumes the presence of central and distributed trainers, which is a core assumption shared by the federated learning technology itself. To bring down the mechanism from the abstraction to more concrete applications, we perform the exercise of mapping the trainer components to specific telecom standard architectures, illustrating the potential of using the mechanism for real telecom use cases that incorporate federated learning. Three example alternative architecture mappings are

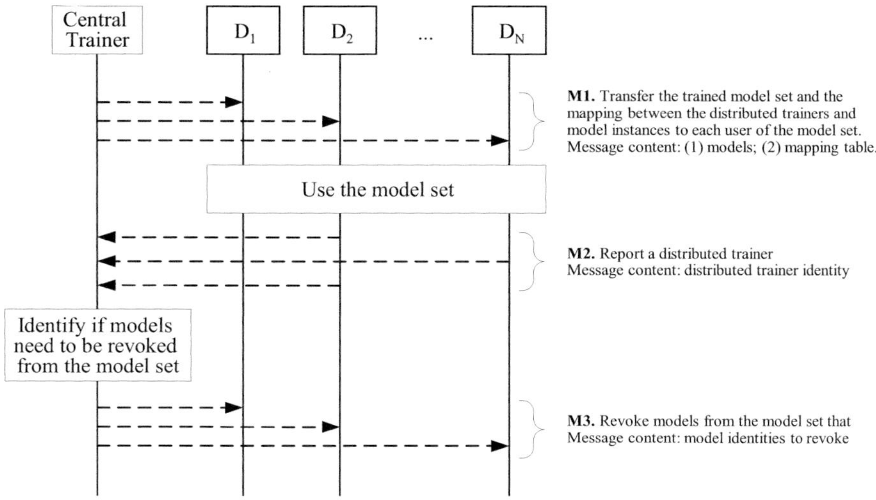

Figure 5.13 Communication during model set management.

shown in Figure 5.14 to depict two O-RAN and one 3GPP scenario. O-RAN and 3GPP were selected due to their active involvement in studying the integration of AI/ML into their systems [6, 15, 16]. In Figure 5.14(a), the distributed trainers are the UEs and the central trainer is implemented in the Near-RT RIC, as an xApp. In this case, gradient transfer, model transfer, and the messages M1-M3 transition are done through the RRC and E2 interfaces. Figure 5.14(b) is a slight variation of this case, with the difference that the gNBs are the data sources, whereas the central trainer remains and xApp. In this case, only E2 is involved. Figure 5.14(a,b) could also be combined. Note that multiple central trainer xApp instances may be created, for example, one central trainer xApp instance to handle UE distributed trainers, and another xApp instance to handle gNB distributed trainers. The third example in Figure 5.14(c) shows a 3GPP core network mapping, where 5G core network functions are the distributed trainers and the central trainer is implemented in the NWDAF.

5.5.2 Model integrity protection

A prominent scenario of federated learning is when the distributed trainers all continue to be users of the model that is the product of the federated training process. In telecommunications systems, distributed trainers may be the UEs or gNBs and the central trainer may be a network function such as the 3GPP NFs or systems (e.g., gNB, NWDAF, and OAM), or O-RAN functions (e.g.,

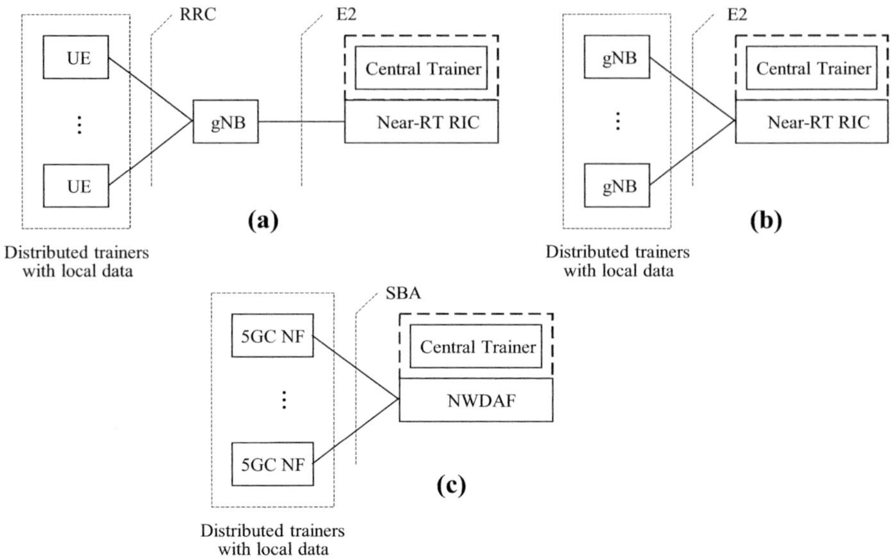

Figure 5.14 Deployment options for integrating the general model set management mechanism into standard telecom architectures.

RIC or SMO). The scope of the trained model may be to perform a prediction that is relevant for UE-network communication (such as channel estimation via AI) or gNB-CN relation (such as domain-specific service quality measurements). In this case, the central trainer entity in the network is interested in ensuring that the distributed trainer entities continue to use the exact model that was trained in collaboration during the federated learning process, and not a different (potentially poor quality) one, to ensure the integrity of the AI-based operation. However, normally the central trainer has no means to verify whether the distributed trainer (or any other entity using the ML model) is actually using the model they created collaboratively. Therefore, the distributed trainer can simply use a different model or not use a model at all. Moreover, a maliciously distributed trainer may even provide deliberately wrong outputs and mask them as if they were produced by the common ML model. Accepting such wrong outputs may cause functional problems in the central trainer or whichever entity is going to use them for their own logic.

As an example (Figure 5.15), a model supervisor entity (MSE) is enabled to verify whether a model execution entity (MEE) is using a specific ML model. Both the MSE and the MEE have an identical instance of the specific ML model whose usage is subject to verification. When the MSE receives a prediction output (that is, a result of applying the model to input

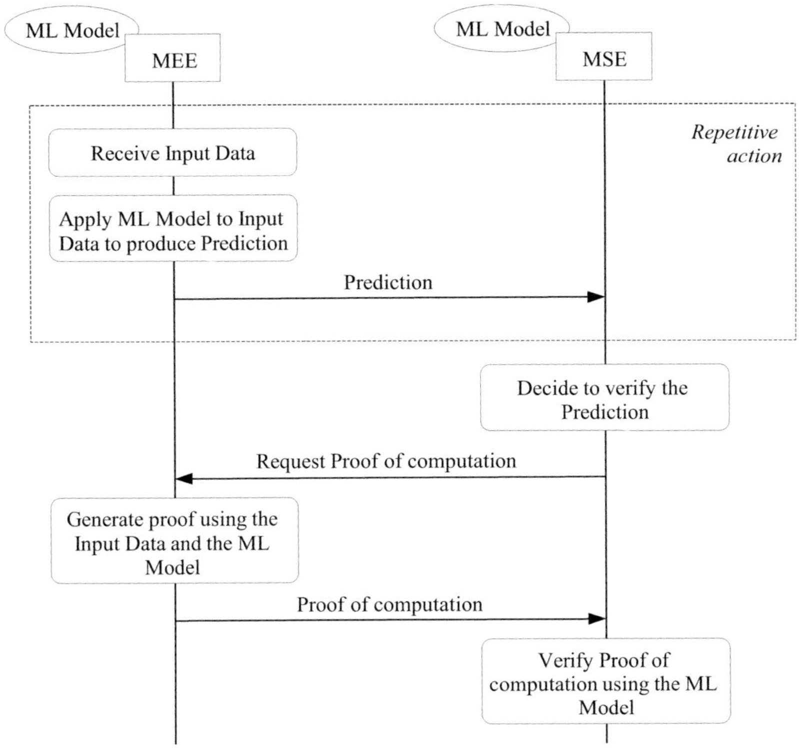

Figure 5.15 Model identity verification.

data) from the MEE, the MSE has the capability to retrospectively ask the MEE to show proof of its computation. The proof of computation verifies that the MEE produced the prediction output by applying the specific ML model to the input data. The verification method is designed so that the MEE can only show the proof if it previously used the specific ML model to produce the prediction output; that is, the MEE cannot trick the method by selectively using the specific ML model only when it is under verification and use some other (potentially lower accuracy) model when it is not being tested. Since the MEE does not know which of its prediction outputs will be verified later on, it is not worth to risk producing a wrong prediction output because it may be detected retrospectively. As the verification method provides a 100% detection rate for wrong outputs, even a single wrong output that is subject to verification will render the MEE untrusted by the MSE.

There may be two levels of proof produced by the MEE for the MSE: a basic proof, which is available even in a black-box model scenario, and an extended proof, which is available in a white-box model scenario. The black-box scenario means that the entity using the ML model has no access to the model internals, also meaning that no model internal state can be observed; the only action that the entity may perform with the model is to apply it on input data and observe the model's output. The white-box scenario means that the entity using the ML model can at least observe the model's internals, for example, it is able to collect intermediate computation results from within the model's computation pipeline. The white-box scenario therefore allows for additional mechanisms that require deeper insight into the model. However, in some cases, only a black-box scenario can be (or should be) assumed.

The basic proof allows to validate the usage of the ML model even if the ML model internals are not observable, that is, the only available ML model operation is to execute the model on input data and collect the model's output. The basic proof is already a good indicator for the MSE that the MEE used an ML model that behaves identically to the specific ML model; however, it does not provide proof that the very same ML model was used.

The extended proof allows the MSE to validate that the MEE used the specific ML model (not only one that behaves identically to the specific ML model) to produce a previous prediction output. Producing and verifying the extended proof requires that the MEE and MSE both have access to the internal state of the model itself as the input data passes through it. Encoding the internal model state into the proof ensures the integrity of the entire computation pipeline that is represented by the ML model, as it can only be produced if the exact same model is used for proof generation and proof validation.

The MSE can also arbitrate between requesting a basic or extended proof from the MEE, balancing between proof quality and overhead.

The details of the basic proof procedure are shown in Figure 5.16. The procedure starts after the completion of a federated learning process, where the MSE and multiple MEEs have collaboratively created an ML model, and all participants have an identical copy of the model. In this case, the MSE was in the federated learning central trainer role and the MEEs were in the federated learning distributed trainer role. Alternatively, there could have been an ML model transfer from the MSE to the MEE, regardless of how the ML model was created (i.e., it does not need to be a product of federated learning). The relevant aspect is that both the MSE and the MEE have the same ML model. The same procedure is performed between the MSE and other MEEs, independently from each other.

In step 1, the MEE receives input data. In step 2, the MEE allocates a prediction ID, which is an MEE internal ID referring to the transaction of applying the ML model to a specific input data and thereby obtaining a

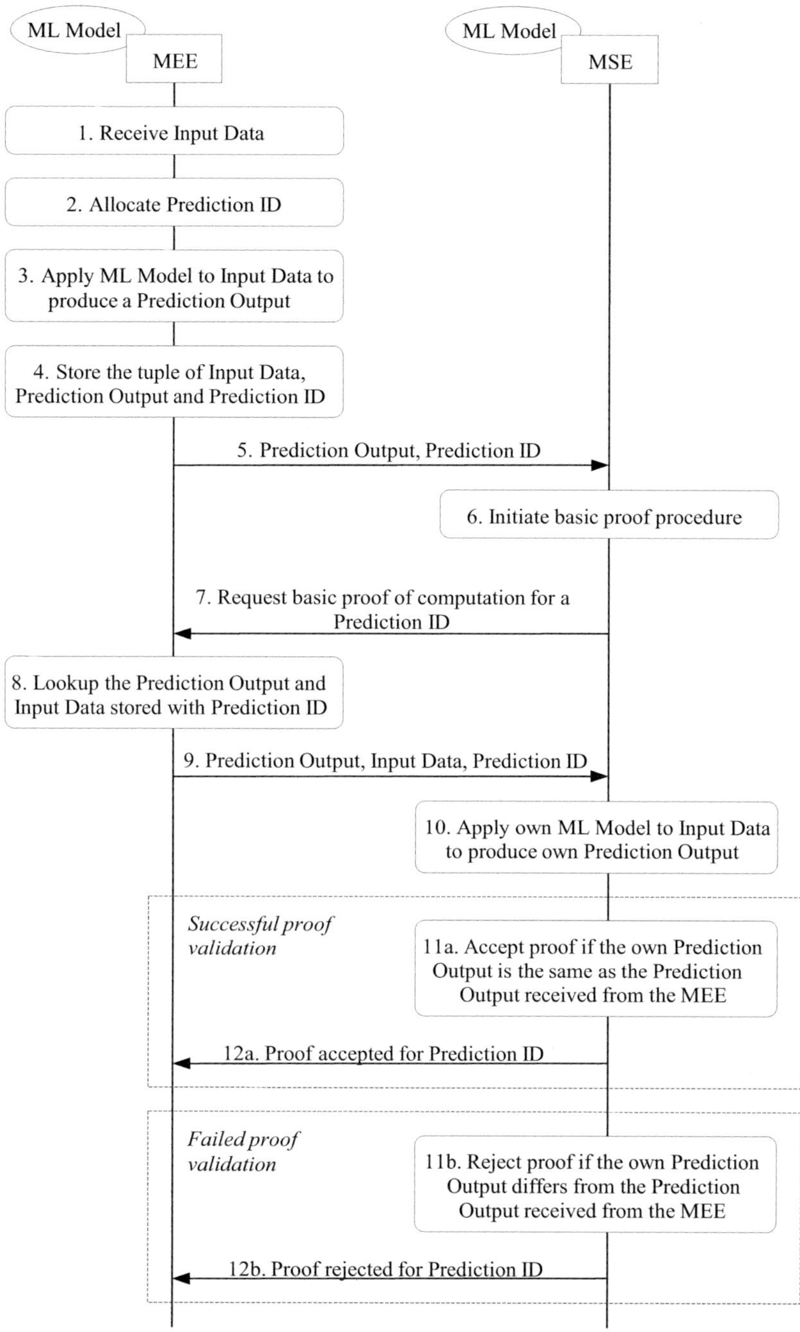

Figure 5.16 Detailed steps for the basic proof (black-box ML model scenario).

prediction output, that is, the model's output to the input data (in step 3). In step 4, the MEE internally records the input data and the prediction output associated with the prediction ID (e.g., in a key-value database where the prediction ID is the key and the combination of the input data and prediction output is the value). The recording may be implemented by a ring buffer that stores a given number of the latest input data, prediction output, and prediction ID tuples. In step 5, the MEE transfers the prediction output and the prediction ID to the MSE. In step 6, the MSE decides to initiate a basic proof procedure for one of the previously received prediction IDs (i.e., not necessarily for the latest prediction ID). The basic proof is requested in step 7, indicating the prediction ID to which the proof should be provided by the MEE. The basic proof consists of showing the input data on which the prediction output was generated that is associated with the same prediction ID. Therefore, in step 8 the MEE obtains the input data based on the prediction ID received in step 7, and in step 9 the MEE transfers the prediction output, input data, and prediction ID to the MSE. In step 10, the MSE generates its own version of the expected prediction output by applying its own copy of the ML model to the input data received in step 9. In step 11a, the proof is accepted if the MSE's own prediction output is exactly the same as the prediction output received from the MEE in step 9. Acceptance may be indicated by sending an acknowledgment to the MEE in step 12a. In step 11b, the proof is rejected if the MSE's own prediction output differs from the prediction output received from the MEE in step 9. In step 12b, rejection may be indicated to the MEE.

The basic proof can be produced by the MEE with low computational overhead (or even zero overhead) as it only involves keeping track of the prediction ID, input data, and prediction output tuples, and executing a lookup for the input data and prediction output based on the prediction ID when requested by the MSE.

The detailed steps and communication of the extended proof procedure are shown in Figure 5.17. The first five steps are identical to the method shown in Figure 5.16. In step 6, the MSE decides to initiate an extended proof procedure. In step 7, the MSE sends the request to the MEE indicating the prediction ID for which the extended proof should be provided. The MEE obtains the input data associated with the prediction ID in step 8. In step 9, the MEE computes a hash value by applying a secure hash function on the internal state of the ML model while the ML model is producing the prediction output.

The hash may be calculated with a well-known hash function, such as one from the SHA-2 family (e.g., SHA-256 to produce a 32-byte hash value). The purpose of the hash is to significantly reduce the amount of data that represents the ML model's internal state.

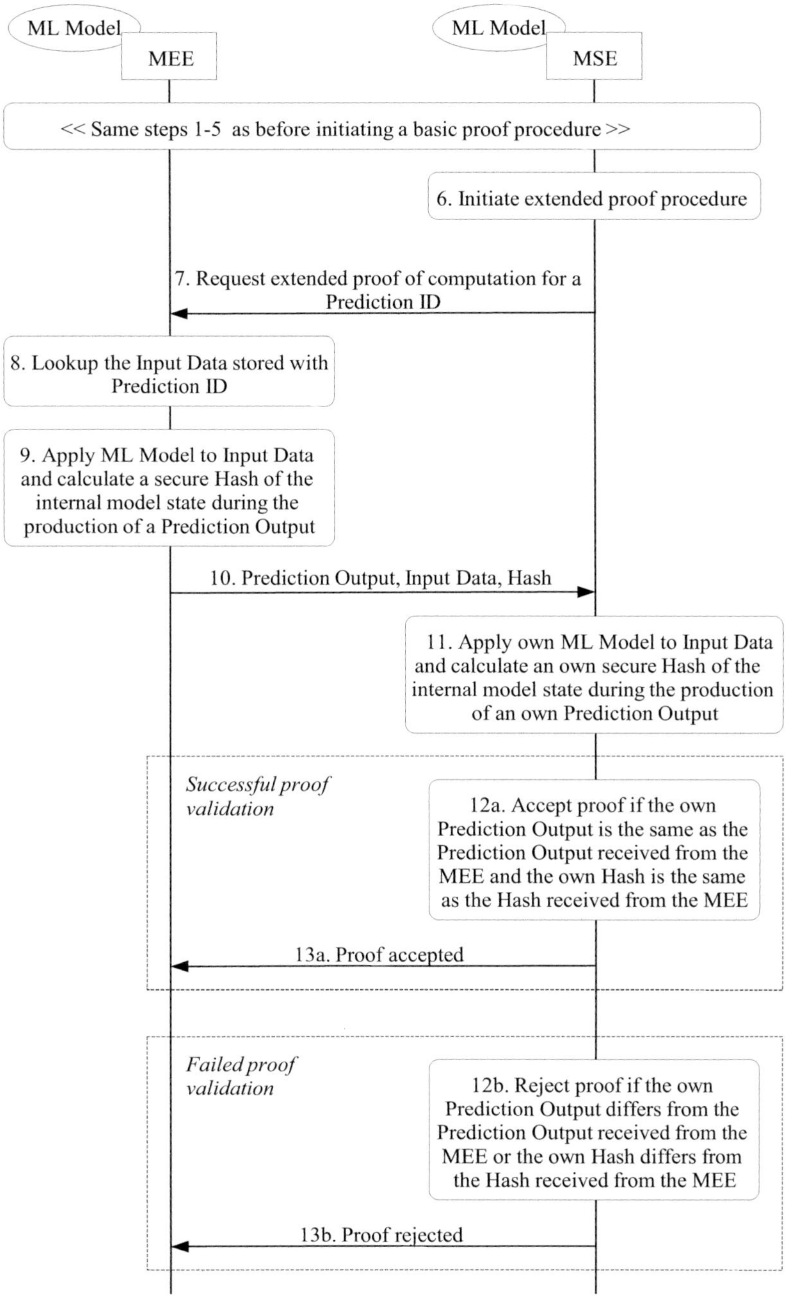

Figure 5.17 Detailed steps for the extended proof (white-box ML model scenario).

In case the ML model is a neural network, the hash may be computed on the output activations (which are the results of forward propagation of the input data through the network) of each neuron in a specific order. If the model is a GNG (growing neural gas) model, the hash may be computed on the code vector associated with the best-matching GNG unit (the one whose data vector is closest to the input data vector). In general, for every ML model type, there is an internal state that gets activated as a result of applying the model to the input data, and the hash should be computed on that.

Since the MSE and MEE share the exact same ML model, it should be possible for both of them to share an understanding of how the hash is calculated on the model. The shared understanding could also be negotiated offline (unrelated to the extended proof procedure). The MEE and MSE must also use the same hash function, therefore, it may be negotiated as part of requesting the extended proof (e.g., the MSE sends a list of acceptable hash functions in the order of preference, and the MEE indicates the hash function used to compute the hash in its response to the MSE).

Continuing with step 10, the MEE transfers the prediction output, and hash value, obtained in the previous step, and the input data, obtained in step 8, to the MSE. In step 11, the MSE applies its own ML model to the input data and computes its own hash value and prediction output, in the same way as the MEE did. In step 12a, the proof is accepted if the MSE's own prediction output and hash value are exactly the same as the prediction output and hash received from the MEE in step 10. Acceptance may be indicated by sending an acknowledgment to the MEE in step 13a. In step 12b, the proof is rejected if either the MSE's own prediction output or its own hash value differs from the prediction output or hash received from the MEE in step 10. In step 13b, rejection may be indicated to the MEE.

For the MEE, producing the extended proof has higher computational overhead than producing the basic proof, but it provides unequivocal proof for the MSE that the MEE is using the specific ML model on previous input data.

Neither the basic proof nor the extended proof requires that the MEE shows the model to the MSE, which makes both proof methods applicable for ML as a Service type of solutions (i.e., when the MEE provides access to a service via a remote interface or API without exposing the model itself).

In a further example, the MSE may have access to the same data source as the MEE, which gives the MSE an additional checkpoint to verify that the MEE's proof does not use forged input data but really the input data it is processing with the ML model. The basic proof method complemented with input data verification is shown in Figure 5.18. In the beginning, at steps 1

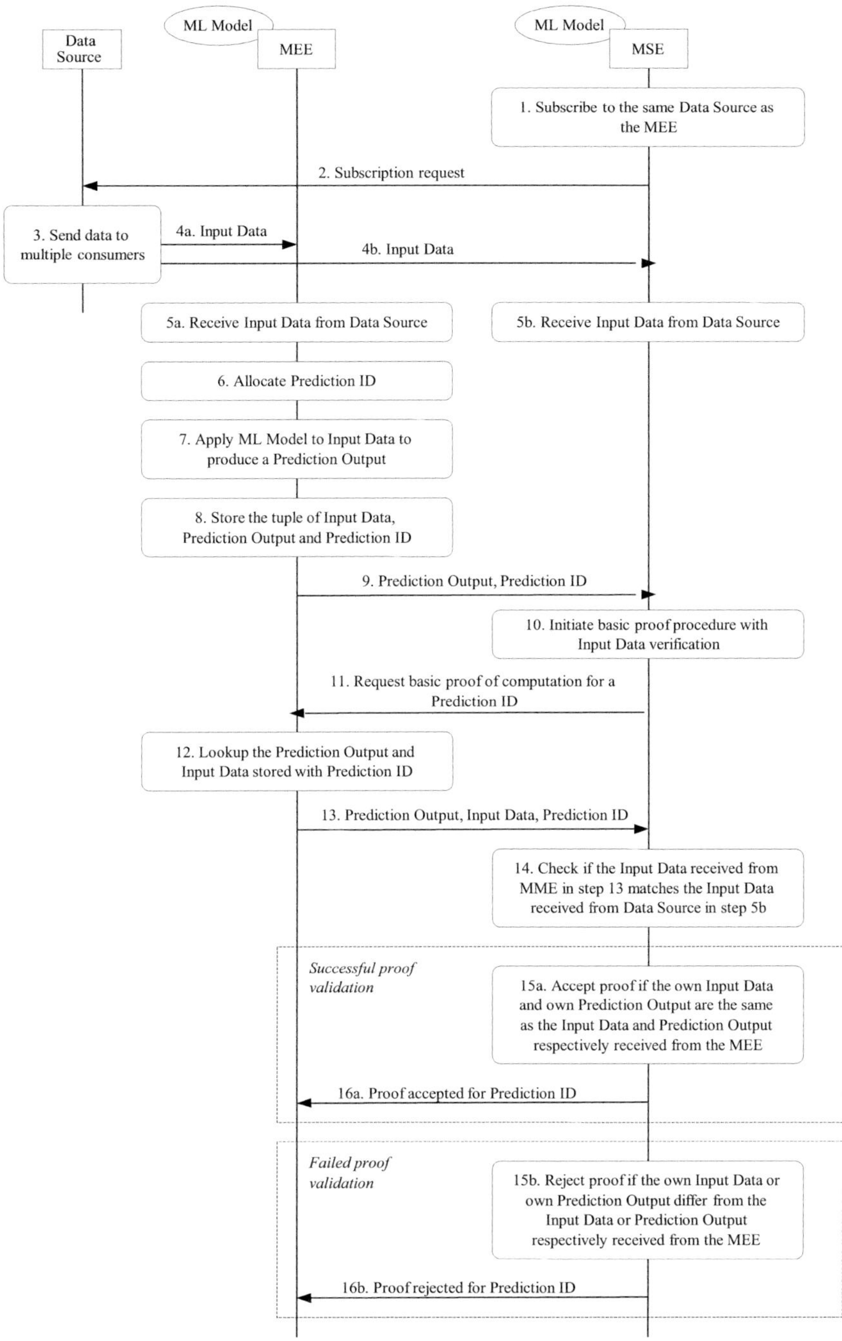

Figure 5.18 Basic proof method complemented with input data verification.

and 2, the MSE subscribes to the same data source that is providing the input data to the MEE. Therefore, the data source sends the same input data to both the MEE and the MSE in steps 3 and 4a/4b. The input data is received by the MEE and MSE in steps 5a/5b. Steps 6–13 at the same as in the normal basic proof method described in Figure 5.16, with the exception that in step 10 the MSE initiates the basic proof complemented with input data verification (however, this difference is only internal to the MSE and not visible to the MEE). In step 14, the MSE checks if the MEE has reported the proof for the same input data that was also received by the MSE in step 5b. In steps 15 and 16, the acceptance of the proof is complemented with the condition that the MEE must have sent the same input data to the MSE as what the MSE had received from the data source in step 5b. If this is not true, it means that the MEE tries to forge proof for input data that was not part of the true input data but was created by the MEE in order to produce a wrong prediction output. This should be considered an especially malicious attempt by the MEE.

In another (or additional) attempt to detect input data forgery by the MEE, the MSE may take advantage of being connected to multiple MEEs that operate in the same or similar environment. The MSE may build statistics of the input data sent by various MEEs (i.e., the input data received in step 9 of the basic proof procedure, Figure 5.16, or step 10 of the extended proof procedure, Figure 5.17). If a specific MEE sends input data as part of the proof that is significantly different from the distribution of input data from other MEEs, the MSE may suspect that the specific MEE commits input data forgery.

The MSE may not have access to the ML model but take advantage of being connected to multiple MEEs that are all supposed to have and use the same ML model (e.g., the distributed trainers participating in a previous federated learning procedure). The MSE may instead engage in an MEE set interaction procedure, shown in Figure 5.19. In this case, the MSE may send the input data received from a first MEE to a set of additional MEEs requesting that each MEE in the set of additional MEEs provides the prediction output (and optionally the hash of the ML model internal state) for this input data, as indicated in steps 10, 11, and 12. In step 13, The MSE compares the various prediction outputs (and optionally hashes) received from each MEE in the set of additional MEEs. In step 14a, if all prediction outputs (and optionally hashes) are the same (respectively), the MSE may conclude that (1) the set of additional MEEs are providing honest response (or, they are all under the same malicious control – which is unlikely if the MEEs have sufficient vendor, model, location, access diversity); and (2) it may use the prediction output (and optionally hash) to continue with the proof validation

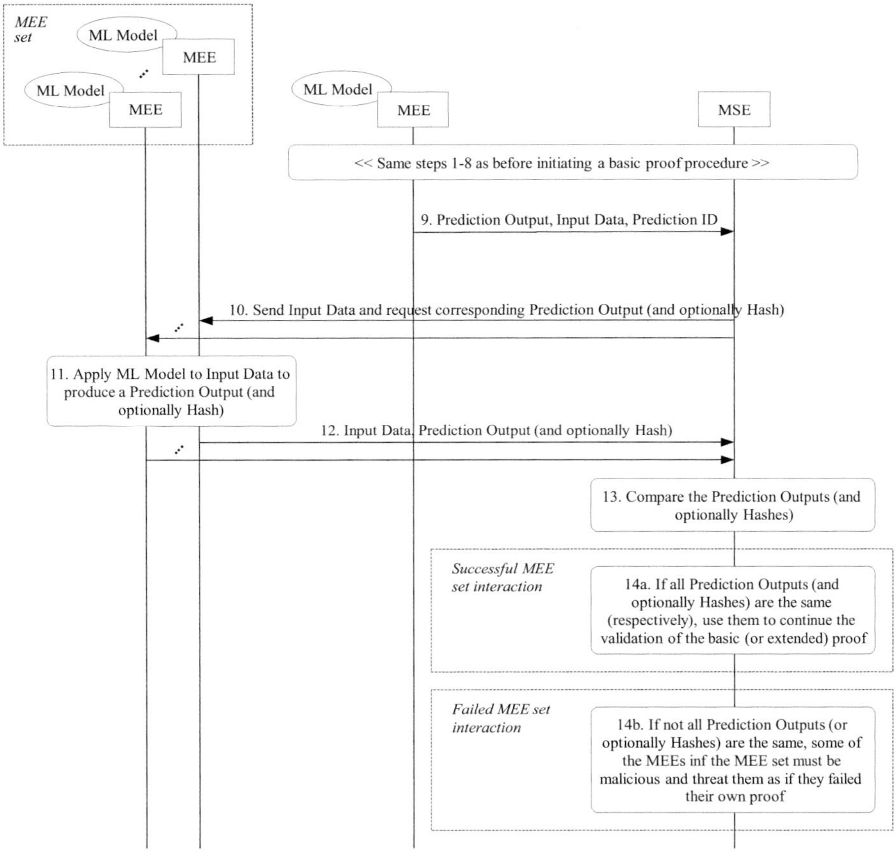

Figure 5.19 MEE set interaction procedure.

according to the basic (or optionally extended) proof procedure. In step 14b, if not all prediction outputs (and optionally hashes) are the same (respectively), then the MSE may conclude that there are malicious actors in the set of additional MEEs and act accordingly (e.g., treat them if they failed at a proof validation).

5.5.3 Local data protection

One of the main reasons for using federated learning to train an ML model is the need to keep the local data secret due to its sensitivity. Therefore, the primary interest of the distributed trainers is to not let any other entity, including the central trainer, learn or derive any information (directly or indirectly)

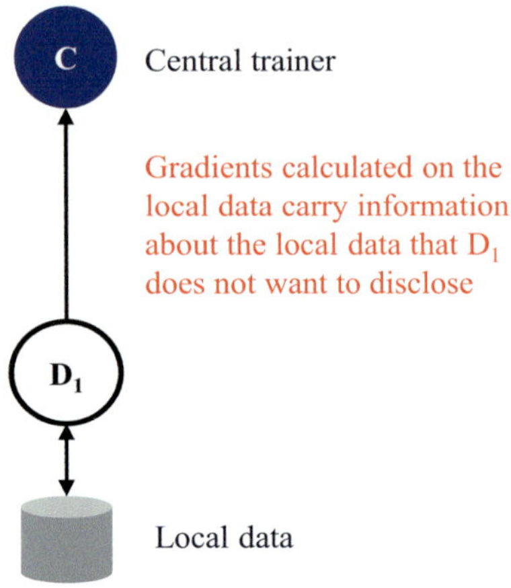

Figure 5.20 The problem of leaking local information through gradient updates.

about their local data during the training process. However, gradients transferred from the local trainer to the central trainer may expose some information about the local data, which could be used by the central trainer to infer statistical information about the local data or conduct membership attacks. This vulnerability is most prominent if the central trainer performs its ML model creation as a service, that is, the distributed trainers have no control over how the central trainer uses the shared gradients. The problem is illustrated in Figure 5.20.

The federated learning process may be modified to help prevent the leakage of information about the distributed trainer's local data. The modifications are concentrated on the distributed trainer's side and they are transparent to the central trainer, therefore the modified method is fully compatible with an external (uncontrolled, service-based) central trainer. The modifications contain three key steps: (1) selective gradient sharing, (2) mixture of sensitive and nonsensitive data, and (3) local data transformation. A distributed trainer may apply one or more of the modifications, and its selection of the applied modifications does not need to be synchronized with other distributed trainers (which may independently choose to apply a different set of modifications). The three key steps are detailed below.

1. *Selective gradient sharing*: In each training step, the distributed trainer only transfers a subset of the gradients it calculated on its local data to the central trainer. The distributed trainer may select a different subset of the gradients in each training step. As a result, the central trainer will

not be able to trace the gradients through the entire ML model architecture (between the input and output layers) as the back-propagation chain will be punctured due to missing gradients. If the central trainer tries to infer some statistical data about the local trainer's data from the selective gradients, the inferred information will be inconclusive because there could have been many different local datasets that would have resulted in the same selective gradients.

2. *Mixture of sensitive and nonsensitive data*: In each federated training step, the distributed trainer adds some nonsensitive (e.g., publicly available or locally available but not classified) data to its normally sensitive local dataset and calculates the gradients on the mixture of data. As a result, the gradients shared with the central trainer will represent data from a distribution that is different from the (sensitive) local data of the distributed trainer. In every training step, the distributed trainer may arbitrate the nonsensitive data samples it mixes with its local dataset. The distributed trainer may also choose to contribute only a subset of its sensitive local data to the mixture and arbitrate the contributed local dataset per each training step. This modification may be combined with the selective gradient sharing by only sending a subset of the gradients (calculated over the mixed data) with the central trainer.

3. *Local data transformation:* The distributed trainer applies a linear transformation (e.g., a local transformation matrix) to its local dataset before it calculates the gradients in a training step. The transformation is locally defined by the distributed trainer and it is kept secret during the federated model training and afterward. As a result, the central trainer will not be able to infer any statistical information about the original local dataset, only about the transformed one. The consequence of using this modification is that, after the federated ML model has been created, the distributed trainer must continue to apply the same transformation on new data that it ingests into the ML model. Therefore, the best application of this modification is when the distributed trainer continues to be a data source for and user of the ML model. This modification can be combined with any of the previous ones, for example, by only sharing a subset of the gradients with the central trainer, or by applying the transformation to the nonsensitive (e.g., public) data as well.

The process is illustrated in Figure 5.21 showing all three proposed federated learning modifications applied by a distributed trainer in a training step.

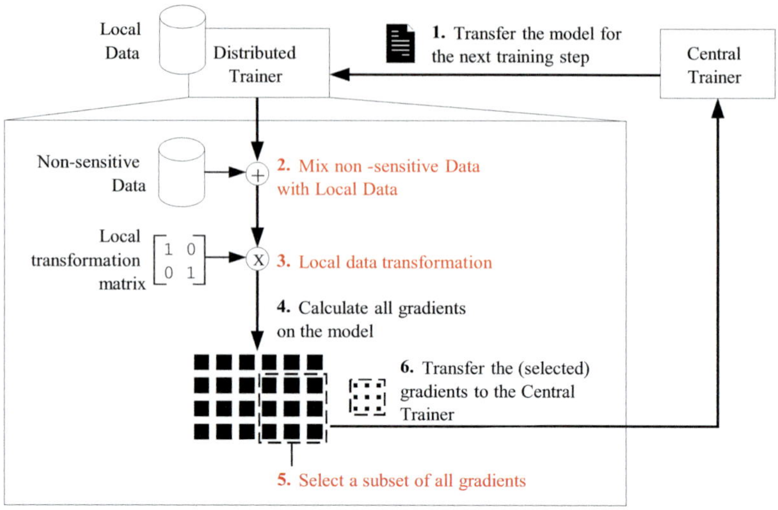

Figure 5.21 Illustration of the three federated learning method modifications.

Steps 2, 3, and 5 may be performed selectively as per the distributed trainer's configuration, policy, or implementation.

A prominent scenario of federated learning is when the distributed trainers all continue to be users of the model that is the product of the federated training process. In telecommunications systems, distributed trainers may be the UEs or gNBs and the central trainer may be a network function such as the 3GPP NFs or systems (e.g., gNB, NWDAF, and OAM), or O-RAN functions (e.g., RIC or SMO). The scope of the trained model may be to perform a prediction that is relevant for UE-network communication (such as channel estimation via AI) or gNB-CN relation (such as domain-specific service quality measurements).

The functionality of the distributed trainer during the selective gradient sharing is shown in Figure 5.22. In order to keep the selective gradient sharing transparent to the central trainer, the number of gradients cannot be changed as it is a function of the ML model architecture and the central trainer expects to receive all of them. Therefore, instead of sending a limited number of gradients, the distributed trainer sends all gradients but sets the value of those that it does not want to send. Each gradient may be zeroed with a certain probability, such as 10%, which means that on average every 10th gradient is set to zero. The random selection of whether to zero a gradient may be re-evaluated independently for every gradient and every training step.

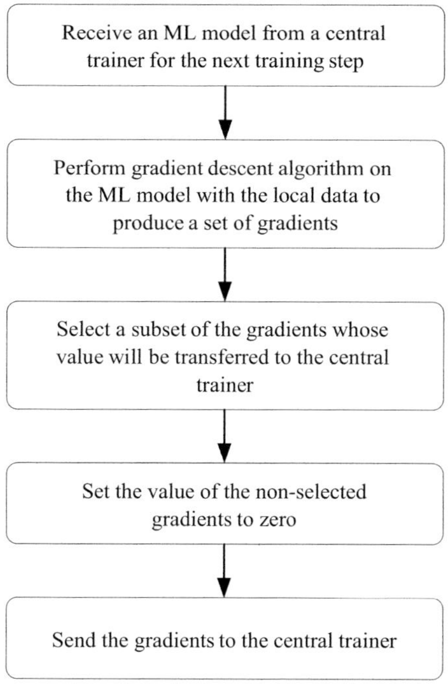

Figure 5.22 Steps of the selective gradient sharing.

The mechanism of the mixture of sensitive and nonsensitive data is shown in Figure 5.23. In every training step, the distributed trainer creates a new dataset that is valid for the training step only. In the new dataset, the distributed trainer includes one or more data samples from its original local data and one or more data samples from a separate nonsensitive dataset. The distributed trainer does not need to include all of its local data in the new dataset, and in every training step, it may include a separate (e.g., randomly selected) set of data samples from its local data into the new dataset. The nonsensitive dataset may be a public dataset that has similar characteristics to the data in the local dataset (at least the data syntax such as numerical representation should match, but also a level of semantical similarity is desired). It is not a problem, however, if the distribution of the nonsensitive (public) dataset is different from that of the local data– it would only cause the central model to learn an extended ML task and as such it is even desirable for model robustness reasons.

The local data transformation is illustrated in Figure 5.24. There are two parts of the transformation: a one-time preparation that is executed only

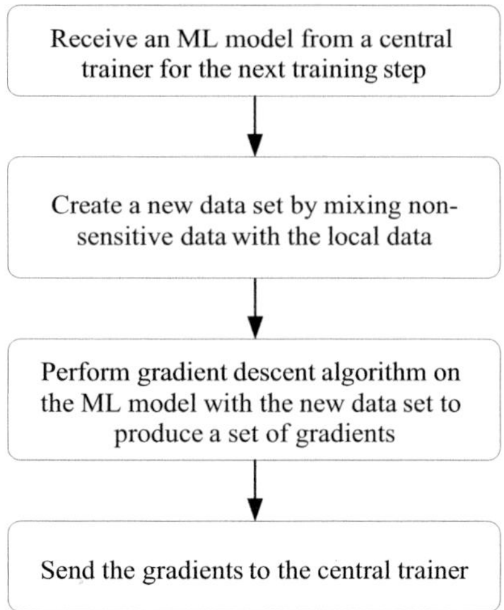

Figure 5.23 Steps of the mixture of sensitive and nonsensitive data.

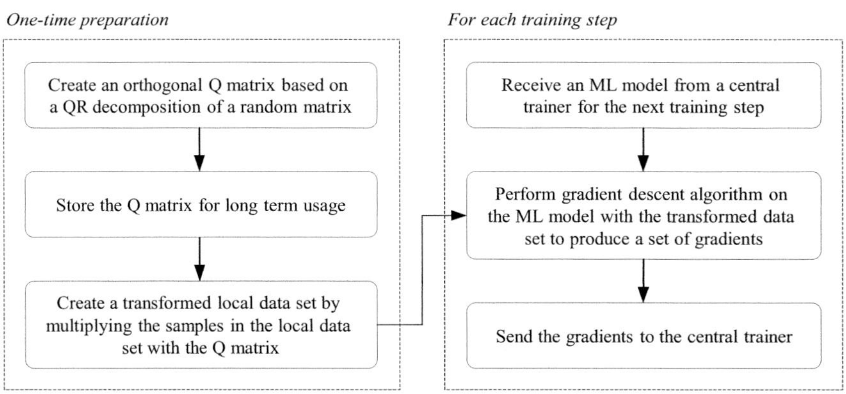

Figure 5.24 Steps of the local data transformation.

once to initialize reusable information; and the steps to be performed for each training step. In the one-time preparation, the distributed trainer generates an orthogonal Q matrix [17], which may be implemented by performing a QR decomposition on a random rectangular matrix. The size of the matrix should be the same as the dimensions of the samples in the local dataset. The local dataset is transformed into a new dataset by multiplying each data sample in the local dataset with the Q matrix. Then this transformed dataset is used in every repeated training step to generate the gradients. The gradients are then shared with the central trainer.

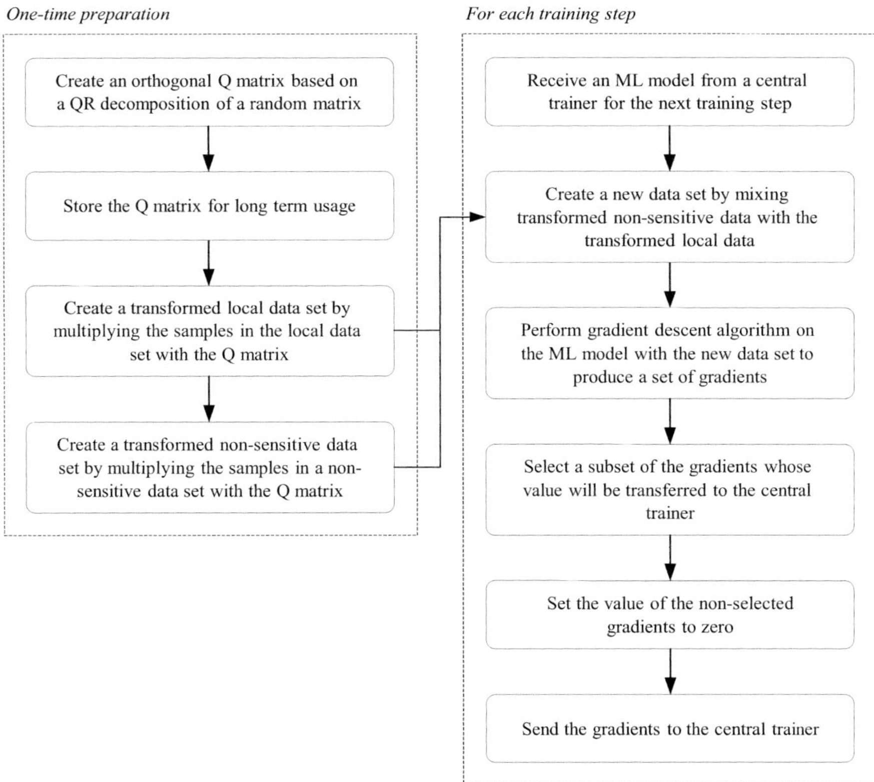

Figure 5.25 A combination of all three federated learning modifications.

A distributed trainer that combines all three federated learning method modifications is shown in Figure 5.25. The combined mechanism is again split into a one-time preparation phase followed by those that are performed for each training step. In the preparation phase, the difference to the local data transformation only (Figure 5.24) is that a second dataset is prepared, which is the transformed version of the non-sensitive dataset. It is more efficient to transform the nonsensitive data once and use the transformed version afterward as the same data sample will be used multiple times during multiple FL training steps. In the training steps performed for each training step, a new dataset is created based on the mixture of the transformed local dataset and the transformed nonsensitive data (the point here is to use the transformed version from both datasets). Then the gradients are computed on the mixed data and the selected zeroing is performed according to the selective gradient-sharing method. Finally, the gradients (some with a value

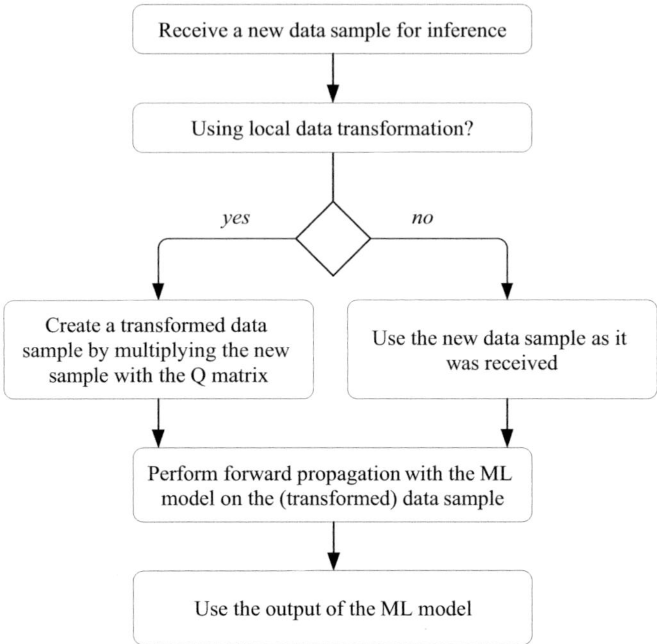

Figure 5.26 The inference performed by the distributed trainer.

set to zero) are transferred to the central trainer. This configuration of the distributed trainer provides maximum protection against speculations about its local data by the central trainer.

After the ML model is trained, the distributed trainer itself may become a user of the ML model. The inference procedure of the distributed trainer is shown in Figure 5.26. The notable difference from a classic ML model inference is that if the distributed trainer used the local data transformation during the training, it has to continue using the same Q matrix to transform the new data samples before they can be fed to the ML model. If the distributed trainer did not use the local data transformation modification of the FL training process, the new data samples may be used as-is during the inference process.

5.6 Summary

The increasing technical complexity of mobile networks has already motivated and driven the adoption of AI/ML in the context of network and management functions, exploiting the abundance of operational data to create new capabilities and automate existing tasks. Native AI/ML provides a paradigm shift in terms of internalizing and owning AI in terms of architecture and operations rather than invoking it as an adjacent technology applied to data exported from the network. Native AI assumes a system design that declares functionalities that directly support AI operations, derived from the requirements of the technology, rather than leaving AI-based operation as an implementation choice. In addition to providing new functional capabilities, AI native systems impose new management aspects such as training data management, model training and verification, model deployment, and performance monitoring, which are modulated by security, integrity, and privacy dimensions. As AI models are software artifacts themselves embedded in deployable software modules, both the AI-driven functionalities and the management of AI are implemented and acted out through software interfaces and APIs. This puts AI native systems on a common evolutionary path with cloud-native systems, where the principles of service-based architecture, scalability, and deployment automation can be leveraged as a mutual benefit for both software management and a foundation for AI management. In distributed systems such as mobile networks, the adoption of distributed AI technologies such as federated learning is critical to leverage the benefits of AI without disrupting the system's primary architectural and design principles. In fact, distributed AI may be the only mechanism that fits the data privacy and computation efficiency constraints exhibited by the system. It is therefore important to analyze and understand the modeling and privacy aspects of distributed/federated AI in the context of the system's architecture, such as 3GPP or O-RAN in mobile systems.

Bibliography

[1] 3GPP TS 32.500 Telecommunication management; Self-Organizing Networks (SON); Concepts and requirements

[2] 3GPP TR 37.817 Study on enhancement for data collection for NR and ENDC

[3] ETSI GS ZSM 002, "Zero-touch network and Service Management (ZSM); Reference Architecture", V1.1.1 (2019-08)

[4] ETSI GR ZSM 005, "Zero-touch network and Service Management (ZSM); Means of Automation", V1.1.1 (2020-05)

[5] 3GPP TR 28.866 Study on Management Data Analytics (MDA) – Phase 3

[6] 3GPP TR 38.843 Study on Artificial Intelligence (AI)/Machine Learning (ML) for NR air interface

[7] ETSI GR ZSM 009-3, “Zero-touch network and Service Management (ZSM); Closed-Loop Automation; Part 3: Advanced topics”, V1.1.1 (2023-08)

[8] ETSI GR ZSM 015, “Zero-touch network and Service Management (ZSM); Network Digital Twin” V1.1.1 (2024-02)

[9] O-RAN Alliance, “O-RAN: Towards an Open and Smart RAN”, White Paper, October 2018, https://mediastorage.o-ran.org/white-papers/O-RAN.White-Paper-2018-10.pdf

[10] O-RAN Alliance, “O-RAN Use Cases and Deployment Scenarios”, White Paper, February 2020, https://mediastorage.o-ran.org/white-papers/O-RAN.WG1.Use-Cases-and-Deployment-Scenarios-White-Paper-2020-02.pdf

[11] O-RAN next Generation Research Group (nGRG), “Research Report on Native and Cross-domain AI: State of the art and future outlook”, Report ID: RR-2023-03, September 2023, https://mediastorage.o-ran.org/ngrg-rr/nGRG-RR-2023-03-Research-Report-on-Native-and-Cross-domain-AI-v1_1.pdf

[12] Open Neural Network Exchange, “The open standard for machine learning interoperability”, Available online: https://onnx.ai/

[13] P. Kairouz et al., “Advances and Open Problems in Federated Learning”, Foundations and Trends in Machine Learning, 14 (1–2): 1–210. arXiv:1912.04977. doi:10.1561/2200000083. ISSN 1935-8237.

[14] Korn Sooksatra, Greg Hamerly, Pablo Rivas, “Is ReLU Adversarially Robust?”, arXiv:2405.03777 [cs.LG], https://doi.org/10.48550/arXiv.2405.03777

[15] O-RAN Alliance, “AI/ML workflow description and requirements”, WG2.AIML-v01.02

[16] O-RAN next Generation Research Group (nGRG), “Principles and Methodologies for AI/ML Testing in Next Generation Networks”, Report ID: RR-2024-04, https://mediastorage.o-ran.org/ngrg-rr/nGRG-RR-2024-05-Principals%20Methodologies%20AIML%20testing%20next%20Generation%20Networks-v1.9.pdf

[17] Karamardian, S. (1976). “An existence theorem for the complementarity problem”. Journal of Optimization Theory and Applications. 19 (2): 227–232. doi:10.1007/BF00934094. ISSN 0022-3239. S2CID 120505258.

[18] M. Ester, H-P. Kriegel, J. Sander, X. Xiaowei, “A density-based algorithm for discovering clusters in large spatial databases with noise”, AAAI Press, Proceedings of the Second International Conference on Knowledge Discovery and Data Mining, p. 226–231, 1996

6

Intent-based Network Management

Intents are objectives declared at a high abstraction level that define outcomes to be achieved by an intent-based network. Intents lack actionable or executable instructions, leaving it to the system to derive the necessary steps to fulfill the intent. As intents remain valid under dynamic network conditions, regardless of any changes in resource distribution, fluctuations of users, or diversity of services, the fulfillment of intents requires a long-term commitment from the network. Autonomous management actions are needed on multiple levels (network, service, system, end-to-end) to keep the system aligned with the objectives of the intents. Therefore, intents and autonomy are inseparable, and so are the technologies that provide enablers for closed-loop automation and the means to define and interpret the intents through new objective-driven human–machine interactions. The intent interfaces and the automation capabilities of the underlying network mutually influence each other: new management capabilities need to be exposed through the intent interface, while the intent interface should also ensure that the fulfillment of intents ingested to the network is feasible with the capabilities and resources of the system. Intent-based composition of closed loops is a potential means to dynamically assemble and invoke the right system components that collaboratively handle specific intents.

6.1 Introduction

Intent-based network management is a paradigm where the operator declares high-level goals and expected behavior for the network, without providing the implementation of the goals through conditions, rules, and executable actions [1, 2, 3, 4]. Rather, the intents should be achieved and fulfilled by the network autonomously, calculating and deriving the necessary steps without executive user input.

DOI: 10.1201/9788770041478-6

The basic concept of intent-driven management is not new as its inception may be tracked as early as the works by M. S. Sloman [5] and John Strassner [6], who both derive intents from policies that govern the behavior of a system while navigating through changes in network state. Strassner introduced declarative policies in contrast to imperative ones. Declarative policies define only the resulting system state, leaving the system with the task of computing the actions leading to the end state. With this property, declarative policies may be regarded as the precursors for intents. Since then, intents have been adopted by mainstream standardization work as they have become a highlighted interest of multiple SDOs, including IETF [7], 3GPP [8], TMF [1], and ZSM [3, 9].

IETF defines intent "as a set of operational goals (that a network is supposed to meet) and outcomes (that a network is supposed to deliver) defined in a declarative manner without specifying how to achieve or implement them" [7]. Intent provides abstraction from low-level devices, technology, and deployment-specific configurations and actions as they omit the means of achieving the goals. However, this creates a requirement for the intent-based system to be capable of reconnecting intents with the actual system's capabilities and operational mechanisms.

3GPP formally started working on intents within the study item [10] created for intent-driven management services, which was followed by producing a specification [8] launched initially in Release 16. Intents are discussed in the well-known management service framework of 3GPP [11, 12]. According to 3GPP's definition, "an intent specifies the expectations including requirements, goals, and constraints for a specific service or network management workflow" [8]. Intents describe what the network needs to achieve in terms of outcomes, rather than defining how they should be achieved. Typically, an intent should be understandable both by humans and machines, posing an implicit requirement for shared semantic concepts between the human and the network.

TMF puts forward intents within its autonomous networks technical architecture. The document defines five levels of network autonomy, where level 5 means a zero-touch system that involves no human control. According to TMF's definition of intents, in the context of autonomous networks, an "intent describes the business objective of operators, as well as the expectations of customers and users" [1]. Likewise, the role of intents is to communicate the business objectives of the operator and the expectations of customers and users to the network [1]. TMF also implicitly defines intents to be declarative so that they define what an autonomous network should achieve, without depending on the network design or specifying how the network operates.

In ZSM, the intent-based approach has been introduced as a means of automation [9]. ZSM differentiates intents from policies by positioning an intent as a "simplified goal-policy" that enables end-users to interact with the system based on nontechnical terms. In this regard, intents and declarative policies are divided by the level of abstraction they capture, policies implementing concrete functions for taking decisions, whereas intent is higher level and more persistent goals. An intent-based network may use policies to translate intents to specific network configurations and actions. The concept of intents is further evolved [3] to discuss intent-driven autonomous networks, such that incorporate intents as a system-level capability. Management services are provided by a logical intent management entity [3], dedicated to the ingestion and validation of intents. The concepts of the intent owner and intent handler are also provided, where the intent owner is the entity (e.g., a human operator) providing the intent to the network, and the intent handler is the network side entity responsible for the network side lifecycle (validation, assurance, fulfillment, etc.) of the received intent. The intent owner and handler concepts are also part of TMF's work on intents in autonomous networks [13]. As a practical approach to intent-based network autonomy, [3] proposes to leverage the synergies between closed loops [14] and intents, in a way that each intent may be associated with a closed loop that is a collection of the necessary functionalities (such as monitoring, decision making, and actions) needed to drive the fulfillment of an intent.

As a common denominator in all reviewed intent definitions, there is a clear contrast between intent-based management and the traditional CM/PM/FM approach. In the latter, the operator provided extensive configurations and commands for the network on the device, domain, and end-to-end system level, whereas intents define only outcomes for which the fulfillment actions should be derived by the network or the network management itself, knowing the environment, context, and capabilities of the network. Intents may provide static goals that are to be maintained for the long term, outlasting the validity of the underlying configuration parameters that provide the right network behavior at any specific point in time. Therefore, during the lifetime of an intent, network configuration needs to be changed to fit the dynamics of the network load, environment, user demand, mobility, etc. Fulfilling an intent continuously while the network conditions are changing is not a one-time effort but a continuous responsibility and tuning, which can only be achieved by closed loops in an autonomous manner [3, 15, 16]. Therefore, intent-driven closed loops [16] are concepts developing organically out of the paradigm of intent-based network autonomy. Closed loops and their integration into the network management architecture will be investigated extensively in Chapter 7.

Intents bring a duality of evolution both for the human–network interface and for network automation technologies. On the one hand, as intents declare outcomes rather than executable instructions to the network, the interaction between the operator and the network should be different from the legacy CLI/UI and config file-based approach. The semantic of an intent may be more abstract than a single configuration parameter, therefore, more abstract semantics should be supported by the human–network interface elements and interactions. More abstraction on the interface also calls for more abstract feedback from the network to the operator. The interface aspects of intents will be detailed in depth in Chapters 8 and 9. On the other hand, the network should have mechanisms to interpret and act on the intents autonomously, which assumes a higher level of responsibility, autonomy, and self-awareness compared to the state-of-the-art provisioning configurations, evaluating conditions, and executing per-programmed commands. The network needs to be aware of its own state, which is a collection of states composed at many levels, including individual network devices, functions, and services, as well as user demand, mobility, and traffic conditions. State models, which are created from network data using AI/ML methods as they were discussed in Chapters 3–5, will be outlined in Section 11. The network, as it is required to act autonomously, should also be aware of its own capabilities to influence its own operation, that is, to know the semantic and consequences of its potential internal actions, such as changing parameters or deploying a closed loop. Semantic modeling is therefore essential part of an autonomous network, and it will be discussed in Section 12.

6.2 Intent-based Network Automation

The scope of automation in an end-to-end system is usually aligned with the overall scope, processes, and outcomes of the system itself. However, as systems are usually composed of individual components with different roles, responsibilities, abstractions, and individual scopes, the automation of end-to-end systems is in fact a product of the integration of smaller autonomous components that interact with each other on a goal-oriented basis.

Concerning a mobile network, the system-level automation goal may be the automation of the mobile network's services and operation as a business (such as one managed by a traditional CSP). However, this is not the highest level of automation that may involve a mobile network; as in an industrial or private network environment, a whole network itself may be only one component in a collection of interworking technologies and subsystems (such as production or manufacturing system, order management system, logistics,

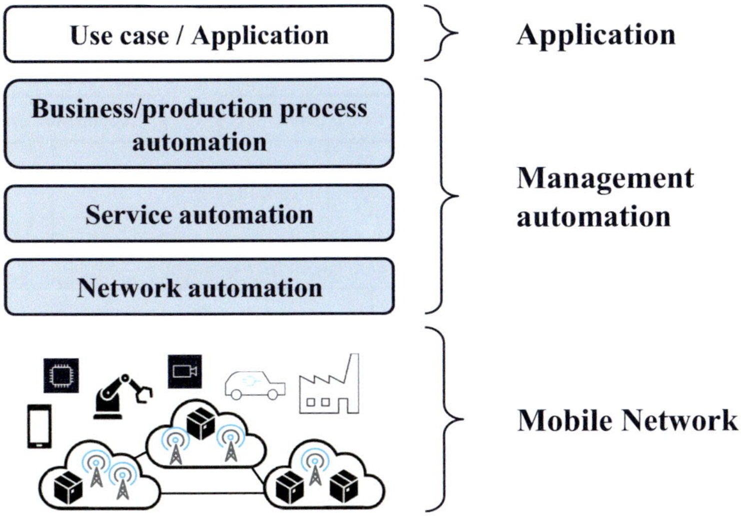

Figure 6.1 Automation scope: Application, business/service, and networking.

and asset tracking, etc. in an industrial site). Therefore, in such scenarios, automation starts with defining a use case or having an application that is directly providing or related to the outcome of the entire (in this example, the industrial) system. At this level, networking or communication services may not be visible at all, as the final product is not related to networking, but networking is merely used as a technical asset to interconnect production systems with a high SLA. Automation at this level may be integrated into the application logic, but it depends on the APIs and capabilities that are provided by the underlying technologies. As networking may be one of those technologies, it is important that networks become consumable (as a service) and that their capabilities can be exposed in a way that makes it possible to integrate with other systems. The technical aspects of network integration and exposure will be detailed further in Section 8.3 and Chapter 13; for now, it suffices to consider consumable networks as a desirable characteristic when it comes to thinking about network automation; that is, the topmost automation goals that will eventually cause actions in an autonomous network may originate from a higher (and nontelecommunication oriented) business level rather than directly from a communication service level consideration or even from an engineering level technological (e.g., network performance) goal. The stack of automation scopes is shown in Figure 6.1.

Automation goals (i.e., goals to be reached autonomously) are communicated to intent-based systems (such as intent-based networks) via intents. As automation scopes may be defined at multiple levels, intents describing

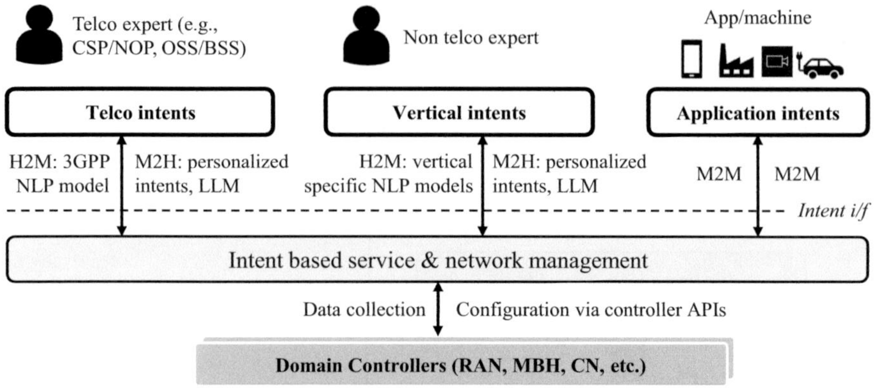

Figure 6.2 High-level categorization of intents.

automation goals may have multiple and diverse origins as per the owner of the intent. A high-level categorization of intents is shown in Figure 6.2, also highlighting some of the key aspects of the interface between the intent's owner and the intent handler on the network side.

The first category of intents is given by telco experts. Although these intents formulate goals about the telco network (on the service or network level), they may come from people with different backgrounds, roles, and responsibilities, therefore these intents are still diverse in their scope and impact. A key objective of the associated intent interface is to be able to adapt to these different backgrounds and roles thus seamlessly supporting the human operators in their roles. One way to achieve this objective is to use natural language processing and language models to allow for intent specification in natural languages and accommodate different domain-specific languages and terms using AI. Generative language models may also be used in the reverse direction, providing feedback with terms that are familiar and relatable to the person providing the intent. These linguistic modeling aspects are discussed further in Chapter 9.

The second category of intents is given by nontelco experts in an environment where networks are parts of bigger systems with a nontelco-oriented goal, such as a private network integrated into an industrial production site. Most of the considerations about telco intents apply here too, with the additional challenge that the domain language of any vertical technology and business (cf. the application layer of Figure 6.1) is both syntactically and semantically further from the telco-specific language describing any of the mobile networks and services. This difference has not only interface aspects but also functionality aspects, as intents formulated in an adjacent technology domain such as machine production must be translated to intents for the telco network.

The third category of intents are those that are given by applications or machines, that is, nonhuman users interacting with the network based on intents. This interface is different from language-oriented human–network interfaces as machine–machine (software-to-software) interaction is less ambiguous and more efficient using formal languages. Still, it is important to keep the attributes of intents (abstraction, outcome-driven, long-term) on the machine level as well, which requires a machine-discoverable and self-contained intent API.

Another angle of intent categorization is along the scope and persistency of the intent with regard to network infrastructure, resources, and services. Although intent taxonomies may go deep into that angle [17], there may be two important categories that are worth highlighting. One type of intent may be referred to as service intents, whereas another type could be called management or operational intents.

A service intent defines requirements related to a communication service, either to a particular instance of the service or to all instances of a given type of service. Actions to be performed by the network autonomously in the context of a service intent are attached to the lifecycle of the service instance or instances; that is, if there are no active service instances of the given type in the network, no action is needed even if the service intent is still active.

A special case of service intents may be referred to as QoE intents. For example, a service intent may declare that a specific application be served "well" in a given service area for up to a maximum number of users or maximum amount of network resources. In this case, the objectives of the service intent are specified in terms of QoE targets, that is, measurable indications of how an application or service performs from the end user's (consumer's, subscriber's) perspective, rather than from the network's perspective (which is usually in the scope of QoS management). The successful handling of QoE intents requires that the network has the right mechanisms to apply differentiated services on the granularity of individual users and applications, and has the ability to classify and separate the data flows end-to-end accordingly. Technology enablers for QoE-specific network and service management already exist, both as general capabilities [18, 19, 20] and specifically for popular applications [21, 22]. Due to the high granularity and agility of service management (i.e., per user, per application, short-lived application sessions, and real time) imposed by the fulfillment of QoE intents, and the fact that services are competing for shared resources (e.g., on the radio interface) [19, 22], managing cross-intent resource contention becomes a prominent responsibility of the network. A detailed analysis related to this special case will be given in Section 12.3.2.

The second major category of intents is management intents. Management intent declares requirements that may be interpreted and applied also outside of the scope of any particular communication service. Management intents may declare goals in terms of energy efficiency, resource optimization, and preference among technological, administrative, or operational alternatives (e.g., favoring the (lower) cost or energy consumption of a service realization over the efficiency of resource utilization). Although the objective of a management intent is well-defined and interpretable outside of the context of any communication service, the scope of the management intent may still be attached to a specific service intent or service instance. By attaching one or more management intents to a service intent, the operator may define additional targets and required means of operation for the network that it must comply with while it fulfills the service intent. Such mechanism may be referred to as "intent overlaying," which causes the same subject (e.g., a service instance) is under the control of the superposition of multiple intents (in this case, the service intent itself which defines what the service should be, and additional management intents that steer and constrain how the network will fulfill the service intent).

Management intents may also define strategies for deconflicting service intents dynamically in case, e.g., network resources at some point become insufficient to sustain all previously accepted service intents. While simple priorities may also be attached to individual intents that could act as one source of information to handle conflicts between intents, such scalars are insufficient to convey more complex intentions about conflict resolution.

6.3 Dynamic Composition of Network Management Capabilities

In intent-based networks, intents provided to the network are fulfilled and assured autonomously by the system. Therefore, the network should be aware of its own dynamically dispatchable capabilities (e.g., management services, analytics, decision models, configuration generation, and other actions); and it should be capable of organizing them purposefully so that the outcome(s) declared by the intent are achieved. How well the network can respond to the intents, and ultimately, what kinds of intents the network can fulfill, depend on the granularity, reusability, and flexibility of its capabilities. For intent-based network management, the capabilities are the network management services and the outcomes they can deliver through the management of configuration, performance, failures, services, slices, domains, etc. At one extreme, if the network management implements monolithic single-purpose end-to-end services, however complex they are internally, only intents that are matching those predefined services (e.g., created as silo solutions for dedicated use cases) could be accepted by the network. Such network management implementations would support only a catalog-order type of usage pattern, where the operator can select items from a predefined list as-is, even if through an interface that exhibits some traits of intent-based operation such as being "declarative" (however, only declarations of preapproved items would be acceptable by the network). This antipattern shows that intent-based networks cannot be created by simply providing a presentation layer over the top of a network architecture that is otherwise incapable of adaptation and flexibility. Instead of implementing network management as a set of monolithic complex services, capabilities may be organized into smaller and reusable components, each component having a well-defined scope (e.g., delivered impact) and well-defined interworking points (e.g., inputs and outputs). Such an organization allows to produce several different complex services or closed loops through a different combination of the same assets, providing a multipurpose toolset for the network to work with.

Defining services and closed loops from the combination of smaller ingredient elements rather than packaging everything into monolithic implementation units improves flexibility and versatility for the network, however, such design does not immediately lead to increased autonomy. For example, if the increased combinatorial freedom of the network assets is locked down by constraining the potential combinations to a few manually approved blueprints, then the means of flexibility are not exploited sufficiently. In fact, reaching the full potential would require exploring the full combinatorial space of the assets, evaluating the impact of every combination (e.g., "what would happen" if that combination was actually deployed), and choosing the combination whose results are delivering the desired outcome. With a high number of potential combinations, especially with assets that are continuously evolving and changing through software development (therefore the combinations do so too), it is impossible to handle such combinatorial optimization manually. Therefore, leveling up the network's autonomy mandates that the combination of its assets to achieve a declared purpose is also automated.

The capability of the network to interpret a declared intent and then produce the right combination of assets that will deliver on the intent is referred to as "self-composition" and illustrated in Figure 6.3. Composable elements

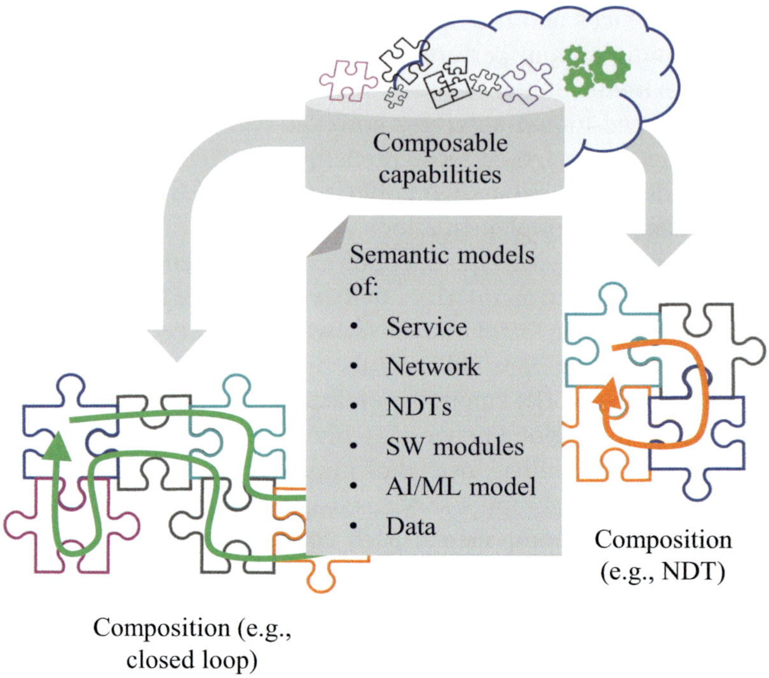

Figure 6.3 Illustration of the composition principle.

may include not only management services but also network functions, communication services, domain controllers, and analytics capabilities, as well as any data sources and stores, AI/ML models, etc. Self-composition is a self-organizing principle that enables the network to bring automation capabilities forward into the assembly of its own assets, which is traditionally a manual job associated with the design phase of creating services and deployable blueprints. In line with the requirements of dynamically responding to an intent with the right combination of capabilities, self-composition enables a network to create dynamic on-demand purpose-built closed loops, in line with the vision set by ZSM [3, 16]. Self-composition does not come as an isolated capability: it requires that the network models and considers all potential combinations of compatible data I/O, service API, management capabilities, software dependencies, and their outcomes, which in turn requires that those capabilities and interfaces are represented in a machine-readable and computable form. The machine-readable and computable representation is enabled by semantic modeling technology, which will be discussed in Chapter 11 in detail.

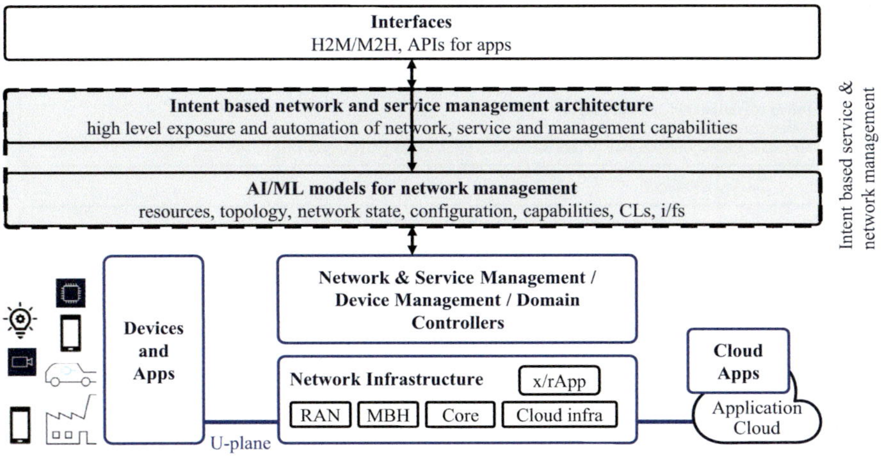

Figure 6.4 Functional architecture of intent-based network management.

A clear benefit of self-composability is not only to avoid having to build point solutions and pre-engineered blueprints per use case but also that the network's combinatorial potentials are identified, surfaced, and exploited to the maximum extent possible by adaptive and flexible automation. That is, each available network functionality may be leveraged in all potential combinations with others, without any a-priori design consideration as the network will dynamically discover and compose the best set of interworking components for each intent.

6.4 Intent-based Network Management Architecture

A possible logical functional architecture of network and service management with intents and AI/ML is shown in Figure 6.4. The interface layer represents the different interactions discussed in the context of Figure 6.2. Below the intent architecture and the AI/ML models is the network itself, including its management functions and services. This is to emphasize that intent-based network management can be introduced without swapping existing means and tools of network management; instead, intent-based mechanisms leverage the existing monitoring and control points of the network to autonomously create an impact that fulfills the intents. If a network already has means to observe and influence its behavior, those means should be exposed toward the intent architecture so that self-awareness and autonomous actions can be exercised as discussed in Section 6.1. This means that intent-based

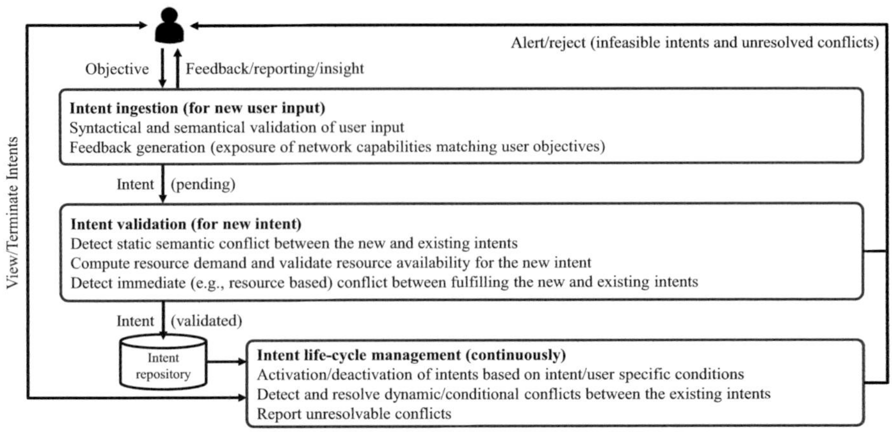

Figure 6.5 Intent-based network management workflow.

network and service management will interact with functions and services managing network functions, devices, domains, services, and in cloudified deployments the infrastructure itself (e.g., to trigger orchestration actions, as discussed in Chapter 5).

The intent-based network management layer consists of two major parts: (1) the intent-based network and service management architecture, which is responsible for presenting the intent interface to operators and users, handling incoming intents, and driving the automation closed loops; and (2) AI/ML models, which provide modeling and learning capabilities supporting network automation. These two parts are only logically separated, and they together provide intent-based management automation capabilities.

The intent-based network management workflow depicted in Figure 6.5 provides a high-level summary of the interactions between the operator and the intent-based network management, as well as the key internal steps of intent creation and management. As a first step, referred to as intent ingestion, the operator provides a machine-interpretable objective that may be formulated in natural language or using other more formal expressions [3]. An objective is not yet an intent as it is not necessarily aligned with the specific capabilities of the network, that is, the network management has not yet validated that it possesses all the implementations (software assets, APIs, resources) that are needed to fulfill the objective. Turning the objective into intent starts with validating the objective, both syntactically and semantically. Syntactic validation means to check that the objective is well-formatted according to the input specification (e.g., it is a legitimate natural language sentence operating with common language terms rather than being an incomprehensible string or properly using formal expressions). Semantic validation checks if the meaning of the objective is comprehensible by the network, for example, it refers to goals for which the network has the software-defined APIs and means to contextualize and internally break them down into specific actions. As the network, even an autonomous one, is only capable of executing logic that is available in the form of implemented and deployable software artifacts, initial objectives may not be fully aligned with the capabilities of the network. Bringing objectives to match existing network capabilities is an iterative process, which requires the network to expose those capabilities that are closest to the requested objective, and the operator to refine its objectives by considering the exposed capabilities. The iteration may be conceived as a form of dialogue between the operator and the network rather than the traditional way where the operator provides a command and the network either executes it as is or provides an error (either upfront or maybe only later during execution). Ideally, at the end of the dialogue, the objective can be reclassified as an intent for which the network management can compose a fulfillment plan in terms of which software assets, data inputs, AI models, and action interfaces need to be involved, and in what combination. The resulting intent is still pending as although it now makes full sense to the network, it is neither to be fulfilled in isolation from other intents nor has access to unlimited resources. Therefore, an intent that is plausibly doable by the network may still be practically impossible or only partially achievable (e.g., only over a restricted service area) due to conflicts with other intents or resource limitations. Conflicts with other intents may be identified or detected during the intent validation phase by static analysis, such as checking for semantic conflict between the goals of the new intent and already accepted ones (e.g., an intent declaring a goal that is the opposite of that of another intent). Initial resource conflicts may also be detected at this stage, such as a lack of compute resources for new software modules that need to be instantiated to provide services on which the fulfillment of the new intent depends. Resource conflict may also arise between existing intents and the new one, for example, when the new intent would require the allocation of physical resources such as slice-specific ones [23] that are already reserved. If conflicts are detected at the intent validation step, they are returned to the operator and the intent can be refined (e.g., restricting its scope to a smaller service area that is free of limitations). If the pending intent passes validation, it is accepted into an intent repository that contains all intents that are handled by the network. It does not necessarily mean that they are active, as intents may be defined only for a future time interval, or for periods at specified times. Inactive intents still need to be supervised by the network to activate them when their time comes or activation conditions are satisfied. This lifecycle of the intents is managed by the network as long as the intent is in the repository, that is, until the intent's owner (operator) explicitly withdraws it, or the intent was assigned an expiration date that is over. During this time, the operator may interact with the intent at any time, such as query telemetry data related to the intent (e.g., to be informed about the amount of resources associated with the fulfillment of the intent, any soft conflicts that were resolved autonomously by the network management but that required extra configuration effort or more actions, or any predictions associated with the foregoing of the intent). Every time the intent is active, the network management has a role to detect (or preferably predict) conflicts that appear dynamically even though the static analyzer during intent validation did not flag any conflicts. This may happen as the amount of resources required to keep the network in a state that is desirable for fulfilling an intent or to enforce an SLA may increase due to changing network environments (especially on the radio interface) or resiliency mechanisms triggered due to intermittent link failures. In case of dynamic conflicts, the scope of the network management is to try to resolve them by rebalancing resources or activating extra (not initially planned) network resources. When resolution cannot be achieved, the conflict should be reported to the operator as at least one intent will be degraded. With priorities defined across intents (perhaps by means of another management intent), the degradation could be administered in a coordinated and contained manner rather than, for example, letting an overload of shared resources destroy all intents that depend on the availability of the resource. If the frequency of such dynamic conflicts increases, or they are regularly associated with specific resources or service areas, the network management should adjust its knowledge about the available resources to better reflect the actual resource availability already during the static analysis phase. It is also an input to longer-term planning efforts that is not necessary within the scope of automation but could help guide manual decision-making.

6.5 AI Models for Intent-based Network Management

Leveraging AI for automation is a technology enabler to evolve a system's capability from executing preprogrammed logic (however, complex the logic is) to being able to adapt its logic to events and conditions that are learned from the specific network operation. Adaptable parts of the network may be implemented via AI models whose parameters are kept trainable after deployment, or by regular updates to AI models that deliver new model versions incorporating information that was collected since the latest model update.

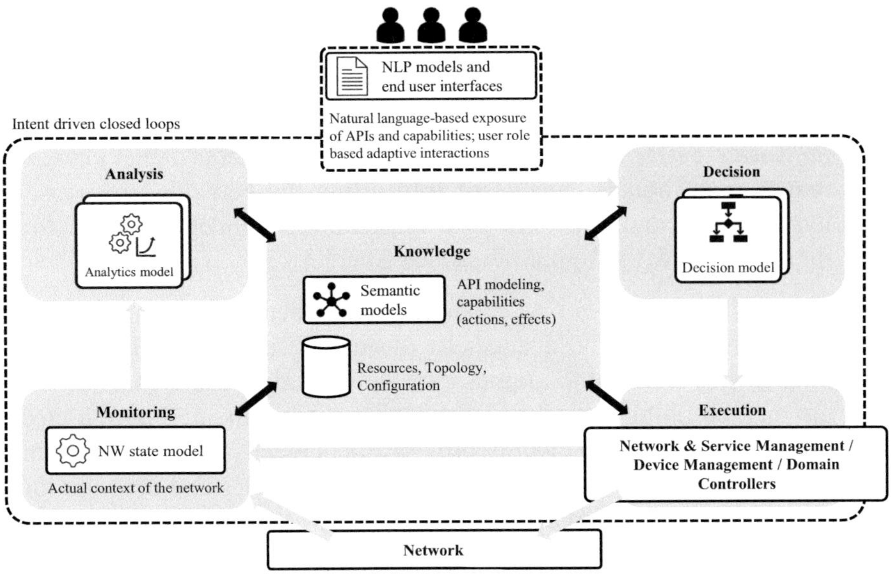

Figure 6.6 AI models in an intent-driven closed loop.

AI models may be integrated into various stages of an intent-driven closed loop [14, 24, 15, 16], as illustrated in Figure 6.6. The main capabilities brought in by the models at each stage are the following:

- *Knowledge:* In addition to information or models about the network topology, configuration, and resources, intent-based closed loops need to model the network's active capabilities such as potential actions and controls, along with their intended effect, as those controls will need to be exercised autonomously. An enabler to capture the dynamic capabilities of the network is to use semantic models (see Chapter 11). The main role of such models is to attach semantics to APIs (including internal network APIs that are not exposed for manual invocation), data (including deep network data that is not collected persistently), and impact (outcomes expected when specific actions are triggered). Semantic models enable to automatically build a connection between the semantic of intents provided by the operator and the APIs, data, and impact that are within the reach of the network, as it will be described in Chapter 11 in more detail.
- *Monitoring:* The dynamic state of the network may be captured using network state models using technology that will be detailed in Chapter 10. The scope of the state models is to create an abstraction of the network (devices, functions, services) on multiple levels and

domains based on real data collected from the network deployment, essentially creating a machine-readable representation of the network that can be a basis of autonomous operations (e.g., event predictions, analysis, and decisions). Network state models digitalize not only the network's current state but also capture its dynamic behavior which makes such models capable of forecasting the network's response to hypothetical conditions. For these reasons, such models are also a foundation for network digital twins (see Chapter 13).

- *Analysis and decision*: AI models quite evidently lend themselves to providing value in these stages by means of creating insight (analytics output) that drives autonomous decisions. Analytics and decision models may be highly specific to the use case implemented by the closed loop, therefore these models provide specialized capabilities defining the purpose and utility of the closed loop. Analytics and decision models are further detailed in Chapter 12.
- *Execution:* The closed-loop delivers impact through the invocation and utilization of existing network APIs, controllers provided by network and service management, device management, or domain-specific resources. These control capabilities are represented in the knowledge stage of the closed loop and are considered by analytics and decision models when an autonomous control action is triggered. The closed loop should also collect feedback about the impact and efficiency of its autonomous actions, as detailed in Chapter 7, therefore the loop is completed through a logical link back to the monitoring stage where the outcome of the actions may be measured and quantified.

The AI models providing the capabilities behind the closed loop stages can be rendered into a high-level logical system architecture that also exposes network functionalities supporting the closed loop operation in more detail (Figure 6.7). The first category of supporting network functions is the scalable and efficient data and knowledge collection at multiple locations, domains, and aggregation levels, which were already discussed in Chapter 3. Data includes both operational data (such as numerical measurements, logs, and events) and actionable information (such as metadata about configurations, software artifacts, APIs, and management services). These pieces of information are input for the network state models and semantic models that are part of the Knowledge and Monitoring stages of the CL model. The second category of supporting network functions is the exposure of programmable

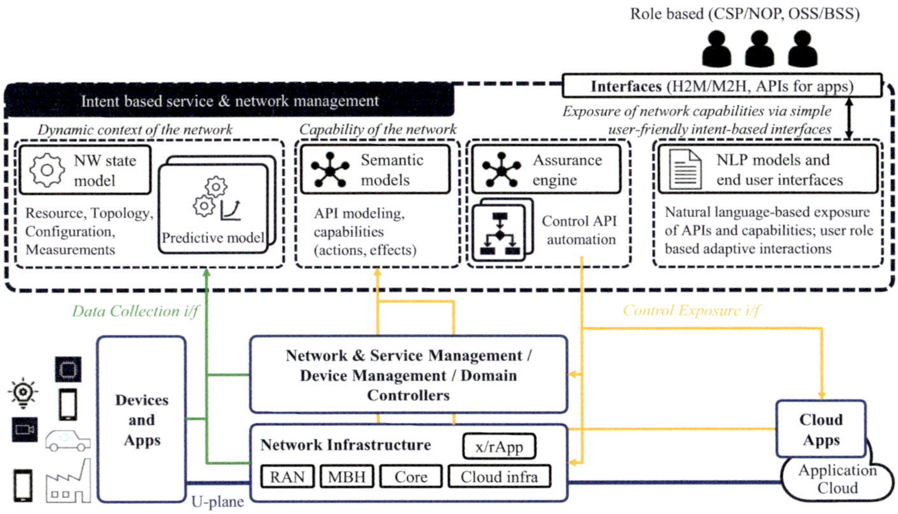

Figure 6.7 AI models for intent-based network management.

interfaces to enable closed-loop control over network configuration and services, which are driven by the analytics and decision and execution stages of the CL model. On the top, the NLP models and intent-based interfaces provide the means of governance for the closed loops.

6.6 Summary

Intent-based networking is a paradigm attempting to reduce the technological complexity exposed to the network operator by providing declarative goal-oriented means of governance rather than requiring imperative executable commands or directly applicable configurations. Intents not only increase the autonomy of networks through easier human–network interactions but also drive the evolution of automation technology within the network to make it capable of handling much higher-level abstract requests and transforming them into continuous actions of intent assurance.

This chapter provided an overview of the standardization landscape of intents, showing a great level of convergence across the SDOs, indicating the maturity of the concept. Intents were shown to be not only relevant in the relation of a telecommunication network and its traditional network operator in a communication service provider role, but intents could be applied in the context of private networks enabling end-to-end industrial solutions where the scope of intent is not confined to a telco data service but to an enterprise system objective. In such cases, intents should be interpreted in the context of the entire solution of which telecommunication services are only enablers rather than the goal itself.

Intents are closely related to the concept of capability composition, an automation mechanism that unlocks the full potential of a system by finding the best matching combination of all existing services (internal and external) and mechanisms that collectively produce the outcome declared by the intent.

This chapter provided a logical architecture as a framework for intent-based network and service management, which is in line with both the ZSM architecture and the ZSM concept of closed-loop automation. The architecture also represented the means of automation in terms of AI models that provide the system's capability of dynamic context awareness, its own capabilities such as means of automation and control, and suggested a language-based intent interface toward human users and operators.

In the next chapters, deep dives will be presented to technical enablers of network autonomy, starting with the closed loops that provide a framework of all autonomous capabilities.

Bibliography

[1] TM Forum, "Autonomous Networks Technical Architecture", IG1230, Version 1.1.1, December 2022

[2] TM Forum, "Intent Life Cycle Management and Interface", IG1253C, Version 1.1.0, November 2021

[3] ETSI GR ZSM 011, "Zero-touch network and Service Management (ZSM); Intent-driven autonomous networks; Generic aspects" V1.1.1 (2023-02)

[4] P. Szilágyi, "I2BN: Intelligent Intent Based Networks", Journal of ICT Standardization, Vol. 9 2, 159–200. River Publishers

[5] M. Sloman, "Policy driven management for distributed systems", Journal of Network and Systems Management, Plenum Press, Vol. 2, No. 4, 1994, pp. 333–360, Available at https://core.ac.uk/download/pdf/1587309.pdf

[6] J. Strassner, "Intent-based Policy Management", Available at https://datatracker.ietf.org/meeting/95/materials/slides-95-sdnrg-1

[7] Alexander Clemm, Laurent Ciavaglia, Lisandro Zambenedetti Granville, Jeff Tantsura, "Intent-Based Networking - Concepts and Definitions", October 2022, https://www.rfc-editor.org/info/rfc9315

[8] 3GPP TS 28.312 Management and orchestration; Intent driven management services for mobile networks

[9] ETSI GR ZSM 005, "Zero-touch network and Service Management (ZSM); Means of Automation", V1.1.1 (2020-05)

[10] 3GPP TR 28.912 Study on enhanced intent driven management services for mobile networks

[11] 3GPP TS 28.532 Management and orchestration; Generic management services

[12] 3GPP TS 28.533 Management and orchestration; Architecture framework

[13] TM Forum, "Intent in Autonomous Networks", IG1253, Version 1.3.0, August 2022

[14] ETSI GS ZSM 009-1, "Zero-touch network and Service Management (ZSM); Closed-Loop Automation; Part 1: Enablers", V1.1.1 (2021-06)

[15] ETSI GR ZSM 009-3, "Zero-touch network and Service Management (ZSM); Closed-Loop Automation; Part 3: Advanced topics", V1.1.1 (2023-08)

[16] ETSI GS ZSM 016, "Zero-touch network and Service Management (ZSM); Intent-driven Closed Loops" V1.1.1 (2024-10)

[17] Chen Li, Olga Havel, Adriana Olariu, Pedro Martinez-Julia, Jéferson Campos Nobre, Diego Lopez, "Intent Classification", October 2022, https://www.rfc-editor.org/info/rfc9316

[18] P. Szilágyi and Cs. Vulkán, "Application Aware Mechanisms in HSPA Systems", ICWMC 2012, The Eigth International Conference on Wireless and Mobile Communication, pp. 212-217, June 2012

[19] N. Radics, P. Szilágyi and Cs. Vulkán, "Insight Based Dynamic QoE Management in LTE", 2015 IEEE 26th International Symposium on Personal, Indoor and Mobile Radio Communications (PIMRC'15), Aug 30 – Sep 2, 2015, Hong Kong, China

[20] P. Szilágyi and Cs. Vulkán, "LTE User Plane Congestion Detection and Analysis", 2015 IEEE 26th International Symposium on Personal, Indoor and Mobile Radio Communications (PIMRC'15), Aug 30 – Sep 2, 2015, Hong Kong, China

[21] P. Szilágyi, Cs. Vulkán, "Network Side Lightweight and Scalable YouTube QoE Estimation", International Conference on Communication (ICC'15), Jun. 8, 2015, London, UK

[22] B. Héder, P. Szilágyi and Cs. Vulkán, "Dynamic and Adaptive QoE Management for OTT Application Sessions in LTE", 2016 IEEE 27th International Symposium on Personal, Indoor and Mobile Radio Communications (PIMRC'16), Sep 5 – Sep 7, 2016, Valencia, Spain

[23] 3GPP TS 28.530 Management and orchestration; Concepts, use cases and requirements
[24] ETSI GS ZSM 009-2, "Zero-touch network and Service Management (ZSM); Closed-Loop Automation; Part 2: Solutions for automation of E2E service and network management use cases", V1.1.1 (2022-06)

7

Closed Loop Automation

Closed loops are mechanisms to execute business logic in systems autonomously yet not independently of human governance and supervision. The objectives for closed loops may be the control of measurable parameters, performance indicators, or even complex management goals at the domain, network, or service level. Closed-loop execution of existing system capabilities enables to increase in the level of network autonomy by removing humans from operational loops. The applicability and validity of closed loops during changing network conditions depend on the flexibility of the implementation within the closed loop mechanisms. Self-learning closed loops are capable of adaptation and optimization based on models that describe the correlation between autonomous actions and their impact on the system and the measurable objectives of the closed loop itself. Such closed loops usually incorporate AI technology as the key enabler for modeling parts of the system based on its past observations captured in historical network data. Combined with intent-based governance, self-learning closed loops provide a melting pot of the key technology trends that increase the level of network autonomy and provide substantial benefits in terms of repositioning manual effort from low-level operation to high-level system supervision.

7.1 Introduction

Network automation refers to a set of technologies and mechanisms that enable a network to operate according to external requirements and specifications but without receiving external instructions on the operational steps it needs to perform. According to TMF's six-step maturity model [1], a network may conform to various levels of autonomy, from level 0 to level 5. The levels evaluate whether execution, awareness, analysis, and decision are manual or autonomously made, as well as whether intents are present as a means of driving automation. Up to and including level 3, at least decisions may be partially made

DOI: 10.1201/9788770041478-7

manually, making such systems at most "conditional automation networks." The term also captures that when automatic actions are driven by manually defined conditions they do not constitute autonomy as the network in fact did not make any decision. Rather, the network only executed a predefined operational logic that consisted of conditions (such as in the form of policies and rules). The simplified operation in these kinds of networks might be modeled with open loops [2]. An open loop starts with a manual input, which sets off various workflows and processes that are executed by the network until they arrive at a decision point. The decision is surfaced back to the human operator, who provides manual input to the network to proceed, completing the open loop.

Level 4 is the first where networks are required to make decisions autonomously, earning the term "high autonomous networks" [2]. Such a level of autonomy may be described through closed control loops [2, 3], which enable the network to proceed to decisions (and apply them) without soliciting manual instructions on how to continue. Level 4 is also the first level when the network may incorporate intents as a means of receiving expectations from the operator. It is not a coincidence that closed loop autonomy and intents meet: as discussed earlier in Chapter 6, it is not possible to have autonomous networks without elevating the abstraction level of the interactions between the operator and the network, where intents may serve as a bridge. To conclude the levels of autonomy, level 5 does not introduce any new automation capability; it, however, mandates (instead of suggesting) intents as a means of interfacing with the system, and requires that all operational scenarios are autonomous (and intent-driven) rather than allowing to limit them to selected scenarios.

Closed loops are mechanisms to control parameters, entities, or behavior of a system and automatically adjust them to reach or keep a desired outcome [2, 3]. Closed loops are key enablers of system autonomy as they execute a full chain of operations from observations and measurements through decision-making up to changing, all without manual intervention. Closed loops may be simplistic and operate according to predefined conditions and actions, in which case they implement a specific and narrow control functionality that is capable of adapting to a restricted set of system or environmental conditions. CLs may also be self-learning [4], in which case they collect and retain knowledge about their actions and learn from feedback obtained directly or indirectly from the system in which they operate.

A general functional model of closed loops was provided in [3] in the context of network management automation, reproduced in Figure 7.1 and invoked previously in Figure 6.6. The closed loop consists of four stages: "monitoring," "analysis," "decision," and "execution." The closed loop

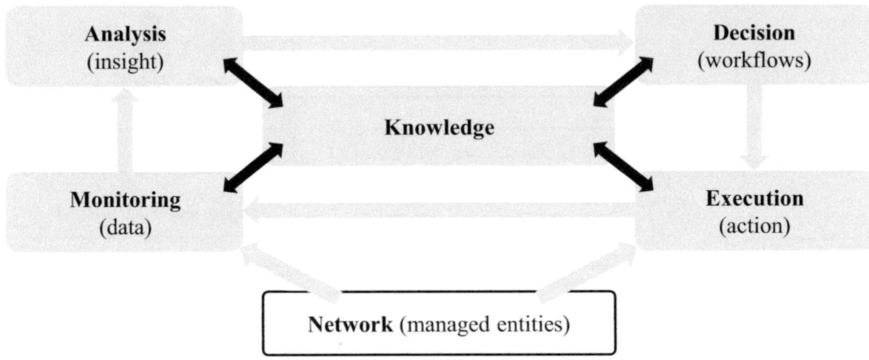

Figure 7.1 General functional model of network management automation closed loops.

manages network entities that may be not only equipment or functions but also services or even other closed loops. The monitoring and analysis stages are responsible for producing information for the closed loop through data collection and insight derivation. The decision stage identifies, derives, or potentially synthesizes workflows as a response to the information produced by the analytics stage. The workflow is executed, impacting the managed network entities, which is then reflected back to the closed loop through the next observations collected by the monitoring stage. In addition to the four stages of the closed loop, a "knowledge" component is defined for the persistence and sharing of data, insight, or any information that enables coherence across the stages of the closed loop.

The roles of closed loops in intent-driven networks were discussed in [5], building on the taxonomy and logical architecture that defined the actors and roles involving intents [6]. The intent management entity (IME) is the network-side logical component receiving the intent from the intent owner (e.g., the operator), implementing the intent handler role [6, 7]. The interaction between the intent owner and intent handler takes the form of a management service, that is provided by the IME (intent handler) and consumed by the intent owner.

7.2 Closed Loops for Intent-based Network Management

In intent-based network management, closed loops play an important role in automating various stages of the intent lifecycle [7], right from the initial touchpoint between the intent owner (e.g., an operator providing the intent) through the handling and fulfilling of the intent until the intent is withdrawn or terminated (cf. Figure 6.5). Based on their roles and goals,

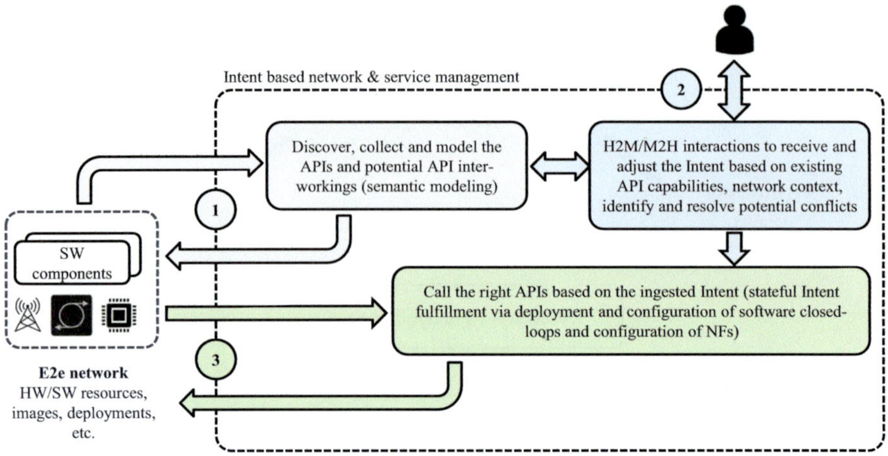

Figure 7.2 Main closed loops that build and exercise the capability of network management to dynamically handle intents.

various types of closed loops may be identified (logically owned and executed by an IME [6]) that enable autonomous intent-based network management (Figure 7.2):

1. Closed loops to drive the discovery and semantic modeling of the network's own capabilities (including management services). As a continuous internal activity, the IME scans and discovers the network's own internal APIs (exposed by the network functions, domain controllers, management services, other software-defined closed loops, etc.) to build and update semantic models (cf. Figure 6.6). The semantic models capture what each modeled SW entity is capable of achieving (in terms of outcomes or output), and what are its dependencies in terms of the capabilities of other entities and input data. The semantic models enable the autonomous composition of closed loops based on a desired outcome (see Chapter 11 for more details). New capabilities are added to the network every time a new software module is onboarded, or a software module is updated to a new version supporting a new API. With new capabilities, the network becomes capable of responding to new intents as the diversity of potential intent handling closed loops increases [6].

2. CLs operating over the human–network interface: Interaction with the intent owner (e.g., the operator) is also a closed loop in intent-based systems, as the definition of the intent is an iterative/dialogue process,

which is a closed loop where both the intent owner and the IME participate. This is an equivalent of TM forum's concept of intent control loops outlined in [7], which is essentially a closed loop coupling the intent owner with the intent handler.

3. Intrinsic intent fulfillment CLs of a system: Intents that are handled by the network (i.e., are in the intent repository as in Figure 6.5) also have corresponding closed loops that are deployed by the IME during the workflow of fulfilling an intent. These are the equivalent of the intent instantiation and maintenance CLs [6], which are attached to intents (i.e., having a 1:1 mapping between intents and Intent I&M CLS) and whose purpose is to implement the assurance of the intent during the rest of the intent's lifecycle. These CLs cannot be catalogized and blueprinted upfront, as that would mean anticipating all possible intents and premake a CL for all of them. Instead, the IME should compose the CL at the intent ingestion phase (cf. Figure 6.5), when the intent owner's objective is translated to intents that the network can handle.

The CLs composed in number 3 above already reflect the intent in their implementation, that is, they control resources and functions of the network that can make an impact toward the intent's declared goal.

7.3 Self-learning and Closed Loops

Self-learning in systems with intent-based closed loops may happen at multiple levels. One type of self-learning commences within the IME (intent handler) during the workflow of composing the right closed loop for an intent that is received from an intent owner. Although potential intents and the corresponding intent fulfillment closed loops may be mapped statically as pre-provisioned knowledge in the IME, this would result in a limited choice of intents that could be served, degrading intents to a catalog-based selection of declarative policies and all inflexibility that comes with it (see Section 6.1 and [8]). Instead, the IME could compose the intent fulfillment CL by matching the intent's desired outcome with the potential outcomes achievable by the network, which are captured in the semantic models (see Section 7.2 and Chapter 11). As reaching a desired outcome may be conceived through multiple alternative closed loops, the IME has to choose from the available alternatives and monitor its choice during intent fulfillment to account for its validity, utility, and efficiency. The monitoring should quantify how efficiently the closed loop is achieving the outcome of the intent based on factors such as the percentage of time during which the intent's outcome is missed (if not fulfilled all the time), or the amount of resources (both network resources and cost or energy) associated with the operation of the closed loop. The IME may try different CL alternatives, record their quantified results, and build knowledge that enables to select the best performing CL for newly received intents.

Once a CL is composed, the CL itself may implement its own internal self-learning capabilities to adapt and optimize its operation to the specific network deployment, environment, topology, resources, user demand, and any other local condition that cannot be precoded into the implementation of the CL's constituent software modules. Self-learning CLs do not execute a static precoded logic (however complex that is) but have the capability to change their own behavior based on learning feedback collected from the network during their operation, conforming to the monitoring and analysis phases (see Figure 7.1) of ZSM's closed-loop model [3].

The concept of self-learning CLs appears in the advanced CL topics discussed in [4]. Self-learning CLs consider their past actions and their consequences when they decide on future actions. This comes from the observation that the utility of a predefined action is not absolute; an action that is very useful in some cases may be not effective or even counter-productive in other cases. Supposing that a CL with a set of objectives may choose from a list of actions through which it may impact the network and services, a self-learning CL should discover which is the best action under a given context that maximizes its utility and reaches the objectives. Such self-learning capability depends on well-defined metrics that quantify the utility of the action (within a given context).

Self-learning CLs require training feedback from the system to adapt their behavior to the dynamic environment in which they operate. Such feedback is defined [4] as the efficiency and the impact related to the action as illustrated in Figure 7.3. The efficiency and impact-based self-learning may be a means to create learning feedback both on the level of purpose-oriented intent fulfillment closed loops (that are created as a response to intents) and on the high level of the IME deciding which closed loop is better to address a given (type of) intent.

Efficiency means that the action executed by the CL is successfully completed with the specific scope and target (e.g., UEs, cell, service area, and network slice). Self-learning in CL is supposed to filter out actions that are inefficient in a given context. For example, a vertical handover action triggered via reconfiguring radio thresholds is an efficient action only if the UEs targeted by the action can execute the handovers (e.g., they support the

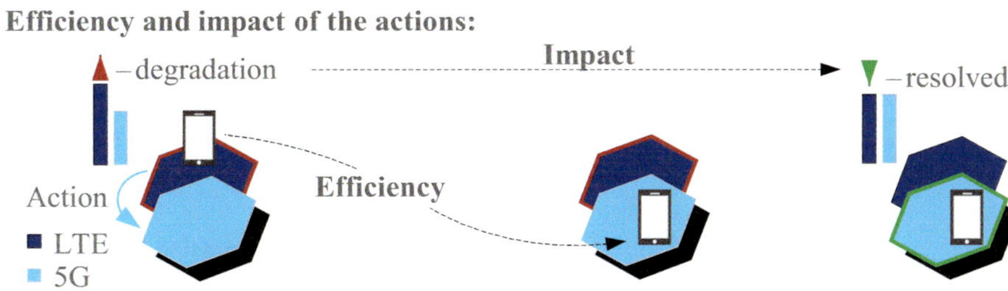

Figure 7.3 Example: the impact and efficiency of an automated action executed by a self-learning CL.

frequencies and technologies involved on the radio layers, and they are at physical locations where the radio propagation environment indeed makes the configured thresholds cause handovers). If some UEs were to reject the handover (e.g., due to lack of capability or lack of real coverage from the targeted frequency layer), the action would be less efficient or not efficient at all, even if on a procedural level the handover configuration action was successful.

Impact means that the action has reached its goal (e.g., resolved a system state degradation due to radio resource overload on one of the radio layers, which was the cause of selecting and triggering the action by the CL). Self-learning in CL is supposed to filter out actions that have a low impact in a given context. For example, if the vertical handovers were efficiently executed and they also resolved the degradation by decreasing the load in the resource layers, the action was impactful. Otherwise, even if the action was efficient (i.e., it did successfully change what it was intended to change) the impact is low or, if the degradation further escalates, even negative.

In the above example, efficiency and impact are defined specifically by the action and the context in which the action was executed. There are two observations related to the example. First, the calculation of efficiency and impact is specific to the action and to the CL's logic itself, which is context and implementation-dependent. However, the quantification of the efficiency and impact (as measurable values) should be uniform across different CLs, even if they operate with their own set of actions and implementations, to enable the evaluation and comparison of CLs. This motivates the definition of a common action utility function that can be attached to a self-learning CL and provides the CL with a uniform efficiency and impact metric as training feedback. In this case, self-learning CLs need to consider a single type of efficiency and impact feedback to implement their learning capability, whereas the utility functions could be separately developed and reused

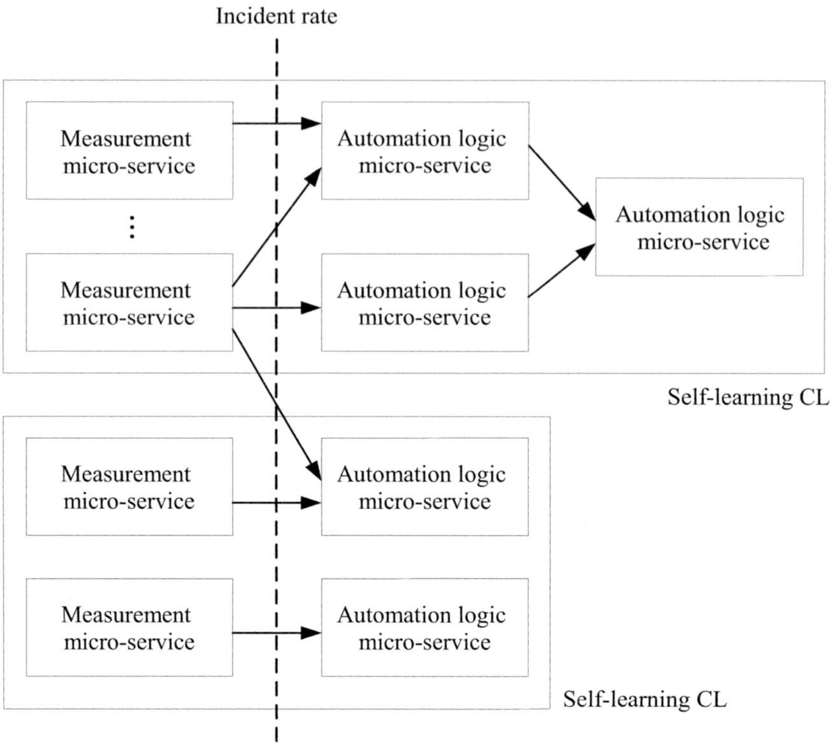

Figure 7.4 Micro-service-based self-learning CL decomposition.

across CLs. In practice, such separation can be achieved by decomposing the CL into interworking micro-services, where one or more micro-services are responsible for action utility measurements and one or more micro-services are responsible for the CL's automation logic (Figure 7.4). An automation logic micro-service may consume measurements generated by a measurement micro-service and produce decisions and actions. Additionally, an automation logic micro-service may produce insight that is consumed by one or more other automation logic micro-services. All these automation logic micro-services together with the utility measurement micro-services may collaboratively implement a complex distributed automation task, which is the business logic of the self-learning CL.

Measurement micro-services are reusable components potentially providing input to multiple unrelated automation logic micro-services in separate self-learning CLs. Each measurement micro-service is specialized to evaluate network, service, traffic, user, equipment, or any other network/user entity state or performance from a specific perspective and provide a common utility metric to any interested automation logic micro-service. The common utility metric is proposed to be the so-called incident rate. The incident rate is a metric defined as a function of (1) the number of events that are considered negative and (2) the total number of events. For example, the function may produce a ratio of (1)/(2). The definition of an event and when it is considered negative is defined by the implementation of the measurement micro-service.

Each measurement service has, besides its code implementation, three attributes: (1) objective, (2) input domain, and (3) scope, defined as follows.

Objective: Any particular measurement micro-service is implemented to generate incidents compatible with a specific objective (e.g., SLA assurance objective requires incident definition related to the quality of the service; power efficiency objective requires incident definition that is related to the power consumption of the services; etc.). The objective is static (design time) metadata that is part of the micro-service implementation.

Input domain: The implementation of the measurement micro-service also defines the input domain from which the incident measurements are generated (e.g., NF PM counters of a specific network function type such as gNB-CU, cloud infra VM resource counters, and VNF application metrics). The input domain is also a static (design time) metadata and part of the micro-service implementation.

Scope: The scope of a measurement micro-service is defined dynamically when the measurement micro-service is deployed in a system (e.g., by an orchestrator management function). The scope of a measurement micro-service is the intersection of its input domain and its deployment area (e.g., a geo-area and a network slice). That is, a deployed measurement micro-service will generate incidents from the intersection of its input domain and the deployment area (e.g., for all gNB-Cus within a network slice) where the generated incidents are compatible with the measurement micro-service's objective (e.g., SLA assurance).

An automation logic micro-service autonomously makes decisions and actions to converge a network or service toward a specific objective. In order to make the automation logic micro-service part of a self-learning CL, it should be coupled with the right measurement micro-service that generates incidents based on the same objective. This requires that automation logic micro-services are also released with metadata defining their objective and input domain, similarly to measurement micro-services. This enables a management function to automatically pair automation logic micro-services with compatible measurement micro-services (based on matching objective and

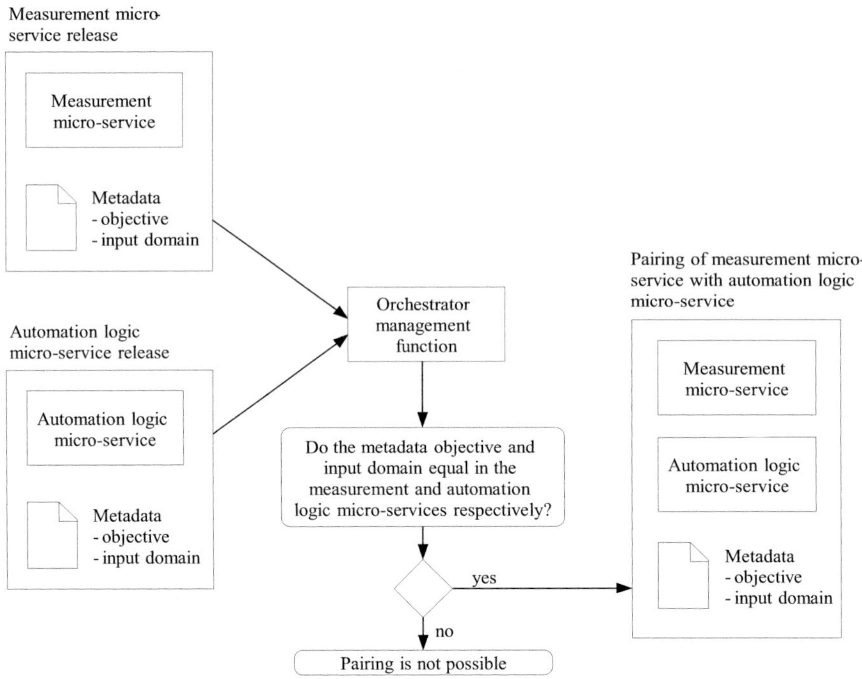

Figure 7.5 Pairing of a measurement micro-service with an automation logic micro-service based on micro-service metadata.

input domain in their metadata), assembling the self-learning CL from the disaggregated micro-services (Figure 7.5). The loose coupling between the measurement micro-services and automation logic micro-services promotes an extendable marketplace where a growing variety of incident measurements can be implemented and published by different measurement micro-services (by a multitude of vendors), but all exposing a uniform API (the incident metric) toward the automation logic micro-services (by the same or different vendors).

The deployment of a self-learning CL is performed by the intent management entity [6]. The prerequisite for the deployment is to have all micro-service implementations and attached metadata (both for measurement micro-services and automation logic micro-services) available to the IME. The deployment of a self-learning CL commences on an intent request coming from an intent owner (e.g., from the operator) received by the IME. Within the intent ingestion process (cf. Figure 6.5), the IME identifies the CL as an implementation that can produce the right management actions to fulfill the intent. The IME also defines the deployment scope of the CL based on

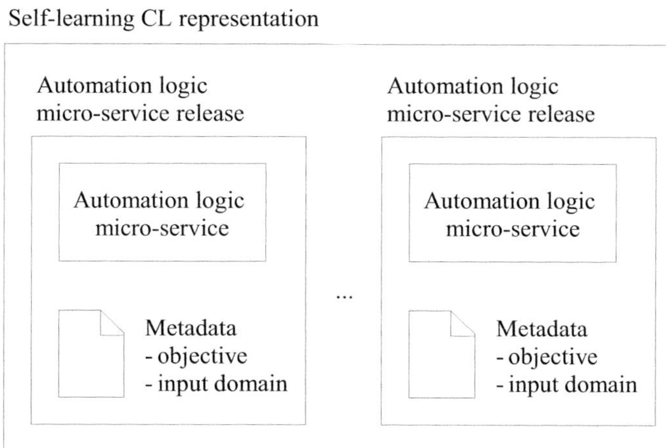

Figure 7.6 Self-learning CL representation for deployment.

the intent (e.g., the service area where the intent should be fulfilled). The CL is represented by the list of automation logic micro-services, wherein each automation logic micro-service is represented by its implementation and the objective and input domain metadata (Figure 7.6).

The first step of the self-learning CL deployment (Figure 7.7) is to collect the measurement micro-service dependencies of the self-learning CL, that is, the list of measurement logic micro-services that are needed to supply the incident rate to the CL's automation logic micro-services. A measurement logic micro-service can supply the incident rate to an automation logic micro-service if the objective and input domain of the two micro-services are respectively the same. The right measurement micro-service for a given automation logic micro-service may be found by searching through all known measurement micro-services and comparing the metadata of each measurement micro-service with that of the automation logic micro-service. On multiple potential matches, the intent owner (e.g., the operator) may be presented with a choice option so that it can select the preferred implementation.

7.4 Benefits of Intent-based Closed-loop Management Automation

Intent-based network management automation, which is essentially what intent-based network management means, provides multiple benefits to the owner and consumer of the network. The benefits may be viewed from

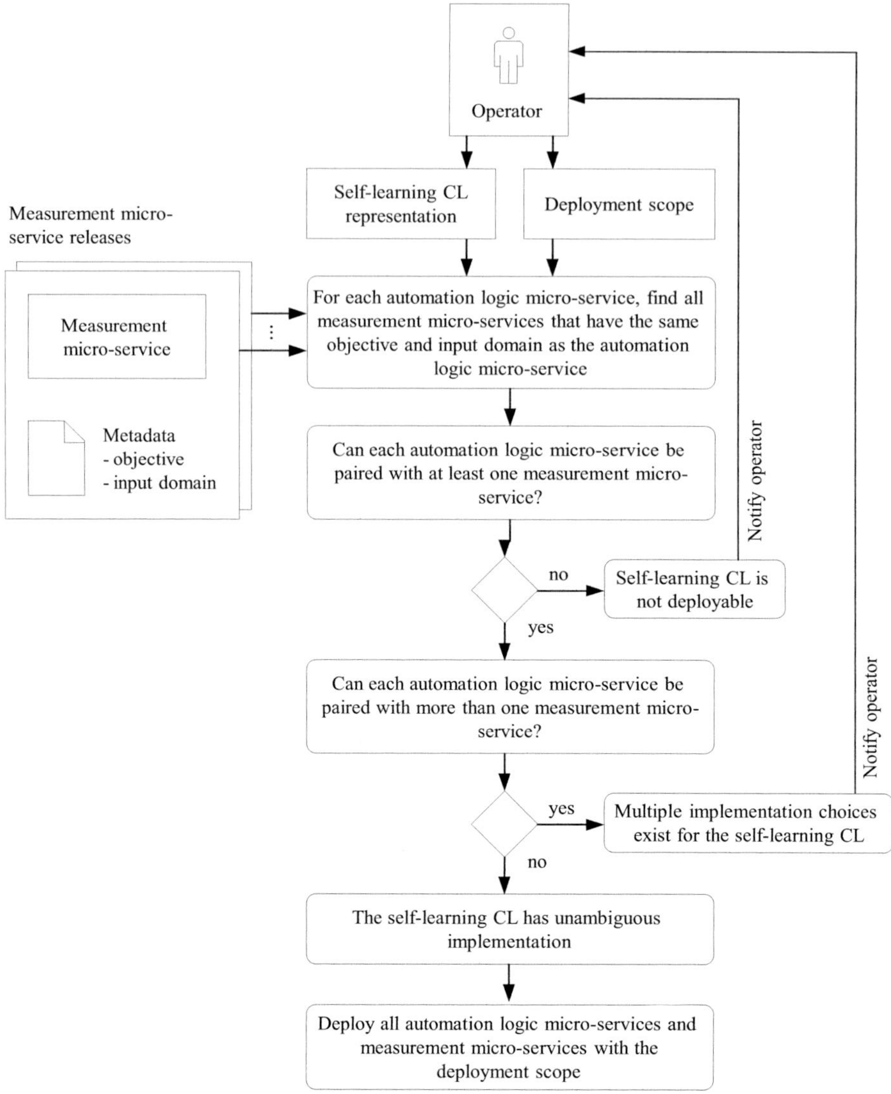

Figure 7.7 Steps taken by the intent management entity during the deployment of a self-learning CL.

multiple angles: first, from human experience related to the interactions with the network; second, from a business perspective related to the implementation of services (in case of CSP deployment) or vertical business/technical outcomes (in case of industrial private networks).

From a human experience perspective, intent-based network management automation brings simplified operation, as shown by the diagram in

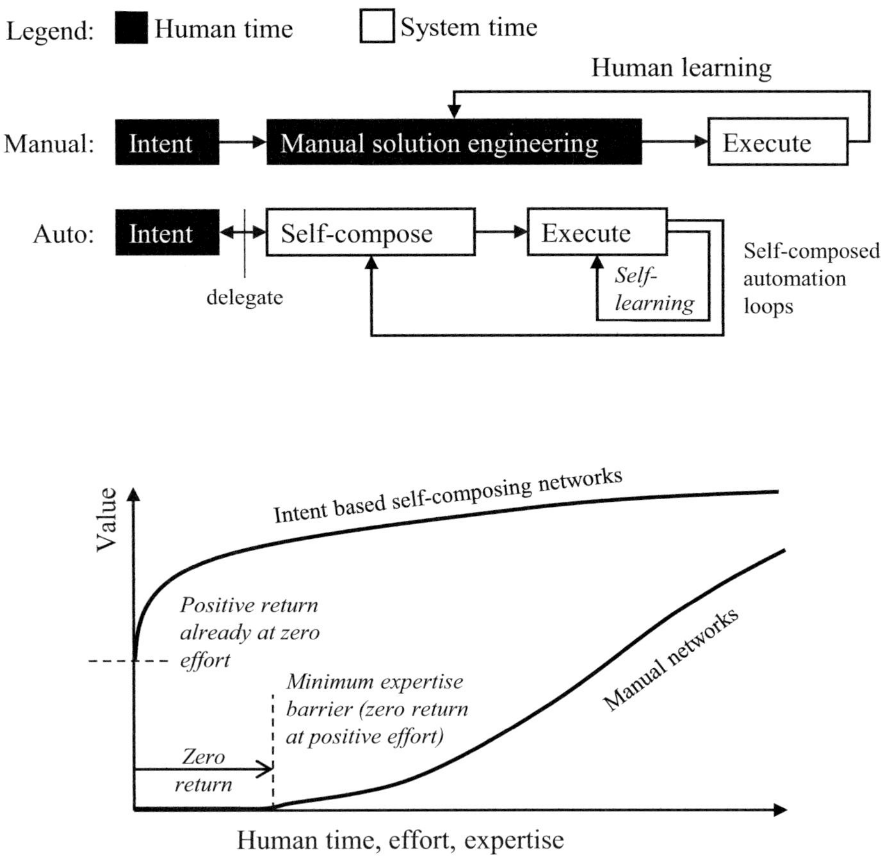

Figure 7.8 The benefits of intent-based network management.

Figure 7.8. Tasks that involve substantial manual effort and consume human time in the traditional open-loop management paradigm are automated via closed loops. Instead of the human operator having to create a detailed execution plan (configurations, scripts, tooling) for the network, it is sufficient to formulate an intent, and the planning of the execution is taken over by the IME. This creates more value per human time/effort investment as less time is spent with repetitive error-prone manual configuration tasks and more time is left for formulating the right intents, which is a more creative process. It also lowers the entry barrier for new staff to start engineering work with networks, which has special relevance for enterprise networks where the level of network expertise may not be in-house. The intent-based management also improves the operator experience by personalizing its interfaces to the role, expertise, and authority of the intent owner, as will be detailed in Chapters 8 and 9.

From a business perspective, intent-based network management automation improves operation efficiency and agility by continuously and dynamically adapting the network operation and behavior to the dynamic context, network state, and available resources to keep the intents fulfilled, by autonomous contextual decisions and actions leveraging deep network data with AI, rather than relying on configuration defaults or pre-sets that may provide suboptimal operation in specific cases. Automation prevents some of the human errors too that would occur from manual (mis-)configurations, typos, or wrong calculations, which translates to less operational failures.

Intent-based management automation simplifies the definition of complex optimization targets by defining different types of targets one intent at a time, yielding multiple related intents to the network that need to be fulfilled simultaneously. For example, by specifying an SLA-type of intent that defines service level attributes, and an additional management intent about resource or energy efficiency that is to be jointly interpreted and achieved with the SLA intent, the network will be required to deploy closed-loops that keep both targets optimized. In a manually managed network, solving joint optimization problems is very complex, and (due to the time it takes to reach a solution) the process will result in a solution that is limited both in space and time, and it may already be deprecated as the network states may have changed while creating and deploying the solution.

7.5 Summary

This chapter presented closed-loop automation in the context of network autonomy, showing how closed loops are inevitable to a high level of autonomy where network management and operation no longer rely on extensive and often error-prone human intervention. The naturally emerging relation between closed loops and intents was also highlighted, positioning intents as an intuitive means of governing closed loops.

Automation via closed loops does not necessarily mean high flexibility and adaptability to new operational contexts and network conditions. However, self-learning closed loops, discussed extensively in this chapter, are closed loops incorporating mechanisms (usually with AI/ML) that optimize their own operation based on the experience of their impact on the system. Self-learning closed loops are therefore capable of improving themselves on the field without having to manually upgrade their control logic in an open loop manual engineering process. Self-learning capability requires that the closed loops have the means to quantify and measure their impact and efficiency on the system to derive learning feedback from their operational environment. This chapter provided a generic means for the definition and assessment of a closed loop's impact and efficiency, which is applicable to a wide range of closed-loop objectives.

The Section concluded with a summary of the benefits of intent-based closed-loop management automation. Closed loops not only improve the efficiency of the system through automation but also enable to optimize the return of investment on human time, allowing to lower the minimum level of required network technological skills and thus the barrier of generating value through interaction with the network.

Bibliography

[1] TM Forum, "Autonomous Network Levels Evaluation Methodology", IG1252, Version 1.2.0, June 2023
[2] 3GPP TR 28.867 Study on closed control loop management
[3] ETSI GS ZSM 009-1, "Zero-touch network and Service Management (ZSM); Closed-Loop Automation; Part 1: Enablers", V1.1.1 (2021-06)
[4] ETSI GR ZSM 009-3, "Zero-touch network and Service Management (ZSM); Closed-Loop Automation; Part 3: Advanced topics", V1.1.1 (2023-08)
[5] ETSI GS ZSM 016, "Zero-touch network and Service Management (ZSM); Intent-driven Closed Loops" V1.1.1 (2024-10)
[6] ETSI GR ZSM 011, "Zero-touch network and Service Management (ZSM); Intent-driven autonomous networks; Generic aspects" V1.1.1 (2023-02)
[7] TM Forum, "Intent in Autonomous Networks", IG1253, Version 1.3.0, August 2022
[8] J. Strassner, "Intent-based Policy Management", Available at https://datatracker.ietf.org/meeting/95/materials/slides-95-sdnrg-1

8

Human–Machine Interactions and Interfaces

Automation increases the complexity of the system by introducing technologies (most prominently but not exclusively AI) that come with their own technological, infrastructure, resource, and operational overhead. Well-designed human–machine interfaces conceal low-level technological complexity and provide intuitive bidirectional human-friendly interactions for the various roles present in a network operator or private network owner organization. The operator roles include different experts at communication service providers such as planners, business developers, technologists, deployment and operational staff. While service providers are in general knowledgeable about the telecommunication technology they operate, the complexity of an operational network has accumulated through merging generations of standards, domains (such as radio, fixed, and cloud), and technologies adopted from IT/OT and AI itself. Additionally, verticals and enterprises as owners of industrial and private networks have their core expertise in their own technology domains, looking at mobile networks to add value to their own business without creating additional integration and management overhead. Intent-based interfaces therefore should be capable of bridging semantics and objectives declared in the language, taxonomy, and vocabulary of the network operator (including industrial owner) and the operational capabilities of the network and its management system.

8.1 Introduction

Interacting with technology has always been and continues to be a human need for all, including end users, operators, integrators, and technology professionals. As technology evolves, the means, scope, and role of human–machine interaction (both in human-to-machine, H2M, and machine-to-human, M2H direction) needs to evolve as well. On the consumer or end-user side, high interface user experience including ease of use, quick and intuitive take-up

DOI: 10.1201/9788770041478-8

(ideally without consulting any user manual) and personalized responses are the norm. Interface and ownership experience (along with design and likeability) is a key differentiating factor among consumer products; excelling in usability may be even more important than excelling in some of the less obvious technical parameters. Therefore, product design spends considerable effort to keep user interactions as simple and intuitive as possible while adapting to the technical evolution of the products [7]. On the professional side of technology, such as in industries and particularly in operating and managing telecommunication networks, less emphasis has been put so far on trimming the exposed technical complexity. Since technology is generally considered to be run by experts anyway, who are working in diverse teams with a range of specializations and expertise, it may seem less critical to spend effort on making lean and simple interfaces that should best fit a professional consumer. However, interaction with technology at scale from the operational side also becomes complex, therefore, also costly and slow, especially with telco networks that consist of a heterogeneous set of technologies such as multiple generations of multivendor telco HW and SW, ranging from physical on-site installations to nation-wide data centers.

As networks and their management are digitalized, softwarized, and virtualized, current H2M/M2H interactions between the operator personnel and the network and its management flow through digital interfaces exposed by the various tools and functions that implement networking and management capabilities. With the traditional means of network management (i.e., mostly via manual or manually scripted operations and workflows), H2M/M2H interactions are confined to the UIs, SDKs, and graphical or command line interfaces provided by the vendors of the management tools. These implement interaction models that are specific to the tool or product, and they require a learning curve from their users (e.g., from operator personnel) before they can be mastered to make the network deliver the desired operational goals. New releases of the same or different tools also require continuous adaptation from the human operator, therefore, the complexity of operating networks and the associated human cost and effort are partly upheld by the continuous flux of changes on the technical interfaces that are supposed to be operated by humans. The more technical and specific an interface is, the higher the associated costs and the more human effort and expertise are needed to operate them.

8.2 Intent-based Human–Network Interactions

Intents have the potential to simplify the network operation due to the automation [1] as discussed in Section 7.4 along with the benefits of intent-based network management. The outcome-oriented intent interface exposes more abstract and less technical interaction patterns compared to traditional tooling, and as such improves the operator experience. However, rather than becoming yet another technology-oriented interface that its users have to learn, the design of the intent interface should first consider the patterns, workflows, and roles associated with network management as it is done by an operator and be supportive of those patterns rather than enforcing the operator to adapt to a specific implementation of interaction with intents.

Network operation, at least on the CSP scale, is a distributed teamwork across diverse groups of experts with different responsibilities, organizational roles, and work shifts. There is not a single engineer who is responsible for the entire RAN including all the CM/PM/FM of every single radio head and baseband unit in all radio layers and technology generations that are deployed. There is not a single person who defines all the business goals, data plans, and cost models associated with mobile subscriptions. Also, there is not a single person who solves all the performance degradations or anomalies that pop up during operation. All of the practical operative tasks that emerge in an operational network are distributed among different people who may not even know each other personally. Therefore, a key design principle of the intent interface is to support the collaborative management of the network and its services in a way that incorporates and harmonizes diverse outcomes dictated by considerations from business, operation, technology, efficiency, and service quality perspectives. Combining this starting point with what intent-based network management can deliver enables to derive a list of requirements toward intent-driven H2M/M2H interfaces and interactions. A summary of the requirements is given in Figure 8.1.

The most obvious requirements reflect the diversity of experts in different roles at a CSP. That is, the intent interface should allow the expression of high-level declarative goals matching the role and expertise of the various experts, who may represent different organizational roles such as planning, BSS, OSS, technical expert for troubleshooting, etc. Technically, this requires that each expert is entitled to use their own terms (such as technical domain language, taxonomy, KPIs, and goal definitions) to express intents so that they can remain within their comfortable domain abstractions. However, defining an intent is not the starting point in an intent-based network management workflow, as it requires that the intent owner already knows (at least roughly) what kind of intent and for what goal it is to be defined for the network. Defining intent assumes that the intent owner already possesses insight into the network, which should be the kind of insight that is required to support the intent owner in its specific role and expertise. Therefore, an intent-based network should provide role-specific insights to support the expert in

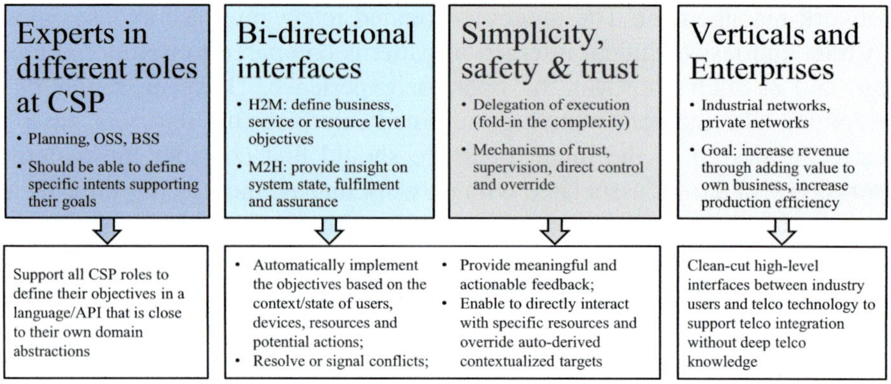

Figure 8.1 Summary of requirements for intent-driven H2M/M2H interfaces.

defining, monitoring, and managing the specific intents. Likewise, when it comes to defining an intent, the network should highlight that part of its own capabilities (cf. semantic models in Figure 6.6) that match the role of the expert (BSS, OSS, etc.) rather than exposing a flat list of all capabilities ranging from low-level device configurability to high-level abstract end-to-end service management goals. Regarding intents that are already defined by the intent owner and handled by the network, the network management should report insight related to the fulfillment/assurance (e.g., failures, conflicts, costs, efficiency, and impact) of the intents and also about the relevant network services, domains and resources. In the case of multiple operator tenants, the intent interface should enforce multiuser concepts such as full privacy of intents, immutability (real-only) access of selected intents, and if exist, priorities and hierarchies among intents defined by different tenants.

Another set of requirements for the intent interface can be associated with bidirectionality, safety, and trust. During intent ingestion, the intent handler performs syntactical and semantical validation of the intent owner's input (cf. Figure 6.5). This is already a dialogue where potentially many cycles or interactions are executed between the two endpoints before the intent is concluded. In the next steps of the intent lifecycle, such as intent validation, conflict detection, and intent assurance, the intent interface should provide capabilities for conflict reporting and interacting with the user to collect its feedback for conflict resolution (such as requesting user input to refine or prioritize selected intents). Finally, the interface should support safety and trust mechanisms, such as methods of cross-validation of the autonomous actions performed by the network management in the context of a given intent; arbitration between manually versus automatically controlled management interfaces; and coexistence of manually and automatically controlled domains.

A third set of requirements is related to private networks that are not operated by CSPs with the primary goal of selling telecommunication services but as part of a bigger technical solution owned by verticals and enterprises with a nontelco (e.g., production or manufacturing) purpose. In such a setup, the intent-based management of networks has an extended role as it needs to bridge the semantic gap between nontelco objectives and telco services, discussed in the context of Figure 6.1 (the application layer) and Figure 6.2 (vertical intents). This requires domain adaptation on the intent interface not only to different flavors of the telco domain (as with diverse CSP roles) but to adjacent domains that do not even use terms directly associated with telco. As part of this domain adaptation and beyond, also during the intent fulfillment lifecycle phase, there is a considerable challenge on the network management side to adapt to the complexity of the heterogeneous vertical use cases, business objectives, and service requirements, which are different from CSP services. The intent interface and the intent handler are expected to provide integration points between vertical business intents (defined by vertical experts) and network management intents (defined by OSS experts), with automated translation from vertical intents to telco services.

8.3 Network Application Embedding

Network application embedding is a mechanism that enables to enrich and extend the capabilities of the network's functions and management services using application programming practices. Network application embedding exposes the technologies and workflows involved in the autonomous composition of intent fulfillment closed loops to applications provided by various players of the telecommunication ecosystem. The central component of network application embedding is to take API discovery and machine-to-machine interactions from being manual design time blueprinting and deployment planning activities to become a flow of dynamic and automated runtime software composition.

The taxonomy of the most prominent actors, APIs, and applications used throughout the description of application embedding is shown in Figure 8.2. The most traditional applications are the network functions and the management services, provided by the vendors. These systems provide vendor APIs, which are partly standardized (e.g., by 3GPP such as NEF [2]) and partly vendor-specific implementing differentiators and value-added capabilities. On top of the vendor APIs, or even independently from them, operators

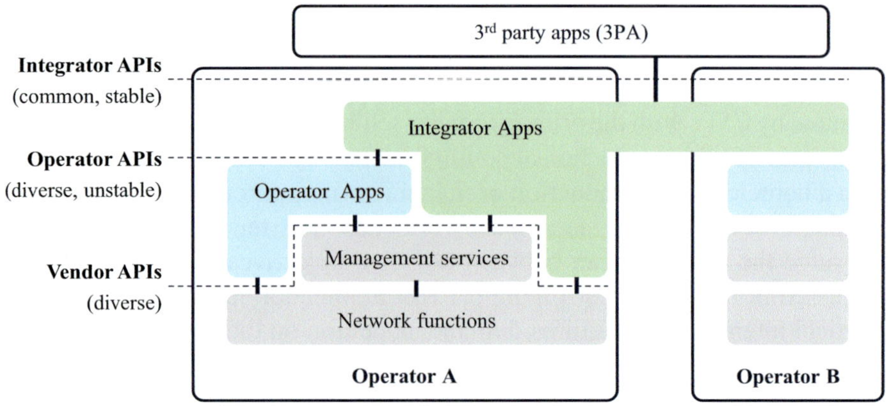

Figure 8.2 Taxonomy of applications.

(including enterprise private network owners) often implement their own internal tools, workflows, management and reporting services, security solutions, etc. These can be leveraged to provide subscriber-facing services (e.g., self-service and SIM swap protection) or internal services (insight, analytics, reporting, BI, planning, optimization, etc.). The resulting APIs, being nonstandard, operator-specific, and internally driven, are both diverse and unstable. Instability is not to imply a certain level of quality but to be subject to change without notice. Those APIs would be used by external applications (e.g., 3rd party ones) with the scope to leverage the network for their own purposes). Developing 3rd party applications over diverse and unstable operator APIs would therefore require integration. The integration may be handled by the 3rd party application itself, but that would put extra implementation and maintenance load independently on each application, which could be prohibitive due to the effort that would be required to maintain the integration itself. A better approach is to insert a separate integration layer that can be implemented as a set of applications unifying the diverse operator and vendor APIs into a set of common and stable APIs that 3rd parties can rely on. This is the role of integrators, who provide enablers by means of applications (implementing compatibility layers, missing functionalities, etc.) to ensure that a capability is available at multiple operators via the same API.

The operator and integrator applications together are regarded as network applications (NwApp) as these apps are developed and deployed on top of existing network functions and management services, with the scope to extend and customize a network's intrinsic capabilities (including standard and vendor products). The scope of network application embedding, illustrated in Figure 8.3, is to enable NwApps to discover and utilize vendor

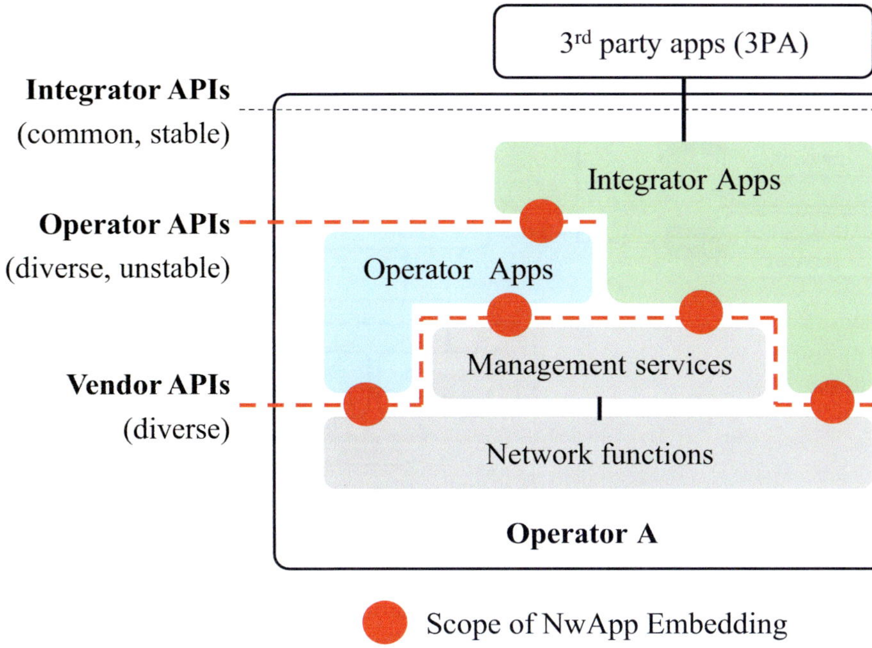

Figure 8.3 Definition and scope of network application embedding.

APIs (and for integrator apps, also operator APIs) using semantic APIs and semantic composition.

The general NwApp embedding functional architecture is shown in Figure 8.4. A key technology enabler of NwApp embedding is semantic modeling and semantic composition. Semantic modeling captures the capabilities of existing network functionality and management services in a machine-readable and computable manner. A semantic model enables to softwarize the manipulation and comparison of semantic, allowing algorithmic selection of network APIs that match a capability required by an upstream application such as an operator app or integrator app. The computational services around semantic models are integrated into a Semantic GW module. The Semantic GW is fronted by the embedding GW, whose role is to mediate between applications (NwApps and traditional network functions and service), the semantic GW (to source the knowledge about which APIs exist, what they achieve and how to combine them to an operational closed loop or software system) and the orchestrator (to request the deployment of required but missing system components).

The animation of the functional NwApp embedding architecture is possible at multiple stages, yielding different levels of bonding between NwApps

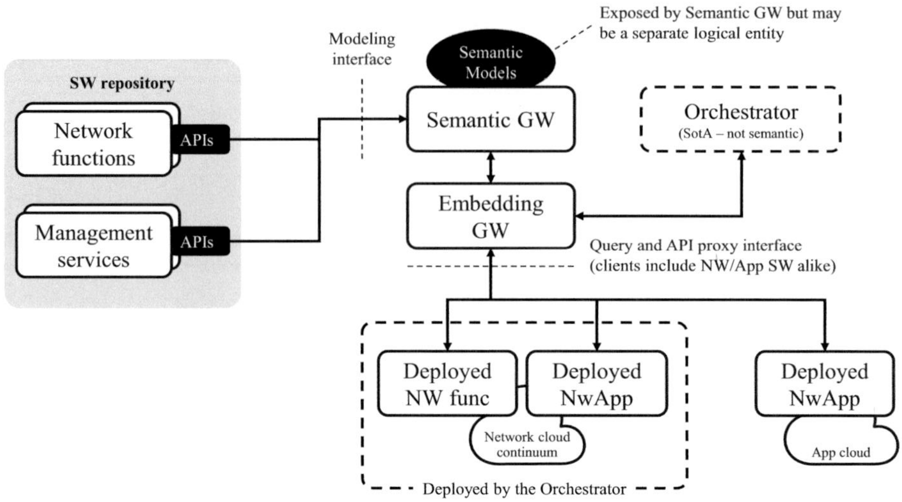

Figure 8.4 General network application embedding functional architecture.

and the network. Stage 1 implements a traditional exposure pattern, where the goal is to enable a NwApp to discover and utilize capabilities of the network (e.g., provided by its NFs, x/rApps, or by controllers, and management functions). The discovery is a semantic query process, where the NwApp declares its expectations for the network capability, rather than trying to invoke an API resource directly. The API resource is delivered by the network (through the interplay of the semantic GW and the embedding GW) as a result of an API resolution, where the best matching vendor API or operator API is identified for the NwApp's semantic description. After the NwApp accepting the result, the embedding GW may need to initiate the deployment (e.g., instantiation or scaling) of some of the network software modules that implement the requested APIs. Those modules that actually provide the resources and functionalities for implementing the vendor/operator APIs will be recorded to enable steering the NwApp's API calls toward the right serving modules. The embedding GW may remain a proxy between the NwApp and the actual network resources (as shown in Figure 8.5) or, in a trusted NwApp-network relationship, have direct access to them.

In slight variations to the main motif of NwApp embedding, the bonding between the NwApp and the network may become deeper. State 2, showcased in Figure 8.6, displays a scenario where a first NwApp, denoted as NwApp1's, has already been embedded into the network; additionally, NwApp1's own APIs have been semantically modeled and incorporated into the semantic models curated by the Semantic GW. Therefore, NwApp1 has

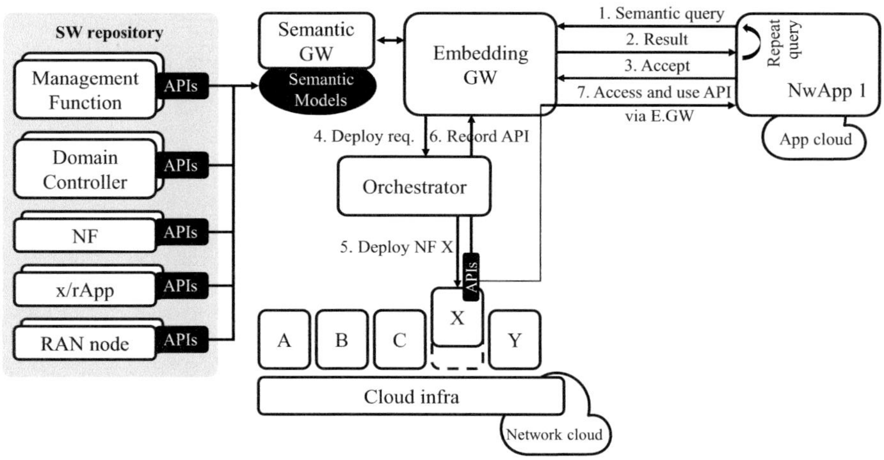

Figure 8.5 Stage 1 – access to vendor and operator APIs.

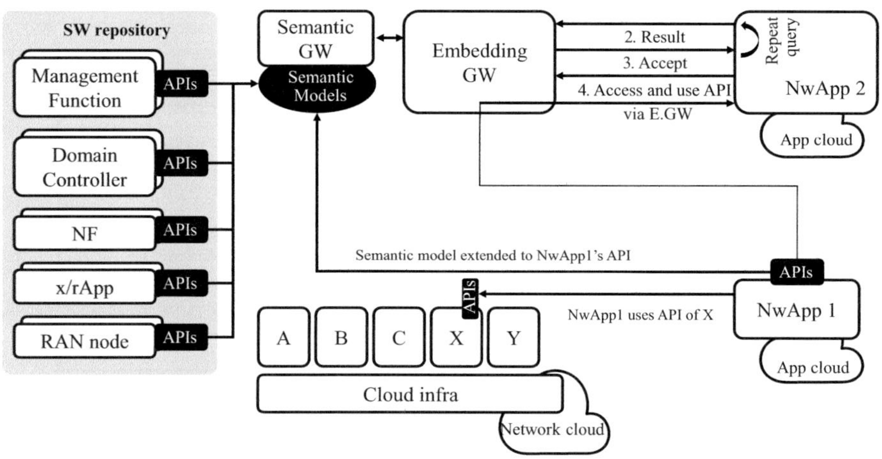

Figure 8.6 Stage 2 – access to other NwApp APIs.

become a logical part of the network's toolbox and its APIs have become discoverable to other NwApps, as it is shown in the figure for NwApp 2. Yet, the NwApp 1's host including the deployment and execution infrastructure remained separate from that of the network, maintaining independence both in terms of resources and lifecycle management. However, this is an important step that allows NwApps to become part of a service chain at intermediate locations and not only be the end consumer.

At Stage 3, illustrated in Figure 8.7, the deployment and lifecycle responsibilities (orchestration, hosting resources, execution) move into the

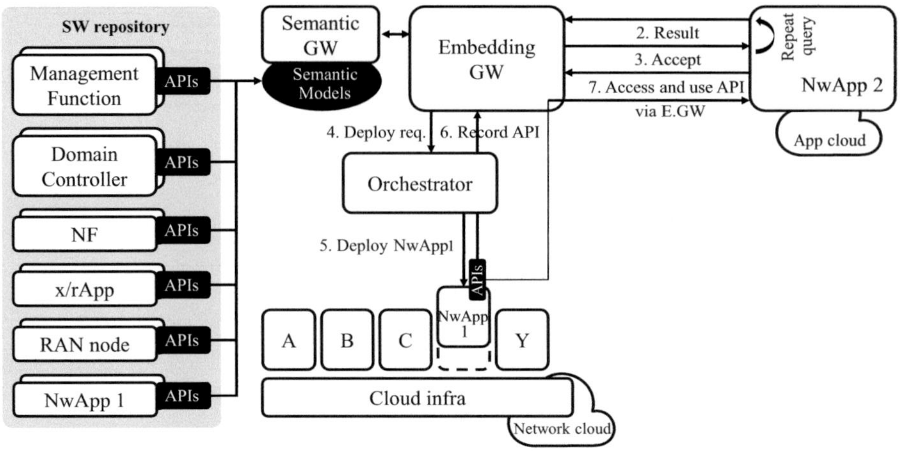

Figure 8.7 Stage 3 – orchestration of NwApps.

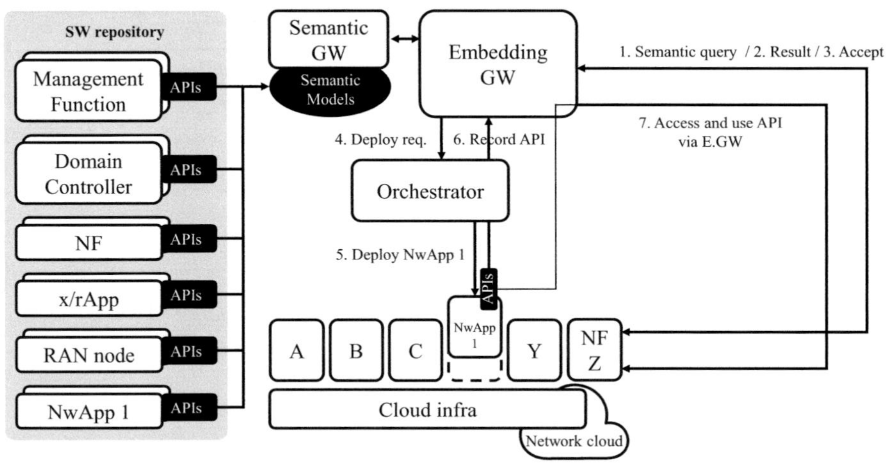

Figure 8.8 Stage 4 – NwApps used by the network functions and services.

infrastructure of the network. This makes the network's orchestrator capable of instantiating and scaling a NwApp, in the likes of managing a network function or service. This enables NwApp providers to focus on their business logic and not care about hosting and resources.

Finally, at Stage 4 (Figure 8.8), a further step is taken in deepening the NwApp embedding by not only incorporating a NwApp's API into the semantic models and offering it to other NwApps but also to use it by the network itself (e.g., by a management service). This move blends the boundaries between NwApps and what is traditionally vendor or operator-provided software module and creates a single infrastructure and ecosystem of collaborative applications.

The benefits of NwApp embedding for the NwApps (and their providers) start with the ability to provide improved, optimized, and potentially new functionalities through accessing deep network APIs that otherwise would be hard to leverage. The integration with the network (vendor and operator APIs) and other NwApps is made easier by semantic query, which liberates the use of rigid syntactical APIs in favor of declaring the expectations toward APIs and making the binding with the actual API at runtime. With the level of embedding shown in Stage 4, orchestration along with the network resources optimizes access to network APIs (including data) and resources.

The network benefits from application development practices, such as a fast development cycle, modularity, experimental functions, and implementation freedom, to extend its own functionality. At Stage 4, the network may optimize its own operation with NwApp awareness, using the information collected from the NwApp's APIs.

Integrators benefit through having a single system experience, that is, no network versus application fragmentation in terms of design, composition, management, and orchestration. They can easily access and offer the full potential of the combined network and NwApp capabilities, including all semantically feasible compositions of multiple networks and NwApp modules.

8.4 Machine–Machine Interactions

So far, the intent interfaces were discussed from an H2M/M2H perspective, considering interface requirements from a human intent owner's perspective. In networks with intent-based management automation, there are also many machine-to-machine interactions between software components. As the fulfillment of intents is intertwined with closed loops, one type of M2M interaction is between components of the CL. Also, there is interaction between different CLs as discussed by ZSM009-1 Section 8.2.2 [3], either in a hierarchical or peer (federated) relationship. Components of intent-based network management CLs also integrate in runtime with network and service management, domain or infrastructure controllers, device managers, databases, etc. to collect insight necessary to their internal operations and to execute actions that are needed to fulfill their objectives.

The M2M interactions may be technically based on a protocol stack, a procedure, or a service-based API. This is the usual means of realizing interaction over software-defined N-bound interfaces that were designed as APIs (e.g., a N-bound interface of an SDN controller). Such interfaces usually implement imperative configuration, command, or query interactions, which are suited to the traditional means of cascading ever-detailed information from upper layers, to be executed (with success or failure) at lower levels in the management hierarchy.

The M2M interactions could also be adopted to follow the intent-based paradigm. This requires implementing declarative, goal-oriented interfaces (preferably as consumable service APIs) by software modules. The interfaces should expose what the software module can achieve on its own, rather than how the module can be operated via external stimulus. The software modules should also declare their dependencies, that is, what needs to be provided as a prerequisite for the SW module (e.g., input data or expected behavior of other SW modules) so that it can operate. Dependencies should not be imperative (such as requiring that a certain version and identity of another software is present) but declarative too, defining what capability should be present in the module on which it depends. Any module that has the required capability should be a suitable dependency for the requesting SW module in a specific deployment.

Moving M2M interfaces toward implementing declarative intent-based interactions is enabled by the semantic models that were introduced in Figure 6.6 and that will be further explained in Chapter 11. As semantic models can represent both capabilities and data in machine-readable form (e.g., to capture "what would happen if this API was called" or "what is the meaning of this data"), they are a natural platform for M2M interactions where the interacting SW modules are not hard-coded but selected automatically based on semantic compatibility (e.g., one module declares the semantic of what it can do, which is compatible with the semantic of a dependency declared by another SW module). Software modules with dynamically bound M2M interfaces may provide the backbone of Intent Instantiation and Maintenance CLs as depicted in ZSM011 Figure 5.2-2 is referred from [4] that are made-to-order [3] by the IME based on an intent received from the intent owner. Passing intents from one management function (MnS consumer) to another management function (MnS provider) is also part of the general intent-based network management architecture of 3GPP SA5 as shown in 3GPP TS 28.312 Figure 4.2.2-1 is referred from [6].

8.5 Coexistence of Automatic and Manual Control

Intent-based network management deploys various Intent Instantiation and Maintenance CLs [4] that are responsible for the lifecycle and assurance of the corresponding intent. According to the intent architecture (Section 6.4 and Figures 6.4 and 6.6), the CLs generate impact (e.g., perform a management action) by integrating with management or resource controller interfaces such as SDN controller, RAN domain controller, service orchestrator, and virtual infrastructure manager. In a real network deployment, not all existing controller interfaces will be controlled by a CL, for example, due to the lack of compatible CL implementations or due to the preference of the operator to keep certain domain controllers out of automation. Therefore, some controller interfaces may be controlled automatically, while others remain uncontrolled by intent-based management CLs. The latter ones must be manually controlled or configurated, otherwise part of the network under their scope will remain partly configured. However, the dynamic instantiation of CLs and their on-demand runtime binding with controllers makes it hard to keep track of which interfaces and controllers are subject to automated CL controls and which require still manual attention. First, even if a type of controller (e.g., RAN domain controller) is managed by a CL automation, its management scope may not be universal in the entire network (e.g., it may apply to a single cell, or a larger geo-area or within a vendor boundary, rather than the whole network). This is due to the scoping of intents, which may also require certain network behaviors to happen locally rather than globally. Second, the dynamic instantiation and adjustment of CL management, which happens automatically, means that the boundaries of automated control are not static and thus certain interfaces may get out of automated control or become subject to automated control dynamically. When a previously manually controlled interface gets under automated control, there may even be conflicts between the previously manually provisioned configuration and what the automation would provide. If the automation withdrew from an interface, it would require manual provisioning, otherwise, the latest automated configuration would prevail past its validity. Such cases would introduce inconsistent end-to-end network configuration and performance.

Section 7.3 introduced self-learning CLs with objective, input domain, and scope. Two CLs have been discussed: measurement CL and automation logic CL, which are implemented as micro-services. The CLs (micro-services) are automatically chained together to form an automation service, based on compatible CL interfaces and unified converged measurements. The automation logic CLs operate existing controller interfaces that are not in between components of the CL components but are provided the network and service management layer (cf. Figure 6.4). The coexistence of manual and automated control of those controller interfaces needs to be solved.

[5] introduced the concept of intent manager (IM) and a hierarchy of IMs to automate the fulfillment and assurance of intents. Intents are received by the IM at the top, cascade to IMs at the bottom (while being specialized and contextualized), and get fulfilled by operating the N-bound interface of existing domain controllers. The IM hierarchy is exactly a set of CLs that is constructed on-demand as a response to an intent, and the set of CLs collectively control a set of domain controllers. However, as each CL hierarchy is a product of automating the fulfillment of a specific intent [4], the extent of their control over the domain controller interfaces is partial (restricted to those interfaces that need to participate in the fulfillment of an intent). This also requires a mechanism that deals with existing control interfaces that do not become automatically controlled at all and with the consequences of interfaces getting in/out of automated control due to the dynamicity of automatically constructing CL hierarchies. As a practical illustration of such a mechanism, in the following, a potential example is discussed to detect control interfaces in a network that are left without automated control and thus require manual control or configuration.

A control interface may be an API of a specific network element or network function, an API of a domain or resource controller (RC), an API of a network management function or management service, or any other software-defined network interface. Automated control is exercised over a control interface if there is a closed loop that claims ownership over the control interface, that is, the CL provides configuration or triggers actions over the control interface. Control interfaces for which no CL exercises control must clearly be subject to manual control to avoid the use of system defaults or inconsistent/obsolete configurations.

In addition to the above control interfaces, the interfaces of the CLs themselves are also considered as potential subjects of automated control. According to ZSM009-1 Section 8.2.2 [3], CLs may have a hierarchical relationship, where a CL may be controlled by another CL. CLs without another controlling CL must also be subject to manual control. This approach ensures that adding automation to a system via CLs does not generate hidden uncontrolled interfaces. Ideally, the only interfaces that remain for manual control in a system are the high-level declarative intent-based interfaces, and all low-level domain controller interfaces become CL-controlled. If an interface (be it a low-level domain controller or that of a CL) does remain uncontrolled, however, the operator should be aware of it and may decide whether to onboard additional CLs that control of those interfaces automatically or the operator is willing and capable of undertaking those interfaces for manual control.

A process to identify control interfaces that require manual control due to the lack of automation is shown in Figure 8.9. The left side depicts an intent-based management architecture. The architecture is shown as a graph with nodes comprising closed loops (labeled by C with an identifier number) or resource controllers (labeled by R with an identifier number). The difference between closed loops and resource controllers is that CLs may control other CLs or resource controllers, whereas resource controllers cannot (as they are controlling NFs or other configurations outside of the scope of the intent-based system). The directed graph edges represent control relation, where control is exercised by the node at the arrow tail over the node at the arrowhead. The graph edges also represent the capability of the controlling node to use the interface of the controlled node to exercise automated control. The right side of Figure 8.9 provides the main steps to detect the interfaces not covered by the intent-based management CLs. The first step is to create a data structure called the control matrix, which encodes the existing control relationship between one or more first CLs and one or more other CLs and resource controllers. The relationship is represented by a tri-state control digit: it is 0 if the first CL cannot control the second CL or RC; it is 1 if the first CL could but does not control the second CL or RC; it is 2 if the CL can and does control the second CL or RC. The method proceeds to calculate the highest control digit in each matrix column, which represents the highest level of automated control exercised over the CL or RC represented by the matrix column. If the highest control digit is 0, it means that the CL or RC must be controlled manually as there is no CL capable of automated control. If the highest digit is 1, it means that the CL or RC may be controlled manually but there is also a capable CL that could be deployed to control it. It is the choice of the network operator whether to proceed with manual control or deploy a capable CL. If the highest digit is 2, the CL or RC is already controlled by a capable CL, and no manual action is needed.

The control matrix structure is further detailed in Figure 8.10. The values in the matrix elements correspond to the example graph of Figure 8.9. Interfaces are represented as APIs as NFs and management functions are software-defined entities. It is to be further noted that in case a CL or RC has multiple APIs that offer different control interfaces, these different APIs should be represented by separate matrix columns. That is, a matrix column should represent a CL or RC as-is only if the CL or RC has a single control API; otherwise, the CL or RC should be sliced into multiple matrix columns, each column representing one API of the CL or RC. This is to ensure that partial control over a CL or RC is properly represented, and the uncontrolled

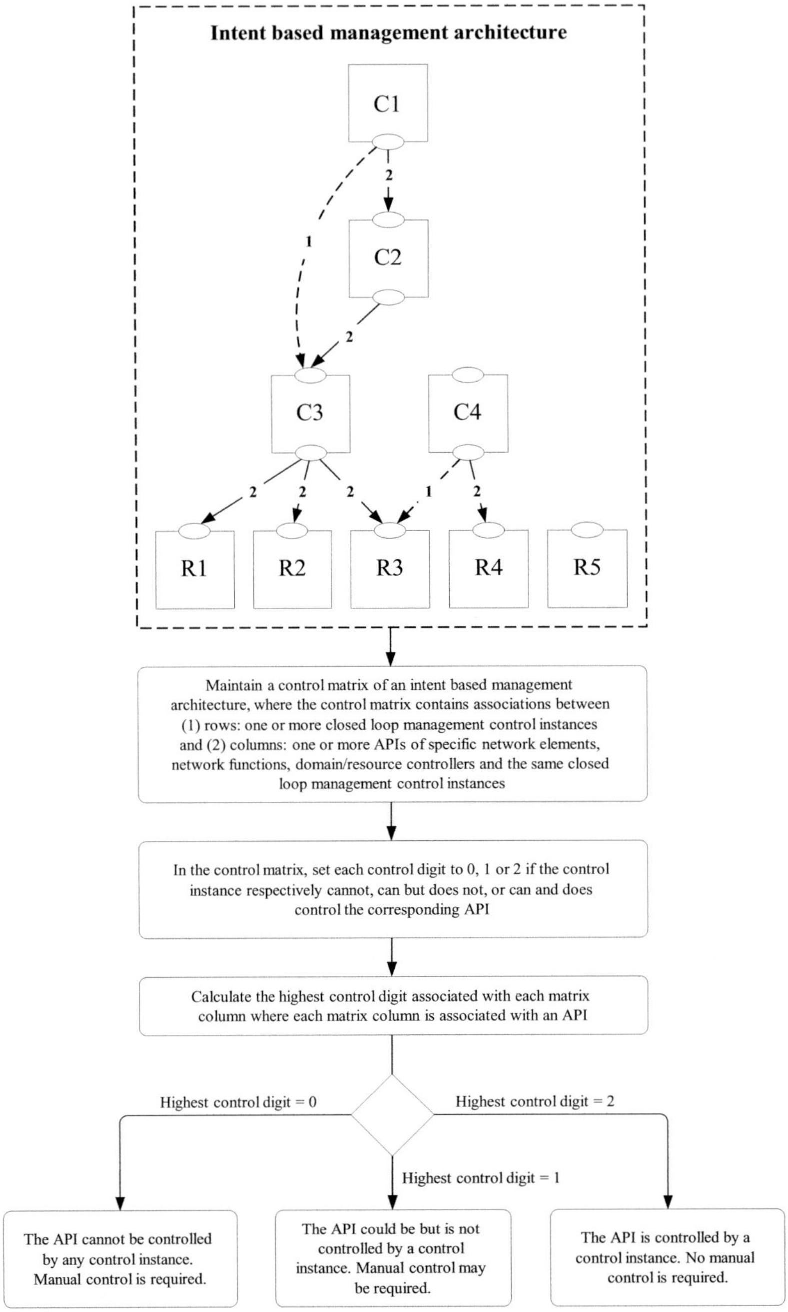

Figure 8.9 Process to identify control interfaces that require manual control.

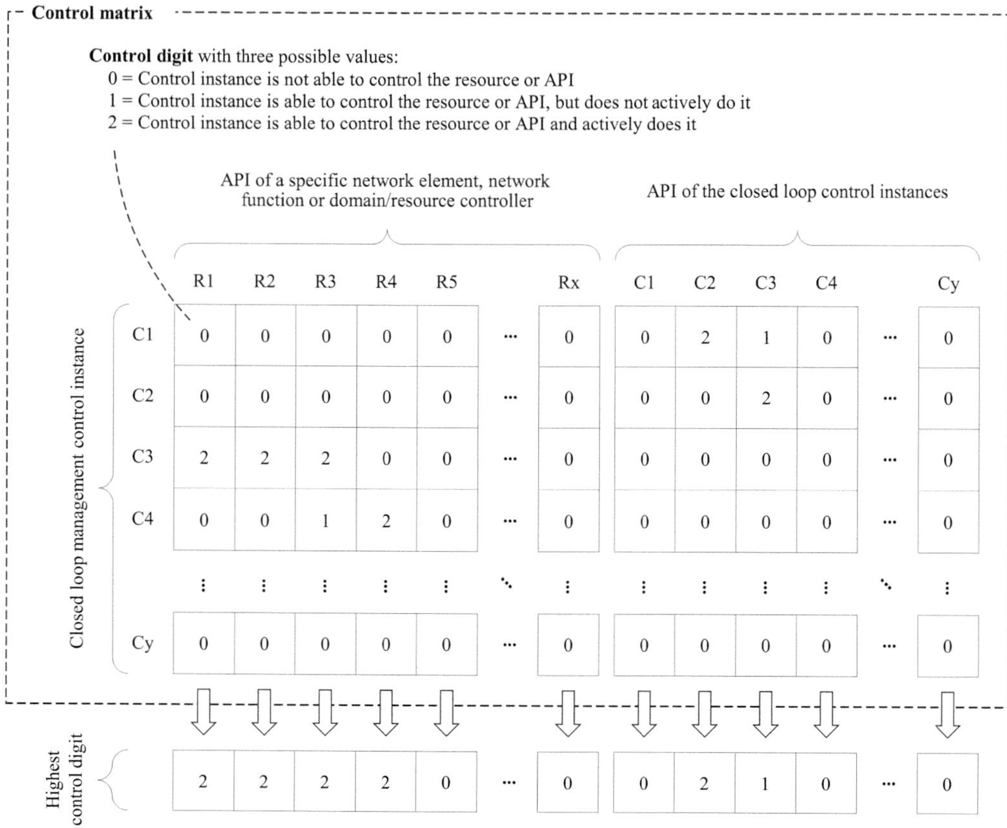

Figure 8.10 Control matrix data structure maintaining tristate control digit associations between any CL control instance and any controllable API, including the APIs of the CLs themselves.

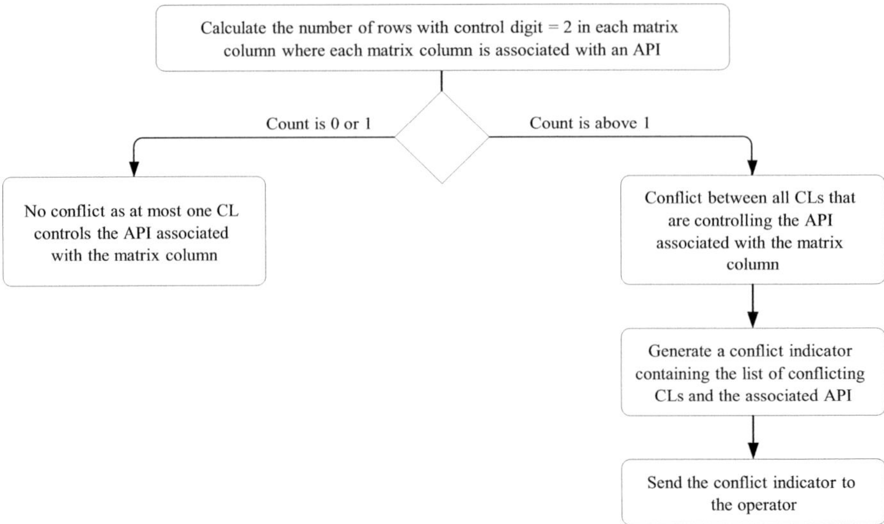

Figure 8.11 Detection of potential conflict between CLs that control the same API.

part of the CL or RC is indicated to the operator as potentially needing manual control.

The control matrix data structure enables a further method to detect potential conflicts due to multiple automatic controls deployed over the same interface. The corresponding steps are shown in Figure 8.11. The method is executed for each matrix column, where each matrix column represents an API of a CL or RC. Next, in a given matrix column, the method counts the number of rows in which the control digit equals 2, that is, the method counts the number of CLs exercising automatic control over the same API. If the count is at most 1, there is no conflict as the API is either controlled by a single CL or is subject to manual control. If the count is more than 1, all CLs that claim automatic control over the same API are potentially conflicting with each other. In this case, the method generates a conflict indicator that contains the list of CLs that are in conflict as well as the API over which the conflict occurred. Such conflict detection can be integrated into the static analysis phase of intent validation (cf. Figure 6.5) and the resulting conflict indicator is sent to the operator as feedback.

The control matrix may be a dynamically changing data structure: when a new CL is deployed in the network, a row is added to the control matrix representing the CL, and columns are added to the control matrix representing the APIs of the CL (Figure 8.12). Control digits associated with the row of the CL are set to 0 or 1 based on the capability of the CL to control the API

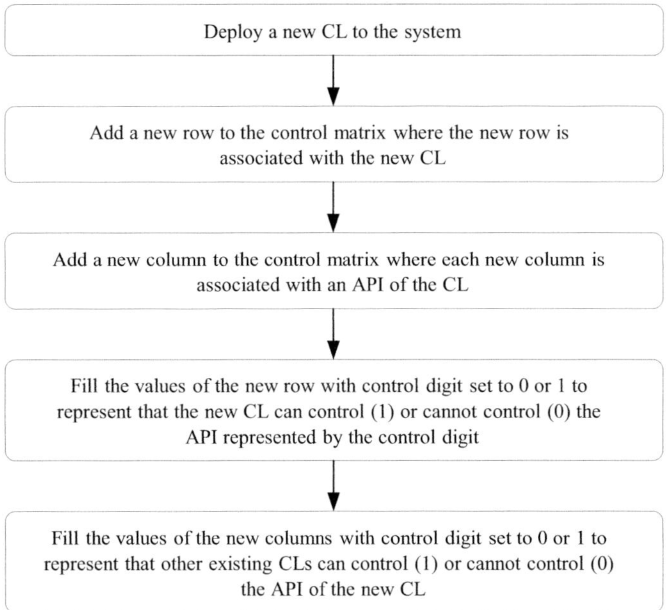

Figure 8.12 Maintain the control matrix upon deploying a new CL.

corresponding to the control digit's column. Likewise, control digits associated with the new columns of the CL's API are set to 0 or 1 based on the capability of other CLs to control the API of the new CL. When the CL starts to control an API, which is only possible if the control digit has been 1, the control digit is set to 2. When the CL stops controlling an API, the corresponding control digit is reset to 1.

When a CL starts to control an API, it means that the API's ownership transitions from manual control to automatic control. The CL should consider how the API was controlled manually up to the point of taking over the control and it should try to avoid sudden disruptive changes. Even if the CL would exercise a largely different control over the API, it should transition toward the automatically computed goal gradually, if possible. When a CL stops controlling an API, it means that the API should return to manual control. This may be due to a change in the CL's scope (triggered by the CL itself), or due to the operator's explicit request (triggered by the operator) to take over the control to manually handle an exceptional or temporary case for which existing automation logic lacks the required insight. In those cases, the operator should consider the latest control actions or configuration that the CL has administered over the interface so that disruptive changes are avoided. If a return to manual control was not triggered by the operator, an alert should be sent to the operator to avoid the API remaining uncontrolled or continuing to run based on obsolete information.

8.6 Summary

Interfaces represent the surface of technology that is definitive both from usability and operational perspective. Human–machine interfaces provide not only the means to consume the services provided by the technology but also the means to govern, supervise, and direct the technology. Although the two types of usage (consumer vs. operational) may seem different in terms of their target audience, both have in fact been driven by the need for simplicity and efficiency. On the consumer side, interfaces are often at the forefront of development efforts to both maximize the appeal of products through aesthetics and design and to lower the effort of usage or consumption through ergonomics and simplicity.

While traditionally design aspects have not been a priority on the operational side leaving a lot of technical complexity and heterogeneity directly exposed to the operator, lately this has also been reconsidered due to economic reasons, resulting in the rise of the intent-based management paradigm that enables the leverage automation capabilities for improving the operator experience of large and complex networks.

This chapter has provided an overview of the key requirements and design principles with regard to the operator interfaces, emphasizing the need for interactions to adapt to the role, scope, knowledge, and authority of the operational staff to maximize the efficiency of human time spent with managing the system. The role-based approach requires that interfaces not only take input but also provide responses and reports on the level of abstraction that is comprehensible and actionable for the interacting person. Applying this principle to private network owners who traditionally do not have telecommunication domain knowledge enables networks to become consumable by OT experts and become integrated into end-to-end industrial solutions with less effort than what is required through the layer of deeply technology-specific APIs. The approach was shown to naturally develop into the concept of network application embedding, where core network functions and over-the-top applications may consume and provide services to each other regardless of their origin. The interactions between the various software components could also be adopted to follow the intent-based paradigm, by declaring capabilities that are either provided or required by a module, rather than integrating through low-level APIs and dedicated glue code.

Bibliography

[1] TM Forum, "Intent in Autonomous Networks", IG1253, Version 1.3.0, August 2022
[2] 3GPP TS 29.522 5G System; Network Data Analytics signalling flows; Stage 3
[3] ETSI GS ZSM 009-1, "Zero-touch network and Service Management (ZSM); Closed-Loop Automation; Part 1: Enablers", V1.1.1 (2021-06)
[4] ETSI GR ZSM 011, "Zero-touch network and Service Management (ZSM); Intent-driven autonomous networks; Generic aspects" V1.1.1 (2023-02)
[5] P. Szilágyi, "I2BN: Intelligent Intent Based Networks", Journal of ICT Standardization, Vol. 9 2, 159–200. River Publishers
[6] 3GPP TS 28.312 Management and orchestration; Intent driven management services for mobile networks
[7] Shelley, C. (2015). The nature of simplicity in Apple design. *The Design Journal*, *18*(3), 439–456. https://doi.org/10.1080/14606925.2015.1059609

9

Intent Interface Evolution and the Role of Language Models

Intent interface has the role to bridge the communication between human actors providing intents (such as operators and private network owners) and the network management that handles the fulfillment of intents. While there is consensus within the industry that intents in general mean to declare objectives on network, service or system level without providing instructions to be executed to achieve the goals, the design of an interface to transfer intents from humans to the network is far from being standardized. In fact, there is a lot of room open for innovation and original mechanisms. Considering the fast-paced evolution of AI to model traces of human cognition such as semantic and reasoning, and especially natural language as a form of their expression, human–machine interfaces experience a rapid uptake of natural language processing and generative language models. It is expected that this evolution also penetrates intent interfaces for autonomous networks. Creating AI models that enable the expression of intents in natural language that is directly comprehensible by humans requires not only the modeling of the vocabulary, taxonomy, and special formulas internal to the networking technology, but also to connect and relate the general concepts of networking (such as the ones defined in open standards) to the implemented capabilities of a specific network deployment.

9.1 Introduction

The evolution of intent interface is driven from two directions. First, there is the human need to be able to use technology intuitively, via interactions that are human-native (such as language, speech, and gestures) rather than machine-native (such as data structures, procedures, and APIs). This driver is most prominent on the consumer device and product market, enabled by the

DOI: 10.1201/9788770041478-9

Digitalization of everyday interactions driven by consumer and human needs

Metaverse

Digitalization of technologies and their management driven by business needs

Enterprise and network automation

Figure 9.1 Interaction with technology: digitalization, automation, and consumability.

digitalization of everyday interactions, and it was discussed in Section 8.1. However, as engineering and operating new technologies becomes increasingly complex, this human need is also present among telecommunications and industry professionals. Second, in the network and enterprise industries there is a need for increasing cost and resource efficiency through system and process automation. In general, higher system autonomy means that the system can be operated at a more abstract level, that is, the system can reach the same outcome with less amount of information or less detailed commands provided by the system's operator. Consequently, in network management automation, the communication between the operator and the network management should reflect this shift through using higher abstractions, which is a driver toward increasingly declarative and intent-based interfaces. The duality of the interface evolution drivers (consumer and enterprise) is illustrated in Figure 9.1.

What emerges at the intersection of the two interface evolution drivers is the need for an interface that is both human-native and intent-based. As a network management interface, it boils down to a network whose autonomy is governed by intents expressed in a format that is inherent to how humans naturally interact: via natural language.

9.2 The Utility of Natural Language in the Intent Interface

Using natural language at the intent interface is already suggested by ZSM011 Section 4.2.4 [1], which argues that the full value of an intent is realized by merging three interface goals: using human language; supporting flexible intent parameter negotiation; and finding the right intent handler, that is, network management capability that can fulfill the intent. In this section, these three interface aspects will be further elaborated in the context of the intent architecture that was discussed earlier in this book.

The efficiency of using natural language between humans is inevitable, not only during everyday communications but also in professional task-oriented scenarios. Dividing a complex process into multiple dependent subgoals, delegating them to teams of experts, and solving them efficiently are all achieved via human-to-human interactions based on natural language. From verbal interactions through emails and messages to documentation, what makes human capable to collaborate is to express intents in natural language on the one hand, and to interpret and achieve them on the other hand.

Delegation through human language (e.g., between customers and service providers, or between team leaders and experts) rarely follows a one-way command-and-ack scheme. Often an initial intent communicated from a human intent owner to a human intent handler generates feedback, questions, and need for clarification at the handler's side, which requires response from the owner's side. This effectively turns delegation-related communication into dialogue, with clear roles between the participants (owner, handler) but with equal capacity at both sides to initiate communication related to the intents (new ones or those being already handled for a while). While the speed of human actions and communication is of course lower than those executed by machines, the pattern and semantic of the information flow can be very similar. If the intent owners are to remain humans, while the intent handlers are to become software-based network management entities and closed loops, this is the humanly natural communication pattern to which the handlers should align.

In an organization, a single expert (who may act as a human intent handler) is rarely a universal actor as the expertise and experience of a single person, however strong and long they are, cannot possibly cover all the knowledge that is needed to act according to any possible intent that otherwise could be very well realized by the collective knowledge present at the entire organization. Also, the availability, capacity, and scale of a human person are limited. Therefore, in the human world, handling intents (e.g., tasks) requires teams of different people to sample the range of expertise that is needed to handle much more types of intents than what any of the individuals could do, leveraging everyone's specialization to the extent it is needed intent per intent (Figure 9.2).

When it comes to the automation of intent handlers, it boils down to the digitalization of the human thought process while solving network

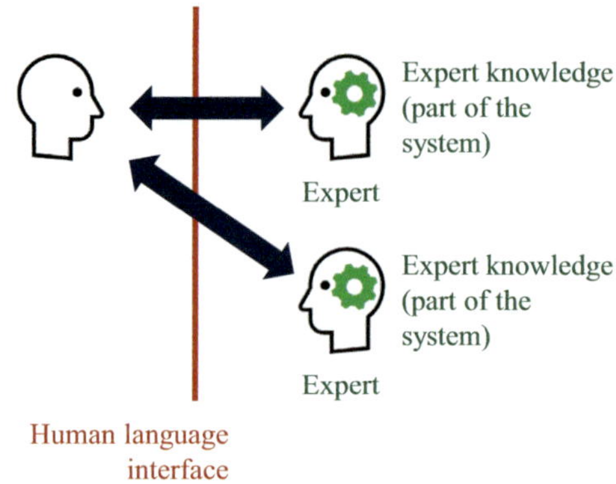

Figure 9.2 Expert knowledge and human-to-human expert interactions.

management tasks. Complex technological tasks such as network management ones involve different types of cognitive activities. Usually, the first thoughts to a problem (such as during troubleshooting) or open question (such as during planning) are generated by the most human specific capabilities: creativity and intuition, which result in ideas and intents with desired outcomes. The next step is to formulate an execution plan that, when completed, will yield the outcome (e.g., solving a degradation, or having a new management capability rolled out). The execution part is a deductive process producing the configurations, commands, and actions that, when executed, fulfill the intent.

When the solution of a technical task is done by a single expert – the creative and deductive processes are not shared between distinct individuals – the transition from intuitive creativity to deductive productivity may be subconscious and effortless, as one only needs to come to terms with their own "internal" concepts and taxonomy. When execution of a task requires interaction – e.g., when the result of the creative process needs to be transferred to someone who needs to execute the deductive task – the transition must be acted out, resulting in one of the aforementioned human language interactions (e.g., verbally, by messages or documentation, etc.). Still, the transition remains a human level interaction. The execution steps, however, normally need to be meticulously implemented into the network management system using computer-defined tools and interfaces, which are nonintuitive, error prone, and require a significant amount of time to articulate a plan in every last detail.

The scope of intent-based automation naturally aligns with the split at the creative and deductive parts. Intuition requires knowledge,

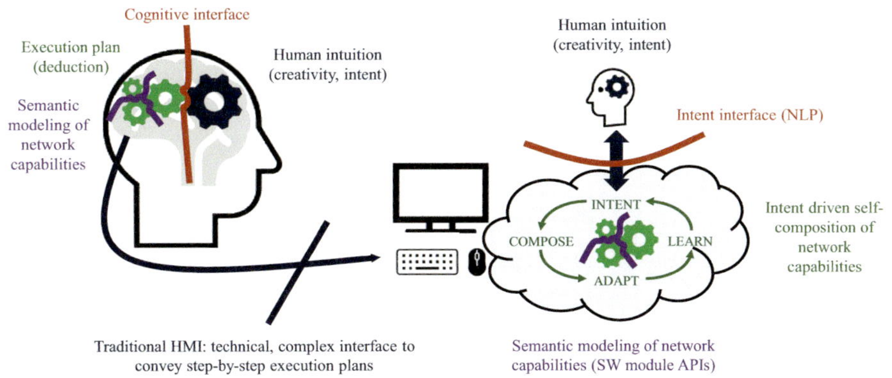

Figure 9.3 Delegation and automation of the methodological part of the human thought process.

experience, and real intelligence; therefore, it is hard to mimic or replace with machine learning. Also, this is at the level of defining network management strategy. Creating strategies is part of the governance of networks, which desirably remains under human responsibility and control. The deductive part, however, requires methodological steps that more resemble computer-friendly tasks such as searching, calculating, evaluating, comparing, and optimizing or more complex procedures/processes that can be decomposed to these tasks. Automating such processes is possible and can bring significant benefit and can be driven by the intents set by the creative person/mind. As the most natural interface between the creative and deductive parts is natural language, inherited from human-to-human communication, the most seamless human-network integration would be if the network would simply become a surrogate for the executor by becoming capable of interpreting and generating the same natural language interactions as if it was impersonating a network expert. The transition from manual creativity and productivity to manual creativity with productivity by network autonomy is illustrated in Figure 9.3.

Mimicking a natural language interface is not only a matter of a presentation layer. What enables a human expert to define the execution plan is that experts have built an actionable model of the network (or at least the part that belongs to their expertise), which they can virtually interrogate as part of their thinking process (Figure 9.4). Part of this network model includes semantic models of network capabilities, which an expert acquires through reading documentation, consulting other experts, and executing actions (such as performing configurations, writing and running scripts, using tools and APIs, etc.). Without semantic models that define what a network can do and

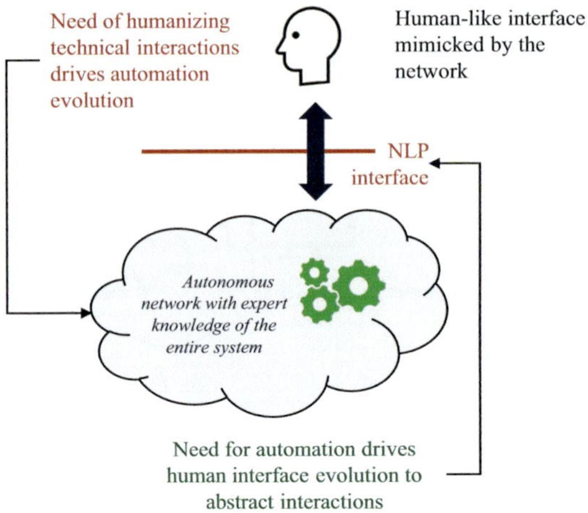

Figure 9.4 Emulation of the expert knowledge.

through which interfaces, no one would be able to define how a given outcome can be reached. It can also be observed that because some network functionalities (particularly in the network management domain) are vendor- and deployment-specific, an operator's knowledge is not automatically transferrable to another system due to local variations of the same high-level concepts or actions. The semantic models will be detailed in Chapter 11.

Most knowledge about the semantic of the network capabilities is obtained by reading or listening to information presented in natural language, as the information is produced by humans with the intention to be read by other humans. A good example is the collection of public 3GPP standards, which is available only as a set of English documents, therefore the official description of how cellular networks operate is only available to someone (or something) that understands the telecommunication jargon of the English language. Additional sources include internal documentations of tools and scripts that are developed in-house by an operator to automate custom workflows. If the execution plan of intents is to be automated, there needs to be a machinery that is able to obtain semantic models of the networks from the same sources as humans do today, which is by interpreting natural language documents. This technical driver naturally aligns with the human need for more intuitive interfaces, making a strong case for the idea of natural language-based intent interfaces [1]. Additionally, a network with natural language-based intent interfaces should also model the operational expert knowledge and implement learning capabilities so that natural language intents are not only interpreted (as in: obtain their semantic in a machine

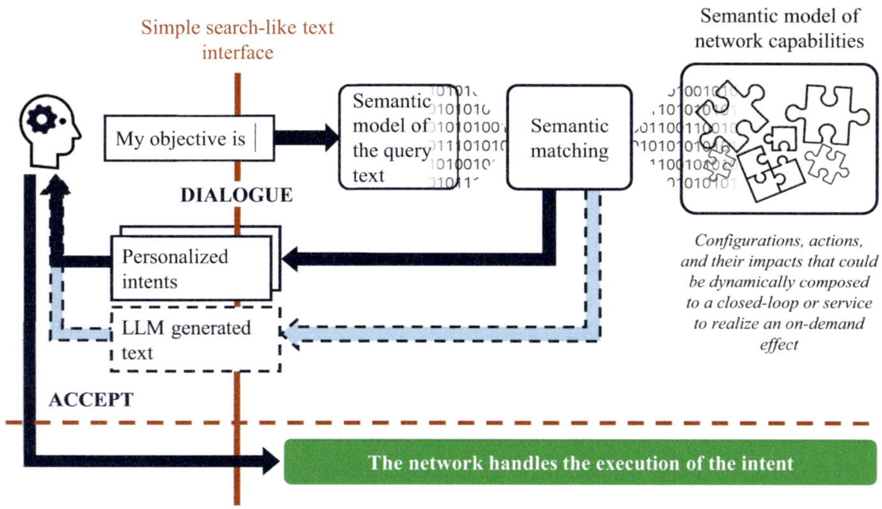

Figure 9.5 Intent definition: dialogue using natural language.

readable form) but also acted upon (as in: derive the right actions dynamically and based on the current network context so that intents become fulfilled). Such a network could be thought as an entity that merges the expert knowledge of all individual experts that would be available to consult in a human-to-human interaction case.

In a natural language-based interface, defining intent becomes a dialogue between a human and the network management (e.g., the IME as in [1], as shown in Figure 9.5). The operator enters natural language questions or requests (objective in general), and the network returns the corresponding network capabilities (i.e., what is it that the network can do that best matches the operator's need). The results are selected by comparing the semantics of the user's objective and the semantics of all network capabilities. The semantics of the user's objective is generated on-the-fly by applying a natural language model to the query text. The network capability semantics are continuously scraped by one of the intent-based network management closed loops (see Section 7.2 and Figure 7.2). The best semantic network capability matches are returned to the human operator as personalized intents that the network would be able to handle once the operator accepts them. The personalization of intents comes from the network's semantic matching strategy, which considers not only pure semantic models but also the user's role, previously accepted intents, etc. similar to how a web search engine profiles a particular user based on the results they most frequently follow.

The user experience of a natural language-based intent interface is indeed similar to that of well-known web search interfaces, where the search results are ranked by how much they match what the user was searching for. Just as web search engines would not create new web pages as a result of a query but they would try to serve up the ones which would be considered relevant by the user, intent handlers would not create new network capabilities based on intents received from the operation. However, intent handlers have an advantage over web search engines, which comes from their different roles. The intent handler can compose made-to-order [2] network capabilities by orchestrating closed loops of modular software entities (e.g., management services), such as a pipeline of data collection, analytics, decision, and action, with self-learning components included in the decision stage. Each component is configured to match the user's intent as much as its configurability allows, thereby providing a customized composite capability (hence the term made-to-order). Therefore, the selection and combination of the components provides the first level of adaptation by the network to the user's intent. This adaptation is an iterative process as it is part of the dialogue between the intent owner and the network management: the intent owner is likely to modify or refine their intent based on the insights gained from the network's best response (another similarity with web search user experience, where people often refine their search phrase based on the returned results).

Once the user accepts the network's offered capabilities to handle the intent through the selected components, the network takes over the intent's execution. When the components are put in operation (e.g., instantiated by an orchestrator), each component may implement a second level of contextualization and adaptation – such as including self-learning capabilities that change the component's behavior based on past experience, or by activating or deactivating parts of the implemented functionality selectively based on available data or available controller interfaces. With the two layers of adaptations, the high-level objectives (intents) become contextualized and implemented autonomously by the network as much as possible with the existing network capabilities (i.e., without having to develop additional functionalities).

A more detailed representation of the intent definition process is shown in Figure 9.6, which focuses on the iterative (dialogue) nature of the workflow and the user role-based adaptation of the interface. The figure also highlights the difference between objective and intent. An objective is primarily a human-understandable expression of the goals, formulated freely without considering the capabilities of the network. Intent is a human- and machine-understandable construct, which is aligned with the capabilities of the network and its management services. The indent definition process helps

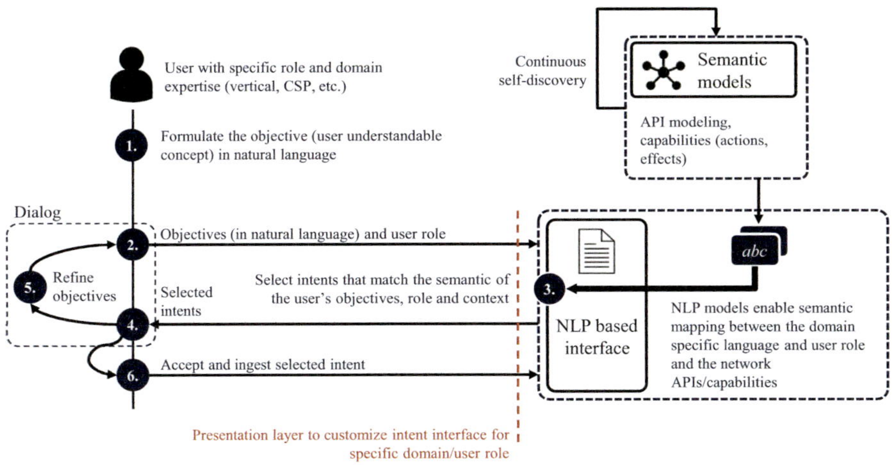

Figure 9.6 NLP-based intent definition process: from objectives to intents.

the user transition from objective to intent while remaining fully human-understandable (using natural language) at the interface. Adaptation to the user's role, profile, etc. is possible by tailoring the selected intents based on previous interactions with the same user – e.g., considering the user's historical selections in the same context. Previously defined intents (where the user and network have already aligned the objectives and the user accepted the resulting intent) can also be cached to serve as a template for resubmitting as-is or to be used as an inspiration for new but similar intents.

9.3 The Role of LLMs for the Intent Interface

The natural language intent interface can use language both to accept input from the users and to provide feedback, insights to the users in the same language. Producing natural language responses is a property of generative large language models (LLMs), which have billions of trainable parameters that are trained on an enormously huge corpus of text [3]. The models may be suitable for different use cases, such as predicting the continuation of a text that was given to the model as input, providing a summarization of a bigger chunk of input text, or answering questions about a piece of text [4]. In most of the existing LLMs, as illustrated by the above examples, the models are able to produce text output from text input. This capability can be leveraged directly on the intent interface when the network management exposes the semantic models of the network (i.e., the network capabilities that match a given intent), because the semantic models themselves are generated based on text descriptions of APIs and other documentation (see Section 9.2). For example, LLMs trained for question-answering could be used to answer questions posed in natural language about what the network can do in a particular context or to achieve a particular goal.

There are two technical challenges when it comes to the application of language models and generative LLMs for intent interfaces. First is the adaptation of the model to the domain, which is in general the telecommunication domain and in particular includes deployment- and implementation-specific capabilities that are present only in one network deployment. Second is the text-to-text nature of the models, which enables LLMs to automate engineering with text but lack the native capability to turn nontextual information (such as numerical measurements, network state, or events) into text.

Domain adaptation of a generative LLM may be achieved by fine-tuning. The models may be first trained on text with no particular domain of interest (which usually means a mixture of many different domains). At this stage, the model is already capable of producing text but may not be accurate when it encounters terms and phrases that were not a significant part of its training. Fine-tuning is performed as a second round of training the model on a smaller but domain-specific corpus. E.g., for the telecommunications domain, the corpus of all publicly available 3GPP documents (specifications, TDocs, email discussion, etc.) could be the basis for fine-tuning an LLM model. LLMs fine-tuned on the 3GPP corpus produce much more reasonable and accurate output when they are interrogated via queries, questions, and input text related to cellular networks, which inevitably contain 3GPP jargon.

The text-to-text nature of LLMs is both an advantage and disadvantage, depending on the use case. As explained above, the text input and output (I/O) of LLMs could be leveraged when network capabilities already represented as text are exposed, (e.g., summarize, generate description of). Some textual representation is always available from API descriptions and documentation. This attribute of LLMs become a challenge when the objective is to generate text about something that is not represented as text. For example, when the network gives feedback about the fulfillment status of intent, the task is to generate natural language description of what is happening in a network. The context and state of the network should be cross-examined with the objective of the intent, and it should be phrased in a humanly comprehensible text. Since network context (e.g., measurements) and states (e.g., clusters of network behavior) are not represented in text, additional layers of modeling are required to bridge between nontextual input and textual output.

Two non-text-to-text use cases are considered below, representing the evolution of the interface toward an LLM-based M2H interface: LLM synthesis and

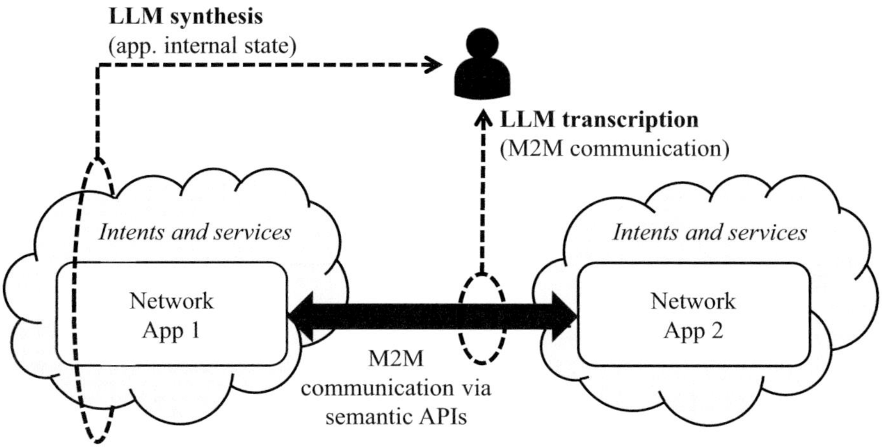

Figure 9.7 Intent interface evolution: from NLP-based intent H2M to LLM-based M2H.

LLM transcription, as shown in Figure 9.7. In both cases, the main requirement to produce a suitable LLM is to define the right type (and source) of training data on which a suitable model could be trained. Such models will be nonconventional LLMs in the sense that their input is not text, only their output is.

The scope of LLM synthesis is to produce auto-generated human-consumable insights into the internal state and output of software entities (e.g., xApps, xNFs, micro-services), network services, and intents. Such a model is applicable to answer queries such as what is happening in the network, function, or in a closed loop that was made-to-order for an intent (and therefore explaining what happens in the closed loop would tell what is happening in context of the corresponding intent). A model like this needs training data that binds numerical (or in general nontextual) representations of network states with textual information, so that the model learns how to describe (in text) events or states that are internally represented nontextually (e.g., as numerical time series or ad-hoc categorical events). A source of such training data may be a correlated collection of machine-generated syntactic tokens and corresponding human-language representations – e.g., quantified performance measurements and logs that are produced by the same software entity (e.g., a NF, xApp, or CL). A deeper source of information could be a trace of API calls that a software module performs and the text description of the API calls.

The scope of LLM transcription is to generate human-understandable representation of the M2M communication between software entities. This is an advanced use case with the purpose of making the network (especially its autonomous parts) more transparent to the human operator. Here the training data could be based on the information elements of the protocol and procedures (essentially also API calls) that take place between two software entities such as applications. In this regard, it is similar to the LLM synthesis use case when applied to traces. The resulting model would be capable of producing human-readable text about the semantic model of the interapp APIs.

9.4 Summary

Intent-based interfaces enable a simplification in the interactions between the operator and the network. Intents have been designed to shift human–machine interaction from the level of executive actions, commands, and configurations addressed to the system through a set of distributed technical interfaces to the level of declaring abstract goals for the entire system without enclosing an executive implementation plan.

Compared to traditional network management, intents bring a significant benefit in terms of decreasing the complexity and frequency of human–machine interactions. Complexity is reduced through outcome-driven abstract goal representation, whereas the frequency of interactions is also lowered due to the longer validity time of intents that are detached from the dynamics of their implementation. These characteristics resemble the way humans and teams efficiently collaborate in solving a task using compact and targeted communication to achieve efficient distribution, delegation, and reporting of work.

This chapter discussed a further evolutionary step closing the gap between machine and human interactions through the introduction of natural language in the intent interface. Enablers for such transition include classical NLP techniques and more recently LLMs that collectively provide the system with semantic modeling and generative text capabilities. However, the training or fine-tuning of language models should be representative of the domain of application, therefore these technologies and models should be carefully adopted (rather than simply reused) to be efficient for telecommunication use cases.

Bibliography

[1] ETSI GR ZSM 011, "Zero-touch network and Service Management (ZSM); Intent-driven autonomous networks; Generic aspects" V1.1.1 (2023-02)

[2] ETSI GS ZSM 009-1, "Zero-touch network and Service Management (ZSM); Closed-Loop Automation; Part 1: Enablers", V1.1.1 (2021-06)
[3] Yiheng Liu et al., "Understanding LLMs: A Comprehensive Overview from Training to Inference", arXiv:2401.02038 [cs.CL], 6th Jan 2024.
[4] Berivan Isik et at., "Scaling Laws for Downstream Task Performance of Large Language Models", arXiv:2402.04177 [cs.CL], 6th Feb 2024.

10

State Models

Network autonomy relies on machine-readable and actionable representation of the system's state across multiple domains and at many abstraction and aggregation levels (network function, technology domain, e2e network and service level, individual traffic flows, users, cells, service areas, system level, etc.). The modeling of states starts with the digitalization and quantification of high-dimensional, multimodal network data, mapping raw data points, counters, performance indicators, logs, and any other network and management data to machine-readable representations that enable correlation among time, space, network function, and user identities. Modeling techniques span from classic statistic through machine learning to complex AI models, resulting in pipelines that encompass the diversity of data sources and formats, such as numerical and textual information. Models should consider the dynamic and temporal behavior exhibited by the various network and user entities to enable prediction of future events in addition to detection and classification of impactful events. Unsupervised self-learning techniques are required to handle the abundance of unlabeled data, which contains a mixture of known and unknown patterns, as well as traces of both normal and abnormal events. The interpretation of state models is facilitated by special self-annotating mechanisms producing text descriptions in addition to technical model output.

10.1 Introduction

Network state is a quantified representation of selected aspects (e.g., performance, behavior, failures) of a network (or part of it, such as a slice or a service) at a given granularity [1]. Network state modeling is a process to create models that produce the network state based on network telemetry such as dynamic observations (e.g., measurements) and configuration data. Network

DOI: 10.1201/9788770041478-10

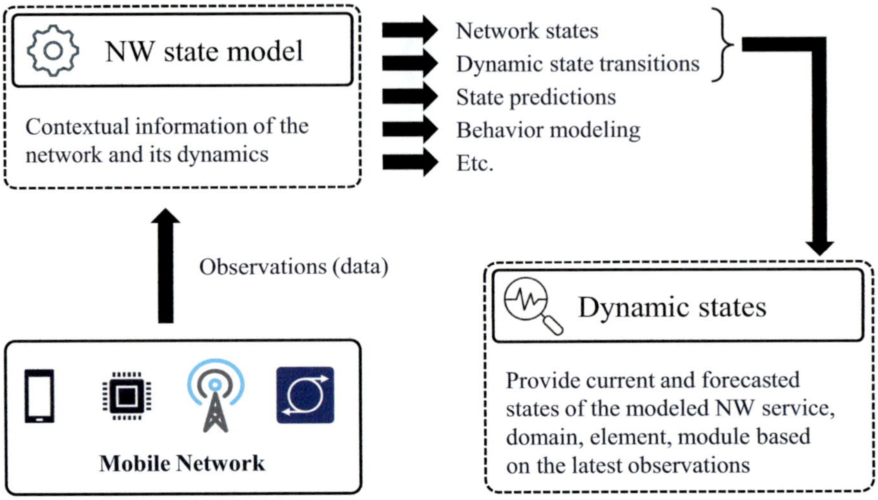

Figure 10.1 Network state modeling.

state models digitalize and quantify the characteristic of (part of) the network at a selected aggregation and abstraction level.

The state models capture correlations within the measured data that describe static (i.e., time-agnostic) or dynamic (i.e., time-based and therefore often context-based) characteristics of the modeled system entity (end-to-end, per domain, network segment, and network function) in order to capture its relevant observable patterns, which are the states of the entity. Beyond the quantification of the modeled entity's states themselves, state models may produce dynamic state transitions, state predictions, behavior, or any other downstream insight that is based on contextualizing the states themselves. Dynamic state transitions provide insight to the dynamics of the modeled entity, which enables capabilities such as detecting trends and providing early indications on which direction the entity's state is likely to evolve. State predictions provide the capability to directly forecast the next state or even multiple states ahead of the current one, including confidence in the predictions. Behavior models provide a capability to emulate how states would present or evolve given different hypothetical context and operational conditions of the modeled entity, such as under different configurations. The state models and their utility are illustrated in Figure 10.1.

Network state models are essential for management automation as they produce context awareness for the network. Network state models provide an automated mechanism to capture the current and expected states of the network and provide it as an input for the management automation mechanisms

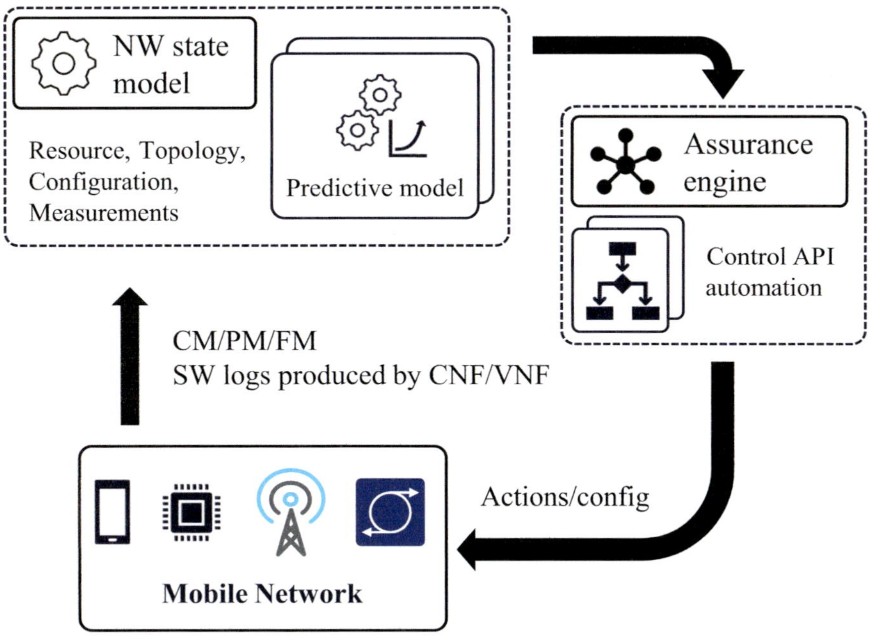

Figure 10.2 Network state models in a network and service management closed loop.

(Figure 10.2). The output of state models may be consumed by automated analytics, decision and execution control capabilities, providing a complete closed loop [2] as illustrated in Section 6.5, Figure 6.6 in general and in Figure 10.2 in particular.

The output of a network state model depends on the exact task for which the model was trained. A basic network state model may be trained simply to quantify the potentially large numerical space projected by all the collected measurements and counters, so that a momentary state of the network can be better represented (e.g., by automatically classifying all measurements into 100 different states or clusters instead of dealing with the potentially infinite measurement space). Additional layers of the state model may include transitions between the states to describe not only the momentary state of the network but also its trajectory in the state space – which, given the low (limited) number of states, is still manageable. Learning the transitions gives the state model prediction capability, when it is trained to predict the next state given a past sequence of states (such training can be performed as self-supervised training, based solely on historical data without human annotations, and is therefore very efficient in terms of human effort).

Incorporating context information and data from related sources (such as data from RAN and Core function instances serving the same end-to-end PDU sessions) provides the model with context-based prediction and behavior modeling capabilities, where the predicted next states are a complex, nonlinear (but learned – not preconfigured) function of the network's dynamics.

Context information that is useful for state models may include:

- Identity of the entity/domain/system to which the state applies
- The configuration of the entity/domain/system
- Time and location (both geographically and topologically) when/where the state applies
- Identity of other relevant entities (e.g., a RAN node and its CN counterparts) to enable state correlation

State models should capture the dynamic behavior of the system, including long-term seasonality and trends. Additionally, the models should be sensitive to the dynamics of the system, as that the order of traversing the states may carry additional information on top of the states themselves. For example, a state representing low traffic load at a radio cell may come naturally (and expectedly) after the load gradually decreased to the usual minimum point; however, the same state comes unexpectedly in the middle or rush hour surrounded by other states that represent high traffic. In order to make state models sensitive to such local contexts, the state transitions should also be modeled and learned from the same data that is used to model the states themselves.

A context-based, dynamic and predictive state model can be a building block in a set of capabilities and services that together implement a use case or intent, such as being an enabler of closed-loops with context-based decisions and actions. In such cases, state models are not "visible" as their output is consumed by another component in an automation stack.

10.2 Comprehension of State Models

The scope of a state model is defined by both the data on which it is trained and on the entity from which the data originates. The state models may be trained on network or management data, such as PM counters, alarms, logs, or any other data that is produced and collected in the system (see Chapter 3). For example, training a model on PM counters produced by 5G RAN nodes

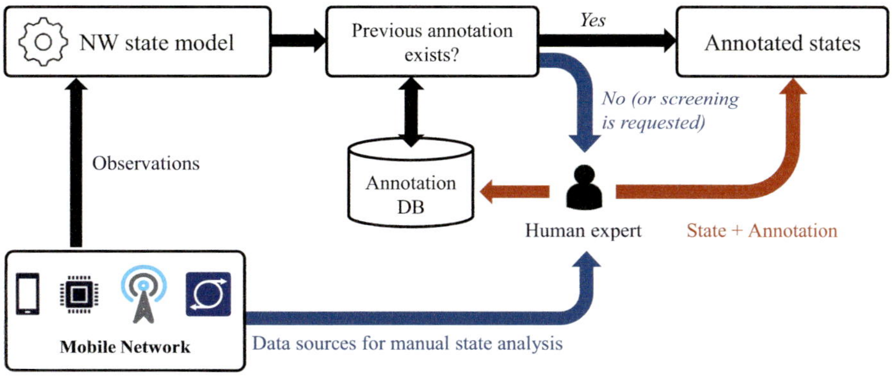

Figure 10.3 Manual or semimanual annotation of network states.

of a specific network deployment will yield a model that could be used to predict the performance of those nodes given their behavior in the past up to the current point in time (observed through the same measurements that were used for training the model). Depending on the scope of the data and models, it is possible to create network state models (capturing network level patterns, such as correlations within performance data of an entire network domain such as RAN), NF states (based on data from a single instance or type of NF), software state models (based on software trace events and logs), UE mobility models (based on the location data of terminals), etc.

Since most data produced and collected by mobile networks is not annotated or labeled, network state models must be trained using unsupervised methods. For this reason, such models must autonomously discover and quantify the characteristic patterns within their ingested data (that is representative of the entities producing the data).

Due to the use of unsupervised AI/ML training to create state models, the raw outcome produced by state models is an abstract state. In order to attach semantic to the states, additional annotation mechanisms need to be in place (Figure 10.3). Annotation may be manual, semimanual, fully automated, or a combination of these approaches. Manual annotation requires experts to look at the original data mapped to specific states, and/or correlate the states with additional information (available at separate management tools, reports, etc.). Although this is a cumbersome activity, applying it selectively at the early phase of developing state models helps build trust in the model's performance and accuracy. It may also help drill down to specific nontrivial but high-impact cases – e.g., when a state correlates with errors visible to subscribers. In semimanual annotation methods, hints are produced by the model (or an additional logic attached to the model's output) and the hints are used to speed up the manual annotation process. These hints may include automatically selected representative examples (e.g., specific network function instances and timestamped data points) where the operator should direct manual inspection efforts to maximize the efficiency of the invested human time. Other types of hints may include a few selected measurements that show high correlation with a network state (e.g., when a state model is built using time series data from several hundred different measurements, which is easily available from standard PM KPI data [3], pointing at 2–3 of those KPIs that are strong indicators can significantly help a field engineer bootstrap the manual investigation. Finally, fully automated annotation requires the state model to produce explainable and autonomously interpretable descriptions attached to states or their combination. The descriptive statements could even be in natural language, generated by data-to-text models as mentioned in Section 9.3. Additional ways to obtain human-readable state annotations will be provided in Section 10.4.3.

State models created from operational network data are inevitably most sensitive to the patterns present in their training data. As real network deployments evolve or seasonality causes new types of patterns to emerge, a previously trained state model may drift out of its applicable zone. To prevent such model deprecation, state models should evolve by adapting to new behavior that they encounter while being operational. The model may be updated through various mechanisms, such as regular retraining of the model (or parts of it), in-situ federated reinforcement leaning, or creating ensemble models specializing on different training data. In all cases, annotations that were already attached to states produced by previous versions of the models should be carried over to ensure annotation continuity during model evolution.

10.3 Network State Models for Anomaly Detection

Anomaly detection autonomously detects and indicates (network) states that are unexpected and, usually, undesired in an operational system (Figure 10.4). By nature, anomaly detection needs to discover relevant and previously unknown deep insights from the (network) data with no a-priori knowledge on either the data itself or the insights to be discovered. This requirement derives from the state-of-the-art in data production, collection, and curation in mobile networks. While data is abundant, it is not human-friendly (as opposed to, e.g., imagery data), creating a barrier even for engineers to have an understanding of how the system operates expressed in

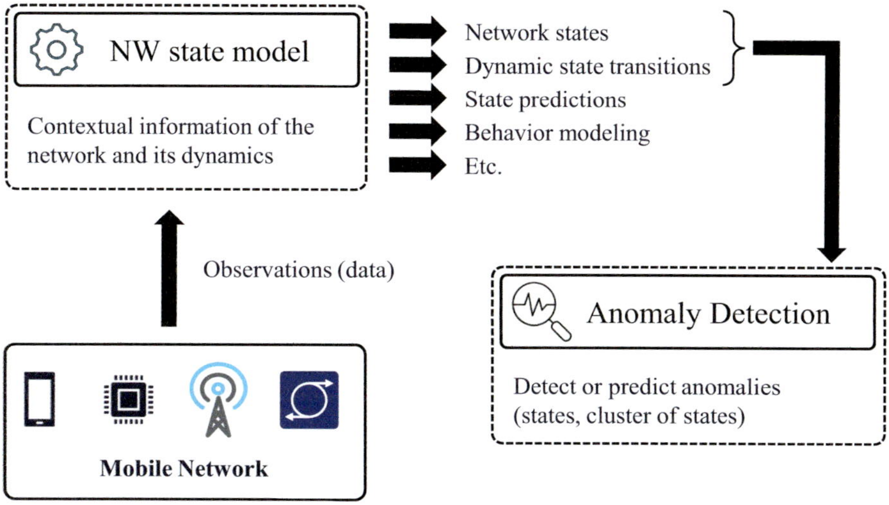

Figure 10.4 Network state model capabilities leveraged by anomaly detection.

terms of the data that it produces. Even though engineers typically possess a blend of theoretical, observation-based, and intuitive knowledge about (parts of) the system, the sheer scale of all observations make their experience based on only a small sample compared to the total amount of digital information produced in the system. In particular, corner cases that do not amount for a representative size of the total available data may carry some of the most impactful information with regards to anomalies, yet may be easily missed by manual inspection unless these data points are already known and actively sought after. Unsupervised state modeling has the benefit of scale and therefore a proper modeling technology can capture such unknown unknowns (i.e., unknown states that were not known to exist, but they are very much informative once discovered), enabling anomaly detection to benefit directly from state modeling technology.

AD models may be trained on various data sources (as detailed further in Section 10.4), but what's common is the unsupervised (or self-supervised) nature of the training. Since the purpose of AD is to autonomously discover "unknown unknowns," it would be impossible to expect annotated data samples (such as examples of normal/expected or anomalous/unexpected) at the quantity that is required by contemporary AI models. Therefore, the model's ability to autonomously ingest unlabeled and mixed (normal/anomalous) data is a fundamental prerequisite. This also means that the model should have no expectation about the content of the input data in terms of patterns or correlations that would or would not be present in the data – detecting patterns and correlations is the purpose of the model itself. Having no expectation and thus showing flexibility on the model's side is an obvious benefit for the user or engineer working with the model; however, it also means that the model will learn the behavior of the entity as it is exposed and represented by the data and the data only. No additional knowledge that the operator may implicitly or explicitly have will be captured by the model. Therefore, it is important to set the right expectations for AD and not to expect the emergence of knowledge that is not represented in the data.

10.4 State Modeling Techniques

The following sections provide overview of selected techniques that can be used to train and use state models. Three prominent model types will be discussed that align well with data that is usually available in mobile networks: numerical state models, suited to analyze time series counter/KPI data or measurements; log models, which can ingest text logs, messages, call traces or events; and self-annotating state models, which combines the previous two to automate part of the annotation process as discussed in Section 10.2.

10.4.1 Numerical state models

Numerical state models are trained on numeric datasets. Numerical data has been the traditional (and for some time, the only) means to monitor the performance of mobile networks. There are a large number of standardized PM counters [3] that provide a numerical value at regular data collection intervals, such as every 1 hour, 15 minutes, 5 minutes or at even higher frequencies. Such data has two key properties:

1. Time series: data points are aligned at specific time intervals; even if there is nothing to report, the value zero (or some other indication) is produced by every counter, KPI, or measurement that is part of the data collection. Time series have certain well-studied characteristics that provide a toolbox of analytics methods [4], with deep recurrent neural networks being the state-of-the-art.

2. Multidimensional: data points at each specific time interval consist of multiple (potentially many, multiple hundreds or even thousands) of measurements, which describe a measure over the same time interval. High dimensionality enables self-learning methods to explore and extract cross-KPI correlations and discover multidimensional patterns that would be impossible for a human to provide a-priori.

The two attributes often appear simultaneously, making multidimensional time series modeling an area of high interest for numerical state modeling.

10.4.2 State models for log analytics

The technology trends of software-defined network and management capabilities, coupled with cloud-native network functions have produced an environment where telecommunication services are also software entities. SW-based implementations import all the practices from development through continuous integration to deployment and operation into the telecommunication domain. Traditional counter-based telecommunication PM monitoring and more recent (but already established in the IT and cloud domains) software management practices coexist in a modern mobile network, providing extra opportunities (and challenges) when it comes to network state modeling. Logs are especially important in 6G due to extreme softwarization and close integration with non-telco SW (e.g., industrial controllers and applications at the edge continuum).

Due to their software-based implementation, network and management functions are producing a lot of text logs while they are performing their functionality. Logs are generated at multiple points, starting with the OS/infrastructure layer (e.g., kernel syslogs, container orchestration logs) and ending with the application processes (e.g., debug or info logs).

Logs differ from numerical data significantly enough that log data requires different learning approaches and architectures. Log data has the following attributes:

1. Primarily being text information, but may be mixed with numerical and other nonlinguistic symbols and data structures (braces, slash/dash, IP addresses, hash values, etc.). Such input cannot be converted to real numbers that would make any subsequent numerical analysis meaningful; therefore falling back to numerical analytics methods is not feasible.

2. Logs, although are often timestamped, do not constitute time series because log entries are not produced at regular time intervals. Instead, they may appear irregularly, in batches or in any other pattern that makes their sequential analysis more difficult than regularly slotted time series.

The above two key attributes are in sharp contrast to the main characteristics of numerical timer series, therefore log analytics requires a different technical approach on two fronts: first, the modeling of the data requires the modeling of text (or a mixture of text and numerical input); second, the modeling of irregular sequences time is needed to represent the order of logs. Note that the same approach is applicable to other log-like data such as alarm sequences and call traces.

The content of logs may be arbitrary and change frequently through the SW CI/CD pipeline – even with known logging standards [5, 6], the content of the log messages is freely defined by the programmer. Therefore, design considerations on log analytics methods may be based on common software logging practices:

- Logs are programming statements – they are a subsample of the statements (inserted between other statements). Therefore the order of logs is a rough indication of the order of program statements and branches/ loops (if, while).
- Known error paths are usually explicitly logged (warnings, errors) – enables to infer negative sentiment (e.g., “fatal error in …”).
- Hidden anomalies (not explicitly logged) may be indicated by a change in program code execution order (different code branches are executed, in different pattern, which are also reflected in the order of log lines.
- Log sources (e.g., different program modules, processes, containers) need to be separately processed (de-multiplexed from a common log stream such as syslog).

According to the above SW logging practices, with sufficient amount of data, profiling the usual order of logs and detecting anomalies as irregular ordering would generate insight to suspicious parts of the logs [7, 8]. Human attention could then be directed to those parts of the logs that are found suspicious by the algorithm.

Modeling the log lines (i.e., creating “log states” or “software states” based on logged events) is a nontrivial task with no single potential approach. In case the logs are inherently text-heavy, intended to be read by engineers, mapping text to vectors is a logical step to represent logs in a way that is suitable for subsequent machine learning models. Mapping text to vectors could be performed using multiple algorithms; however, semantic-preserving mappings have proven [7] to be better than one-hot encodings or template-based representations. Semantic log mapping, coupled with self-supervised learning to predict the most likely next log lines, have created a practically usable log anomaly detection pipeline [7].

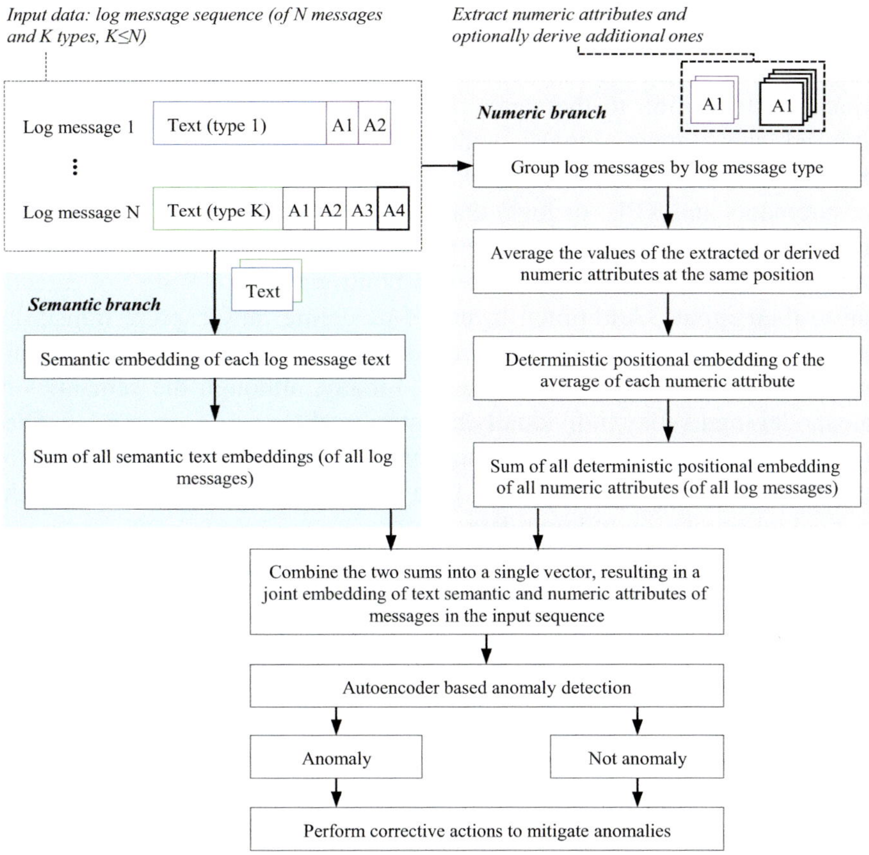

Figure 10.5 Log modeling with separate semantic (text) and numeric branches combined at the final modeling step to leverage the full content of log entries.

When logs contain a mixture of text and numerical attributes – where the numerical parts also have significance – it is desirable to model both the semantics of the text and the numerical content (Figure 10.5). Otherwise, logs that have the same log structure and text content but different values for their numerical part would be the same for the model, causing modeling errors and misclassifications in downstream tasks such as log-based anomaly detection. It was shown [8] that semantic modeling of the log's text part combined with the positional encoding of numerical attributes yields a log model where the full content (text and numeric) of the log entries was learned and represented. Such model, extended with capturing sequential information, was reported to be successfully used for anomaly detection in logs [8].

10.4.3 Self-annotating network states

The goal of self-annotation is to automatically attach human-interpretable semantic information to the states that are output by a state model. Well-produced labels (annotations) provide explainable and relatable descriptions for the states. State models usually work from interpretable data (such as measurements and KPIs, or logs) that individually have well-defined meaning. Since state models combine multiple inputs in a nonlinear way into a quantified state, labeling these states is nontrivial, as they do not directly map to their inputs. Additional layers of modeling may capture transitions between states to derive dynamic state models, creating more complexity between interpretable inputs and states. Finally, although the semantics of state model inputs may individually be interpretable (e.g., as they are defined by a standard or by an in-house procedure), the volume and diversity of the data itself cannot be comprehended by a human examiner, limiting even the practical interpretation of input data.

Self-annotation may be based on multiple methodologies. One approach could be to try to decode the relationship between the states and the interpretable components of the input data, such as individual KPIs. By measuring the contribution of a KPI to the state (e.g., using correlation metrics), states that correlate well with a low number of KPIs could be associated with the (combined) semantics of the KPIs themselves. Explainable AI methods such as SHAP [9] may also be used to assign importance value to input features with regards to specific states.

In cases where the same network entity produces both numerical and log data, there is also a potential to exploit the correlation between these data streams. For example, a numerical state model may be made more explainable by borrowing semantics from a human-readable log stream that is produced by the source that also generates the numerical data. In this case, training a state model which predicts both states and corresponding logs (i.e., which logs the modeled entity would produce given the predicted future state) could be a means to import the semantic readability of logs in the context of numerical modeling. Such model may be regarded as self-annotating as it learns and generates its own annotations rather than requiring an external state annotator. Besides, such model may provide more granular annotations (multiple potential logs per the same state) compared to a traditional one-to-one state-to-label annotation scheme. An artistic map showing the output of a self-annotating state model is presented in Figure 10.6.

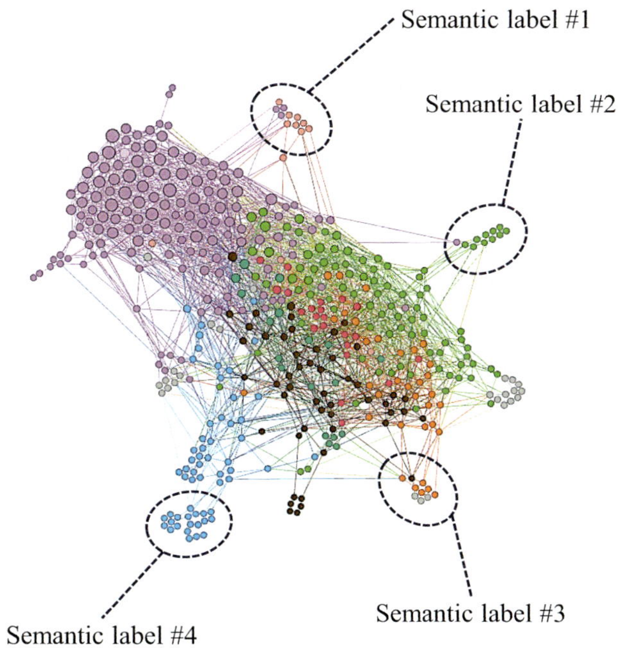

Figure 10.6 Artistic view of the output of a self-annotation state model.

10.5 Summary

Network autonomy is a product of autonomous system capabilities (realized as closed loops) with local (starting at individual network equipment or function level) and global (end-to-end, network, or service level) scope. State modeling is a fundamental enabler of network autonomy by representing all relevant contextual information (measurements, states) that are directly or indirectly relevant for the system's operation and dynamics.

State modeling includes configuration awareness (ability of the system to model its internal architecture, resources, topology, and logical relations between system components) and behavior awareness (ability to model its own current state, predict future states, and consider the dynamics and correlations of states and events). This already enables many downstream use cases such as event prediction, trend analysis, or anomaly detection.

This chapter provided an overview of network state modeling techniques applicable to various types of data commonly available in operational networks (CM, PM, and FM, software logs, sequences, events, etc.) and discussed the importance of correlating multiple data sources to maximize the potential value extracted from the collected data. The explainability of network states (e.g., through human readable annotations) is important to maintain the transparency of self-awareness and to enable further analytical steps resulting in network autonomy. The concept of self-annotating network states, along with potential enablers, was also discussed.

Bibliography

[1] ETSI GS ZSM 012, "Zero-touch network and Service Management (ZSM); Enablers for Artificial Intelligence-based Network and Service Automation", V1.1.1 (2022-12)
[2] ETSI GS ZSM 009-1, "Zero-touch network and Service Management (ZSM); Closed-Loop Automation; Part 1: Enablers", V1.1.1 (2021-06)
[3] 3GPP TS 28.552 Management and orchestration; 5G performance measurements
[4] Hannák, G., Horváth, G., Kádár, A., & Szalai, M. D. (2023). Bilateral-Weighted Online Adaptive Isolation Forest for anomaly detection in streaming data. Statistical Analysis and Data Mining: The ASA Data Science Journal.
[5] Rainer Gerhards, "The Syslog Protocol" https://www.rfc-editor.org/info/rfc5424
[6] World Wide Web Consortium, "Logging in W3C httpd", October 1995. Available online: https://www.w3.org/Daemon/User/Config/Logging.html#common-logfile-format
[7] G. Horváth, A. Kádár, P. Szilágyi, "TeleDAL: A regression-based template-less unsupervised method for finding anomalies in log sequences", The Journal of Supercomputing (Springer), 15th May, 2023
[8] G. Horváth, A. Kádár, P. Szilágyi, "The Sub-Sequence Summary Method for detecting anomalies in logs", IEEE Access, Volume 11, pp. 37412–37423, 14th April 2023
[9] Scott M. Lundberg, Su-In Lee, "A unified approach to interpreting model predictions", Proceedings of the 31st International Conference on Neural Information Processing Systems (NIPS'17), December 2017, pp. 4768–4777 https://dl.acm.org/doi/10.5555/3295222.3295230

11

Semantic Models and Semantic Composition

Network autonomy is based on closed loops that provide outcomes and actions in the network and management system without explicit human instructions and intervention on the operational level. Closed-loop actions not only assume that the network evaluates its own state in the context of automation goals but that the available actions are also modeled together with their impact on the system, services, and measurable outcomes. Such models provide the network with a representation of its own capabilities (and their consequences) that can be programmatically invoked by automation loops; therefore, these models capture the semantics (meaning, utility, and potential cost) of the actions. Semantic models enable the network to manipulate its own state by autonomously choosing the best action at any given time, context, and current network state. Given the software- and cloud-native implementation of many system capabilities, semantic models are closely related to programming interfaces and software modules. Building semantic models to represent network APIs and their potential interdependencies gives the system a self-programmable operational fabric that can be controlled through automated software operations such as deploying a set of modules triggered by the dynamic need for a certain management capability.

11.1 Introduction

Semantic models are machine-computable representations of the system, including its software components, automation loops, AI/ML models, data, and network and service management capabilities.

Semantic models may be functional or nonfunctional, depending on the type of system capabilities they represent. Functional semantic models capture structured knowledge of the network and its constituent components,

DOI: 10.1201/9788770041478-11

including what are their inputs and output, what is the impact they deliver to the system, what are the outcomes they can provide, and what are their dependencies on other components. Functional semantic models can be used to ensure that two system components (e.g., software modules) are able to interwork not only based on syntactical compatibility but also in terms of conforming to the same semantic concepts. Nonfunctional semantic models describe qualitative attributes related to the delivery of functionality represented by the semantic models. Nonfunctional semantic models capture aspects such as the volume or load caused by functional interactions between two system components, supported frequency of interactions or transactions, supported aggregation levels and methods over a given type of data that is used as input/output, scalability requirements, and SLAs related to interactions such as expected or tolerated delay and quality in completing a transaction or sourcing a requested data. The functional and nonfunctional semantic models together provide a semantic layer for describing the system components and their potential interactions. It is important to note that this semantic layer is an additional one on top of the syntactical descriptions of components and interfaces (such as SW APIs), as syntactical correctness and compatibility of configurations, API descriptions, interfaces, and runtime interactions remain mandatory requirements. While checking syntactical correctness is a state-of-the-art automated capability built into software systems, enforcing semantic correctness is usually left to human engineers (software developer and integrator) based on human knowledge and understanding.

Semantic modeling in general is applicable to any part of a system, given a suitable modeling technique that generates the semantic (functional and nonfunctional) representation of the system components. A specific area where semantic modeling is particularly helpful for the purpose of autonomous networking is in modeling the semantics of system components that can be individually orchestrated and composed into a larger structure, such as a multistage closed loop [1]. If a closed loop is composed of entities that are interworking through syntactically correct and semantically consistent interfaces, the CL may implement a use case, provide a service, or in case of intent-driven closed loops [2], deliver an outcome declared by an intent. Implementing composition as an integral part of a system gives the system self-composing capabilities, as illustrated in Figure 11.1. A self-composing system autonomously selects which components are required to produce a desired outcome. The composition considers the potential functionality of the system components, such as the output they provide or impact they deliver, which are captured in the semantic models. The composition matches the semantic of the potential functionalities with the semantic of the desired

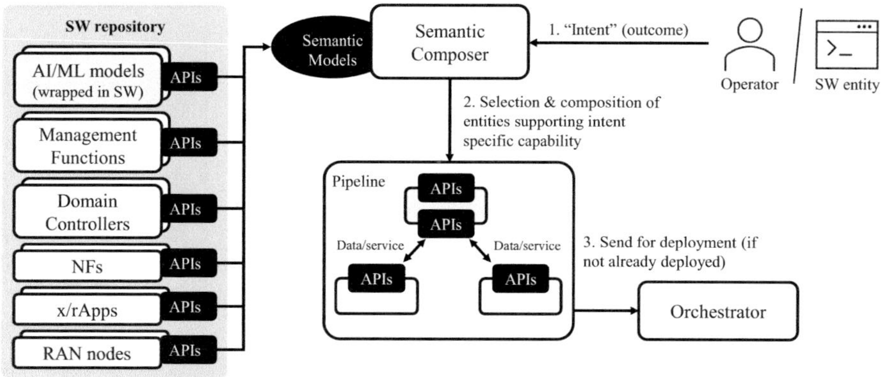

Figure 11.1 Intent-driven functional semantic closed loop composition.

outcome to decide on the right set of components. The composition is then complemented with all necessary dependencies and configurations that produce an executable set of components, ready for orchestration (including both deployment of new components and scaling of already running ones). Self-composition elevates the level of autonomy [3] of the system by autonomously responding to intents with autonomous design capabilities, giving the flexibility to dynamically and automatically provide customized closed loops that optimally deliver the needed system capabilities. This is in contrast to the state-of-the-art practice of manually predefining a set of blueprints (which are essentially compositions themselves, but produced manually and prior to the need for deploying them). Even if selecting a blueprint as a response to an intent may be an automated process, the outcome of the blueprint is not tailored to the intent itself as closely as it would be possible with a composition that has the freedom (but also means) to produce the best matching but still syntactically and semantically correct interworking of functionalities.

11.2 Full API Models: Syntax and Semantic

Network functions, edge applications, management services, and monitoring and reporting systems are increasingly (if not already fully) implemented as cloud-native software modules. Cloudification and softwarization have been part of the core design of 5G through the integration of virtualized network functions and service-based architecture (SBA) [4–6]. When applying the self-composition concept to networks, the composition needs to work with the software modules implementing various parts of the network capabilities, whether 3GPP standard network and management functionality, or additional

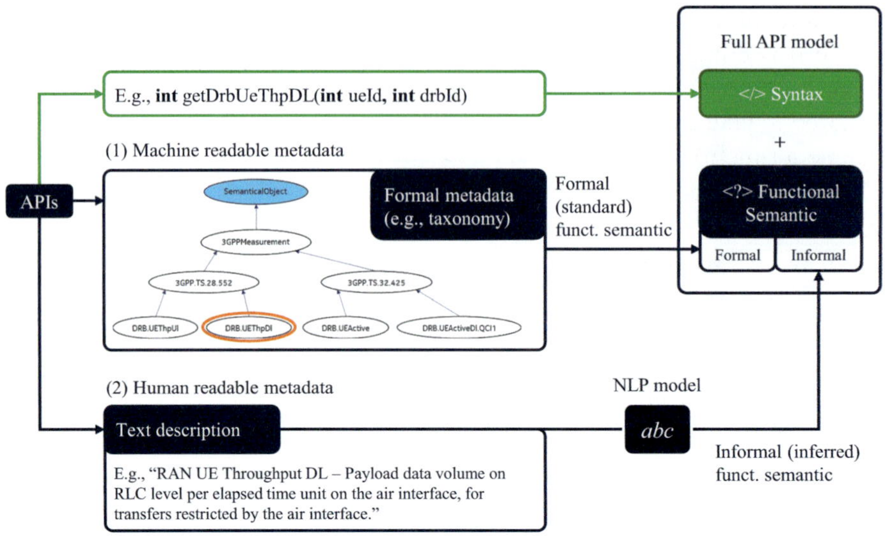

Figure 11.2 Full API model with syntactical and semantical parts.

tools and services developed by the operator, integrators, or even third parties on top of network APIs (see also Section 8.3). Consequently, semantic modeling that enables self-composition will be focused on the software modules (e.g., what they do) and their APIs (e.g., how they interact, what they require or provide) as these are the essential connectors through which semantically correct compositions are produced.

A deployable composition of software modules shall contain only syntactically and semantically correct interworking. Interworking between software modules in cloudified and distributed systems including networks is handled through APIs. Automating software module composition and ensuring both syntactical correctness and semantical consistency requires a full API model that captures both syntax and semantics. A full API model is illustrated in Figure 11.12, with syntactical and different types of semantical elements.

Syntax has always been part of software APIs – in fact, syntax has been the only concern of API definitions considering the machine-readable parts of current APIs such as OpenAPIs [7]. Syntax is the first element of API description in the full API model, marked with (0) in Figure 11.2. This remains to be crucial for ensuring syntactic compatibility between APIs.

Syntax captures data types, IDs, argument orders, and other attributes that can be validated programmatically using basic arithmetic, string and type operations that are inherited from computer programming practices (i.e., the syntax of a program code is also validated by the compiler or interpreter before it is compiled to byte- or machine-code or executed; for APIs there are also schemas [8] that enable similar validation). For example, a function declared to take an integer argument and return a string value can be matched against a function call that provides a floating point as the argument, to find out that the call and the function are syntactically incompatible as converting from float to integer would cause loss of numerical precision. Also, if the return value was going to be used in an arithmetic operation rather than in a string operation, it causes a syntax error that prevents the code from running. Syntax errors are actually singularities to the machines executing any code (including API calls) as syntactically invalid operation is simply not sensible. However, there is no semantic validation of the API calls, which makes it entirely possible to write code or use an API in a way that is syntactically correct (thus passing any compiler or schema validation) but semantically incorrect. For example, if the API's integer argument was meant to be a temperature value but the caller of the function supplies an integer encoding the temperature in Fahrenheit, that's already a semantic mismatch. Additionally the pure syntactic nature of APIs even enables the caller to supply a fully irrelevant value, such as the number of users in a day in place of a temperature value, as long as the type of the two values matches. The only mechanism today that prevents the creation of such semantically incorrect chain of API calls is the human expert who is writing the code, and it is up to the knowledge and expertise of the coder (and to practices such as code reviews and extensive test automation) to prevent or catch any semantic errors. If such errors pass through these practices, they cause unexpected runtime issues that may be hard to debug and yield to serious consequences [9].

The second API element, marked by (1) in Figure 11.2, attaches formal semantic to APIs. Formal semantic is metadata that was designed to be machine readable with the purpose of encoding the meaning of what the API does (e.g., what data it produces, what impact it has on the system, what outcome it delivers, etc.). Structured representation of semantic may use taxonomies or ontologies, or may be encapsulated by knowledge graphs [10] to provide a potentially or partly standardized set of semantic concepts that unambiguously denote meaning interchangeably. This representation may be beneficial for APIs where an exact semantic match is essential and even subtle semantical differences cannot be tolerated, as they can lead to broken interfaces. Exact (and thus formal) semantic dependencies may also be required for regularity and transparency reasons.

The third element of semantic representation, marked by (2) in Figure 11.2, is informal semantic. Informal semantic is acquired from sources that provide semantic context in an originally non-machine-readable format, but through data modeling, it is possible to transform them into a machine-readable representation. A prominent and practically usable example of acquiring informal semantic of APIs is the application of NLP models to the text that describes an API. API descriptions are the state-of-the-art means to convey an understanding of what the API does, what is the meaning of the components (e.g., parameters) of an API call, what would happen if the API is used, etc. Even OpenAPI definitions contain human-readable text descriptions to capture semantic information about the API (in addition to syntactic information that is meant for both humans to read and machines to enforce). API descriptions are mandatory to enable its adoption for system engineering; therefore, there is good potential that existing APIs do have a human-readable description. The modeling mechanism that can transform text to machine-computable representation in a semantically preserving way is to use NLP techniques such as word or sentence embedding [11, 12]. In order to produce accurate semantic representation, the embedding model has to be trained on a corpus that is representative of both the vocabulary and the linguistic patterns exhibited by the API description's domain language. Due to the special taxonomy and vocabulary of technical speech that is commonly used in APIs, publicly available NLP and language models may not be sufficiently accurate in representing the meaning of text (e.g., important words may be missing or misrepresented by applying every-day semantic to something that has a special meaning in an industry-specific domain language). Therefore, it is best to train an NLP model on a corpus that is collected from the domain language itself. In the telco domain, published standardization documents and related interim working documents represent a sufficiently large corpus that enables even a from-scratch training of a word or sentence embedding model. Fine tuning of an existing embedding model with a smaller but good quality and comprehensive corpus is also an option. Since the semantic extracted from human-readable text depends on the applied AI model used, this type of semantic is referred to as informal semantic.

In a full API model, the attributes of formal semantic (e.g., based on taxonomy) may very well coexist with informal semantic, but formal semantic may take precedence whenever they are present in the API model of all software modules that participate in an interworking (e.g., implement different endpoints of an interface).

Collecting the APIs and building the full API models is required to make the network aware of its own capabilities. The steps for producing the semantic model of APIs and software modules can be separated into two major parts. The first part is a discovery process that creates awareness of the

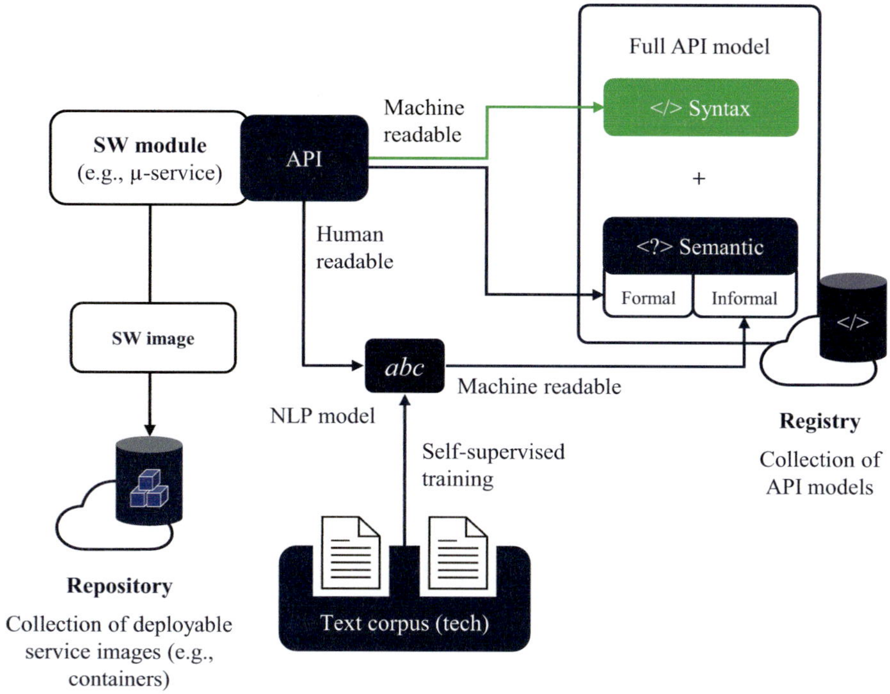

Figure 11.3 Software module discovery and API modeling.

available software modules, whereas the second part is the modeling step that creates the semantic models of the discovered modules (and their methods). The steps and the link between them are illustrated in Figure 11.3.

The discovery process ensures that any software module that could be the subject of composition (i.e., it can be dynamically deployed and interconnected to other modules – practically any container, pod, or cloud native entity) is identified and the relevant software artifacts and metadata are collected. The discovery can be proactive by defining registration hooks into the onboarding process of new or updated modules (in which case the module's artifacts and metadata are pushed into selective databases); or discovery can be reactive in which case the system should run an attestation process that collects the information from compute and management nodes based on databases and logs. The proactive process is much more efficient, lightweight, and accurate, and thus recommended. Each discovered (or registered) software module is split into two logical components: the deployable and executable software image, which provides the implementation of the module logic; and the API description of the software module, which will be the subject of semantic modeling according to the discussed method-based granularity.

11.3 Semantic Composition of Software Modules

Full API models are used by the composition to ensure that software modules selected into a closed loop (interworking set of software modules) share syntactically compatible and semantically consistent APIs. As composition has to consider the granularity of deployable software modules, where each software module may implement a set of different APIs, there is a need for modeling software modules as an abstraction and aggregation above the API level. Composition needs to consider that deploying a software module, all of its APIs will potentially become useable; and likewise, dependencies on other APIs (implemented by other software modules) may need to be satisfied.

A software model that follows software technology and coding practices is to consider a hierarchy of APIs, methods, and modules. APIs represent the semantic models (formal and informal) of individual capabilities accessible within the system; methods represent aggregations of APIs that are exposed by specific methods; and modules represent collections of methods that are implemented (packaged) into deployable units. A formalization of the API, method, and module abstraction levels enables the system to exercise self-composition to its fullest potential and efficiency, that is, selecting SW modules based on the lowest granularity of capability (i.e., a single API) while also considering what comes as a package (through the architecture of the SW module being a combination of APIs and methods) producing compositions that are deployable and executable. The formal modeling architecture has multiple scopes: (1) to capture the semantic of the APIs provided by the SW module (in addition to its syntax); (2) enable semantic models to explicitly include the impact (behavior and actions) of the SW module (making the SW module's impacts both consumable and dependable); (3) to enable semantic dependences between SW modules, rather than having to declare explicit SW package names and versions as implementation dependencies).

Starting at the API level, the basic building block of the semantic API model is the semantic object (SObject). A SObject represents the semantic of a physical or virtual (abstract) entity or capability, identifying with all of its relevant attributes. The equivalence between two SObjects therefore means that the two entities that they represent are truly interchangeable, whereas it does not necessarily mean that they are identical – they may still differ in irrelevant attributes that are not identified by the SObject. SObjects may also be organized into hierarchies through one or more taxonomies that represent relations between SObjects. A common taxonomy is representing the "is-a" relation between SObjects, producing a hierarchical tree graph where ancestor-descendant relationship between SObject represents that the descendant SObject is a specialized version of the ancestor SObject (carrying all of its attributes extended with additional more specific ones). Other taxonomies with different organization principles can be constructed as well to model different types of relations between SObjects.

The next abstraction level of the formal SW model is a method. A method represents a black-box implementation of a block of code, functionality, or business logic, performing its operation partly as responses to API calls from external entities (e.g., other methods) and/or autonomously as a closed-loop.

There are two key aspects that need to be considered in the formal model of a method: (1) data aspects, and (2) effect aspects. The data aspects deal with the input and output of the method in terms of data consumed and produced, without causing any side effects in the system. Side effect, an established programming term applied to methods, refers to a method having an impact on the underlying system that lasts beyond the call of the method itself. Methods that have no side effects are stateless and they can be chained together to compose powerful pipelines of data transformation and analytics, or be the implementation of monitoring, analysis, decision, and execution stages of closed loops [1] (see also Figure 7.1 and Figure 6.6). The effect aspects capture the impact of methods by representing the semantic of the outcome of actions. Methods with side effects naturally yield the composition of the execution stage of CLs, prepended with stateless methods on the monitoring, analysis, and decision stages. The outcome-oriented semantic modeling makes the semantic API model well aligned with the outcome-oriented intent definition, which will be an essential property leveraged in self-composition for the selection methods that are essential for the fulfillment of an intent.

Modeling the effect as part of the method's side effect allows capturing the dependency of the method on other side effects that are produced by other methods. This is a hidden dependency that is implicitly resolved by manual programming but needs explicit representation when moving toward autonomous method and module composition. It is important to note that modeling the dependency of a first method is different from declaring or naming a second method as its dependency: the latter means to state that a specific method is to be considered as dependency, whereas the former (and desired model) means that any method that can produce the required side effect may be considered to resolve the dependency. The difference between the two approaches is that modeling dependency on side effects (of any other Method) rather than explicit other methods eliminates the manual administration overhead of maintaining a set of potential dependencies for each method, as declaring dependency on a side effect does not require the knowledge of any other specific method that provides the required side effect. In fact, it is possible to release a method with a dependency on a side effect without any other method existing at all that could provide the required side effect and implement the dependency later in a second method (possibly by another organization and in another SW module than what produced the first method).

Returning to formalism, a method is represented by four interface elements: input, output, effect, and dependency, which are abbreviated by I, O, E, D, respectively. The semantic of each element are as follows:

- Input (I): represents data that the method consumes in order to perform its own operation.
- Output (O): represents data that the method produces as a result (or by-product) of its operation.
- Effect (E): represents the impact of the method, which is a means to model the purpose of the method.
- Dependency (D): represents the semantic of the effects that must be present (i.e., caused by other methods) in order for this method to fulfill its own operation goal (e.g., produce its output data or carry out its own effect).

Each I, O, E, and D interface elements may consist of zero, one, or more SObject pairs, denoted by (SO|C). In the (SO|C) SObject pair, SO indicates the semantic of the interface element (e.g., the semantic of the input/output data for I/O; the semantic of the effect/dependency for E/D), and C indicates the semantic of the context of the corresponding SO. The context models the method's nonfunctional attributes, such as its configurability (e.g., specific conditions) with regards to producing/causing the SO (in case of output/effect SO) or expecting the SO to be received/caused by another SO (in case of input/dependency SO). If one or more of the I, O, E, or D interface elements is empty, it indicates that the method does not consume/produce the corresponding input/output or effect/dependency.

A method may be represented as a graph node as shown in Figure 11.4. The method's interface elements can be separated into two categories. On the one hand, the purpose of the method can be described by the output and effect of the method, as these are the reasons why the method is invoked (i.e., it produces some data or ensures an effect or impact). Therefore, the method's effect and output are grouped under the semantic API that is provided

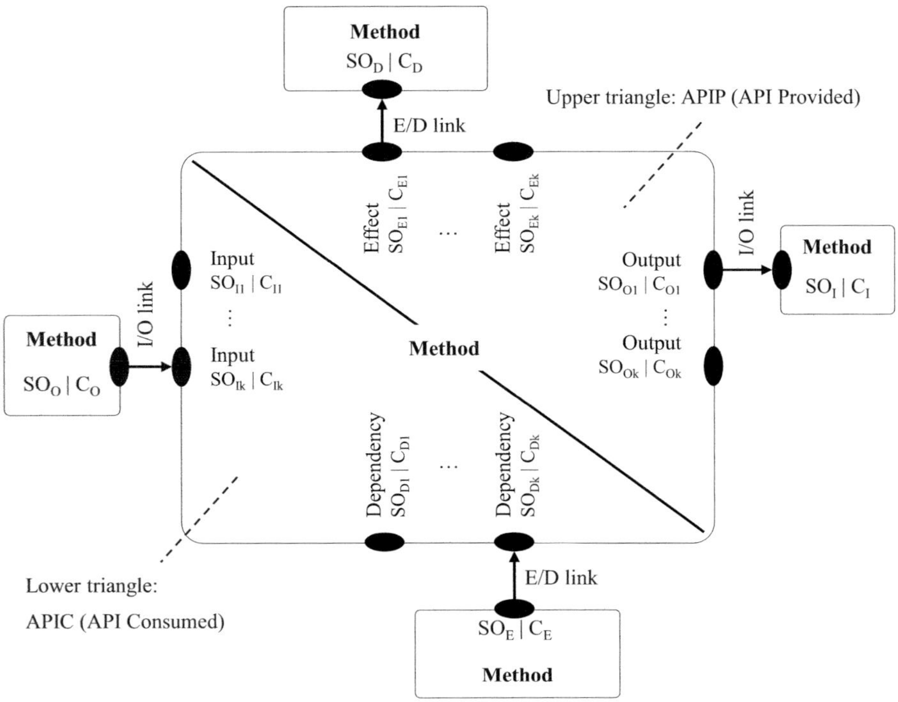

Figure 11.4 Graphical representation of the semantic API model of a method.

(APIP) by the method. A method of course may provide zero, one, or multiple data (with their own semantics) or be capable of causing zero, one, or multiple effects; therefore, in general, there is a multiplicity (zero, one, or more) of both output and effect semantics associated with the method. On the other hand, the method may require input data or may depend on effects ensured by other methods. These constitute the semantic API that is consumed (APIC) by the method, again potentially with a multiplicity (zero, one, or more) of inputs and dependencies. Two method graph nodes may be connected via one or more edges where an edge represents semantically equivalent (SO|C) SObject pairs at both connected methods. Two (SO|C) pairs are semantically equivalent if the SO and C elements of the two pairs are respectively equivalent. Such links may be created between I/O or E/D SObject pairs, that is, where an output (SO|C) of a first method is connected to an input (SO|C) of a second method, or an effect (SO|C) of a first method is connected to a dependency (SO|C) of a second method. Such links are referred to as I/O link and E/D link, respectively. The links are directed in the O→I and E→D direction.

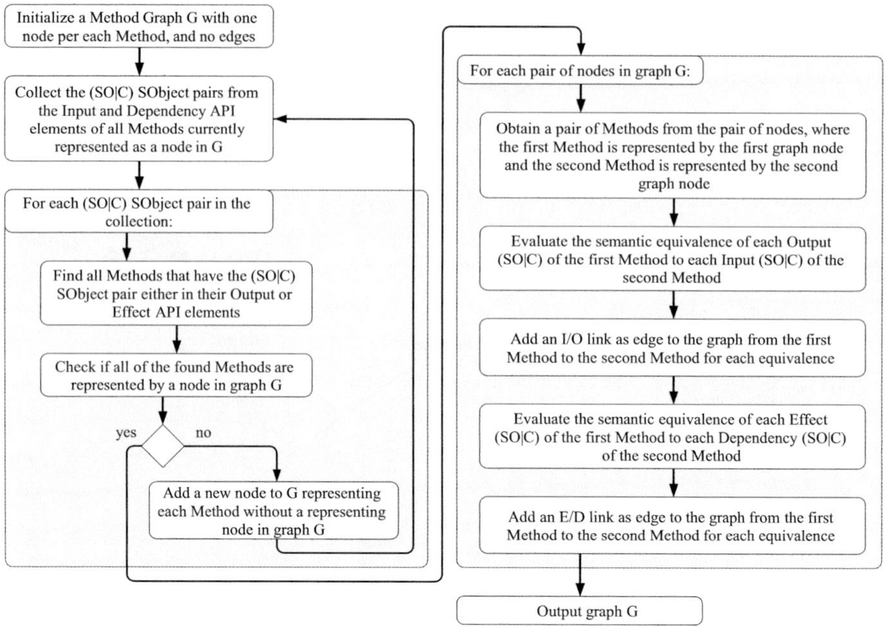

Figure 11.5 Steps of the full method graph discovery and assembly (D&A) method.

The highest abstraction level of the semantic API model is a SW module. The SW module is conceived as a collection of methods, thus the semantic API model of a SW module is defined as the union of the APIs of its methods. The API of the SW module is partitioned into the same four I, O, E, and D elements, each defined as the union of the respective API elements of the constituent methods.

Based on the semantic API model, a discovery and assembly (D&A) procedure (Figure 11.5) can be specified that automatically discovers the full set of syntactically and semantically compatible method combinations that exist within a set of available SW modules. The D&A method creates a so-called method graph, where each node represents a method and each edge is an I/O or E/D link between two semantically equivalent (SO|C) SObject pairs within the API of the two connected methods.

Since the full method graph contains all syntactically and semantically compatible method interfaces, the method graph is fully defined by the input methods (i.e., there are no alternative method graphs). A method graph, however, may be reduced to one of its subgraphs to represent a subset of the potential method capabilities. Particularly interesting subsets of a full method graphs are those that root in a designated direct method (DM), and contain only those additional methods and links that are required to fulfill the recursive dependencies of the DM. Building a method graph for a direct method uses the same D&A method as shown in Figure 11.5 with the exception that the initialization of the method graph G contains only one node representing the DM itself.

A method graph (either full or reduced to a direct method and its dependencies) can be transformed to one or more SW module graphs where the nodes represent deployable SW modules. The transformation merges nodes in the method graph into one node in the SW module graph if the method graph nodes represent methods that are implemented by the same SW module. Since the same method may be implemented by multiple SW modules, it is possible to generate alternative SW module graphs from the same method graph. Selecting a SW module graph from multiple alternatives may be an optimization opportunity over nonfunctional attributes (e.g., to select the SW module graph with the smallest number of SW modules, or estimate the compute resources or other monetary, resource, license, or other costs associated with the use/deployment of the SW modules represented by each SW module graph). The SW module graph derived from the full method graph is a superposition of every blueprint that can be generated out of the available SW modules and methods. A SW module graph of any kind is a blueprint that is not only syntactically deployable but also fulfills a meaningful purpose through a chain of semantically compatible data flows and complementary effects.

The various graphs discussed above are practically useful to enable intent-based software composition. Intent-based software composition is a mechanism that ingests an intent provided by an intent owner, such as the operator, and assembles the software components that have the collective capability to produce the outcome declared by the intent. The intent-based composition mechanism considers the available software modules and their capabilities (i.e., output and effect), which are captured by the semantic models of the software modules. The mechanism may be implemented by the intent management entity introduced by ZSM011 [12], referred to as the intent manager (IM) in Figure 11.6.

The IM collects and models network capabilities (essentially APIs describing what a network can do); exposes selected capabilities to the user (intent owner); ingests and interprets intents from the user; and deploys, triggers, and configures the right SW modules that will fulfill the intent. The IM constructs semantic API models that represent network capabilities on the levels of callable SW API methods and deployable SW modules. Based on the semantic models, the IM constructs graphs that model which SW methods/

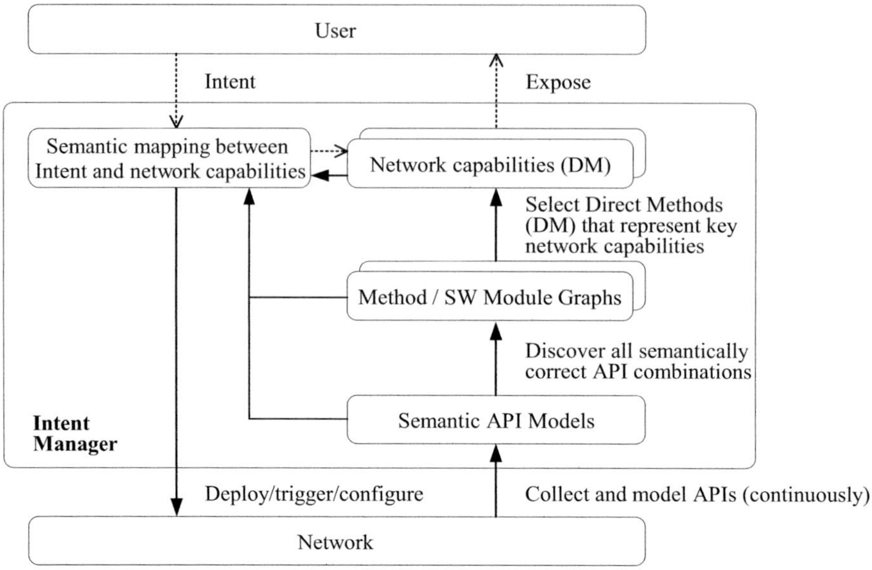

Figure 11.6 The key components and interactions of the intent-based semantic closed loop composition mechanism.

modules may be connected with each other in a way that creates semantically (not only syntactically) meaningful interfaces. Such graphs capture all potential SW blueprints that may be created from the available SW modules by preserving semantic integrity along the interfaces. The graphs also model the dependencies between the SW methods and modules to ensure that only fully implementable interfaces are considered. Based on the graphs, the IM selects and exposes those network capabilities (referred to as direct methods and detailed later on) that represent high-level objectives for which the system has all the capabilities to automatically achieve. The user provides intents to the IM, which maps the semantic of the intent to the semantic of the available DMs. The semantic mapping finds the DM (out of all available DMs) whose semantic is closest to the semantic of the intent, meaning that the DM (and its dependencies) together are the closest interworking set of network capabilities that can implement and fulfill the objective of the intent. If the intent's semantic matches that of the DM, the SW module implementing the DM (and all of its dependences as per the SW module graph) are deployed and/or configured. The dashed arrows indicate a cycle through network capability exposure (from IM to user), ingesting intent (from user to IM) and semantic mapping between the intent and the network capabilities (internally within the IM). This cycle enables iterative negotiation between the user and the IM

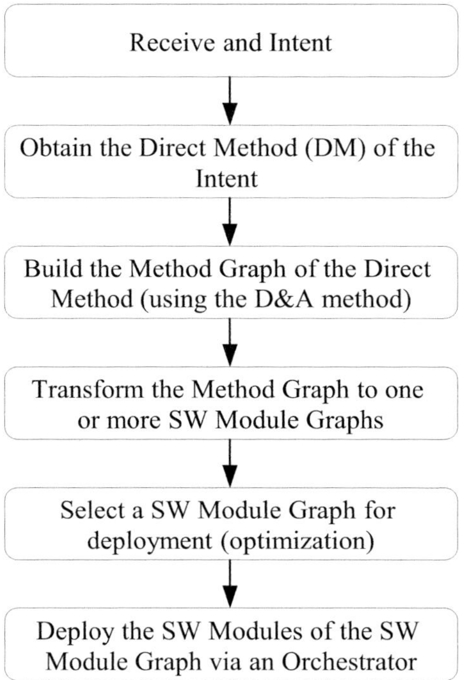

Figure 11.7 Identification and deployment of the SW modules required to fulfill an intent.

(see also Figure 6.5 and Figure 9.6): the user may refine its intent based on the exposed (i.e., available and implementable) network capabilities; and the exposure of capabilities can also adapt to the user's preferences inferred from the previously provided intents (e.g., by ranking capabilities higher whose semantic is closer to the semantic of the intent). Also, the user will want to accept the final semantic mapping between its intent and the network capabilities, authorizing the IM to proceed with the intent's automated implementation and fulfillment.

The IM responds to receiving an intent as shown in Figure 11.7 and detailed below. First, the IM receives an intent from a user of the network (e.g., CSP, enterprise, vertical, etc.). Next, a direct method is derived from the intent by mapping the semantic of the intent to the semantic of all methods. Mapping the semantic of an intent to the semantic of a direct method is possible if the semantic of the intent is represented by the same set of SObjects and taxonomies that are used by the semantic API model. Ensuring such semantic continuity between intents and APIs is possible, e.g., via an intent interface that guides the intent owner toward one of the available method output/effect APIs. The identified DM is the entry point into the system capabilities that are selected and organized to fulfill the intent. The full automation of the intent requires the identification of all other methods that are required to provide input and dependencies for the DM, recursively. This is exactly what's provided by a method graph built for the intent's DM, and its derived SW module graph, which represents the collection of all closed loops that together participate in the fulfillment of the intent. A SW module graph derived from a method graph built for an intent's direct method is a blueprint that, if deployed, can fulfill the objective of the intent.

Note that the SObject-based semantic API of the method does not replace its callable API or override the actual data that is exchanged through the interfaces. SObjects model the semantic of the callable API so that it becomes machine discoverable, semantically comparable, and composable. Additionally, SObjects model the method's effect and dependencies, which are not part of its callable API. A method will still be implemented and called through its programmatically defined and exposed API (e.g., a REST/JSON interface).

The semantic API may have an impact on the APIs designed for 6G network and management functions. Automation capabilities implemented and organized as microservices fit especially well with the principles of semantic API modeling, which enables automatic discovery and assembly of SW module graphs (on-the-fly generated blueprints of closed-loops). For example, the serverless (function as a service) [13] paradigm would simply mean a 1:1 match between methods and SW modules, promoting method graphs directly to SW module graphs.

11.4 Mapping Natural Language Intents to Network Capabilities

According to ZSM011 [12], intents may be formulated in natural language. In the semantic modeling framework introduced in Section 11.2, this means that intents are declared using informal semantic rather than by manipulating formal semantic through a user interface. This observation also points toward the solution of modeling the semantics of the natural language intent with the same NLP modeling technique that can be used to produce informal semantic from the API descriptions that are also natural language text themselves.

The semantic models generated through NLP or defined formally using taxonomies or ontologies provide a computable set of values representing the capabilities of the network. As the capabilities are modeled on the method and software module level, they also provide the building blocks of

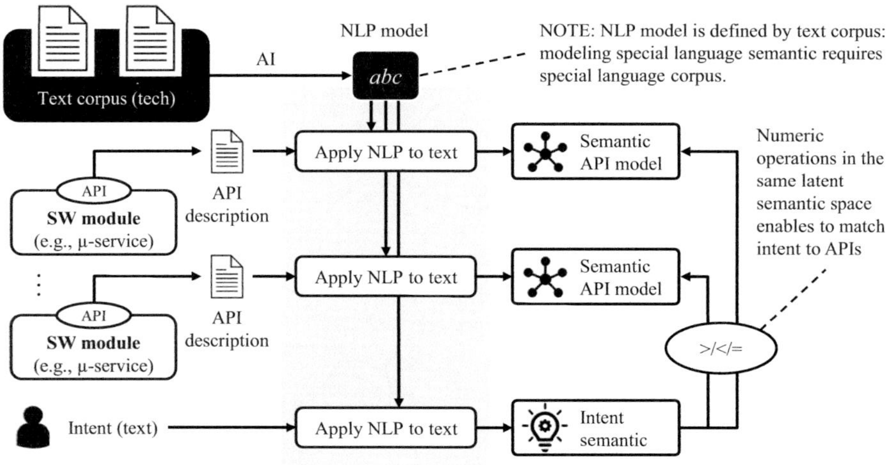

Figure 11.8 Semantic model of intent sharing the same latent vector space with the semantic API models.

composability when it comes to organize a closed loop or set of interworking software modules implementing a capability via semantically meaningful interface relations.

The mechanism to generate semantic models from text-based API descriptions is not exclusive to APIs; however, the model itself produces computable semantic vectors in the specific latent vector space that is designated by the training of the underlying NLP embedding model. Therefore, the mechanism naturally lends itself to the modeling of intents given that the intents are also expressed in natural language. Applying the NLP model that has generated the semantic API models to intent text would result in a semantic vector representing the intent in the same latent space as the APIs; therefore, making the semantics of the intent directly comparable by vector arithmetic operations with the semantic vectors of the APIs representing the composable capabilities of the network. This process, starting with the NLP model training itself, continuing with the API modeling and then completed by the modeling of the intent, is outlined in Figure 11.8.

As the semantic vector representing the intent becomes directly computable within the context of semantic vectors representing the APIs in the NLP model's latent vector space, it is possible to automatically select the best matching API for an intent or create a ranking of the topmost APIs matching the intent. As the APIs are modeled with the method granularity, matching the intent with the API models provides a very fine-grained yet fully automated browsing through the network capabilities to lock on the method best

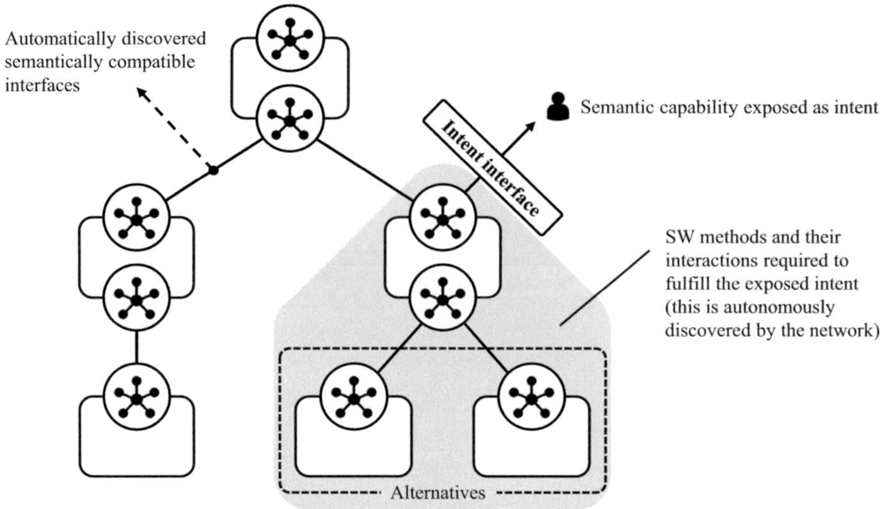

Figure 11.9 Illustration of the module super-graph representing potential module interconnections, and a highlighted subgraph corresponding to a specific intent.

aligned with the intent. This method, referred to as the direct method of the intent, when invoked, would ensure the closest effect or provide the output best matching the intent's semantics. Taking this method would then enable one to systematically generate the list of dependencies and software modules through the process already discussed in Section 11.3. The outcome of the process would be a method graph (or module graph) that represents not only the identities of the required methods (modules) to enable the designated method but also the required interconnections via semantically compatible interfaces (i.e., the I/O and E/D links between methods). Such a graph would actually be a subgraph of a super-graph that represents all existing methods and modules, with all potentially existing semantic interface connections, as shown in Figure 11.9.

In case there are multiple methods that provide the same semantic (e.g., as output data, or effects), they would constitute as alternative implementations and be recorded as multiple I/O or E/D links leading toward an input or dependency connector. Such alternatives may be resolved based on dialogue with the operator who defined the intent, or automated selections driven by policies or previous choices. Another goal could be to avoid software module fragmentation by favoring methods that are implemented by modules that are already required for providing capabilities via additional methods. Additionally, if there is historical performance data collected for both alternative methods and their implementing modules, the best performing, more accurate, least energy consuming, etc. module could be favored (again potentially modulated by the previously mentioned considerations).

The software module level super-graph can be composed and maintained already as part of the software module registration and discovery process as discussed in Section 11.4. Subgraphs related to intents can be quickly identified on-the-fly as a new intent request is processed, based on the semantic intent modeling and intent-to-API matching steps outlined in Figure 11.8.

11.5 Composition of Closed Loops for Autonomous Services

The flexibility of service composition based on intents and semantic modeling is further illustrated in Figure 11.10. As the latest up-to-date knowledge about the composable network capabilities are available as the semantic models, intents provided by the operator can be dynamically mapped (through the previously discussed dialogue process) to the best matching network capability. That capability and all recursive data and effect dependencies together provide a made-to-order closed-loop [1] that can be configured and tasked with the fulfillment and assurance of the intent.

Upon the construction of a new closed-loop, some required components (software modules) may already be up and running in the network as they have already been required for previously requested intents, or they are part of the infrastructure that was instantiated outside of the intent framework (e.g., an initial set of functions required for basic control plane functionality and user plane connectivity may be always up and running, as well as all the infrastructure that is required for the intent framework itself, such as the semantic models, intent managers, orchestrators, domain controllers, etc.). Those already running software modules (cloud-native modules or even PNFs) may be partly reused by the new intent's closed loop as well, and thus the existing modules do not need to be replicated or deployed again. Still, they may need to be configured to provide additional types of data (that they are capable of) or to register with new API endpoints to integrate with the new closed loop's modules. Additionally, upscaling may be required to provide them more resources in case their performance scales with the load caused by the new intent. For example, a low-level measurement agent embedded in the U-plane of the N3 interface may not need to be changed at all, as it is providing original measurements related to packet level performance on the RAN-core interface, which are ingested by a data collection framework that scales and distributes the measurement toward any number of consumers (as

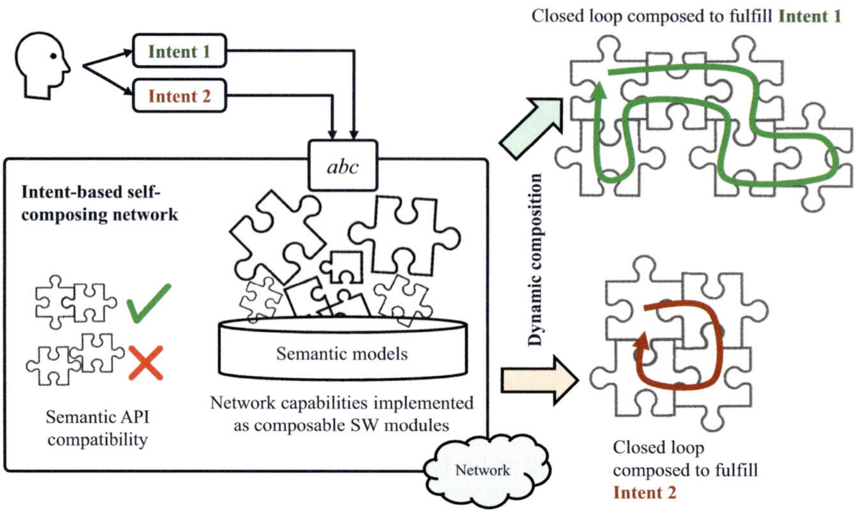

Figure 11.10 Dynamic semantic composition of intent-based made-to-order closed loops.

discussed in Chapter 3). However, an anomaly detection entity that analyzes a stream of PM counters by applying one or more AI models on the collected data is likely to require additional compute resources in case its scope is extended to a larger portion of the network or new types of measurements are turned on and channeled to its input layer. The decision of the necessary scaling falls into the scope of the orchestrator, which may communicate with the software modules to determine the extent of the scaling.

11.6 Summary

Semantic models provide the system with machine-readable and actionable representation of its own internal or external capabilities, their dependencies on other (supportive or helper) capabilities or services, and the impact of deploying them in terms of the achieved outcome. With the increasing adoption of cloud-native implementation in telecommunication systems, the capabilities are implemented by containerized software modules providing services and interacting with each other via APIs. Consequently, semantic modeling of software-defined capabilities essentially captures the semantic models of the APIs. In addition, it is important to also capture the side effects or impacts of the software modules on the greater domain or system level (i.e., beyond the module itself) to enable the modeling of domain/system level outcomes that would originate from the deployment of a given module. This chapter provided a detailed semantic API modeling technique that borrows abstractions from the software implementation world and enriches them with taxonomies and AI-generated semantic representations to create a framework for semantic computation over the field of system capabilities.

Semantic models are enablers for both intent-based composition and natural language intents, concepts that were discussed in detail throughout the book and particularly in this chapter. A joint semantic modeling of network capabilities and intent objectives enables the network to automatically select the key functions and management services whose capabilities directly map to the outcome declared by the intent. Completing the initial capabilities by dynamically selecting and composing all of the required software modules and services into a coherent set of interworking functions provides a closed loop that is dedicated to the fulfillment of the intent. Autonomous and dynamic composition of closed loops provides the system with self-composition capability, increasing the level of autonomy through not only executing ready-made predesigned closed loops but assembling new ones as a response to dynamically received intents. This has numerous design and operational benefits, e.g., not having to prepare a blueprint or closed-loop for every potential intent (which does not even scale), but having the best possible closed-loop generated dynamically based on the available (implemented and deployable) system capabilities.

Bibliography

[1] ETSI GS ZSM 009-1, "Zero-touch network and Service Management (ZSM); Closed-Loop Automation; Part 1: Enablers", V1.1.1 (2021-06)

[2] ETSI GS ZSM 016, "Zero-touch network and Service Management (ZSM); Intent-driven Closed Loops" V1.1.1 (2024-10)

[3] TM Forum, "Autonomous Network Levels Evaluation Methodology", IG1252, Version 1.2.0, June 2023

[4] ETSI GR NFV-IFA 043, "Network Functions Virtualisation (NFV) Release 5; Architectural Framework; Report on enhanced container networking" V5.1.1 (2024-05)

[5] 3GPP TS 23.501 System architecture for the 5G System (5GS)

[6] 3GPP TR 28.834 Study on management of cloud-native Virtualized Network Functions (VNF)

[7] OpenAPI Initiative. Available online: https://www.openapis.org/

[8] JSON Schema. Available online: https://json-schema.org/

[9] Mars Climate Orbiter. Available online: https://science.nasa.gov/mission/mars-climate-orbiter/

[10] Lin, J., Zhao, Y., Huang, W. et al. Domain knowledge graph-based research progress of knowledge representation. Neural Comput & Applic 33, 681–690 (2021). https://doi.org/10.1007/s00521-020-05057-5
[11] Tomas Mikolov, Kai Chen, Greg Corrado, Jeffrey Dean, "Efficient Estimation of Word Representations in Vector Space", arXiv:1301.3781 [cs.CL], 7 Sep 2013
[12] Jacob Devlin, Ming-Wei Chang, Kenton Lee, Kristina Toutanova, "BERT: Pre-training of Deep Bidirectional Transformers for Language Understanding", arXiv:1810.04805 [cs.CL], 24 May 2019
[13] ETSI GR ZSM 011, "Zero-touch network and Service Management (ZSM); Intent-driven autonomous networks; Generic aspects" V1.1.1 (2023-02)
[14] J. Scheuner, P. Leitner, "Function-as-a-Service performance evaluation: A multivocal literature review", Journal of Systems and Software, Vol. 170, Dec 2020, https://doi.org/10.1016/j.jss.2020.110708

12

Decision Models

The capability of automated decision-making unlocks the path to the highest level of network autonomy. Decision models represent correlations between current network states, potential actions, and predicted impact of the actions given that they are invoked in the current operational context. Such representations may be learned using AI/ML from operational experience or (partly) provided through existing system models of known (architecture or standard defined) correlations. The scope of decision models goes beyond the selection of the best action (if any) in the context of any one operational goal or intent. A network has to handle a multitude of intents and services simultaneously rather than in isolation, creating cross-intent and cross-action impacts with complex and unknown dependencies of which action caused what impact and side effect. De-conflicting intents dynamically during their fulfillment is necessary to ensure the stability of the system. Decision models may also consider the larger impact of different actions by incorporating measures beyond a specific intent's goals. Fusing network data with external sensor data describing the wider environment of the network (such as energy and power consumption aspects) allows running autonomous networks at a greater global optimum while also ensuring the fulfillment of specific operational goals.

12.1 Introduction

Network autonomy refers to an evolution of networks where traditionally manual operational and management tasks are increasingly owned and performed automatically by the network [1]. The evolution to autonomous networks is enabled through the development of capabilities such as context and state awareness, analysis, decision-making, and execution, modulated by adaptation and learning abilities. Autonomous networks can be classified

DOI: 10.1201/9788770041478-12

into five different autonomy levels [1] (see also Chapter 7), depending on the extent to which automation takes over manual operational responsibilities. An important distinction point between Level 3 ("conditional autonomous networks") and Level 4 ("high autonomous networks") is that the latter are expected to perform decisions autonomously, whereas the former could still resort to manual decisions. Transitioning from conditional to high autonomy level through the capability of automating decisions marks the importance of decision-making in mastering autonomy; without decision-making, highly autonomous systems cannot be created as they will regularly require external (manual) input to complete operational goals.

Closed loops are logical compositions of stages that incorporate capabilities associated with the increasing level of autonomy, going up to Level 4 of "high autonomous networks." Multiple models exist for closed loops, such as the observe-orient-decide-act (OODA) model [2] and the monitor-analyze-plan-execute with knowledge (MAPE-K) model [3]. ZSM has also defined the closed loops for network and service management in line with these models, referring to the stages as monitoring, analysis, decision, and execution [3] (see also Chapter 7). A common attribute of all CL models is to include decisions as one of the stages ("decide" in OODA, "plan" in MAPE-K, and "decision" in ZSM), showing the potential of CLs to provide the means to achieve high level of autonomy in networks, or in case of the ZSM scope, in the management of networks and services. Note that the highest level of autonomy according to TMF [1], Level 5 "full autonomous networks," adds intent-based operation in all scenarios on top of highly autonomous networks. This is reflected in ZSM through the introduction of intent-driven autonomous networks [4] and intent-driven closed loops [5].

Decisions within a closed loop are captured in the "decision" stage (or equivalent) of the closed-loop models. Those decisions refer to autonomy that is exercised by the CL itself to reach its own operational goals, based on the intelligence it has collected and analyzed during the monitoring and analysis stages.

In an autonomous network, leveraging closed loops as a means of automation, implicitly or explicitly, there is an additional decision scope that is logically above the closed loops, with the purpose of managing (e.g., composing, deploying, monitoring) CLs, and providing inter-CL coordination, including the de-conflicting of closed loops. This decision scope and the provided automation capability are referred to as closed-loop automation (CLA) [3].

In the rest of this chapter, concepts around decisions within closed loops as well as above CLs are analyzed and discussed in more details.

12.2 Automated Decisions Within Closed Loops

Decisions are established as a mandatory component of reaching autonomy [1], with explicit support from the common closed-loop models [3]. Closed loops autonomously trigger actions based on a series of steps including data collection, analytics, and decision. During a CL's decision step, the closed loop may select from a set of actions, where the best action depends on the CL's dynamically changing environment and operational context. In systems with dynamicity (such as mobile networks with mobility, traffic diversity, etc.), the mapping between potential contexts (such as domain specific insights and system states generated by domain intelligence) and actions cannot be defined statically (e.g., as a list of rules) prior to the implementation and deployment of the CL.

CLs are not only expected to act autonomously but they also need to learn from their own actions to become more efficient and capable in fulfilling their operational targets. To learn which action is the best within a given context, CLs should monitor the efficiency and impact of their own actions (see Section 7.3) to generate a self-learning feedback. Efficiency means whether an action has successfully completed the intended changes. Impact means whether the completed changes have caused to reach the goal of the action, which should be aligned with the CL's operational target.

Actions may have different latency until they become effective (i.e., until their outcome becomes measurable); therefore, even an efficiently completed action may not deliver the expected impact in time. Whether an action is efficient and impactful depends on the context in which it is executed. The context may be derived from the CL's collected data, past knowledge, and internal insights created by its analytics step. Learning the context-based efficiency and impact of the actions may be a basis for self-learning and self-optimizing CLs.

Considering the timing aspect of the actions is essential for making efficient and impactful decisions by the CL. In general, if the action is triggered as a remedy to a degradation, the action should complete (take effect) before the issue escalates to degradations noticeable to end users or SLA violations. Therefore, the CL should measure and store the latency of the actions it triggers, and, in any situation, should select actions that have a chance to take effect within the time budget available to resolve the trigger condition.

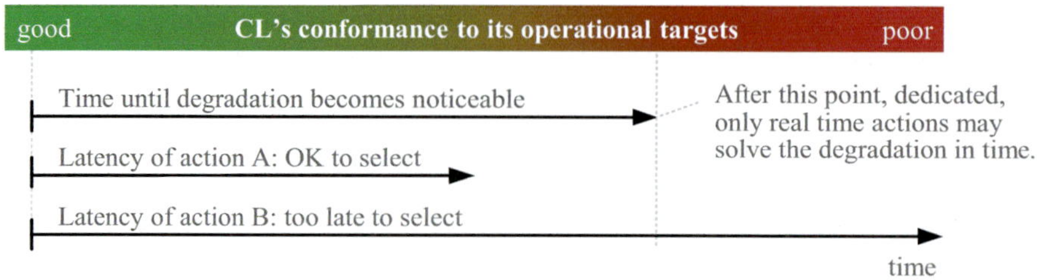

Figure 12.1 Illustration of the concept of considering the latency of actions in CL analytics and decision making.

The timing of actions is also relevant for tuning the action (cf. the earlier control-loop analogy), as tuning an action's parameters requires knowledge on the time constant of the action (i.e., the speed at which changing the action parameters is expected to take effect in the action's observed efficiency and impact).

The concept is illustrated in Figure 12.1 with a situation where, with time, the system would transition into a degraded state, which is monitored by the CL. The objective of the CL is to keep the system out of the poor performance range. Suppose that in the current context, there are two actions that have proven to be efficient and impactful for the CL, indicated by "A" and "B." The latency profiled for action "A" is shorter than the time before the degradation is expected to escalate, making "A" a potential choice for the CL. However, the latency of action "B" has been measured to be longer than the time until degradation. Therefore, even if action "B" was an efficient and impactful one, in the current situation it should not be selected as long as there is a better alternative. Therefore, the CL should go with action "A" in this case. Action "B" is still a valuable tool as a long-term action that, however, is impactful only in cases of slow system changes or as a proactive action.

The self-evaluating and self-learning CL operation concept is depicted in Figure 12.2, combining efficiency and impact evaluation as well as latency considerations and mapping them onto the CL steps of data collection and analytics, decision, and actuation. The contextual knowledge representation is also highlighted.

The CL may be logically partitioned into two interacting internal loops: a cognitive loop and an operational loop. The cognitive loop is responsible for maintaining the context-based knowledge of the CL, based on self-monitoring the actions and their efficiency, impact, and latency. The operational loop has the scope to collect data from the managed entities and observe the context in

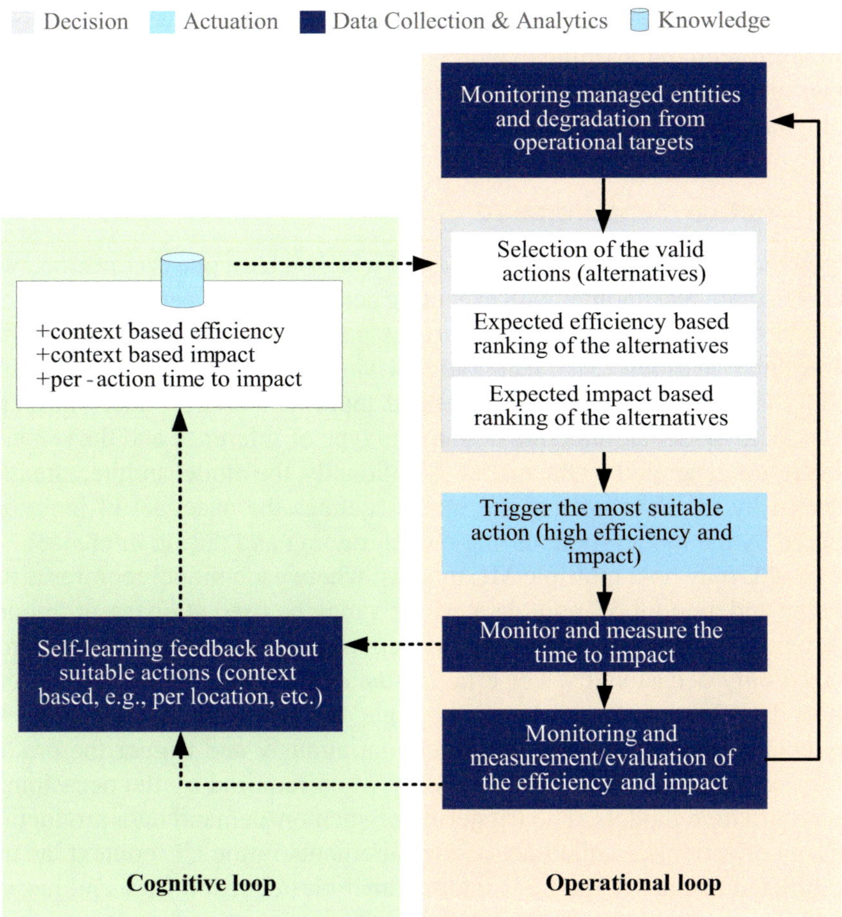

Figure 12.2 Self-evaluating and self-learning CL operation.

which the CL operates; detect if there is any need for an action (degradation from CL operational targets); select, based on the accumulated knowledge, the best possible action in the context; launch the selected action; monitor the efficiency, impact, and latency of the action. The interaction between the two logical loops is to generate self-learning feedback from the operational loop for the cognitive loop, and to retrieve knowledge from the cognitive loop to the operational loop.

Note that at a given decision point, prior accumulated knowledge may be insufficient to support the decision of the CL about triggering actions. In this case, the CL may transition to an exploration mode, where actions are evaluated based on predefined rules or general (not context specific) domain knowledge used for bootstrapping the CL. In theory, random action selection as in reinforcement learning exploration may also be used; however, this may not be suitable in certain CL deployment environments (e.g., business-critical deployments).

12.2.1 Active measurements

Closed loops consist of multiple stages, of which at least one is concerned with data collection and another with executing actions. In between these two steps, multiple others may exist, e.g., analytics and decision-making, which may use machine learning (ML) technology. Using ML usually requires a trained model that takes in a set of well-defined input data and produces inference results. The model architecture defines the type of inference and the semantic of the result generated by the model. Additionally, the model architecture itself (selected by the developer of the model) defines the exact set of input data required by the model (both during model training and during inference).

A CL may host multiple ML models, where each model requires different type and amount of input data. Models may be used at different frequencies, e.g., a default model may be used continuously, and other models may be used only occasionally. For efficient data collection, the CL should only collect data that is going to be used by one of its models. Therefore, the CL may collect data for its default model continuously and trigger the production or collection of additional data only when required by the occasionally used alternative models. The triggering of such on-demand data productions or data collections is called active measurements in the CL context, as they are initiated as part of the CL's internal analytics/decision flow and not as a permanent configuration or deployment option.

In a CL, multiple ML models may exist to cover a wider range of analytics capabilities compared to the possibilities of a CL with a single model. Models could require different input data to deliver their inference result. For example, a model with few input data may be able to deliver coarse analytics results, while another model with more diverse input data may deliver finer analytics results. The two models may be different in complexity and inference speed, i.e., the simpler model may be quicker for basic decisions. Additionally, the simpler model is more relaxed on the data collection requirements, i.e., puts lower load on the data producers (e.g., other CLs or managed entities). Therefore, the mode of operation of the CL could be to normally use the simpler model driven by a limited set of data, whereas it proceeds to use the more complex (and more data intensive) model only in exceptional cases when the simpler model's inference is not satisfactory or conclusive.

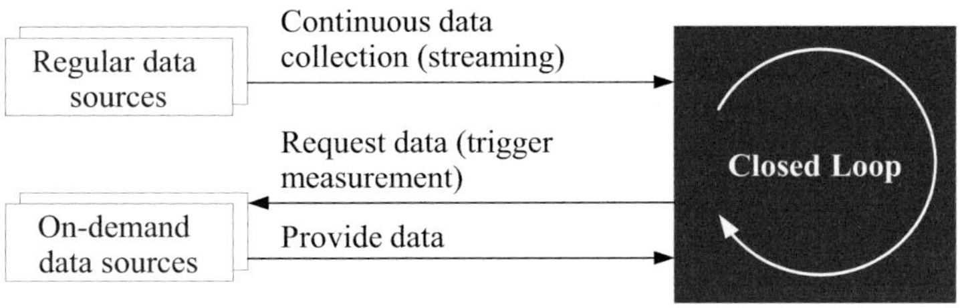

Figure 12.3 Dynamic interaction with data sources.

Optimizing data collection according to the above mode of operation requires that the CL is able to dynamically program data sources according to its internal analytics flow. Accordingly, the CL may use a set of "regular data sources" whose data are collected and analyzed continuously, while additional "on-demand data sources" are utilized only on an as-needed basis and thus their data are collected only on specific request from the CL. Such operation is outlined in Figure 12.3.

The on-demand data collected on need basis may be used in combination with the previously obtained regular data (Figure 12.4(a), when a model has been trained on a combination of regular and on-demand data) or used separately (Figure 12.4(b), when a model is trained solely on the on-demand data).

On-demand data may have at least two availability stages:

1. Existing data. This is data that has been produced by a data source already and has been stored in a database, from where it only needs to be retrieved.

2. Data that needs to be generated on request. This data has not been produced but requires additional actions/procedures (outside of the CL) to be generated.

Requesting existing data is usually more lightweight and available with shorter latency compared to the data that needs to be generated, especially if the latter implies interactions between network functions or measuring/generating user plane traffic. Still, on-demand generated data is useful to enable a CL to perform more detailed analysis.

With certain ML technology, the CL may detect that a model is not able to deliver conclusive or confident results by evaluating the module's intrinsic confidence metric, such as that of a softmax classifier used as the output layer of a deep neural network. Alternatively, the CL may monitor the distribution of model input data encountered on the field and compare it to the current default model's training data distribution to check if the model is dealing with

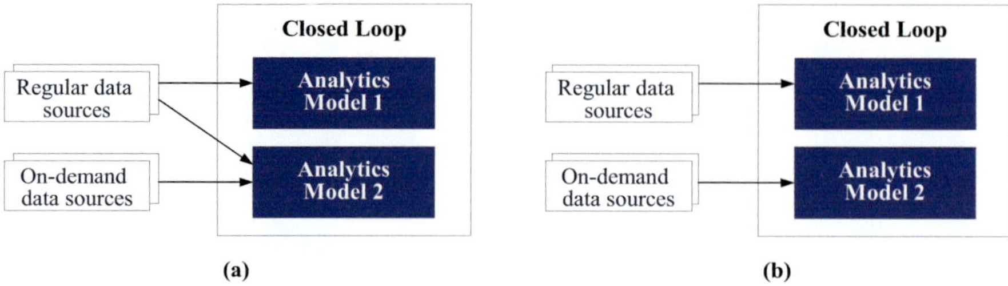

Figure 12.4 Closed loop with multiple analytics models, each requiring different (potentially overlapping) set of input data.

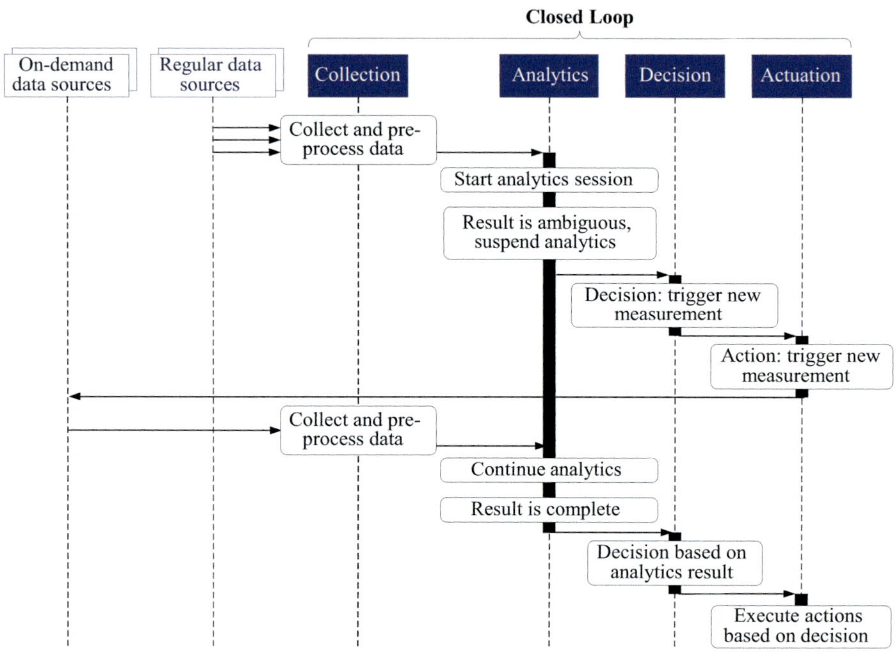

Figure 12.5 Procedure flow for triggering active measurements from a closed loop.

the kind of data it has not been trained for, triggering a switch-over to another model that was trained for the currently received data. While performing analytics, the CL may realize that its currently used model is not sufficient for its analytics/decision requirements. In this case, the CL may switch to another model, which may in turn require additional data.

The flow of command where a CL triggers active measurement as part of its analytics/decision steps is shown in Figure 12.5. The CL is depicted by its multiple internal steps (collection, analytics, decision, and actuation). The analytics step realizes (by means discussed above) that the collected regular data does not lead to conclusive results; therefore, its decision is to trigger a new measurement. The new measurement is shown to be initiated by the CL's actuation step, emphasizing that obtaining the on-demand data may require new data to be generated by entities outside of the CL, not only fetching additional (but already existing) data from a database.

12.2.2 Consideration of environmental context

Softwarization and virtualization have brought new management aspects into mobile networks in addition to the traditional CM [6], PM [7], and FM [8] aspects. Cloudification combined with the new service-based 5G core network architecture [9] produced cloud-native 5G network functions, VNFs, and CNFs that are virtually orchestrated (rather than physically deployed) on compute HW and infrastructure layers [10]. This new virtualized environment in which network functions are hosted produces additional types of telemetry, which could be incorporated into the network's context and state models (see Chapter 10) to enable monitoring, analytics, decisions, and actions (essentially closed-loop operation, see also Chapter 7) based on a wider environmental insight.

Compute HW, like any electronic equipment, is sensitive to temperature; running hot degrades compute performance and may even result in permanent damage. Therefore, data centers and server rooms are equipped with cooling solutions that regulate the temperature of the environment in which compute HW operates. Cooling itself consumes energy, contributing to the total energy footprint of running a given NF at a given data center/server room. A typical datacenter cooling solution is depicted in Figure 12.6. Autonomous networks may become more energy efficient by considering cooling and temperature aspects when deciding about the location (e.g., the datacenter site or server room) for deploying a VNF/CNF.

The total amount of energy consumed by deploying a workload (e.g., a VNF/CNF instance) at a specific datacenter/server has multiple components. A direct component, which is also the most obvious one, is due to the compute load generated by executing the workload on the compute HW (e.g., CPU, GPU). This is specific to the workload and the type of HW (e.g., how efficient is the compute HW, how much energy is consumed per CPU/GPU cycle, what is the HW clock rate, what energy saving options are available/activated, etc.). In addition to this direct component, there is an indirect component that comes from the temperature requirement of the compute HW. Compute HW dissipates heat during its operation, but it requires limited

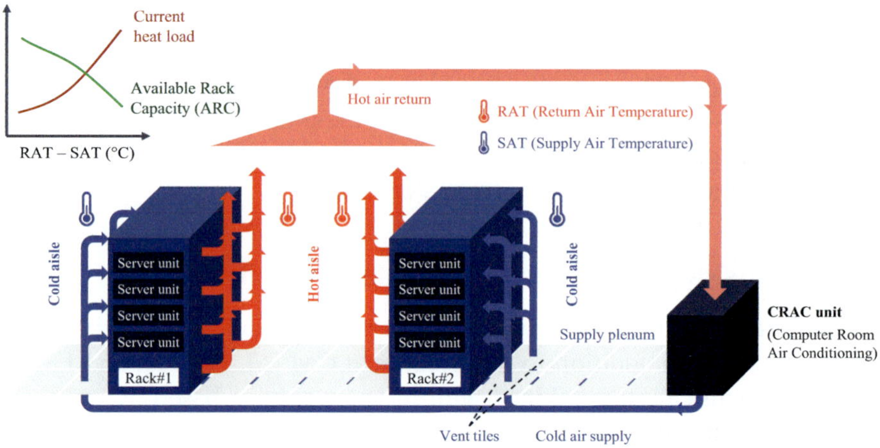

Figure 12.6 Example of a datacenter cooling solution.

temperature to function properly; therefore, a cooling mechanism is implemented to prevent HW overheating. The cooling mechanism also consumes energy, e.g., the energy needed for the mechanical circulation of the coolant (such as air or liquid), or the energy required to exchange heat for lowering the temperature of the coolant heated by the compute HW. The higher the workload (i.e., more CPU/GPU cycles are consumed to execute the VNF/CNF), the more heat is generated, thus, more energy is consumed by the cooling system to keep the compute HW at the same temperature. If the cooling system's capacity was not adjusted to the increased compute load, the HW temperature would increase.

Cooling systems usually use a fixed temperature target (e.g., 20 °C) set for the coolant (e.g., cold airflow) that is regulated all the time. Therefore, cooling power (and thus its energy consumed by the cooling system) is automatically increased with every new compute load, which in turn increases the indirect energy consumption of the compute load via the increased energy consumed by the cooling. However, if the new compute load only slightly increased the temperature, and especially if that increase would be temporary, enforcing the preset temperature target by consuming more energy by the cooling system would be unnecessary. This is even more prominent if increasing the cooling power required spinning up more active cooling components, e.g., an additional air conditioning unit, causing a jump in the energy consumed by the cooling system.

Orchestration function placement decisions may be augmented to consider the energy impact of the cooling systems at the target datacenters that are candidates for hosting new workloads. NF orchestration decisions (i.e., selecting the location where an NF is deployed) typically consider SW/HW compatibility (e.g., presence of accelerator such as GPU for an NF that depends on such HW), compute resource availability (CPU, memory), disk/storage capacity, and in advanced cases the network latency between the new VNF and the UEs or between the new VNF and other VNFs that will communicate with the new VNF. Considering the datacenter's cooling mechanism, temperature, and load on the cooling system (and therefore the cooling energy increase or temperature increase caused by instantiating the NF at a given data center) is less obvious due to the ownership fragmentation between the data center infrastructure operator (owning the cooling system and being aware of its internal state) and network operator (running the orchestrator without knowing anything about the cooling system). Integration between orchestration and cooling systems requires that cooling telemetry data is made available for orchestrators, where the cooling telemetry data could provide insight to the capabilities and state of the cooling system.

Specific technical requirements for integrating cooling considerations into orchestration decisions include:

- Collection of telemetry about the cooling system's capabilities, the coolant type and temperature, the energy efficiency of the cooling mechanism, and any other relevant information about the cooling system at datacenters that are evaluated by the orchestrator as VNF/CNF host candidates.
- Augmenting the orchestration decision using the cooling telemetry data to optimize the total energy consumption of VNFs/CNFs, including both the direct energy consumption of the compute load, and the indirect energy consumption due to increased cooling capacity.
- Triggering cooling actions by the orchestrator, such as deferring the activation of additional cooling units in case the temperature increase caused by a new VNF/CNF instantiation at the datacenter would only slightly/temporarily increase the HW temperature; or on the contrary, proactively switching cooling to a higher capacity when sudden deployment of new compute load is anticipated.

Augmenting VNF/CNF orchestration decisions (e.g., NF placement, scaling, or relocation) by considering the energy aspects of cooling at the datacenters requires different technical enablers. In the context of 3GPP system and existing standards, enablers may be partitioned in four groups:

1. Architecture (interfaces and integration): collect cooling data (e.g., HW and coolant temperature, energy consumption of the cooling system, cooling capacity and load, etc.) from HW/environmental sensors and

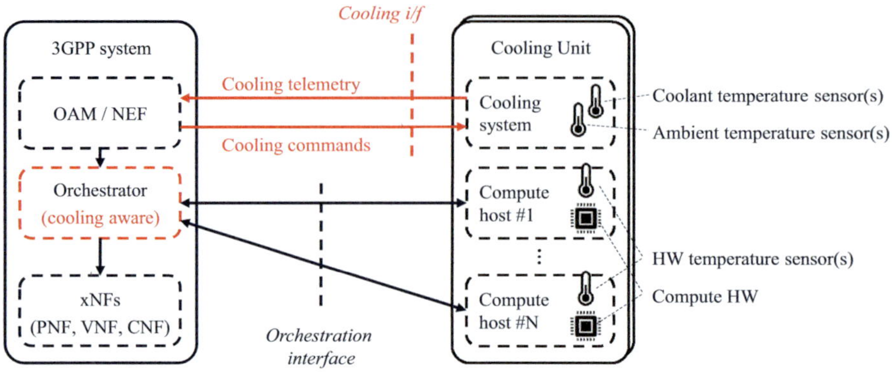

Figure 12.7 An example architecture integrating cooling awareness into a 3GPP system – cooling specific interfaces and capabilities are in shown red.

the cooling system itself (e.g., via AF/NEF interfaces) to enable cooling aware decision making in the orchestrator.

2. Method (in the orchestrator): augment orchestration decisions (function placement, scaling, etc.) by considering the cooling at the potential deployment points in the datacenters (e.g., orchestration to cooler data center locations contributes to lower energy consumed by cooling; orchestration to passive cooling locations takes no extra cooling energy).
3. Method (via the PCF): Extension to noncloud (e.g., PNF/classic RAN) network elements by load balancing driven by cooling conditions (drive traffic away from hot units as they require more costly cooling).
4. Architecture (interface from orchestrator to cooling system): more efficient compute-aware control of the cooling system.

An example architecture supporting cooling aware orchestration is illustrated in Figure 12.7. A cooling unit may be an entire data center room or a corridor within the data center room whose temperature is regulated by a single cooling system. The cooling unit may consist of one or (typically) more compute hosts, which share the same cooling environment (e.g., airflow intake). The xNFs of a system such as a 3GPP core network may be deployed on multiple compute hosts at different cooling units, so in the general case the 3GPP system and the orchestrator must consider cooling data of multiple cooling units. This also provides the degree of freedom for the orchestrator to perform function placement or scaling decisions by considering the cooling options and states.

The architecture provides an interface with cooling-specific elements between the 3GPP system (NEF) and the cooling system of the cooling units. The interface enables the 3GPP system to collect cooling data from the cooling system about its capabilities and measurements, as well as to learn the association between the cooling unit and the compute hosts whose cooling is provided by the cooling unit.

Using the cooling data obtained from the cooling system, the orchestrator's function placement and scaling decisions are augmented to consider the temperature and indirect energy associated with the operation of the cooling system. The cooling interface may also enable the orchestrator to send commands to the cooling system to trigger changes (such as delayed capacity increase) more efficiently in the cooling system.

The cooling system may provide cooling data to the 3GPP system and the orchestrator to enable cooling-aware orchestration and load balancing. The cooling data may consist of (but is not limited to) the following elements:

- Cooling unit ID
- IDs of the compute hosts whose cooling is provided by the cooling unit
- Ambient temperature within the cooling unit: e.g., temperature that someone walking into the cooling unit, such as data center room, would experience
- Ingress coolant temperature: e.g., cold airflow temperature injected to the compute hosts' ventilation system
- Egress coolant temperature: e.g., hot airflow temperature ejected from the compute hosts' ventilation system
- Temperature targets for the ambient, ingress, and egress coolant temperatures (if any)
- Total cooling capacity: e.g., how much workload – e.g., in vCPU units or in Watts dissipated – could be sustained by the cooling unit to keep the cooling unit's designated ambient or ingress/egress coolant temperature targets – if such targets are defined
- Free cooling capacity (out of the total cooling capacity)
- Cooling capacity headroom until new active cooling mechanism (such as an extra AC unit) would be turned on
- Cooling energy per dissipated Watts as a function of specific ambient/ingress/egress coolant temperatures: e.g., correlates with the efficiency

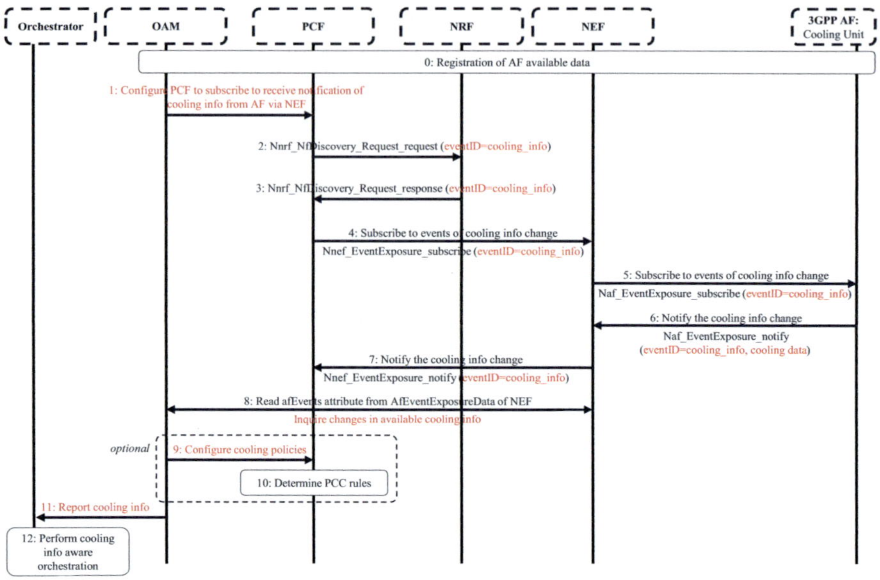

Figure 12.8 Procedures for cooling-aware orchestration.

of the cooling system – passive cooling systems may have it close to zero and flat in function of the dissipated Watts up to some local environmental thermal conduction capacity; active cooling system usually have it scaling with the dissipated Watts linearly for reasonable amounts and then polynomially or exponentially for increased dissipated Watts

Figure 12.8 illustrates the procedures for ingesting cooling data by the 3GPP system and the orchestrator. The cooling-specific parts of the procedures/ information elements are marked in red.

Step 0: A data center room/cooling system may act as an AF and it may register its available cooling data via OAM configuration at NEF. The data that can be collected from the AF includes: AF identification, AF service identification (e.g., endpoint information of Naf_EventExposure), and available data to be collected per application (e.g., identified by Event ID(s)). After the registration of AF-available data at the NEF, NEF generates an event exposure with a new eventID, in this case "cooling_info," to be associated with available cooling data to be collected from the AF. This info is stored in the NF profile of the NEF, which is updated with the new "cooling_info" eventID and associated AF identification, application ID(s). Such update is reflected at the NRF [11].

Step 1: An NF, e.g., PCF, etc. may be configured (e.g., by OAM) to subscribe to notifications on events related to cooling info from AF. In the case of non-trusted AF this communication will be done over NEF. The eventID "cooling_info" referring to the cooling data may be provided in this step.

Step 2: When an NF needs to discover the data made available by AFs and the associated NEF to collect this data from, it invokes Nnrf_NfDiscovery_Request_request service operation, using the NEF NF Type, a list of event ID(s) and optionally AF identification and application ID as parameters. The NRF matches the requested query for available data in AFs with the registered NEF profiles and sends this information via Nnrf_NfDiscovery_Request_response message to NF [11]. In order to discover the cooling data availability, the NF, e.g. PCF shall provide the eventID "cooling_info" referring to cooling data as provided in Step 1.

Step 3: The NRF will respond to the request in Step 2 with the indication of the according NEF where the cooling data from the AF is registered.

Steps 4–7: The NF, e.g., PCF can subscribe to data in AF via NEF by using Nnef_EventExposure_Subscribe and indicating the "cooling_info" eventID. If the event subscription is authorized by the NEF, the NEF records the association of the event trigger and the NF identity. Based on such request, the NEF subscribes to cooling data in AF by invoking the Naf_EventExposure_Subscribe and indicating the "cooling_info" eventID related to cooling data. The AF provides the NEF with the cooling data by invoking Naf_EventExposure_Notify. Once the NEF gets the notification from the AF, the NEF notifies the NF by Nnef_EventExposure_Notify by providing the cooling data as retrieved from the AF.

Step 8: The OAM may retrieve the cooling data from the NEF by reading the afEvents attribute from AfEventExposureData object [12]. The afEvent represents AF event(s) exposed by the NEF after registration of the AF(s) at the NEF. In this way the OAM may inquire the changes in the cooling data.

Step 9: Optionally, the cooling data may be used to derive and configure cooling-aware policies toward PCF, e.g., to balance the load from hotter to colder HW in case of uneven heat distribution at PNFs or VNF/CNF compute hosts.

Step 10: If Step 9 was performed, the PCF determines the PCC rules following the guidelines from OAM.

Step 11: The cooling data is exposed toward the orchestrator to enable cooling-aware orchestration.

After (a single or repeated execution of) Step 11, the orchestrator may perform cooling-aware function placement or scaling decisions. By way of example, two types of operations are discussed.

Type 1: Cooling-aware function placement and scaling.
The orchestrator may consider cooling data as follows (given by way of non-exhaustive examples):

- On the deployment of a new workload (e.g., placement of a new xNF instance, or scaling up/out of an xNF), select a compute host at a cooling unit with the lowest ambient/ingress/egress coolant temperatures. If the compute load increment caused by the new/scaled xNF instance is reasonably small compared to the compute capacity of the compute host(s) at the cooling unit, this strategy ensures that the temperatures across cooling units stay approximately even and at each time the cooling unit with the lowest temperature is loaded.
- On scaling down (terminating instances) of an xNF or multiple running instances, terminate the one running at the cooling unit with the highest temperature (ambient/ingress/egress coolant). This strategy of removing load from the hottest location complements the previous one.
- Place the workload at a cooling unit with passive cooling (and sufficient free cooling capacity).
- Place the workload at a cooling unit with active cooling system where the extra compute load would not cause the activation of a new active cooling unit (such as spinning up extra ACs).

Note that the orchestrator must also comply with SW/HW compatibility, affinity, and other xNF configuration specifications in addition to the above cooling-aware decisions. For example, if the compute HW at the coolest location is not compatible with a new xNF instance, the orchestrator must not try to deploy the xNF there. In general, the cooling-aware logic should come after the potential deployment locations have been prefiltered through hard priorities such as compatibility/affinity.

Type 2: Smart data center/server rack cooling management (via cooling commands).
Since slight variations in temperature may be tolerated by the compute HW, there is an optimization opportunity related to the energy consumption of the cooling system, which is currently not leveraged. If the compute load

increases only slightly, not increasing the cooling capacity would let the temperature increase only slightly – this would save energy on the cooling side by letting the temperature increase. Of course, at some point increasing compute load must be followed by increasing cooling capacity to protect the HW; therefore, postponing the upscaling of the cooling system can only be a temporary action reserved for sporadic compute loads that are anticipated to end before increased cooling becomes mandatory. Even in those cases, the decision of turning the cooling on or up can be made more precisely and only as much as strictly necessary.

12.3 Conflict Resolution Across Closed Loops

De-conflicting closed loops is an important requirement in systems where multiple independently defined closed loops may exist. In intent-based systems, closed loops may be the implementation of intents, providing the capabilities required to ensure the outcomes declared by the intents. As many intents may be provided to a system that need to be fulfilled simultaneously, a need arises to coordinate between the intents, that is, ultimately between the closed loops that are implementing them. In ZSM, coordination between intent-driven closed loops for conflict resolution [5] is declared as an important requirement for intent-based management systems.

According to TMF [13] and in line with [2], de-conflicting among CLs is necessary. Given the individual autonomy of CLs, they focus on delivering their own goals, which could degrade other CLs' capabilities and resources needed to achieve their respective purposes. Potential conflicts between intent-based closed loops include explicit contradictions [13], where the intents already declare opposite or incompatible goals. Such conflicts are obvious from the intent definition and should already be caught during the intent ingestion phase (see Section 6.4). Another, less obvious type of conflict occurs dynamically between closed loops of multiple intents, where the autonomous actions of the CLs may conflict [5, 13]. In such a dynamic conflict situation, intents under the management of the same intent handler could be resolved internally (i.e., within the handler [4], Section 6.4). If intent handling is distributed in the system, one strategy could be to partition the scope of the intent handlers so that overlaps in shared resources and concerns are limited, reducing the potential conflict surface during the operation of the intent-handling CLs. Still, detecting conflicting intents – potentially across the scope of different intent handlers – is needed to at least indicate (e.g., to the intent owner) the presence of conflicts.

12.3.1 Detection of conflicting intents

A practical approach to detect potential conflicts between two or more intents provided to a network (or between the effects of assuring/fulfilling the intents) may consider three main components:

1. The intent target database (ITDB)
2. The state model (SM) of the underlying network
3. The state model-based conflict detection (SMCD) entity

The ITDB is a database that relates intents with measurement values (MVs). That is, it contains a list of intents, and for each intent, a list of MVs that are (likely to be) directly affected by that intent, e.g., because the intent itself aims at changing those MVs. MVs may be performance management (PM) counters, QoS/QoE metrics, latency values, failure counters, and any other observed or derived metric, and their combination that refers to the state of the network or the fulfillment of the intent. Additionally, MVs may be abstract network state descriptors, which may be created by means of applying arbitrary analytics to information coming from, or related to, a network, where the analytics have the ability to provide a state descriptor for the network at any point in time. Intents may have such a network state as a target to be reached (e.g., a desired state) or to be avoided (e.g., an anomaly/faulty state). Thus, intents with different desired states are in conflict. The same state being targeted as a desired state for one intent and being a state to be avoided for another one makes those two intents conflicting.

The SM of the underlying network constitutes a database/graph that represents relationships between MVs of the network. It stores subsets of MVs that are typically correlated or otherwise related. That is, for each MV, *m*, the SM encodes which other MVs are likely to change in a predictable way upon the change of *m*.

The SMCD, upon receiving a set of intents (e.g., a new intent along with already active intents, or a fresh set of intents), performs a lookup in the ITDB for all MVs directly affected by the intents. Subsequently, the SMCD recursively explores the SM for indirectly affected MVs. If the lookup and exploration discover at least one MV that is simultaneously affected by more than one intent, it declares a potential conflict and outputs the conflicting intents (i.e., the intents which would presumably affect the same MV).

The components and functional steps of the method are depicted in Figure 12.9 and Figure 12.10. The ITDB is represented as a table, with each row storing a single intent and its associated MVs that are known to be directly

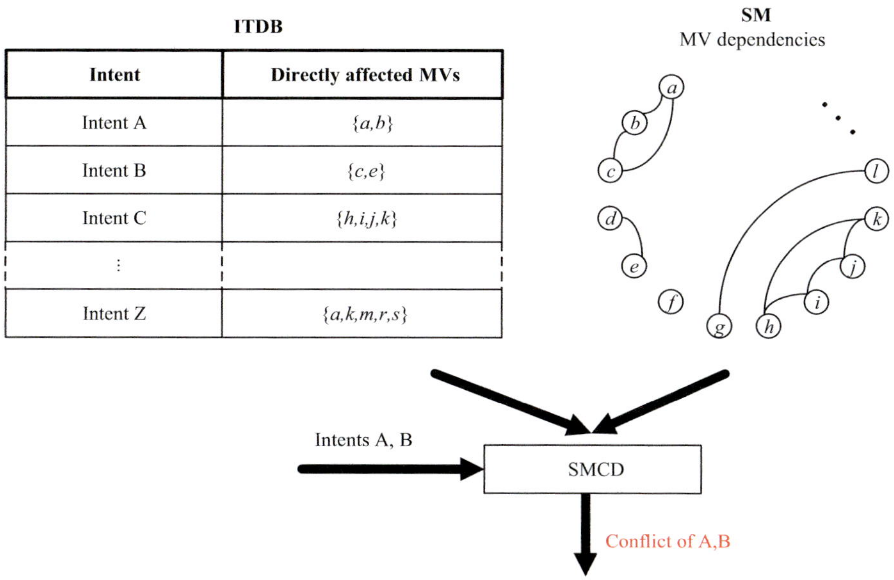

Figure 12.9 The inputs and the outputs of the method, with example intent target database, state model, and measurement value relationships depicted as a graph.

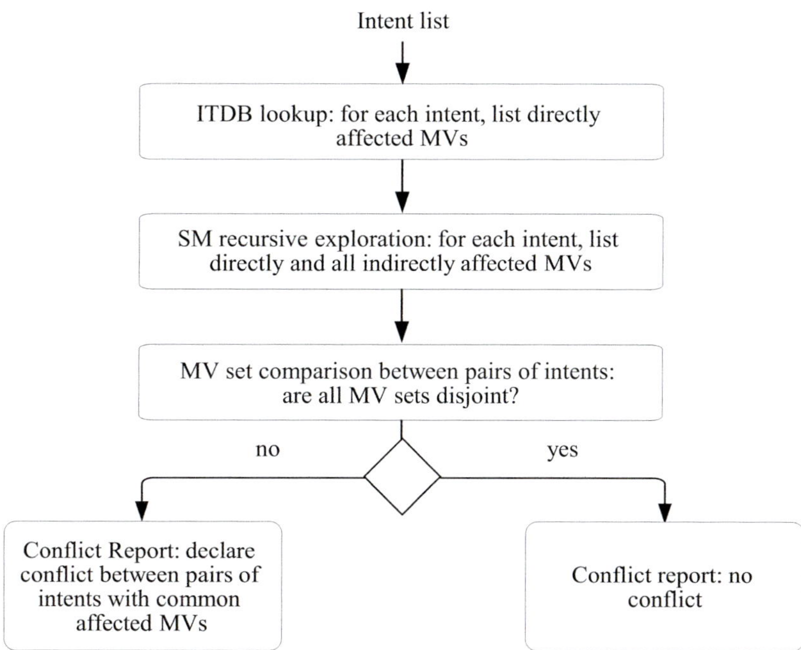

Figure 12.10 The principal functional steps of the method.

affected. The SM is represented as a graph, where each node represents an MV and an edge indicates a correlation between the two respective MVs. In the below example, intent A affects MVs *a* and *b*, and intent B affects MVs *c* and *e*. According to the SM, *a* and *b* correlate with *c*, and so *c* is affected by both intents A and B. Thus, intents A and B are declared to be conflicting intents. With this SM, intents A and C, or B and C, would not be declared to conflict with each other.

The method is hosted by state model-based conflict detection (SMCD) which takes three types of inputs: (1) the intent target database (ITDB), (2) the state model (SM), and (3) a list of intents.

The intent target database is a data structure containing a list of intents and, for each intent, a list of associated measurement values (MVs) that are directly affected if that intent is active (i.e., is being fulfilled or assured). The ITDB might have been created and can be maintained, e.g., from observations on historical intent-related data, domain expert knowledge, and arbitrary analytics on network behavior. MVs can be performance management (PM) counters, QoS/QoE metrics, latency values, and any other observed or derived value, and their combination, that refers to the state of the network or the fulfillment of the intent.

The state model is a data structure that represents relationships between pairs of MVs, e.g., in form of a graph, where a node represents an individual MV and edges represent a strong relationship between the adjacent MVs. A strong relationship between two MVs might be positive correlation, negative correlation, or any complex form of dependency defined by the SM creator/publisher. In the graphical representation, if a path between MV nodes *i* and *j* exist, then the two respective MVs show a level of dependency. The SM can stem from, e.g., analytics on historical network data, expert knowledge, and heuristics.

The SMCD takes a list of intents as the third type of input. Upon receiving a list of intents, it performs a table lookup in the ITDB for each intent to acquire the list of corresponding directly affected MVs. Then, given the list of directly affected MVs per intent, it performs a search/exploration in the SM to find all MVs that are indirectly affected by each intent, i.e., for each intent, it explores the nodes in the SM graph that are reachable (over a path) from directly affected MV nodes. (This search can be performed recursively, e.g., with depth-first search or breadth-first search, or similar algorithms.) Upon listing all affected MVs per intent, the SMCD compares the sets of affected MVs for each pair of intents and creates a conflict report. In the conflict report, it declares a conflict between a pair of intents if their respective affected MV sets overlap, and no conflict otherwise. This procedure is illustrated in Figure 12.11.

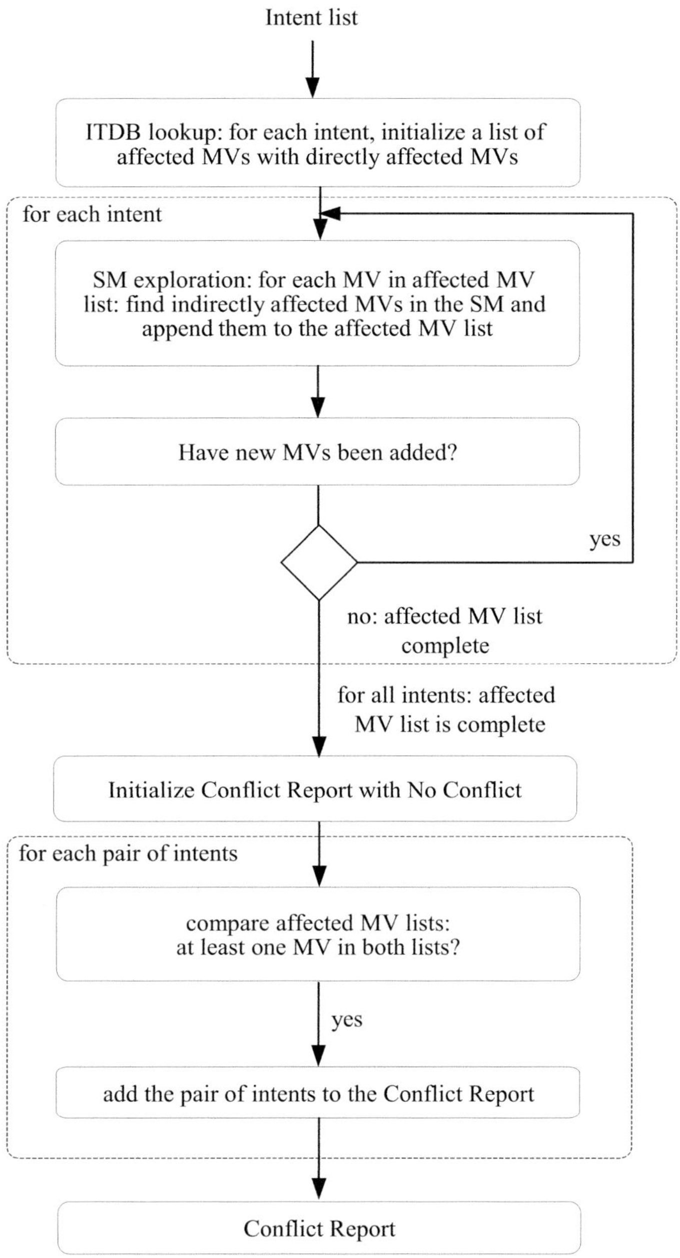

Figure 12.11 The functional steps of the proposed method.

Additionally, the conflict report, which carries pairs of conflicting intents, can be extended to include larger subsets of pairwise conflicting intents. For example, if the conflict report contains the conflicting intent pairs {A,B}, {B,C}, and {A,C}, in an additional step, the conflict report can be developed into containing a conflicting intent subset {A,B,C}.

12.3.2 Conflict detection of quality of experience intents

QoE intents have been introduced in Section 6.2 as a special case of service intents that require the network to dynamically manage the resource contention between multiple intents. QoE intents are objectives declaring that the end-user experience of certain end-user service should be satisfactory. Ensuring good QoE for end-user services is technically a resource management problem, which has to be solved by the intent-based network automatically. QoE-driven resource management requires the network to dynamically allocate a sufficient amount of resources to each end-user service from every resource pool (e.g., RAN PRB, link capacity, virtual CPU) that is used for providing the service. For a given service, the same amount of resources (e.g, RAN PRB) may allow different levels of QoE depending on dynamic UE and network conditions (e.g., UE radio channel quality), which define the resource demand of the service (i.e., the amount of resources needed for the service to have good QoE). Assuring/fulfilling multiple QoE intents simultaneously requires that common resources are scheduled so that each end-user service is allocated at least as much resources from the common resource pool as its resource demand. As the resource demand may vary according to the network conditions, as well as due to end user, application or content level dynamics, the network needs to dynamically change the services' resource allocation or arbitrate the scheduling scheme that defines how common resources are split among multiple services. If such scheduling is exercised over a common resource pool, good QoE is achieved for all services that consume resources from the pool.

There are multiple reasons why such scheduling may not be possible: (1) the resource pool's capacity is lower than the cumulative resource demand of the services using it; (2) the resource scheduler's capabilities are insufficient to split the resources in the right way (e.g., it has an allocation granularity that prevents the allocation of arbitrarily small amount of resources, or it can only operate according to a finite number of allocation presets that prevents stepping in between adjacent configurations). Both types of problems may prevent the assurance/fulfillment of QoE intents, but for different reasons, thus calling for potentially different corrective actions. Intent-based networks

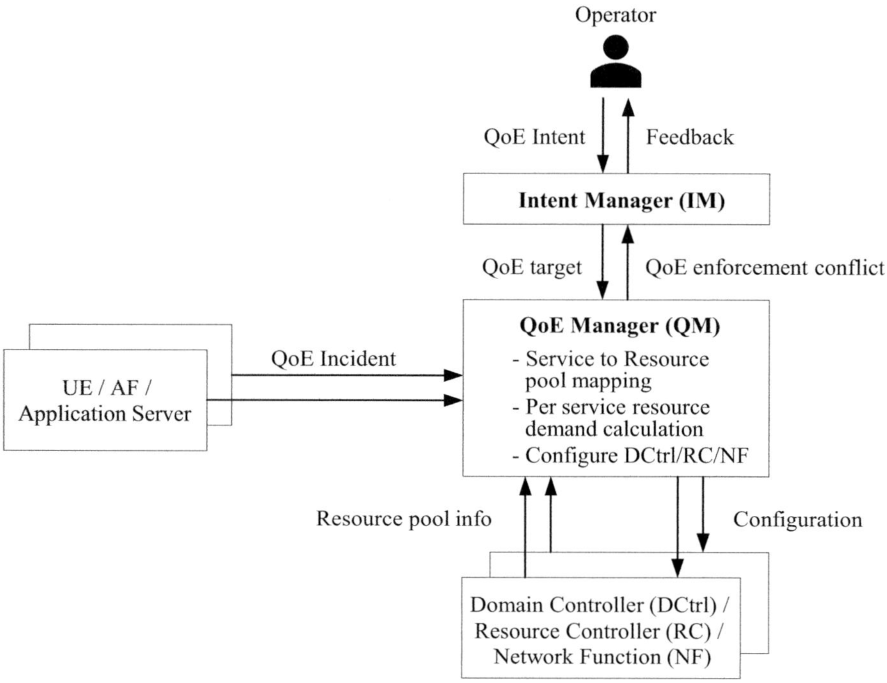

Figure 12.12 The interfaces used by the IM.

should therefore have the capability to detect the type of resource allocation problems in the context of QoE intents and report it to enable resolution.

A potential approach is described for an intent-based network that enables the detection of different types of QoE enforcement conflicts during the assurance/fulfillment of multiple QoE Intents. The key components of the approach are an intent manager (IM) and a QoE manager (QM), which together fulfill/assure QoE intents received from the operator and detect QoE enforcement conflicts if the QoE intents cannot be fulfilled/assured simultaneously (Figure 12.12). A key step in the method is the transformation of QoE intent fulfillment/assurance objectives into a closed-loop, QoE-driven resource management automation task. The IM receives QoE intents from the operator. For each QoE intent, the IM provides one or more QoE targets for the QM. The QM supervises a set of domain controllers (DCtrls), resource controllers (RCs), and/or network functions (NFs) by using their N-bound APIs to influence resource allocation decisions and thereby enforce the QoE targets for the end-user services. The QM obtains resource allocation information from the DCtrl/RC/NFs and QoE feedback from

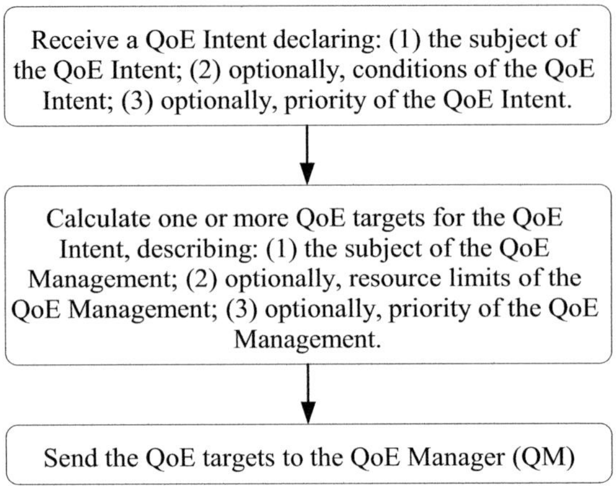

Figure 12.13 The main functionality of the IM.

the UE/AF/application server terminating the end-user service. These inputs are used by the QM to evaluate whether the resource pools controlled by the DCtrl/RC/NFs have sufficient capacity to ensure the QoE of the services, and if yes, whether they are able to enforce the right resource split among the services competing for the same resources.

The QoE intents, received by the IM from the operator, declare that the QoE of certain end-user service or application should be satisfactory. Optionally, the QoE intent may contain one or more constraints on measurable parameters, such as: traffic metrics (up to which the QoE should be enforced, such as a maximum throughput value); time (such as daily time window when the intent should be active); area (geographical area or set of NFs such as RAN entities); user/subscriber category or individual; etc. Optionally, the QoE intent may also contain a priority value to indicate the relative importance of QoE intents.

The IM translates each QoE intent into one or more QoE targets (Figure 12.13). Each QoE target describes: (1) the exact subject of QoE management, e.g., one or more user, application, etc; (2) optionally, resource limits up to which the QoE should be enforced; (3) optionally, priority among the QoE targets to indicate to the QM which target is more important. The resource limit and the priority may be derived from, or carried over from, the QoE intent if it contains constraints or a priority value.

The QM collects resource pool info from the DCtrl/RC/NFs. The resource pool info describes: (1) what resource pools are controlled by the DCtrl/RC/NF; and (2) what is the amount of resources allocated to each end-user service and what is the pool's capacity (total amount of resources).

Resource may represent any measure that is quantifiable, has a finite capacity, and is allocated by the DCtrl/RC/NF (e.g., RAN PRBs in a cell allocated by the cell's radio scheduler).

The QoE feedback is collected by the QM from the UE/AF/application server in the form of a QoE incident, which is an event sent by the source if it momentarily experiences QoE degradation. The QoE incident abstracts away the specific nature of the end-user service and what constitutes QoE degradation (e.g., whether the service requires a certain throughput or delay to enjoy good QoE, and how much or how long a violation of such requirements causes degradation). The uniform QoE incident event enables the QM to handle any end-user service including future ones, making the solution scalable and forward-compatible also for future services and applications.

The main functionality of the QM is shown in Figure 12.14. Based on the resource pool info received from the DCtrl/RC/NFs, the QM maintains a mapping between each service and the resource pools, where mapping means that the service uses resources from the pool. As a next step, executed for each resource pool, the QM calculates the resource demand of each end-user service that is mapped to the resource pool. The resource demand of a service is the amount of resources needed for the service from the resource pool to enable good QoE. The resource demand is used by the QM to check if the resource pool may be a bottleneck limiting the QoE of one or more services, which happens if there is a QoE incident for at least one service, and at the same time, the sum of all resource demands is higher than the resource pool's capacity. In this case, a QoE conflict is declared due to an insufficient amount of resources. Additionally, a different type of QoE conflict is detected if the sum of all resource demands is not higher than the resource pool's capacity but at least one service has QoE incident and that service's resource demand cannot be fulfilled due to limitations in the DCtrl/RC/NF's resource allocation capabilities. If no QoE conflict is present, yet the resource demand of at least one service is not fulfilled by the actual resource allocation, the QM reconfigures the DCtrl/RC/NF to arbitrate the split of the resource pool among the services and align the per-service resource allocation with the service's resource demand.

The QM periodically collects resource pool info from each DCtrl/RC/NF it controls. The resource pool info (Figure 12.15) consists of an indication of the resource pool capacity (total amount of resources) and the current resource use of each service from the pool. The resource pool info has two uses: (1) map the services to resource pools; (2) help the QM estimate the resource demand of the services, as detailed below.

For (1), mapping the services to resource pools, the QM maintains a mapping hierarchy as shown in Figure 12.16. The mapping enables to trace which

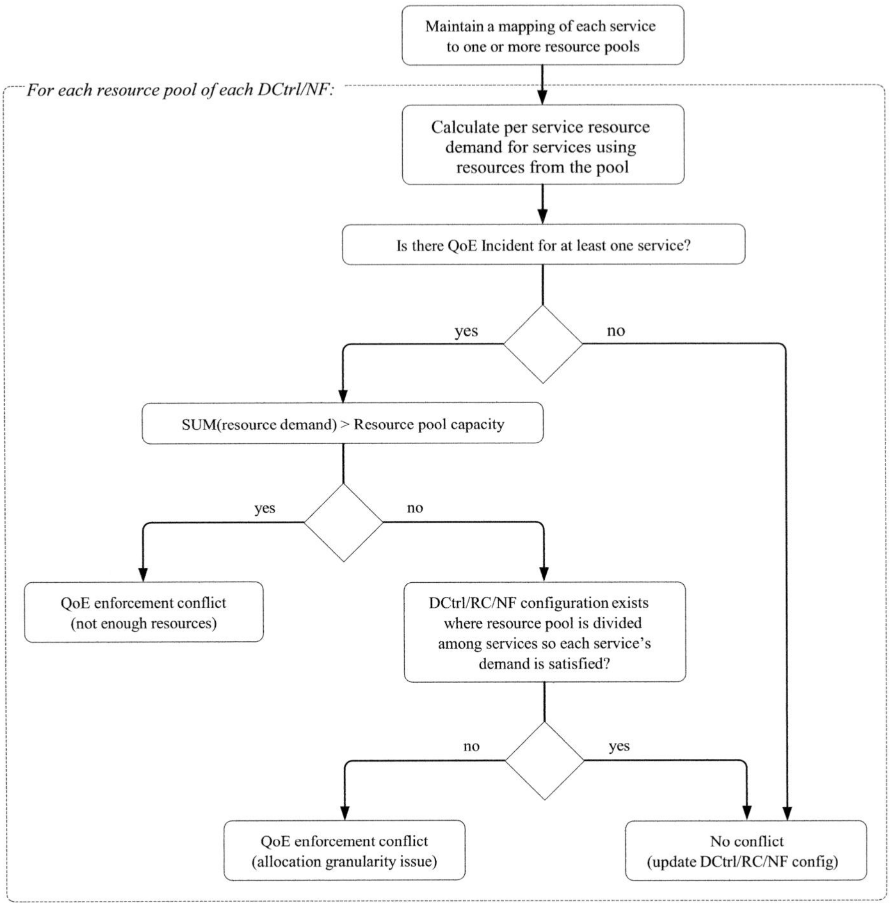

Figure 12.14 The main functionality of the QM.

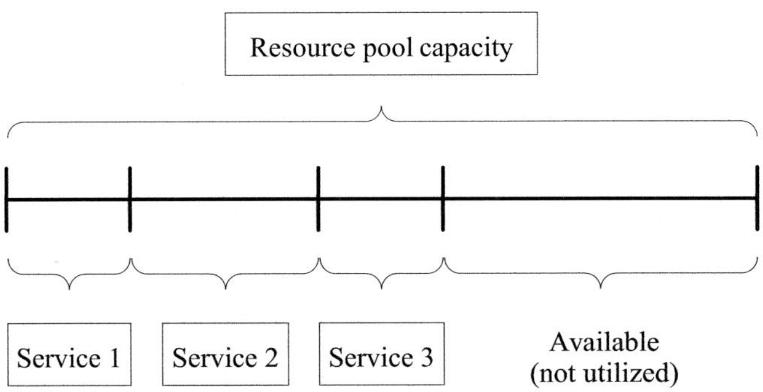

Figure 12.15 Resource pool info sent by the DCtrl/RC/NF to the QM.

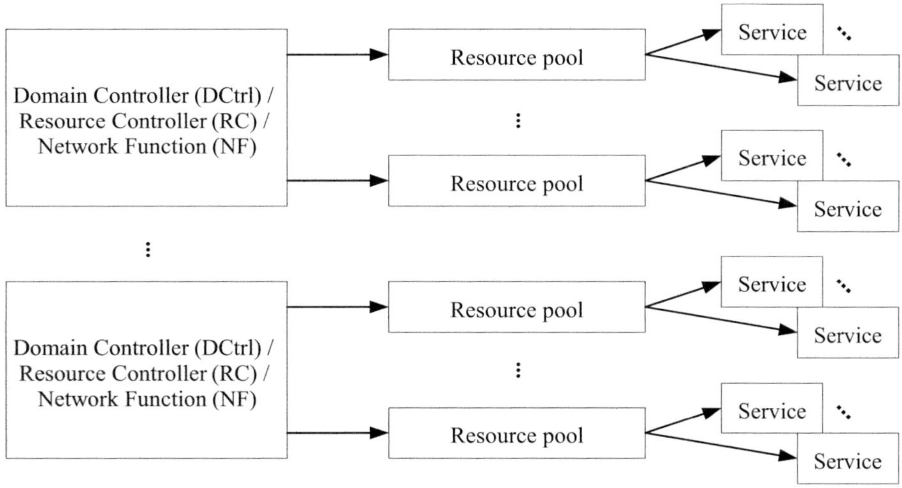

Figure 12.16 S ervice to resource pool mapping.

DCtrl/RC/NF controls which resource pool, and for each resource pool, which services are using it. A service may use multiple resource pools simultaneously.

For (2), calculating the resource demand of the services, the QM may consider that in case a service declares a QoE incident, the current amount of resources it uses is insufficient (demand exceeds usage). Conversely, if the service does not declare a QoE incident, the current amount of resources it uses is sufficient (usage exceeds or equal to demand). The current amount of resources used by a service may be calculated as a rolling average over a time window, rather than using the latest reported data point. The QM may keep an estimated resource demand for each service by tracking the service's QoE incidents in correlation with its current resource usage: the resource usage where QoE incidents appear yields a lower limit for the services resource demand, whereas the resource usage where QoE incidents disappear is an upper limit for the same. An additional indicator the QM may use is whether there is available (unused) capacity in the resource pool: available but unused resource means that the resource is not a bottleneck of the QoE as services could use more resources if they needed more. This however is only a valid assumption if the resource allocation mechanism is work-conserving and there are no service-level limits preventing a service to grow its usage above a certain threshold. Such knowledge of a DCtrl/RC/NF's resource allocation strategy and configuration should be part of the QM's implementation (statically or obtained dynamically at runtime when connecting to the N-bound APIs of the DCtrl/RC/NF) as that is exactly what makes it capable

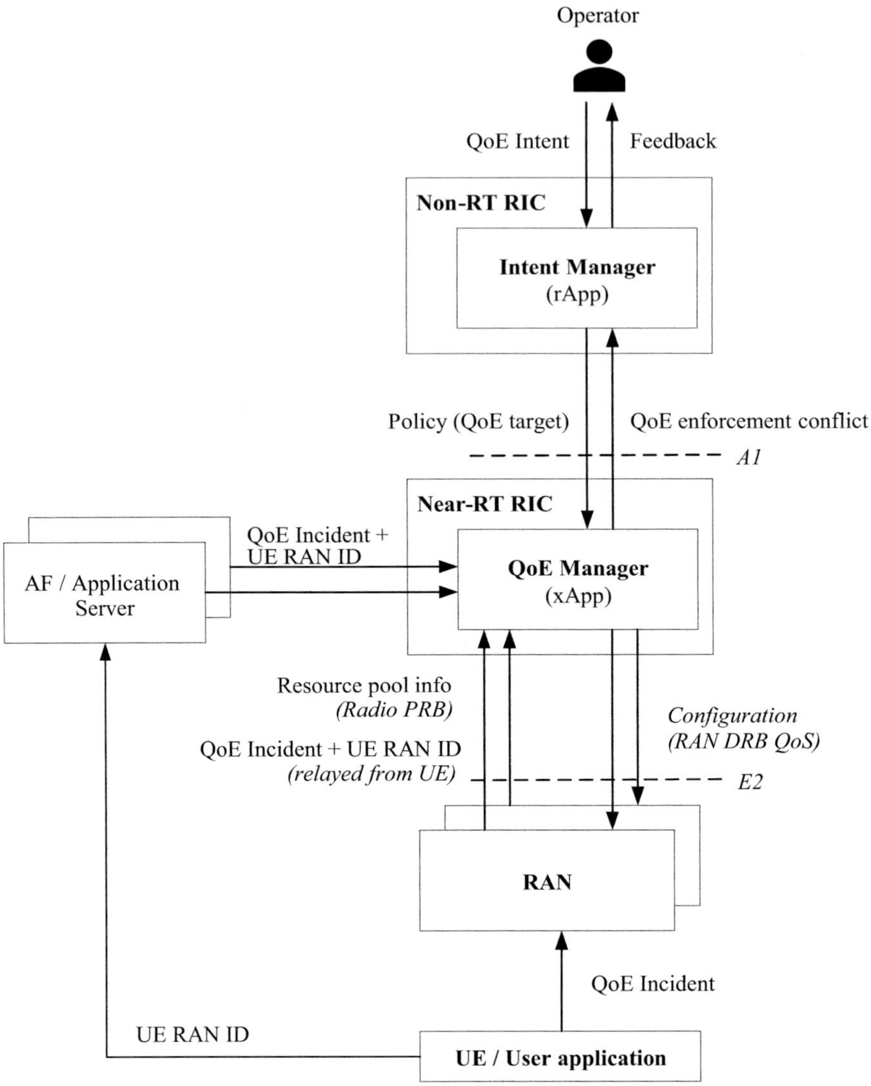

Figure 12.17 Mapping to the O-RAN architecture.

of controlling the DCtrl/RC/NF. There may be additional means to measure or collect the resource demand of a service (e.g., monitoring the patterns in the service's traffic flow to detect if the service is performing well or experiences resource shortage).

The method may be mapped to the O-RAN architecture with non-RT RIC and near-RT RIC having A1 and E2 interfaces as shown in Figure 12.17. In this embodiment, the IM may be an rApp running on the non-RT RIC and the QM may be an xApp running on the near-RT RIC. The IM interfaces with the operator and may receive QoE intents which are targeting groups of users (e.g., gold subscribers), application types (e.g., video), or services (e.g., OTT/Internet or native services). The IM translates these QoE intents to QoE targets, such as a QoE target for a specific user (e.g., identified by UE ID) or a specific application (e.g., YouTube) or both (a specific user's specific application). The QoE targets are provided to the QM on the non-RT RIC as A1 policies through the A1 interface. The QM functions as depicted in Figure 12.14 (and maintains the data structures shown in Figure 12.15 and Figure 12.16). The QM in the near-RT RIC collects QoE incidents from the UE and/or from the external AF/application server. The QM interfaces with the RAN (gNB) to collect resource pool info (Radio PRB allocation) and to provide configuration (RAN DRB QoS profile). An O-RAN-specific technical problem related to the collection of QoE incidents is the identification of the UE to which the QoE incident relates. The RAN, UE, and near-RT RIC are all aware of the UE's RAN ID (the UE's unique identifier within the RAN). However, by default the AF and the application server both lack this information. The UE sends the UE RAN ID to the AF/application server counterpart, and the AF/application server includes this information element in the QoE incident that it sends to the QM. The interface between the UE and the AF/application server may use an in-band interface embedding the UE RAN ID in the uplink user plane data sent by the UE to the AF/application server. Alternatively, the UE itself may transfer the QoE incident to the RAN via RRC and the RAN relays it along with the UE's RAN ID to the QM via E2. The required RRC signaling may be an extension of the mechanism proposed in Annex L (normative) in 3GPP TS 26.247.

12.4 Summary

Decision models enable autonomous networks to turn insights and analytics to actions and thus close the automation loops by not only producing contextual knowledge but also delivering impact to the network. Decision models build on the self-awareness of the system achieved through the state models and semantic models, operationalizing the knowledge about current and predicted states in combination with the network's own capabilities and their local or global impact in the current context.

Decision models are integral components of the planning and decision stages of closed loops, and the quality of their outcome (i.e., selecting the right action) has great impact on the performance of the entire closed loop. Decision models should consider all information that is relevant to optimize their performance; to this end, they may have the capability to dynamically activate additional data sources if the currently available information is insufficient or inconclusive. For example, collecting and fusing measurements about the network's environment such as power consumption or infrastructure temperature enable a more holistic evaluation of a decision's impact, considering not only network performance or service quality KPIs but also their footprint and cost in terms of energy.

Decision models and in general closed loops operating in dynamic network environments cannot afford to execute static business logic or predefined rule-based mapping from the observations and analytics toward actions. The best actions may depend on a set of variables that may change over the time of a network deployment, and new conditions may arise that were not part of the training phase of decision models. Having decision models learning from their own decisions and actions through monitoring their impact and efficiency remains key to networks that are not only autonomous but also adaptable.

Coordination and de-conflicting between closed loops are required to ensure that the decisions taken and implemented within one closed loop do not have a negative effect on others. De-conflicting should be a strategy that is going through the full lifecycle of closed loops, starting with a validation before they are even deployed to catch potential explicit conflicts between existing and new CLs, as well as a continuous runtime operation to keep following the dynamic conditions that may create conflicts during the fulfillment of multiple CLs.

Bibliography

[1] TM Forum, "Autonomous Network Levels Evaluation Methodology", IG1252, Version 1.2.0, June 2023

[2] 3GPP TR 28.867 Study on closed control loop management

[3] ETSI GS ZSM 009-1, "Zero-touch network and Service Management (ZSM); Closed-Loop Automation; Part 1: Enablers", V1.1.1 (2021-06)

[4] ETSI GR ZSM 011, "Zero-touch network and Service Management (ZSM); Intent-driven autonomous networks; Generic aspects" V1.1.1 (2023-02)

[5] ETSI GS ZSM 016, "Zero-touch network and Service Management (ZSM); Intent-driven Closed Loops" V1.1.1 (2024-10)

[6] 3GPP TS 28.513 Telecommunication management; Configuration Management (CM) for mobile networks that include virtualized network functions; Stage 3

[7] 3GPP TS 28.523 Telecommunication management; Performance Management (PM) for mobile networks that include virtualized network functions; Stage 3

[8] 3GPP TS 28.518 Telecommunication management; Fault Management (FM) for mobile networks that include virtualized network functions; Stage 3

[9] 3GPP TS 23.501 System architecture for the 5G System (5GS)

[10] ETSI GR NFV-IFA 043, "Network Functions Virtualisation (NFV) Release 5; Architectural Framework; Report on enhanced container networking" V5.1.1 (2024-05)

[11] 3GPP TS 29.510 5G System; Network function repository services; Stage 3

[12] 3GPP TS 28.541 Management and orchestration; 5G Network Resource Model (NRM); Stage 2 and stage 3

[13] TM Forum, "Intent in Autonomous Networks", IG1253, Version 1.3.0, August 2022

13

Network Digital Twin

Network digital twin (NDT) is a network modeling and management paradigm that enables high degree of automation by adopting the digital twin (DT) technology widely used in aviation, manufacturing, and robotics industries. In addition to the high level similarities between NDTs and DTs, there are also differences rooted in the architectural, topological, and technological specifics of communication systems. The multitude of diverse use cases the NDT can support (network planning, network simulation, management, optimization, security, etc.) require specialized NDTs and at the same time an architecture that allows scaling and on-demand composition of new NDTs out of the existing capabilities. A service-based architecture with intent-based, semantic composition and contextualization has all the capabilities required for an efficient deployment and management of a multitude of specialized NDTs within a communication system. This approach has the benefit of easy deployment of the technology in new public and private systems. As the metaverse is becoming dominant and industry digitalization and softwarization are getting momentum, NDT-managed autonomous networks are going to provide services to industrial DTs, resulting in systems consisting of AI-driven, autonomous DTs and NDTs.

13.1 Introduction

The transformative technological meta-trend, the metaverse itself, is going to speed up the digitalization of the personal, professional, and industrial environments and will allow humans to seamlessly immerse in technology in unprecedented ways and with the consequence of incorporating everything into the network be it public (Internet), semiprivate (CSP), or private (enterprise, industrial). Digitalization of the physical entities or the environment itself will result in digital entities that are commonly referred to as digital twins (Figure 13.1).

DOI: 10.1201/9788770041478-13

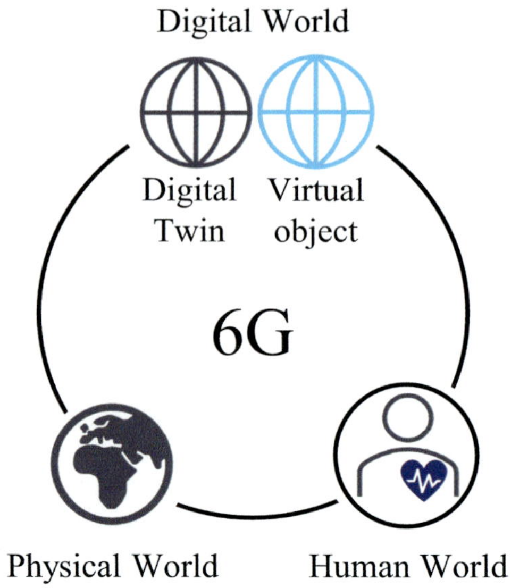

Figure 13.1 Digital twins are the key building blocks of the metaverse.

The digital twin technology has a long history of application within the industry, e.g., in aviation, manufacturing, or robotics [1]. In those industries, digital twins are used to represent the state and capabilities of physical entities, enabling both planning with and controlling physical devices from a digital space [2]. Additionally, digital twins may represent more abstract structures such as a process that is composed of multiple interworking physical entities, leading to a system of interworking digital twins in the virtual space. Digital twins may collect real-time telemetry and state information about the physical entities, either directly from the entities themselves (e.g., using built-in capabilities) or indirectly (e.g., from external sensors attached to or observing the entities).

The concept of digital twins has also been transferred to various networking technologies including 5G [3], stirring interest in different standardization activities [4], [5], [6], [7]. As a common theme in all these recommendations, studies and specifications, a network digital twin follows the general idea of a digital twin being a virtual replica of a real-world ("physical") entity [5], meaning that an NDT is a digital twin with physical counterpart that is a network or part of a network [7]. In the case of networks, one important note is that "physical" does not necessarily mean a physical network function, physical equipment, or a HW entity, but increasingly refers to a part of the network that is already provided as a virtual function or software entity. Still, the analogy between DTs and NDTs holds, as an NDT is not simply yet another instance of a network software (in case the "physical" entity is already virtualized) but captures knowledge about the twinned entity's operational and behavioral aspects that are relevant for the NDT's purpose.

The scope of an NDT may be diverse: it may scale from representing a single unique device (including HW) or function (including SW) in the network, following the industrial approach of per-device DTs [2]; through representing part of a communication network [7]; up to modeling an entire mobile network including devices, radio and transport links, applications, and the environment in which the network operates [3]. In general, the network digital twin may be considered being a virtual representation of a real network, including its functions, management processes, users, services, and its operational environment, in order to provide capabilities in the virtual world that maintains a relevance and utility in the physical world. Depending on the use case supported by the NDT, it may provide analytics capabilities that provide insights or predictions related to a network situation such as the analyzing NDT in ZSM015 [7]; or it may exercise a level of control over the physical network by being incorporated into closed loops such as the controlling NDT in ZSM015 [7], providing decisions, configurations, or other actions that are transferred back to the physical network. Analysis and control capabilities may also coexist in the same network digital twin, which in theory enables an NDT to become a surrogate for certain network functions, emulating partly or fully its behavior while providing additional capabilities such as evaluation of potential actions in a hypothetical scenario.

While the notion of network digital twins stems out of digital twins as defined by the industry [8], there are notable differences between the DT of a cyber-physical device, such as an autonomous robot, and the DT of a network, that is, an NDT. The differences relate to the dynamicity, complexity, and scale of the twinned physical entities, resulting in different requirements and modeling technologies to produce DTs and NDTs.

If the scope of a DT is to map the physical (kinematic, dynamic) properties and responses of a self-contained cyber-physical device, physical models are available (or can be adapted to the specific case) to provide an accurate analytical description of the device's physical operation (such as motion and forces). Such models capture the device's behavior and interaction with its environment based on physical laws, offering a persistent representation that remains as long as the device's physical build stays intact. Also, there is no stochasticity involved in such physical models; therefore, they provide a repeatable and universally usable model of the physical parts of the device. The complexity of the models is specific to the complexity of the device's physical build, e.g., number of axes, freedom of movement, etc., but it does not need to consider factors that are outside of the specification of the device itself.

On the contrary, the scope of NDTs may be to capture the behavior of an entire network or a set of network functions. The operation of a network is a result of the interplay of many heterogeneous components, modulated by events and conditions that cannot be influenced by the network such as the users' mobility, the radio channel characteristics, the behavior of over-the-top applications and traffic, all of which generate a lot of stochastic elements that have to be captured by the NDT. Additionally, the stochastic elements in both the physical network and its environment are dynamic, continuously changing, and evolving, which require that the NDT models are continuously updated. As a result, no analytical model can be created to even describe the operation of a network, which pushes toward the use of AI/ML for deriving models based on observations rather than functional/physical models. However, the size, scale, and geographical distribution of a network (especially in the RAN) prohibits the sourcing of all network data (especially in real time) to drive an NDT that is a one-to-one replica of a network on the low level of details (such as at the level of physical equipment and virtual functions). As a result, NDTs may need to provide various levels of abstraction in terms of the fidelity and granularity of replicating the physical network. In terms of replication, high-fidelity representation of a physical network or one of its entities (e.g., equipment, function) may only be possible focusing on a subset of the physical network (e.g., on one specific equipment instance) rather than aiming to reproduce the behavior and responses of the full-scale physical network in every aspect. The wider the scope of the NDT, the higher abstraction is required to keep the computation complexity of the models manageable and to enable them to operate on real time network data. As with any modeling exercises, the extent and scope of simplification (i.e., discarding information and relations) is driven by the purpose and use case implemented by the NDT.

Despite the above differences between DTs and NDTs, a commonality is that NDTs (just like DTs) maintain a relation to a physical entity (network or part of it) rather than being theoretical platforms that exist only virtually. That is, NDTs are not general simulators or emulators that operate detached from the reality of any particular network deployment (even if they use simulation or emulation technologies internally), but every NDT instance is derived from and specialized for an actual real physical network. The lifecycle of an NDT thus has to intersect at least once with the lifecycle of its physical network counterpart (Figure 13.2). The intersection may be regular

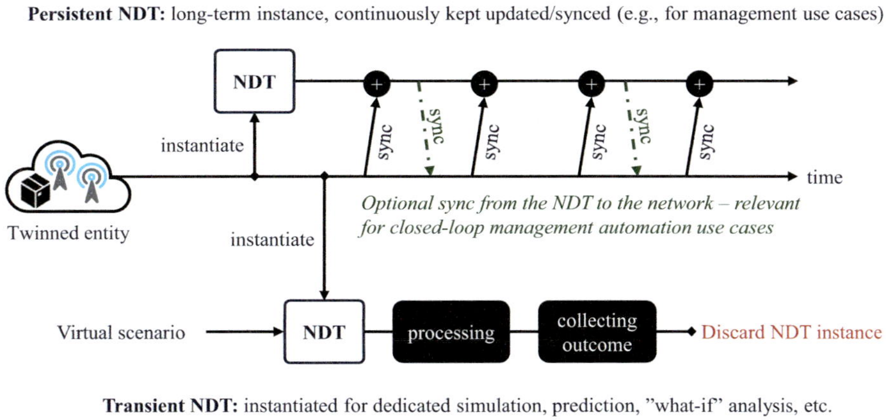

Figure 13.2 NDT physical-virtual synchronization patterns.

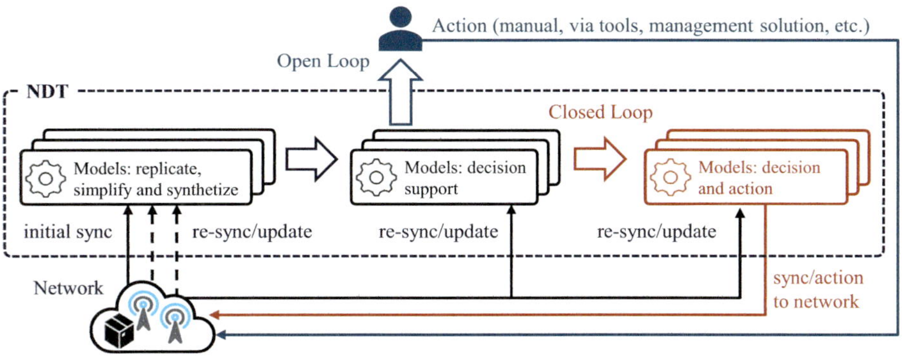

Figure 13.3 NDTs for open loops and closed loops.

and frequent, as in the case of a persistent NDT that is instantiated based on the current state of the physical network (twinned entity) and continuously kept in sync through subsequent updates from the physical to the virtual domain. Such synchronization pattern is useful if the purpose of the NDT is to provide instantaneous insights, recommendations, or even decisions that are relevant in the physical network's present context. In case the decisions are acted out in a closed-loop fashion by the NDT (Figure 13.3), the synchronization becomes two-way, incorporating the replication of states of actions at the NDT space back to the physical network.

NDTs may also be more transient and created on-the-fly for a specific purpose, such as evaluating a network state, the impact of a decision in a hypothetical scenario, or any other condition that benefits from reality-based analysis. Multiple transient NDTs (with different parameters) can also be dispatched in parallel to explore the potential problem space before converging on an outcome. The NDT(s) are discarded when their purpose has been fulfilled. Of course, this does not mean to discard the knowledge (such as AI/ML models) on which the NDTs are delivering their capabilities, but only to discard the specific simulation, emulation, or analysis job that is instantiated and parameterized for the different hypotheses that the NDTs have to prove or contradict. The lifecycles of the persistent NDT and transient NDT match the needs of ZSM015's control NDT and analyzing NDT concepts [7].

The rest of this chapter is organized to provide a deeper discussion across different NDT concepts. Section 13.2 presents an overview of prominent use cases for NDT such as NDTs for network management automation. Section 13.3 explores the architecture principles for NDT, converging toward a service-based architecture that brings the flexibility necessary to customize NDTs to specific use cases while leveraging enablers and capabilities existing in the network. Next, Section 13.4 discusses the problem of avoiding NDT silos per each use case through the investigation of modeling and composition aspects that were already introduced in Chapter 11. Finally, Section 13.5 provides an outlook toward NDTs for enterprise and private network scenarios.

13.2 Use Cases

NDTs provide value to a physical network by providing new capabilities that are operated virtually before (if at all) they are synchronized back to the real (physical) network. The type of capabilities provided by an NDT may be versatile and specific to the use case that the NDT implements [7, 9]. Example use case categories and use cases may be provided as follows:

Network emulation, simulation

- RL training for radio planning and handover optimization
- Impact evaluation of automated decisions: in ZSM015 ML inference-impact emulation; in 3GPP TR 28.915 policy verification and impact estimation using NDT

Network planning and optimization

- Scenario emulation and evaluation (ZSM015 mentions subcases such as network slicing risk prediction, signaling storm simulation and analysis, ML inference-impact emulation, etc.; 3GPP TR 28.915 also reports on simulation and emulation as technologies part of most of the solutions proposed for key NDTs use cases)

- Energy saving (also covered in ZSM015)

Network and service management, and their automation

- Self-annotating network states: a concept covered in Section 10.4.3
- Service-based integration of NDTs with NFs: a concept that will be covered in Section 13.3
- ZSM015 devotes a section on NDT for zero-touch network and service management
- 3GPP TR 28.915 includes specific use cases such as signaling storm analysis, network failure, risk prediction, and network automation

Defensive networks

- NDT as security honeypot: a concept that will be covered in Section 13.2.2
- NDT proxying functionality of NFs: NDTs may involve functional models of the physical network [7] that may become substitutes for the actual network function; C/U/M-plane NDTs [7] also provide integration with the real network that enable the NDTs to be natural

The above use cases and categories are only exemplary and by no means complete; other use cases and subuse cases exist and are expected to be developed further.

13.2.1 NDT for network management

Network management use cases have been the earliest ones to appear in NDT-related standardization works [5, 7], including a dedicated work item on NDT for enhanced zero-touch network and service management [10]. One reason for this may be the focus of the SDOs that were early to launch work items on NDTs, such as ZSM that focuses on network and service management automation. Another technical reason may be an initial touchpoint between the concept of NDTs and the current network management systems. The management systems already represent configuration, states, data, and capabilities of real (both physical and virtual) network functions and provide means to interact with them. Management automation is also implemented in or through such systems, realizing different levels of autonomy [11].

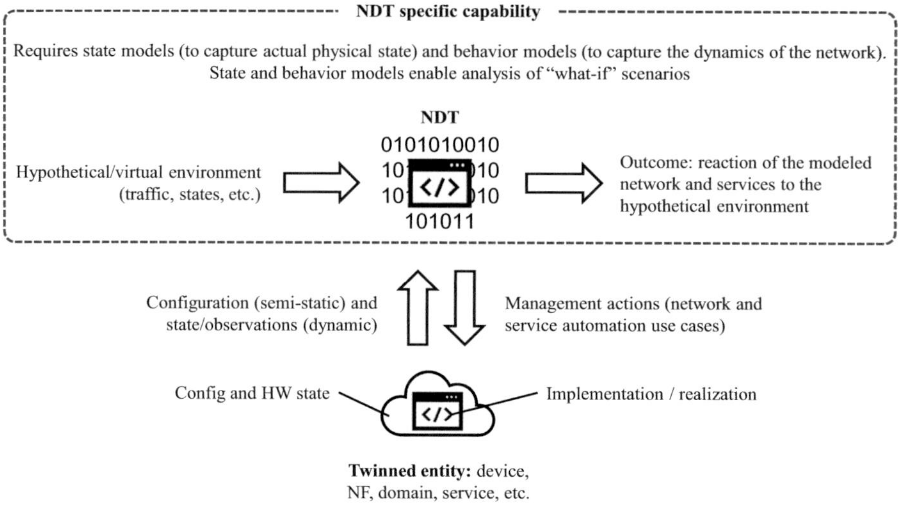

Figure 13.4 NDT use cases for network management automation.

The management systems are, however, not automatically becoming NDTs. Collecting and storing system data and configuration need to be complemented with modeling capabilities that enables the NDT to perform analysis of potentially hypothetical scenarios, such as an analyzer NDT [7]. These analysis capabilities can of course be practically implemented in a network management system itself; therefore, the distinction between management systems and NDTs is becoming less definitive and less important.

The importance of analysis capabilities for NDTs targeting use cases for network management automation is illustrated in Figure 13.4. On the physical network (twinned entity) side, there is a given implementation of a network element, function, or capability, whose behavior is modulated by its configuration, state, and other external conditions that impact the operation of the network (such as traffic, user mobility, and actions). The NDT's goals within network management use cases relate to its capability to analyze how the physical network would perform in a given (hypothetical, or explicitly known) different scenario, that is, in case of any change in the physical network's configuration, state, or changes in the external conditions. The NDT should have access to the relevant configuration of the physical network (which may not be entirely static but is expected to change at a slower pace than the external conditions). The NDT should also be able to collect observations such as measurements, logs, counters, etc. from the physical network. Based on the available (semistatic) configuration and (dynamic) observation data, models can be trained to represent the state of the physical network (see state models in Chapter 10). The state models enable to have a machine-interpretable representation of what is happening in the physical network, or, in case of predictive state models, what is likely going to happen. In addition to the state models, behavior models can also be trained that predict the physical network's typical response in specific states (predictions are possibly modulated and specialized by additional context information such as external conditions, configuration, time, and location). Based on the state and behavior models, NDT enables advanced decision-making [7] and automation when the NDT is synchronized back to the physical network through management actions.

Modeling the network state and behavior is essential but generic capabilities for an NDT that aims to provide extended capabilities for network management. The concrete use case of the NDT defines the exact model type, technology, and architecture; the data used to train the model (in case of AI/ML modeling) and make it fit to the twinned physical network; the input and output (both syntactically and semantically) of the models; etc. Therefore, models for network management NDTs have to be specialized to the actual use case, matching the realities of available data as well as the expectations of the models in terms of representation and expressiveness.

13.2.2 NDT for security

The softwarization of network functions have created security concerns that are rooted in the state of the art of SW technology. In particular, xNFs, x/rApps are software implementations with API/interface exposure to external applications for integration, programmability, and consumability. Such SW implementations may contain vulnerabilities including those imported via the integration of third party/OSS libraries, as well as those added through vendor R&D and CI/CD pipeline. In addition to generic SW vulnerabilities, AI used in the SW implementations may be vulnerable to AI-specific attack vectors (e.g., adversary attacks, model integrity violations). In-line network SW modules (such as UPF, RAN) may also be attacked through traffic (e.g., DoS) or via their protocol stack (e.g., malformed protocol IEs). Management and control interfaces are prone to authorization and authentication weaknesses, which may open the system to penetration attacks and privilege escalation. Overall, any of the above type of attacks may cause network failures, service interruption, unauthorized access to management capabilities, injection of invalid (and harmful) commands, etc.

To defend against some of the above attacks, NDTs may be used as "Fake Nodes" ("NDT-FN") to safely emulate parts of the system functionalities (from individual SW module level to entire xNF/xApps/rApps). The NDT-FN provides the first layer of interfaces through which users (operators, applications) may start interacting with the system, rather than directly accessing the real network and management functions. In this scenario, there are two key requirements for the NDT-FN:

- *(1) Masquerading*: How to masquerade an NDT-FN to look like part of the real system, so it's not obvious for an attacker that this is a fake node? Without masquerading, a hypothetical attacker would have no interest in targeting an NDT-FN but would try to access the real network or go through indirect attack channels such as end-to-end traffic or DoS. On the other hand, an efficient NDT-FN's scope is to look like the right target for attacking, only proving to be impossible to breach and gain access into the real system. Ideally, during an attack, the attackers would not even know that they are not being successful, but they would keep devoting more time and effort to penetrate the NDT-FN, while the real system operates untouched.
- *(2) Session migration*: How to enable benevolent (legitimate) users to bypass the NDT-FN, or more precisely, to transfer their interactions from the NDT-FN to the real system without having to restart/redo their session (e.g., authentication/authorization, already entered commands, etc.) with the real system? Even to nonattackers, it would not be beneficial to reveal that they used to be interacting with an NDT-FN and now they are openly redirected to the "real" system where they need to restart their interaction, as everything that they accomplished was only on a fake node.

The NDT fake node concept may be incorporated into an architecture (Figure 13.5) that enables to masquerade real network components (e.g., NFs, xApps, rApps, management services, etc.) from users that may potentially be malicious. Users of such network components are those that interact with them in order to configure, operate, and monitor them. Such users usually access these network components over remote interfaces, not directly via a physical management console attached to the HW that runs the network components; therefore, the remote interfaces may be accessible to attackers breeching the firewalls protecting unauthorized access to the network components, or may use social engineering (e.g., password extraction) to hijack the login of a legitimate user to perform malicious activities in the name of a valid user. Multiple types of NDT-FNs may be created, each type twinning a

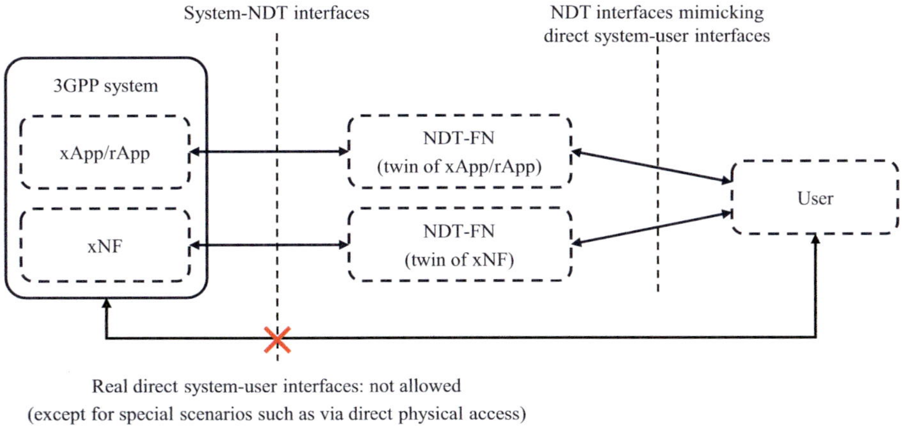

Figure 13.5 The architecture using NDT-FNs to capture all user interactions on behalf of the twinned network components.

different type of original network component, and multiple instances of the same NDT-FN may be deployed in a system to provide multiple entry points via NDT-FNs.

The solution approach for the *(1) masquerading* requirement may be outlined as follows:

- An NDT-FN stands in for all user interactions on behalf of the twinned real network component. Users are not allowed to initiate direct interactions with any network component, especially accessing the network component via remote interfaces. The only exceptions may be users having physical access to the network components (or the HW hosting them), as those users may anyhow have means to interact with the network components that cannot be controlled via IT security means. Note, however, that physical access should not automatically mean authorized direct access to the network components; for example, if the ownership of the network components and the physical HW are different.
- The NDT-FN provides the full interface of the twinned network components in terms of user access, commands, responses, etc. The user may initiate interactions with the NDT-FN (believing to be interacting with the real network component) for which immediate response is expected. Immediate interactions may include:
    - Establishment of connectivity, identification, authentication, and authorization (login procedure)

  - Some commands with real time output (e.g., query of system state, access to stored data, access to logs, etc.)

- Responses to such immediate actions may be emulated by the NDT-FN, i.e., not exposing the real system state or data but instead generating statistically relevant but fake information. Such information could be valid for the system in theory but not in particular – however, for the user this is transparent.
- The user interactions are profiled by the NDT-FN to identify if the behavior or the identified user is valid, according to the user's usual profile (e.g., to detect impersonation attacks) or if there is any activity that is suspicious (e.g., query for data that is not relevant for the user's profile) or malicious (e.g., providing commands to the system with negative side effects or providing management objectives or intents that would create conflicts with the existing ones). User sessions that are classified as suspicious or malicious are not migrated to the real system – interactions are terminated by the NDT-FN and the existence of the user session remains transparent to the twinned real network component. By keeping the user active on the NDT-FN, the attacker's resources are kept busy on targets where no harm to the real system is done.

The solution approach for (2) session migration requirement may be outlined as follows:

- Legitimate user sessions where the user interaction qualifies as nonmalicious should be allowed to make changes to the real twinned network component. However, the user should not be required to redo all interactions that have already been performed with the NDT-FN. The solution leverages the bidirectional state sync capability of digital twins, i.e., changes made to the NDT-FN are replicated to the real twinned network components. Since NDT-FNs are digital twins of their twinned real network components, they are able to not only to sync their states with that of the real network components but also to sync changes from the NDT-FN to the real network components.
- The sync is transparent to the users; therefore, they keep interacting with the NDT-FN. The only difference between malicious and nonmalicious user interactions is that the interactions of nonmalicious users start to be synced back to the network components (after the users are cleared by the NDT-FN to be nonmalicious).

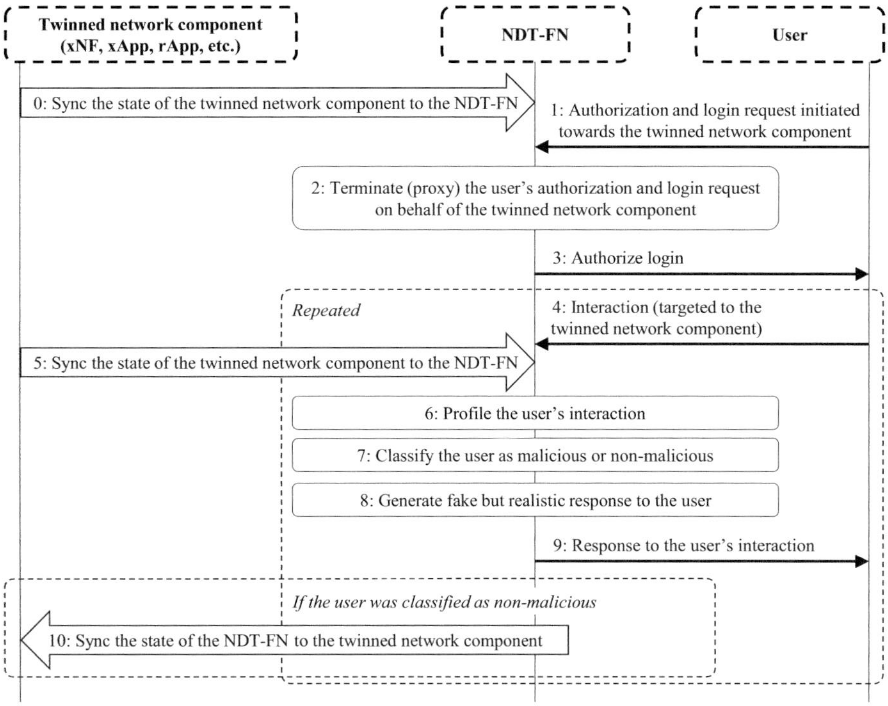

Figure 13.6 System level integration of the NDT fake node concept.

The NDT-FN's interaction with the system and the user are shown in Figure 13.6.

Step 0: The NDT-FN's state is synced from the twinned real network component. This is standard operation of an NDT that is replicating (part of) the functionality of a real network component.

Step 1: The user initiates an authorization and login process addressed to the real network component.

Step 2: Transparently to the user, the NDT-FN consumes and handles the request on behalf of the real network component. In other terms, the NDT-FN acts as a transparent application proxy toward the user, concealing the request from the real network component.

Step 3: Since the NDT-FN is a twin of the real network component, it can respond to the request as if the request was handled by the real network component.

Step 4: The user performs an interaction (e.g., entering commands through CLI, or clicks through a GUI, or any other user interface action). As the user believes, the interaction is with the real network component, but in fact, similarly to the login process, the interaction is terminated and handled by the NDT-FN of the twinned real network component.

Step 5: The NDT-FN may refresh its state by synching it to that of the twinned real network component. This is optional and depends on how frequently the state of the real network component changes and how much that impacts the capability of the NDT-FN to produce realistic but fake responses to the user. Also note that such sync from the twinned real network component to the NDT-FN may happen asynchronously at any time, according to the implementation of the NDT-FN and its interaction with its twinned real network component.

Step 6: A primary scope of the NDT-FN is to trace and profile the user's interactions with the intention to classify it as malicious or nonmalicious. The profiling may consider, e.g., the content of the interaction (e.g., the command given via a CLI), the absolute timing (e.g., time of day), or relative timing (e.g., time since previous interaction) of the interaction; comparison of the user's interaction to historical interactions of the same user or interactions of other users; the interactions of the user in context of the role and responsibilities of the user; etc.

Step 7: Based on the profiling, the NDT-FN may classify the user as malicious or nonmalicious. The classification may not be possible after every interaction, e.g., the NDT-FN may need to profile multiple interactions of the user since the login before the pattern of the interactions becomes definitive of being malicious or not. Malicious behavior may be detected based on one or more of: suspicious content of the interaction (e.g., the command is unusual, such as syntactically wrong or refers to nonexisting resources that the user should be aware of and thus not trying to access, etc.); interaction coming at unusual time of day (e.g., outside of working hours of the user) or in unusual timing pattern relative to previous interactions (e.g., repeated or rapid requests for the same or similar pieces of information from the network component); the interaction was never done by the user before (and the user has a significant history of previous interactions) or by other users with the same role; the interaction does not fit to the ones expected from the user's role (e.g., persistently trying to access the unauthorized information, or trying to write to a read-only resource, trying to repeatedly perform, or work-around a command that was already denied such as mounting a physical drive or accessing a device's classified folders); etc.

Step 8: The NDT-FN generates a fake but realistic response to the user (in case the user's interaction was expecting a response). At this point the NDT-FN may already have the user classified as malicious or nonmalicious, which may impact the generated response (e.g., provide accurate response to nonmalicious user, or provide a statistically relevant but particularly incorrect response to malicious users to keep them engaged with the NDT-FN rather than trying to move to another attack target).

Step 9: The response generated in Step 8 (if any) is sent to the user on behalf of the twinned real network component.

Step 10: If the user was already classified as nonmalicious, the NDT-FN emulates session migration to the twinned real network component by performing a backwards sync from the NDT-FN's state to the twinned real network component. This enables that any action performed on the NDT-FN with side effects (e.g., changing the network component's configuration) is replicated back to the twinned real network component, as if the nonmalicious user has had performed them directly on the real network component.

The *Steps 4–10* are repeated as needed.
Note that the above mechanism also enables the NDT-FN to reclassify a nonmalicious user to malicious and stop syncing its interactions (or even reverting past interactions) with the twinned real network component.

13.3 NDT Architecture

This section discusses architectural building blocks and enablers that are common for NDTs especially for NDTs for network and service management. Building blocks include data sources, common modeling capabilities, and interfaces for the management and governance of NDT.

Figure 13.7 provides an abstract view of a network with three key programmable capabilities that are rendered in the context of NDT enablers.

1. NW state modeling, as discussed in Section 13.2 and in Chapter 10, is a generic enabler to build context-based network automation capabilities. The state models encompass a wide range of modeling targets, including resources, network topology (at different layers), configuration, measurements, and their combination. State modeling is a potential

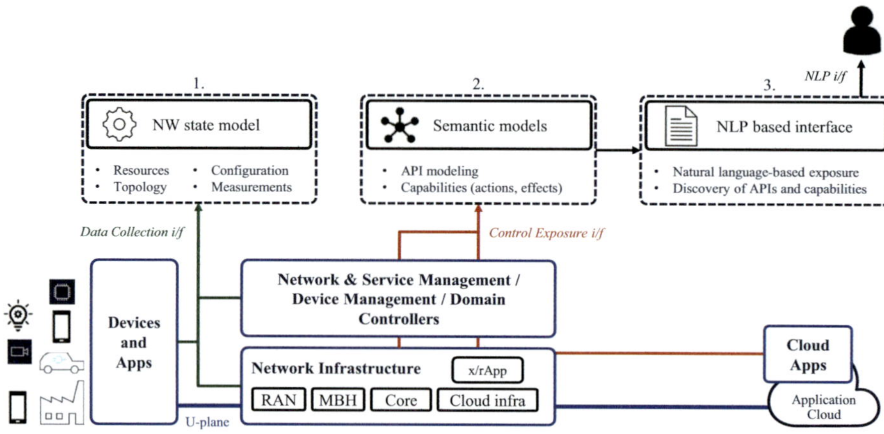

Figure 13.7 Programmable network components leveraged by NDTs.

consumer of all network data; however, not every state model needs to ingest all data that is produced by the network.

2. Semantic models, as introduced in Chapter 11, enable to capture the means to impact existing services and functions in the network through modeling the potential impact of various accessible APIs and capabilities that could be manipulated by an NDT. Semantic modeling is a consumer of the potential API descriptions and control points exposed by the network, such as the interfaces of the network and domain controllers, but also potentially CLIs and other deep interfaces through which network functions, elements or services, tools, and workflows may be accessed and automated.

3. User interface, covered in Chapter 8 in general and in Chapter 9 for intents, which enable interactions with the network for the purpose of constructing an NDT for a given use case (along the principles of semantic composition introduced in Section 11.5 and what will be applied to NDTs in Section 13.4), and later on also to interact with the NDT itself.

The basic logical architecture of NDTs targeting network management automation use cases is depicted in Figure 13.8. The modeling scene is expanded to explicitly show the predictive, analytics, and decision models, which are technical enablers for the NDT to integrate capabilities such as impact analysis, what-if analytics, event prediction, evaluation of different (hypothetical) configurations, etc. These indicate usual NDT capabilities [7] that may be shrunk, expanded, and tailored to the use case implemented by the NDT.

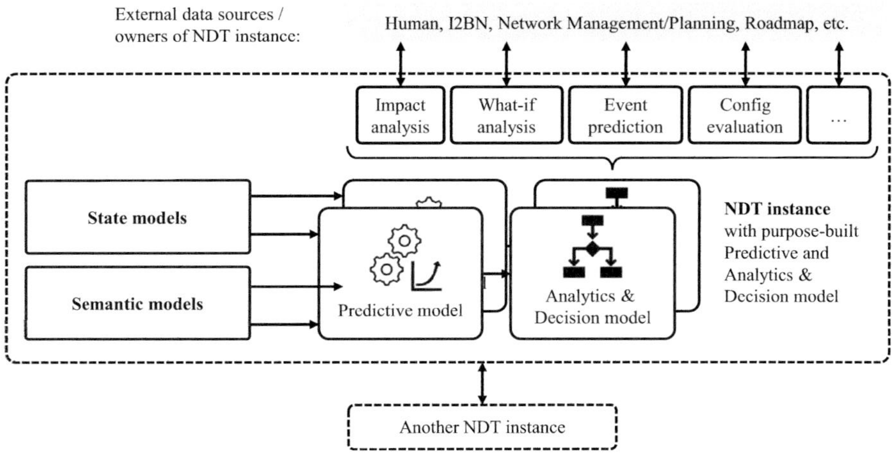

Figure 13.8 Network management automation with network digital twin.

Besides collecting data from the network for building models specific for the twinned physical network, the NDT may also interact with external data sources or the operator to source information that cannot be collected from the operational network (such as planning related information that includes decisions already made about the future of the network to which the NDT also needs to comply). The NDT may also interwork with other NDT instances similar to interworking between services (based on a provider-consumer pattern) where one NDT is producing an insight (e.g., an analyzer NDT [7]) that is consumed by another NDT making an impact for the physical network (e.g., a Control NDT [7]).

A more detailed logical architecture diagram depicting the integration of multiple NDTs with a network is shown in Figure 13.9. The left side of the figure illustrates the various network functions, management services, and applications that act both as data sources and control points in the physical network. A logical data collection layer enables access to all network data that is required for the various types of commonly needed models, such as the already discussed state models. The data collection may be realized according to the principles of Chapter 3. The exposed control points in the network are represented by semantic models. Both the network state models and semantic models could be regarded as multipurpose representations that belong more to the network itself than to a specific NDT use case, as they implement digitalization and machine-readable description of network operation and capabilities rather than providing a use case-specific functionality. Therefore, these modeling capabilities may even be integrated

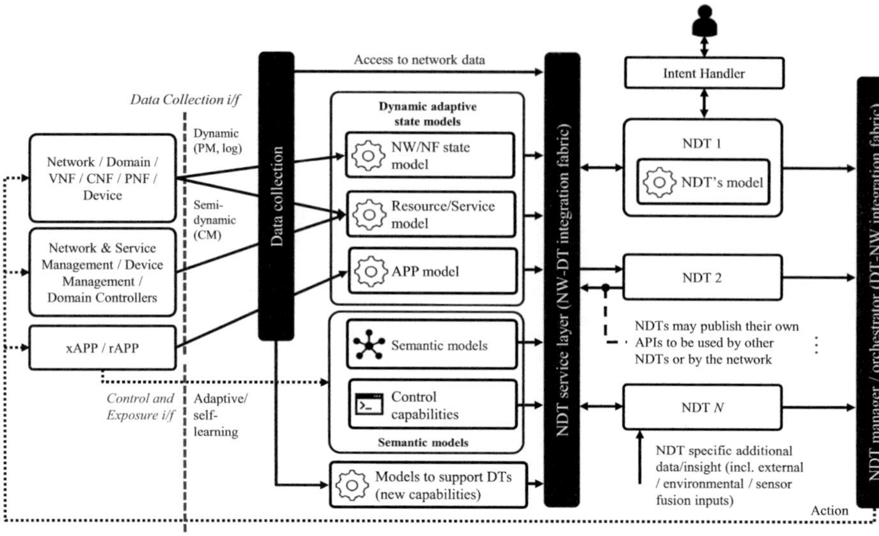

Figure 13.9 Network digital twin general architecture.

with the network (similarly to the service-based integration of trusted 3GPP application functions) and be exposed to the NDT domain though a so-called NDT service layer. The NDT service layer is a logical entity that implements control over access and information flow between the network and the NDTs (as well as between interworking NDTs). The NDT service layer enables to keep security, capability exposure, and integration concerns under control, considering that NDTs could be provided not only by network vendors but also by third parties. In addition to the rather generic state and semantic models (that could be of use by network management automation even without NDTs), the network may host additional NDT-specific models. Those models could still be generic, that is, not specific to any NDT's use case, but consider the requirements of NDTs in terms of bridging between the real physical network and a virtual digital counterpart (e.g., provide models or services for alignment between the different time scales of the real network and a simulation or emulation proceeding in an NDT at a different pace [7]).

The NDT instances consume the state and semantic models as well as potential NDT-oriented other services through the NDT service layer. What makes NDTs specific to their use case is the NDT-specific model (or models) that each NDT owns and integrates with the information flowing from the physical network. In addition to the network's data, the NDTs may also collect information from sources outside of the network (e.g., from environmental sensors that enable an NDT to extend the network representation with that of its operational environment, be it the physical macro environment or related to the datacenter infrastructure that runs the network functions). NDTs may publish their own capabilities (e.g., analysis outcome, or a capability to exercise control over the network) as services to be consumed by other NDTs. This enables interworking between collaborative NDTs, or even collaboration between an NDT and the network (e.g., using an NDT to automate part of the management of the network may be achieved by looping the NDT's services back to the network to look like a native management service).

In an intent-based network where network management is already based on intent, it is natural to use intents also for the purpose of interacting with NDTs. The scope of the interaction may be two-fold. First, for the creation (design) of a new NDT, using the capabilities and models provided by the network and extended with NDT specific models. Second, for the management of the NDT instances, along the principles of native AI management (given that NDTs are likely AI-based themselves) and intent-based network management (given that NDTs are likely to provide use cases that are related to or directly relevant for network automation). Intents for NDTs will be further discussed in Section 13.4 with intent-based NDT composition that unifies the concept of semantic intent-based composition (Section 11.5) and NDTs.

13.3.1 Service-based deployment architecture

Network digital twins may integrate with the network through APIs and interfaces exposed by various network or management functions. Depending on the use case, an NDT may require network integration that enables real-time or in-depth state cloning (a.k.a. synchronization) from the twinned network component onto the NDT and vice versa (syncing data or configuration from the NDT to the real network). This imposes multiple requirements for how and what the network exposes through APIs and interfaces support such tight interworking [7].

1. Providing access to internal network states and real time context, which may need to be accessed by an NDT.
2. NDTs may need access to C/U-plane, transport network, or mobility/ handover context, or data to perform their operation. In these cases, the NDTs need access at least to the SBA and to U-plane flows so that they can initialize or sync their operation to events and packets in the real network.

3. NDTs may also need to interact with each other to build more complex solutions (such as a first NDT acting as an analytics engine on top of the real time data it ingests from the network, and a second NDT consuming the analytics output to perform decisions or actions related to the real network). Inter-NDT interaction however cannot go fully through the SBA as the nature and scope of inter-NDT interactions are beyond the scope of the network's own C-plane.

4. Provide means for the integration between the network (including its NDTs) and an external DT (that is, a digital twin outside of the network). In a network-DT interaction, the DT should not have direct access to each NDT that is attached to the network, similarly to an external untrusted AF not having direct access to the SBA of the network's C-plane but having to go through the NEF. Also, depending on the nature and requirements of the external DT, the functionalities (provided by the NDTs) may need to be filtered or customized considering the identity, role, and authorization of the external DT.

This section provides taxonomy, architecture, and related methods to enable the integration of NDTs with networks on various levels, including management plane, control plane, and user plane. The scope of an NDT may comprise, e.g., e2e network or services; a domain such as RAN, transport network, core, cloud; or any other technological or administrative domain. Additionally, it provides the means for multiple NDTs to interwork with each other to create more complex capabilities than what is efficient with a single NDT instance. Finally, it provides a means to exchange capabilities implemented by (one or more) NDTs with capabilities implemented by external (nonnetwork) DTs and vice versa to facilitate NDT-DT interworking. The service-based NDT integration architecture is shown in Figure 13.10.

The NDTs may implement use cases, capabilities, functionalities, and roles that may be mapped to specific planes such as U/C/M-plane. In that regard, a novel taxonomy is proposed for NDTs that classifies them as *NDT-M*, *NDT-C,* and *NDT-U* [7], and gives their interaction points with the network and with each other.

- *Taxonomy*: NDT-Ms implement advanced planning, management, optimization, recommendation, validation, and other analytics use cases, utilizing the data and capabilities of the network, its services and its management layer. NDT-Ms may support advanced decision-making by what-if analytics, configuration validation, parameter search and optimization, and other planning/ management/

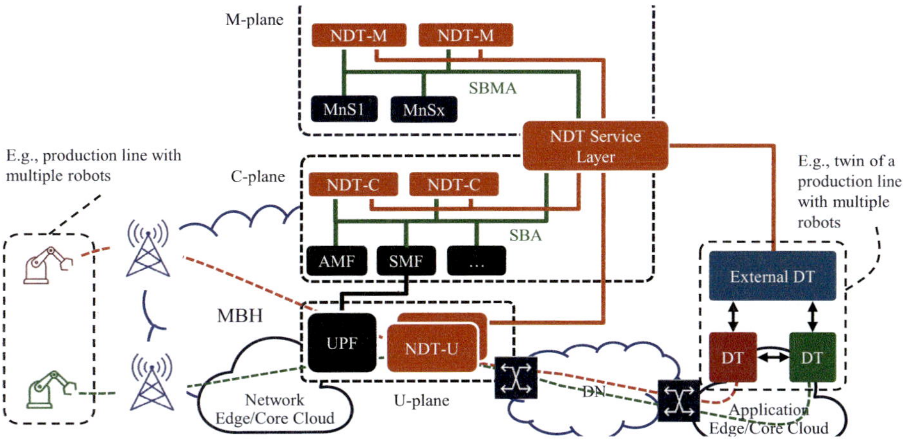

Figure 13.10 The different types of NDTs in the proposed taxonomy and their integration with the network, with each other and with external DTs.

optimization capabilities that utilize real data, real topology information, or real configuration from the twinned network to initialize or drive its twin capabilities.

- *Integration point*: NDT-Ms may integrate with the network on the M-plane attaching to the SBMA, acting as MnS, but also having NDT-specific interfaces between NDT-M instances (e.g., where NDT-M's output is consumed by another NDT-M such as in case of multistep analytics pipelines). The inter-NDT-M interactions may be out of scope of standardization (e.g., part of a single-vendor delivery) and therefore not going through the SBMA and MnS framework.

In the ZSM architecture, an NDT-M may be mapped to the end-to-end service management domain, or to other management domains.

- *Taxonomy*: NDT-Cs implement use cases that exercise control over (parts of) the network according to the use case they implement. An NDT-C may be a model of (part of) a C-plane NF, reusing part of the twinned NF and/or being initialized with the internal state of the twinned NF, with NDT-specific functionality to implement the control logic. For example, an NDT-C may simulate various future or expected user mobility patterns and demand distributions modeling future events, generate relevant policies for the network, and provisioning them to the PCF. The power of NDT-C specifically (instead of any analytics tool) is the NDT-C's ability to accurately evaluate the network's response to future (predicted) demands as well as the network's behavior given the policies generated by the NDT-C. The best policies are then ready for ingestion by the network, which could be done directly by the NDT-C.

- *Integration point*: The NDT-C may integrate with the network via the SBA to leverage data and control available on the C-plane, that is, by partly acting as a C-plane NF. The NDT-C may twin and extend control functions related to FWA, non-3GPP access (such as Wi-Fi), as well as 3GPP domains such as RAN and core, or clouds. Similarly to the NDT-M, NDT-Cs may also interact with each other outside of the SBA for communication that is out of scope for C-plane NFs.

In the ZSM architecture, an NDT-C may be mapped to a management domain.

- *Taxonomy*: NDT-Us implement use cases that are based on extending the behavior of in-line U-plane NFs while maintaining visibility to the real U-plane packets. E.g., an NDT-U may be a virtual clone of a real UPF instance, initialized with the same configuration and internal state as the original one, but having extended capabilities that cannot be present in the original UPF instance (e.g., evaluation of multiple U-plane actions in parallel, based on the real packet level traffic handled by the original UPF, but operating at a time scale slower than real time, due to having no immediate packet handling responsibility). The original UPF must keep operating at real time, whereas the NDT-U, starting from the same initial state and configuration, can afford to take extra time to train or fine-tune ML models driven with the local traffic of the original UPF and evaluate a richer set of hypothetical UPF actions based on its twinned or modeled behavior. Based on the evaluated actions, the behavior of the original UPF may be updated (via twin-to-real sync) to handle U-plane flows better (according to the metrics used by the NDT-U's evaluation algorithm).
- Integration point: Deployed as in-line functions (such as probes or U-plane NFs) that enable both packet-level traffic insight and packet manipulation; or deployed having indirect access (e.g., via port mirroring) to a copy of the in-line traffic (of part of it), which enables read-only packet insight collection (without direct packet manipulation). NDT-U may twin and extend U-plane capabilities in, e.g., RAN, transport network, core, or cloud domains.

In addition to be integrated with the network according to the above integration points, the NDTs may collaborate with DTs from other industries, such as robot DTs, production line DTs, or any other DTs that are twinning a networked physical entity (such as a cloud-controlled robot) or a logical process coordinating networked physical entities. The collaboration between the NDTs and the external DTs may be performed through an NDT service layer, rather than directly connecting the potentially multiple NDTs (each with a different use case and capability) to each external NT. The NDT service layer has two main roles:

1. The NDT service layer provides authentication and access control in front of the NDT capabilities to protect the NDTs (and the network) from uncoordinated access attempts.
2. The NDT service layer acts as a single API gateway that tailors its exposed NDT-based services to the identity, role, and authorization of each external DTs.

As the NDT service layer hides the internal NDT architecture from external DTs and exposes only the functionality that is necessary for specific needs of external DTs, it provides an easy one-stop integration of the network into a mixture of other technologies (e.g., into an industrial automation technology landscape with its own business and technology processes). New NDTs may be created, or new capabilities/use cases may be added to existing NDTs transparently to external DTs.

In addition to the integration of NDTs and external DTs, the NDT service layer may also act as an integration point between different types of NDTs, such as between NDT-M and NDT-C, NDT-M and NDT-U, or NDT-C and NDT-U. This type of indirect cross-NDT integration enables to compose a complex NDT-(M/C/U)-based service from multiple NDT-(M/C/U) instances and offer it as a logically single NDT-(M/C/U) to other types of NDTs.

The scope of the collaboration between NDTs and external DTs may be mutual adaptation and interworking between the network and twinned entities or their DTs.

- On the one hand, the network may adapt its telecommunication service to the exact requirements of the twinned entities. Adaptation to the exact requirements is critical in case the requirements include determinism, such as time sensitivity, high reliability, and predictability (that is, dependability on the fulfillment of service requirements not only momentarily but during the lifetime of critical workflows or operations). Determinism is a requirement that is prominently present in industrial private networks, but it is also relevant in other areas such as distributed real-time audio/video production requiring high synchronicity or group communication between physical entities coordinating a collaborative task (e.g., robots moving in 2D or 3D). In order to adapt the communication services to the exact needs of these use cases, especially in a predictable manner, the network may use its NDTs to carry out the necessary (predictive) analytics and decision process that yield the (re)configuration of network resources and services, via the M/C-plane service-based architecture integration.

- One the other hand, the twinned entities or their DTs may also adapt their behavior to the capabilities of the network, e.g., by selecting a synchronization frequency or a physical motion speed that can be safely maintained through the level or service provided by the network.
- Collaboration between NDT and other DTs may also be a federation of solving an end-to-end industrial process automation task that has complex responsibilities distributed across communication endpoints (and their controllers), the networking itself (via communication and mobility requirements), and other business solution components that are outside of the network's reach or the NDT's reach. In this case, interworking results in a service-based communication between NDTs and DTs where each (N)DT may use the other (N)DT's offered capabilities (data, analytics, or predictions) to leverage for optimizing its own operation.

Figure 13.11 illustrates the sequence of the NDT service layer acting as a single integration point between external DTs and multiple NDTs. First, the NDTs register themselves at the NDT service layer with their available APIs. An external DT may query the NDT service layer for the available APIs, by providing its identity, role, and authorization. Based on this information, the NDT service layer may compose and expose a specialized API toward the external DT, which consists of selected APIs from multiple NDTs. The identity of the NDTs and the source of the APIs are not disclosed to the external DT. Importantly, the API endpoints associated with the offered API methods are terminated by the NDT service layer, not by the original NDTs. The external DT may call the offered API methods at the endpoints at the NDT service layer, which relays the requests to the corresponding NDT, and provides the response back to the external DT.

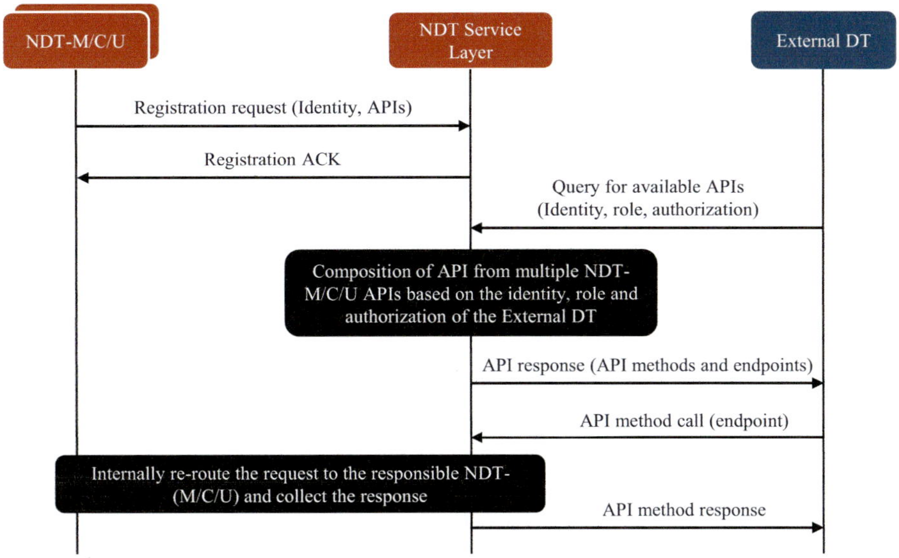

Figure 13.11 Exposure of multiple NDT-(M/C/U) services to external DTs via the NDT service layer.

13.4 Modeling and Composition

One of the principles formulated by ZSM for NDTs is that they should be use case-specific, given that the input and output of the NDT, the data, the models, and other artifacts incorporated by the NDT all depend on the use case [7]. Therefore, the diversity of NDT use cases drives the diversity of the models used or owned by the NDTs. It also increases the complexity of designing an NDT, that is, the composition process that needs to select the right inputs and models, and combine them into an interworking system to produce the NDT for a use case. The selection and combination of inputs and models together is a contextualization process, as the models need to be adapted (e.g., fine-tuned) to the actual physical network for which the NDT is created, rather than simply using a pretrained model as-is.

In addition to the complexity of composing a use case-specific NDT, integrating that into a specific physical network drives a different type of complexity: the complexity of composition between the NDT and the physical network, and the complexity of runtime contextualization. The composition between the NDT and the physical network means to identify and configure those adaptors (such as data sources, action interfaces) that make the NDT able to source or deliver its input/output within the particular physical

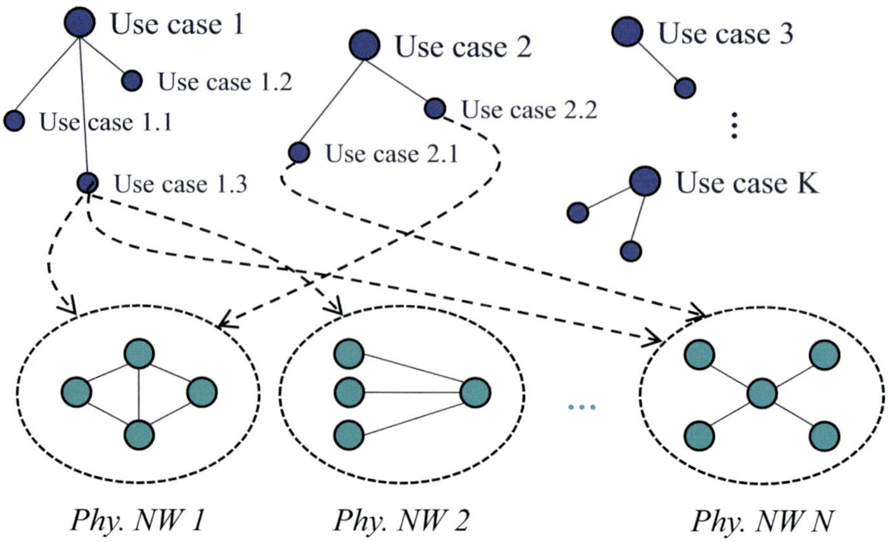

Figure 13.12 Sources of NDT complexity.

network. This is needed given that the same information may be exposed in different network deployments through different mechanisms, e.g., due to the difference in the network management system, databases, protocols, and solutions for access control. As a result of the composition between the NDT and the physical network, the NDT becomes capable of receiving data from the network, process, and analyze them, generate its output, and synchronize it back to the network (if that is part of the NDT's operation and use case). The runtime contextualization happens within the NDT (or within the models owned by the NDT) and it is a continuous process that takes place during the lifetime of the NDT instance. Runtime contextualization means to adjust the NDT (and its models) internally to match it with the dynamic changes and evolution that happens within the physical network so that the NDT's models remain relevant to the network. This reflects but also extends another principle formulated by ZSM for NDTs stating that an NDT is aware of the dynamic changes of the physical twin environment [7].

The different types of complexity involved in creating and operating an NDT in the context of a physical network are illustrated in Figure 13.12.

The diversity of NDT models is further illustrated in Figure 13.13 through an example of model taxonomy. The two main branches of models could be indicated as "descriptive" models and "functional" models. The descriptive models represent data, information, or knowledge about the modeled entity, using a data model or schema. Such models do not produce

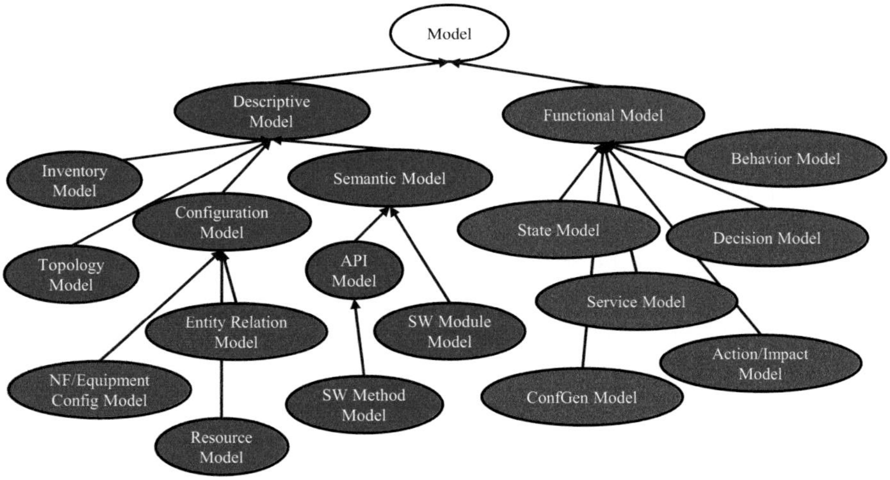

Figure 13.13 Example modeling taxonomy for NDTs.

an action or outcome that requires computation (i.e., does not perform an inference or prediction). The interaction with the model is mainly through queries requesting data, or updating the data to be represented by the model. The functional models represent a dynamic state, process, or functionality in the network, including all the required context and environment aspects that influence the modeled entity. Functional models may compute predictions as a response to hypothetical input, context, or environmental data. While doing so, they may or may not depend on a descriptive model to represent information about the modeled entity.

Within the two main model categories, many other, increasingly specialized model types may be represented. Models that represent static or semidynamic information, attributes and relations, such as the inventory of the devices, the network topology, various configurations, resources, and the semantic models themselves are considered descriptive models in this example taxonomy. For example, under the semantic model category, one can find the models for those entities that constituted the parts of the full API models introduced in Section 11.2. In another example, entity relation models capture important logical grouping and associations between different types of network elements, such as a RAN node and its CN control plane counterpart (e.g., a gNB and an AMF connected via the N2 interface) or a RAN node and its CN U-plane counterpart that participate in the service of the same PDU session (e.g., a gNB CU-UP and a UPF connected via the N3 interface) [12]. Knowing such relations is important to enable the contextualization and analysis of data that is collected from different parts of the network (e.g., network performance measurements or QoS insights sourced from the RAN and the core via different raw data collection systems have to be correlated to formulate an e2e view of the network and service performance, and knowing the relations between the RAN and CN entities is essential to establish such correlations efficiently).

Models that abstract or mimic a dynamic capability, events, or transitions of the network do belong to the other main model category: functional models. State models and behavior models, already encountered in the context of NDTs, capture dynamic changes (state models) and potential responses from the network (behavior model), which make such models capable of delivering a prediction related to what would happen and how the network would react to such changes given evolving conditions in the network operation. When they are modulated with or split along descriptive models, such as topology or configuration models, they become capable of evaluating the impact of hypothetical configurations or changes in the topology, driving what-if analysis which is one of the most coveted capabilities of NDTs. In principle, models may be even generative, such as the example ConfGen model that may produce alternative network configurations suitable for specific hypothetical scenarios, such as an expected future load, demand distribution, or resource situation.

Due to the complexity of NDTs driven by the diversity of use cases and models, there is a risk to think of individual NDTs as independent systems with their own lifecycle, infrastructure, and resources. Such an approach, however, would result in NDT silos that contain a dedicated instance of every instrument, from data collection to modeling, with the involved network and infrastructure resources, that are needed to produce and operate the NDT. Figure 13.14 (a) shows this stage, where not only two NDTs are constructed fully independently, but also their constituent models are trained and maintained independently, even though there are potential synergies both at the models and at the data collection front. Such implementation is inefficient as it results in double design (i.e., designing and training Model A twice) and triple data collection overhead (collection of the same data that is used for both instances of Model A and for Model A'). A better but still not perfect situation is indicated by Figure 13.14 (b) where the synergies in data collection are leveraged, however, the modeling overhead is still kept as each NDT exclusively owns (that is, trains and manages) all models that it uses. Creating and sharing reusable models between NDTs and only owning (thus exclusively producing) models by NDTs that are specific to their use case is represented as the last step in Figure 13.14 (c). In this case, Model A is not

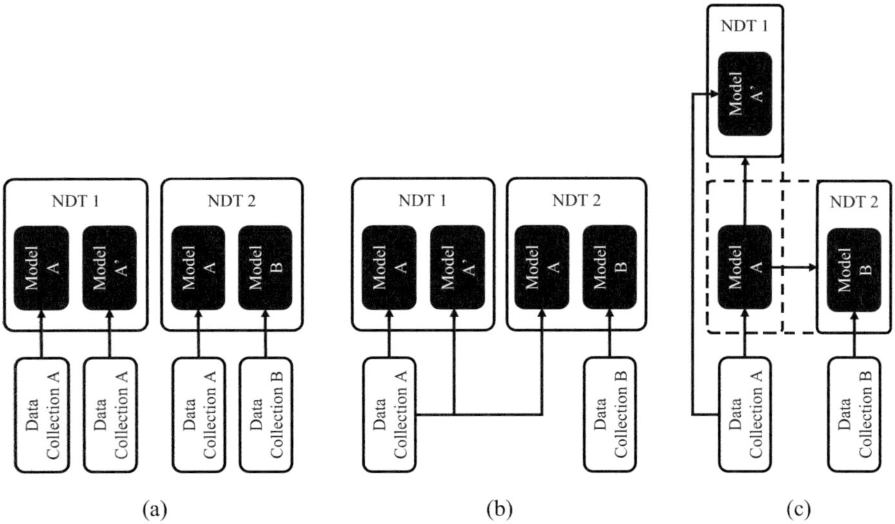

Figure 13.14 Illustration of reusing data collection and models for building different NDTs.

owned exclusively by any of the NDTs but rather belongs to the category of models to support NDTs (and that was associated with the network rather than with any of the NDT instances in the architecture vision of Figure 13.9). Such models may be provided as a service, according to the discussion in Section 4.5. The setup of Figure 13.14 (c) also maximizes the synergies in terms of data collection for different models (Model A and Model A').

Breaking the NDT silos is not only important for resource efficiency but also for business scalability. The latter refers to the effort required to transfer a use case NDT that was already successfully implemented in one physical network and environment to another one, where either the same use case needs to be provided but on a slightly different basis in terms of physical network and environment, or a slightly different (but business-wise still very closely related) use case needs to be provided. In both cases, the challenge is how to reuse as much as possible from the already implemented NDT, including its models if possible, and only build new models or adapt existing ones to the new scenario as little as needed. If only the physical environment changes but the use case stays the same, there is a runtime contextualization challenge that requires model integration and adaptation (but probably no new model). For example, if an NDT of a private network supports the production at one manufacturing site of a company, and the NDT needs to be transferred to a second manufacturing site for the same company, the network environments at the two sites are probably different;

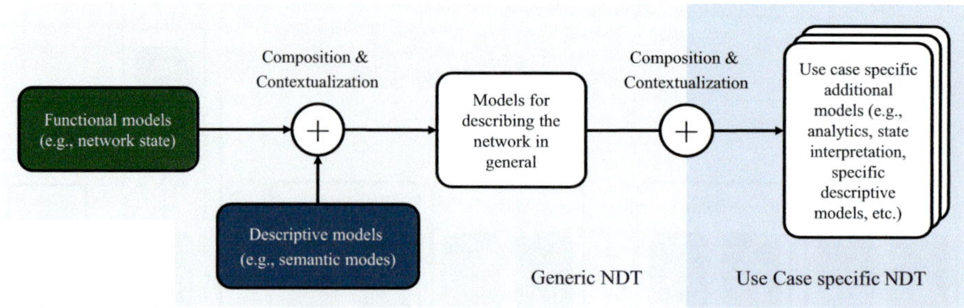

Figure 13.15 Model reusability for efficient NDT engineering.

however, the available data types and integration points toward both the network and the business processes are the same. If, however, the use case itself evolves (while the physical environment might even stay the same, e.g., by remaining at the same private network of the first manufacturing site), or the NDT needs to be transferred to an adjacent business where the data and integration points are semantically different, there is likely a need for training and including new models in the NDT (thereby creating a new version of the NDT as well).

Generalizing NDTs to be applicable for multiple use cases (rather than creating a full separate NDT silos per use case) requires the integration of both reusable models (providing generic common network modeling capabilities) and specialized models (built exclusively for the use case), as illustrated in Figure 13.15. The combination (composition and contextualization) of multiple descriptive and functional models may create a basis of models that are generally applicable for a network in terms of producing its network states or capturing its APIs. Those are then leveraged toward a specific purpose by applying additional models (such as use case-specific interpretation of the same network states, or use case-specific control of the same APIs), thus creating a use case-specific NDT as a composition of the generic models and the use case-specific models. The rest of the section explores the concept of composition and contextualization in more details.

13.4.1 Composition and contextualization

After reviewing the general concepts around the relation of models, NDTs and use cases, this subsection focuses on technical enablers for automating the composition of NDTs and their integration with the actual physical network they are representing.

In the context of NDTs, composition means the automated selection of the right models that have the combined capability of providing the functionalities defined by the NDT use case at the expected level of replication, simplification, and synthetization. Composition enables to create a use case-specific NDT and to adapt the NDT's functionality to the real physical network (e.g., identification of the right interfaces for data collection to sync between the network and the NDT).

Another central term related to NDT composition is contextualization. Contextualization means adaptation to a local context, whether that is the set of available capabilities, services, and models from which the NDT could be composed; or resources and interfaces of the physical network; or potential conflicts caused by other NDTs, services, management actions, or policies established in the network. Accordingly, contextualization is involved at multiple stages during the lifecycle of an NDT: starting with the formulation of the need that could be fulfilled by an NDT; through the composition of the NDT; up to and including the runtime deployment, execution, and operation of the composed NDT. These three stages of contextualization could be conceptualized as follows:

1. Intent contextualization: identifying the need for an NDT (e.g., triggered by an intent defining a use case or capability to be fulfilled through an NDT). Intent contextualization matches the need (intent's objective) with the network's capabilities, the network-owned models that are created for supporting NDTs, and the potential NDTs and use case-specific models. The intent contextualization is resulting in one or more potential composition(s) of NDT(s).
2. Composition contextualization of (or within) the composition itself: identification of all required synchronization points, APIs, and interfaces (both data and action-wise) between the physical network and the NDT. Based on the synchronization points and their capabilities, the nonfunctional requirements such as data availability, quality, load, latencies, resources, etc. are considered. Static de-conflicting such as detection of resource unavailability happens in this stage as well. The output of composition contextualization is the "best" (such as most resource efficient or least conflicting) composition inherited from the previous contextualization stage.
3. Runtime contextualization within the composed models and closed loops internal to the NDT: models and autonomous logic owned by the NDT may be fine-tuned or adapted to the actual data that is sourced

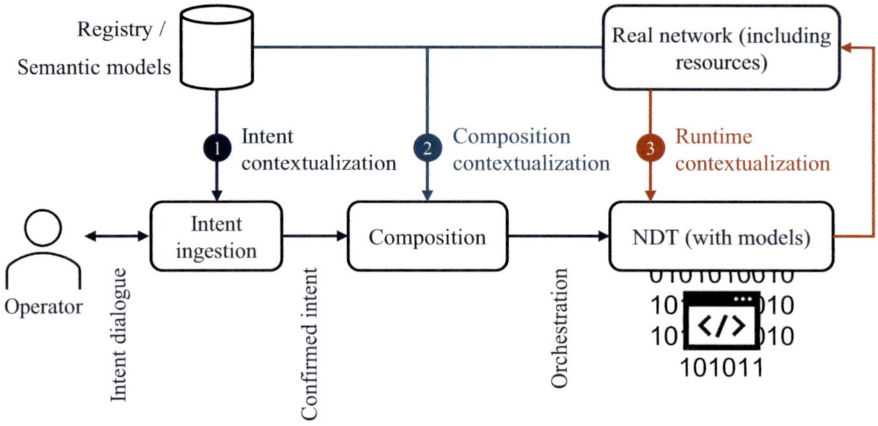

Figure 13.16 Composition and contextualization.

from the physical network on which the NDT operates. Depending on the NDT use case, runtime contextualization may be a continuous activity that takes place until the NDT is terminated (e.g., if the NDT has to follow the evolution of the network states, new states need to be automatically incorporated to the NDT's logic). For NDTs that do not need to keep in sync with the network after their inception (e.g., they operate on hypothetical future scenarios seeded from the physical reality), long-term runtime contextualization may not be important.

The different stages of contextualization and their relation with the NDT's lifecycle and composition are shown in Figure 13.16.

In the context of the NDT general architecture depicted earlier in Figure 13.9, the contextualization stages and the intent-based composition are represented in Figure 13.17. The integration between the components of the composed NDT, as well as between the NDT and the physical network, are through a service-based deployment architecture, according to the principles presented in Section 13.3.1. Note that for the sake of simplicity, the NDT service layer is omitted from this view; however, it could also be part of the integration between the NDT and the physical network.

13.4.2 Intent-based semantic NDT composition

Composing NDTs based on intents fits into the general concept and technology of intent-based semantic composition. The subject of the composition, as discussed in Chapter 11, may be any software module, data, AI model, or

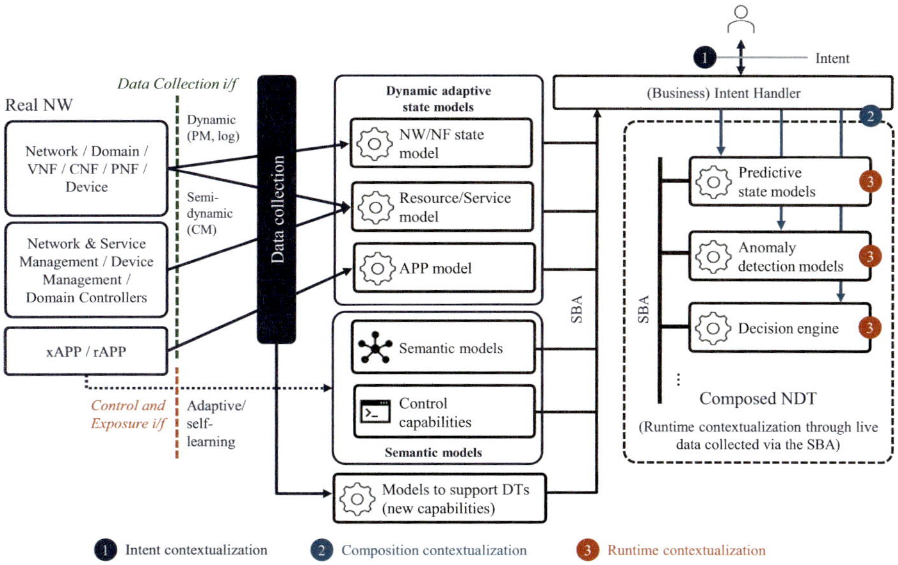

Figure 13.17 Composition and runtime contextualization within the NDT architecture.

other asset that can be represented within a semantic model. The semantic model enables the automatic discovery of all potential interworking points between the components, as well as the matching between the semantic of the intent and the right components that need to be included in the composition. Therefore, intent-based semantic NDT composition is possible with the same semantic framework that was established in Chapter 11.

The intent owners may bring different views and requirements; they may have various roles and represent different organizations, as illustrated in Figure 13.18. The illustration naturally rhymes to Figure 6.2 from Section 6.2 where intent-based network automation was introduced and discussed, with the extension of intents over capabilities provided through NDTs. This also improves the level of integration between NDTs and between telecommunication systems and enterprise/industrial environments.

Regardless of the origin of the intent, the intent handler of the network preforms the contextualization and composition steps that produce the set of services and capabilities required to fulfill the intent. An advantage of composable NDTs is that composition can universally treat NDT-specific components (such as models, software modules, or even data sources) and non-NDT-specific ones such as network applications, management services, network functions, etc. This mixed scope is shown in Figure 13.19, with a remark that an intent that would result in the composition of an NDT may be

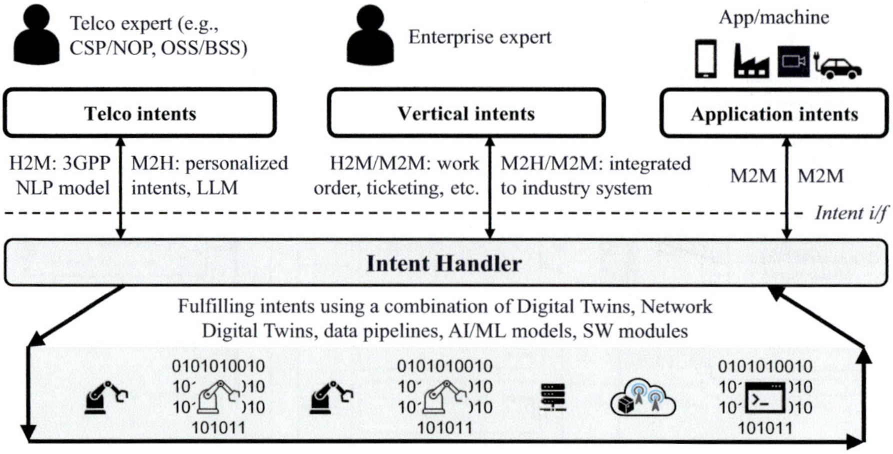

Figure 13.18 Intent-based NDT composition architecture.

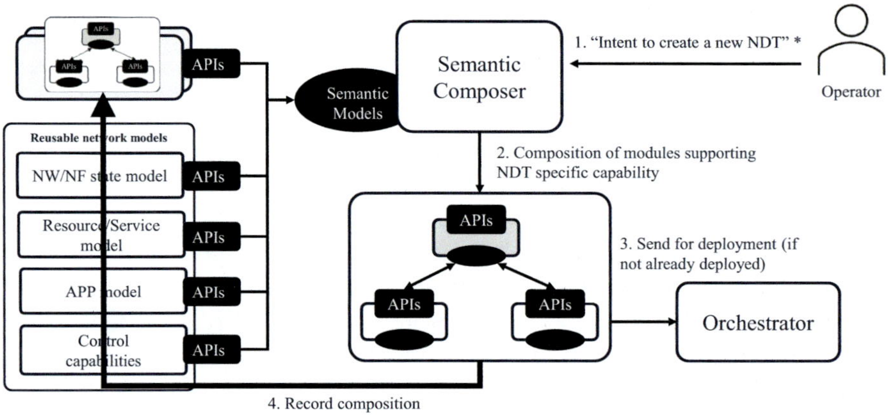

Figure 13.19 Intent-based NDT composition method (compose to create an NDT).

only a "dry-run" to check the feasibility of a composition rather than acting out the composition by contextualizing and deploying it. This hypothetical composition capability can be considered as the digital twin of a real composition that can be used as a what-if analysis for evaluating potential compositions without actually delivering them.

The result of an NDT composition may be stored and promoted to become a composable component on its own. This means that subsequent composition processes may utilize the previously composed NDT as a

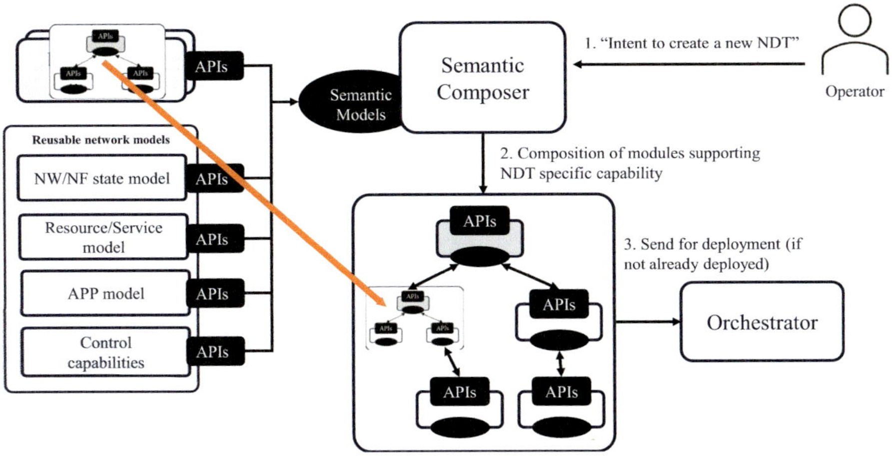

Figure 13.20 Intent-based NDT composition method (compose by reusing an NDT).

logically single component that provides its own capabilities, along with the dependencies, input, and output, as discussed in the topic of semantic modeling (Section 11.2). The reuse of a previously composed NDT as a standalone component in the next composition is illustrated in Figure 13.20, which further evolves the example scenario displayed in Figure 13.19.

The deployment of an NDT composition, i.e., going from virtual blueprint to a deployed system of software modules is illustrated in Figure 13.21. The figure shows the practical impact of physical function placement and scaling versus the initial logical composition, e.g., component #4 is running in two instances deployed at two different cloud locations. These decisions are delegated to the orchestrator (note their presence in Figure 13.19 and Figure 13.20), along with the responsibility to maintain the software instances according to the relevant high availability, redundancy, and computational performance requirements.

Figure 13.21 also illustrates that some of the composed software modules may be inserted into the U-plane as they have a role that requires access to traffic. Such modules may perform dedicated measurements based on packet flow observations that are not present in a standard system, and therefore require the use of purpose-made modules (similarly to network probes), or may act as traffic sources themselves (e.g., by means of active measurements, see Section 12.2.1). Other software modules provide control or management type of capabilities, such as analytics, prediction, or closed-loop automation via actions executed by integrating with the already present network controllers.

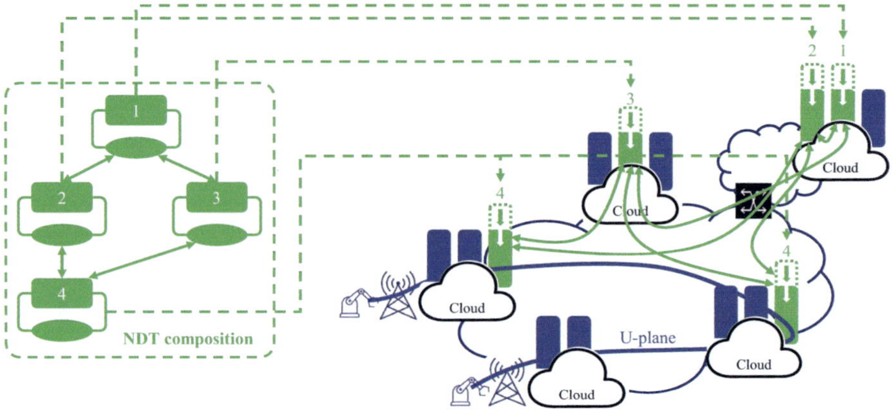

Figure 13.21 Distributed deployment of an NDT composition.

13.5 Enterprise

The digital transformation and automation of industries, characterized by Industry 4.0, has the potential to exploit synergies across multiple technologies that have their own history of evolution, such as digital twins, 5G, private networks, and network digital twins. Out of these four areas, digital twins have been driven by the manufacturing and production industry itself [1], [2], and were adopted and transformed for networks by the telecommunication industry [4]. Although DTs and NDTs may exist separately in their own technological and business domains, there are scenarios where they may become connected as part of the same system and thus exploit the benefits of interworking. Such scenarios are when 5G is deployed as a private network solution [13], to help factory and process automation [14].

Industrial private networks have the scope to provide services to support the enterprise business and technical processes, such as motion control, mobile robotics, sensor data collection, AR/VR, closed-loop process control, and monitoring and asset management [14]. As the integrity of industrial processes traditionally depend on wire-grade communication between the assets, industrial private 5G networks have to support stringent and unique requirements (not present in commercial public CSP networks) related to quality of service, such as deterministic services, time synchronization, and reliability [14]. Such stringent requirements could only be provided through tight control loops in the 5G network and service assurance, based on real time awareness of both the network status (current and predicted), potential conflicts in resources, availability of mitigation actions, and fully autonomous operation

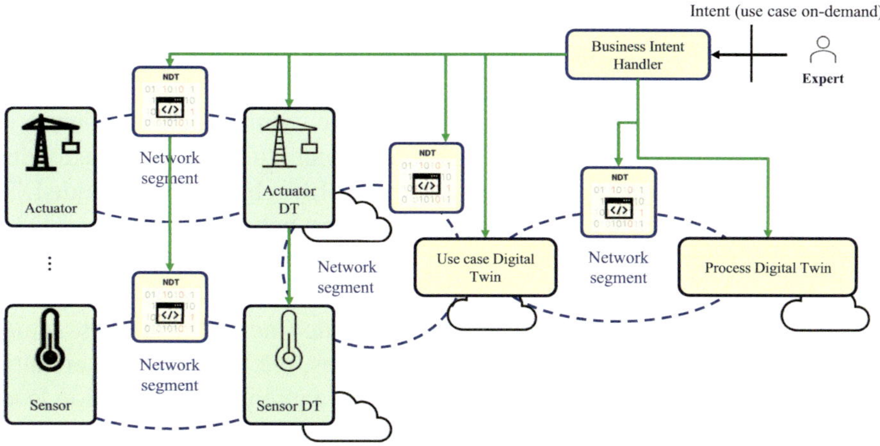

Figure 13.22 System view: network of DTs and NDTs.

of network, and service management mechanisms. As discussed earlier, one of the primary use cases for NDTs is to improve network automation by providing a fully network-situational aware, data-driven virtual engine equipped with analytics and decision capabilities that maintains relevance with the physical network (Section 13.2.1). Therefore, NDTs are well positioned to support high level network and service automation in 5G industrial private networks as well.

With NDT added to enterprise networks, it becomes a system of digital twins (Figure 13.22). DTs and NDTs are not independent entities operated in silos (such as being part of an industrial domain with its own IT/OT system, and part of a telco domain with its own separate management system) but entities that could be managed and governed as a converged system. This means that the system does not provide a separate industrial and telco technological interface (or even a separate industrial and telco intent interface) to the private network operator, but a single intent interface that represents the entry point to the converged system and is therefore capable of system-wide assurance of high-level intents (acting across all components, whether industrial or telco origin). Being an industrial network, the intents given to the system may be to fulfill the industrial and operational goals (that existed even before the integration of 5G and NDT into the industrial system), but the means to achieve such objectives is now extended with a mixture of industrial and telecommunication capabilities that are dependent on each other and thus have to be operated in concert. Such intents are referred to as business or vertical intents (see also Figure 13.18), hence the business intent handler component in Figure 13.22 that acts as the intent handler [15] for business intents.

Handling business level intents in a system of DTs and NDTs (as well as the physical assets controlled by the DTs and the twinned physical network) requires that the concepts of composition and contextualization are extended to cover not only NDTs (as discussed in Section 13.4) but to also include DTs and potential interfaces that enable interworking between NDTs and DTs. This means that the semantic modeling of capabilities such as data sources, AI models, controllers, software modules, applications, etc. are not only built for the network side but also for the industrial side (including sensors, actuators, robots and robot controllers, DTs, processes, etc.). Integrated semantic models enable a business intent handler to receive intents at the solution level rather than at the network or communication service level. As composition will operate over all capabilities (including the NDTs and DTs themselves), it will deliver a blueprint of a solution that contains an interoperable mixture of network and industrial components. Practically, such composition can be deployed only if software modules, processes, and interfaces are harmonized and modeled uniformly at the API level. Otherwise, if there are no compatible interfaces between any two components where one is produced by the network side and the other is originating from the industry, the composition itself cannot bridge the semantic gap between network and industry. The composition will fail (in the lack of a capability suitable to assure the intent) or it will only deliver siloed set of networking vs. industrial components with no interworking and thus no real harmonization in between.

In a successful interworking of NDTs and DTs, they may target different scopes internally but leveraging information sourced from the other (i.e., NDT from the DT, and DT from the NDT). The flow of information may of course also be unidirectional, e.g., the NDT providing network insights to the DT and the DT not providing any industrial insight to the NDT, or vice versa – such use cases may also be valid. The NDT's scope may be network and service automation, with insights received from DT used to adapt the service to the (dynamic) needs of the DTs. For example, a DT can inform the NDT about planned manufacturing activities, such as an anticipated order intake or an upcoming initiation of an industrial process. To this, the NDT may react by preparing network resources for a future surge in time-sensitive traffic between the actuators and their controllers. The DT may also inform the NDT about special requirements or SLAs, e.g., the need for multiconnectivity to improve resiliency and robustness for critical communication flows. The DT may receive network insights from the NDT that it can use to optimize the scenario of the physical factory floor, e.g., by planning routes for automated guided vehicles moving goods

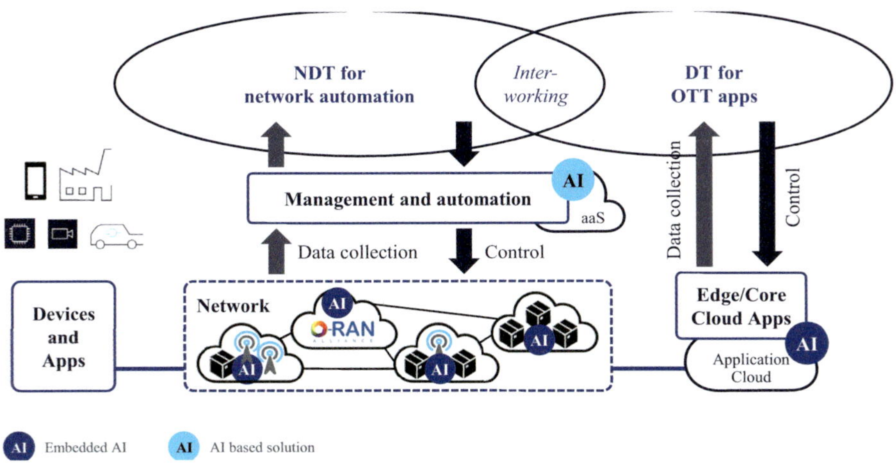

Figure 13.23 Interworking of NDT and DT.

around a warehouse so that they remain under coverage and thus always connected to their virtualized controllers. The DT may also adapt the control process of its physical twin according to the intrinsic latency of the communication link at different locations within the network's coverage, e.g., by falling back to slower physical motion that can be still controlled with the necessary precision within the available latency budget. The idea of interworking between DTs and NDTs is illustrated in Figure 13.23.

Merging the application embedding concept (Section 8.3) with composition and NDT-DT interworking results in a scenario (Figure 13.24) where the intent for composing an NDT is provided by the DT of an industrial process (i.e., an application rather than a human user/operator). The NDT is built according to the composable NDT concept (Section 13.4), and the capabilities of the composed NDT are exposed to the process DT through an API in terms of the application embedding concept (Section 8.3). The interworking between the process DT and the NDT is realized by the process DT consuming the NDT's API (which may also include bidirectional interworking between the DT and the NDT, as the NDT's API may both expose information from the network and receive insight from the DT).

13.6 Summary

A network digital twin is a virtual representation of an operational network that evaluates operationally relevant hypothetical scenarios without disrupting the real (physical) network. NDTs incorporate a variety of functional and

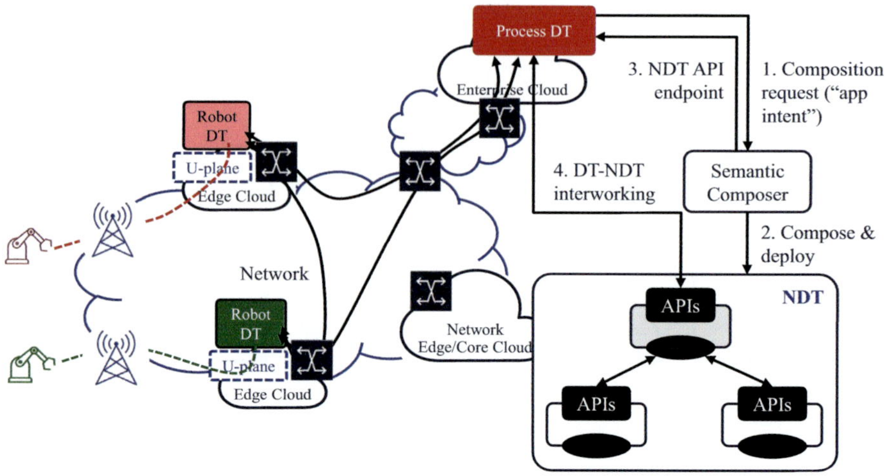

Figure 13.24 NDT composition for enterprise DTs.

descriptive models to abstract and represent both the semistatic configuration and capabilities of the network (e.g., topology, entities, and relations) and its dynamic behavior (e.g., state models) and capabilities (e.g., semantic models). The NDTs maintain a level of synchronization to the real network. At their initialization, they may start from a state that is copied from the real network, and they may remain synced by regular updates from the real network. NDTs may only provide analytical capabilities, or even deliver impact back to the real network, effectively becoming an advanced closed loop attached to the network.

An NDT supports a specific use case such as network and service management automation, what-if or impact analysis of potential decisions before executing them, validation of hypothetical or generated configurations, or even to become a surrogate of a certain real network function to extend it with new experimental or security-related capabilities.

NDTs fuse relevant, accurate, and timely data collected from the real network, its environment, and about the use case. Due to scalability reasons, NDTs are not monolithic entities that reimplement every data processing, modeling, and analytical capability from scratch for every use case. Rather, NDTs are composed from a set of general models that provide reusable abstraction and analytics capabilities, complemented with use case-specific models that are relevant only for the particular use case supported by the NDT. The semantic intent-based composition concept is also applicable to NDTs by modeling the NDT's analytical and automation capabilities similar to that of services. Therefore, NDTs are established as part of the digital assets available for composition to build a closed loop for intents.

As the NDT concept is rooted in the digital twins of the operational/industrial technology, NDTs and DTs can naturally be interworking components of the same system, especially in industrial private networks. In such cases, NDTs support the automation of the entire business procedure by automatically creating (and maintaining) the network communication services required by the industrial components.

Bibliography

[1] B. R. Barricelli, E. Casiraghi and D. Fogli, "A Survey on Digital Twin: Definitions, Characteristics, Applications, and Design Implications," in IEEE Access, vol. 7, pp. 167653–167671, 2019, doi: 10.1109/ACCESS.2019.2953499 3GPP TR 28.867 Study on closed control loop management

[2] S. Olcott, C. Mullen, "Digital Twin Consortium Defines Digital Twin", Digital Twin Consortium, December 3, 2020. https://www.digitaltwin-consortium.org/2020/12/digital-twin-consortium-defines-digital-twin/

[3] M. Sanz Rodrigo, D. Rivera, J. I. Moreno, M. Àlvarez-Campana and D. R. López, "Digital Twins for 5G Networks: A Modeling and Deployment Methodology," in IEEE Access, vol. 11, pp. 38112–38126, 2023, doi: 10.1109/ACCESS.2023.3267548

[4] ITU, "Digital twin network – Requirements and architecture", ITU recommendation, ITU-T Y.3090

[5] C. Zhou et al., "Digital Twin Network: Concepts and Reference Architecture," draft-irtf-nmrg-network-digital-twin-arch-05, 4 March 2024, https://www.ietf.org/archive/id/draft-irtf-nmrg-network-digital-twin-arch-05.txt

[6] TM Forum, "Digital Twin for Decision Intelligence (DT4DI)", IG1307, White paper, IG1307, Version 1.0.0, December 2022

[7] ETSI GR ZSM 015, "Zero-touch network and Service Management (ZSM); Network Digital Twin" V1.1.1 (2024-02)

[8] Digital Twin Consortium, "Digital Twin Consortium Defines Digital Twin", Accessed: 2 July 2024, https://www.digitaltwinconsortium.org/2020/12/digital-twin-consortium-defines-digital-twin/

[9] 3GPP TR 28.915 Study on management aspect of Network Digital Twin

[10] ETSI GS ZSM 018, "Zero-touch network and Service Management (ZSM); Network Digital Twin for enhanced zero-touch network and service management", V1.1.1 (2024-12)

[11] TM Forum, "Autonomous Network Levels Evaluation Methodology", IG1252, Version 1.2.0, June 2023

[12] 3GPP TS 23.501 System architecture for the 5G System (5GS
[13] 5G-ACIA, "5G Non-Public Networks for Industrial Scenarios", 5G-ACIA White Paper, July 2019
[14] 5G-ACIA, "5G for Automation in Industry", 5G-ACIA White Paper, July 2019
[15] ETSI GR ZSM 011, "Zero-touch network and Service Management (ZSM); Intent-driven autonomous networks; Generic aspects" V1.1.1 (2023-02)

14

Summary and Outlook

Network and service management automation and the autonomy of cellular mobile networks are not only key enablers to operate them efficiently and economically at scale, but also to reach new markets through their integration into the end-to-end solutions and systems of relevant vertical industries. Automation is challenging due to the multiple degrees of network and system complexity, such as technological, topological, multidomain and multivendor, that the network operator has to handle. The main technologies adopted to contain the complexity through automation itself, most prominently AI, have led to further complexities. On the one hand, ensuring smooth integration and interworking between traditional telco architectures and AI technologies while maintaining an increasing diversity and density of telco-grade services poses its own technical and engineering tasks. On the other hand, the AI technology pulls in its own open challenges especially in terms of resource and data intensity, and lack of model transparency, leading to security and trust issues when applied in closed-loop automation.

This book explored the megatrends and wireless evolution that has been jointly influencing the development of mobile networks, focusing on the requirements, enablers, and means of network and service automation, covering both technological and standardization aspects. A series of technological deep dives unpacked the details of key technology enablers such as data and knowledge management; native AI and the related management, security, and trust aspects; intent-based management and closed-loop automation with advanced human-network interactions; various modeling technologies to provide networks the necessary cognitive capabilities to interpret their own context, their own capabilities, and to make operational decisions under the governance of intents; and network digital twins, uniting all technologies in a framework of composable and consumable networks.

Having mapped out some of the influential technology trends and enablers for autonomous networks, the question of continuation

DOI: 10.1201/9788770041478-14

naturally emerges. Guidance is available from, among others, the International Telecommunication Union [1], the agency promoting the harmonization of global spectrum usage, technology standards, and regulations to enable worldwide interoperability of telecommunication systems. ITU is a trend-setting organization that formulates vision, requirements, and recommendations toward mobile networks, defining a series of International Mobile Telecommunication (IMT) standards specifying a set of usage scenarios and capabilities expected from conforming technologies, including 3GPP cellular networks. 3GPP is a collaborative effort across vendors, operators, device manufacturers, and other industry partners, developing technical standards for the generations of cellular mobile networks throughout 2G–5G, with 6G standardization already being started. Although 3GPP is not an affiliate of ITU, they work closely to ensure that 3GPP standards maintain parity with the IMT standards of ITU. For example, 5G (starting with 3GPP Release-15) conforms to IMT-2020 [2], which was referred in Chapter 2 as one of the influences shaping the trends on current cellular networks.

Looking forward, ITU has already outlined future technology trends of terrestrial international mobile telecommunications systems toward 2030 and beyond, that is, what would become the IMT-2030 standards [3]. Among the emerging technology trends and enablers, they reconfirmed the priority of several ones that have already been identified and discussed in this book. Among others, these include AI-native networks and proliferation of intelligence; the continuation of network and computing convergence; intent-based network and service management automation; support for digital twin networks and occupying a strong position in vertical industries; privacy, security, and trustworthiness. Therefore, it is expected that the evolution of these technologies will continue in the future, maturing through continuous cycles of research, development, verification, and standardization. Megatrends and technologies emerging outside of the telecommunication industry are also expected to continue their influence on cellular networks and management architectures. Steady trends and expectations, however, may always be disrupted by unpredicted innovations that change the course of technology, products, or entire markets. Therefore, while building on the past and presence of technology gives a strong foundation to understand the ongoing research and development directions, looking into the future remains open and exciting.

Bibliography

[1] International Telecommunication Union, Online, https://www.itu.int

[2] International Telecommunication Union, Radiocommunication Sector, "Detailed specifications of the terrestrial radio interfaces of International Mobile Telecommunications-2020 (IMT-2020)", Recommendation ITU-R M.2150-2, December 2023

[3] International Telecommunication Union, Radiocommunication Sector, "Future technology trends of terrestrial International Mobile Telecommunications systems towards 2030 and beyond", Report ITU-R M.2516-0, November 2022

Index

A

AI native 13, 22, 95, 97–102, 104, 106, 133

Analytics 15, 29, 31, 35, 46, 48–51, 54, 56, 63, 66, 67, 74, 83, 90, 142, 144, 150, 151, 157, 176, 200, 209, 214–216, 229, 245, 246, 248–251, 260, 262, 271, 272, 277, 290, 294, 295, 298, 309, 311, 314

anomaly detection 55, 212, 213, 216, 217, 219, 240

artificial intelligence 27, 54

automation 1–4, 6, 7, 13, 15, 19–21, 27–29, 31–33, 35, 37–42, 46, 47, 63, 70, 71, 73, 74, 79, 95–97, 133, 135, 137–140, 144–146, 148, 151, 152, 155–157, 162–166, 168, 169, 171, 172, 181, 183–185, 189, 190, 194–197, 208, 210, 221, 225, 236, 244, 265, 271, 275, 280–283, 289–293, 297, 298, 307, 309–315, 317, 318

autonomous networks 13, 20, 21, 40, 73, 92, 136, 137, 156, 193, 243, 244, 251, 271, 275, 317

autonomous service 239,

B

big data 56

C

closed loop automation 20, 155

cloud 1, 6, 10, 11, 13, 14, 16–18, 22, 29, 31, 38, 46, 54, 63–65, 83, 97, 133, 163, 171, 215, 221, 223, 227, 239, 240, 251, 294, 296, 297, 309

cloud native 97, 227

conflict resolution 142, 174, 259

contextualization 200, 275, 299–301, 303–307, 312

D

data fusion 32

data lake 55, 56

data management 47–50, 53, 56, 66–69, 79, 97, 102, 106, 133

E

enterprise industries 194

F

federated learning 13, 32, 39, 45, 92, 105–111, 113–116, 118, 124–128, 131, 133

I

intent-based networking 151

intent-driven closed loop 149

intent interface 32, 135, 140, 146, 152, 173–175, 193, 194, 200–204, 235, 311

M

machine learning 55, 58, 62, 80, 82, 96, 105, 110, 111, 197, 207, 216, 248
model integrity 115, 283

N

natural language 12, 32, 140, 146, 193–195, 197–202, 204, 212, 236, 237, 241
network digital twin 15, 31–33, 40, 42, 275–277, 291, 292, 313
network exposure 35
network management 3, 14, 15, 17–19, 21, 29, 32, 34–36, 40, 41, 45–47, 73, 75, 96, 99, 135–137, 142–148, 151, 156–158, 165–168, 172–175, 181, 182, 184, 193–201, 204, 280–283, 290–293, 300
network slicing 280
network state 89, 136, 149, 150, 168, 202, 207–209, 211–213, 215, 219, 221, 260, 279, 283, 291

O

open RAN 38
Operational Efficiency 29

P

programmability 36, 39, 48, 283

R

RAN (radio access networks) 11, 13, 16, 18–20, 27, 34, 35, 38–40, 45–47, 62, 63, 103, 108, 115, 128, 133, 173, 183, 210, 211, 239, 254, 264, 266, 267, 270, 271, 278, 283, 294, 296, 301, 302
RIC (RAN intelligent controller) 38–40, 115, 116, 128, 270, 271

S

SDN 18, 182, 183
self-configuration 3
semantic composition 32, 177, 221, 228, 240, 275, 290, 306
semantic model 177, 204, 226, 237, 301, 307
service-based 10, 18, 29, 35–37, 83, 126, 133, 162, 181, 223, 251, 275, 280, 281, 292–294, 298, 306
service management 1, 2, 5, 14–18, 21, 27, 29, 31, 32, 34, 37, 39, 42, 46, 71, 83, 95, 96, 141, 145, 146, 150, 152, 174, 181, 183, 209, 221, 244, 281, 289, 295, 311, 314, 317, 318
SON 20, 96

T

trustworthiness 71, 73, 74, 81, 93, 318

About the Authors

Csaba Vulkán is a research department head at Nokia Bell Labs. His main research focus is network automation including AI/ML-based network management, intent-based autonomous networks, and network digital twins. Csaba's contribution to the research of human–network interworking done together with Péter Szilágyi led to the Natural Language Networks concept, an AI breakthrough that can reconfigure networks through human speech. His and his team's work on applying machine learning in network management resulted in the Nokia Anomaly Detection Service awarded with 5G World award for the most innovative machine learning software product. During his 25 years of professional career, he has also worked on network dimensioning, network automation and optimization, and quality of experience management for which he has received the Nokia Technology Excellence Award. As a research manager, he is promoting joint innovation with academia, an activity recognized by the Budapest University of Technology and Economics with the Pro Facultate Award.

Csaba has created over 30 patents and coauthored over 30 publications in book chapters, journals, and conferences.

Péter Szilágyi received an M.Sc. degree in Software Engineering from the Budapest University of Technology and Economics (BME), Hungary, in 2009. He is a senior research engineer and Distinguished Member of Technical Staff (DMTS) at Nokia Bell Labs, with a history in telecommunications and software, artificial intelligence, data analytics, 5G and verticals, connected vehicles (V2X), end-to-end system engineering, rapid prototyping, high-profile public presentations and tech demos, intellectual property creation, standardization, and technical management. Péter was researching, prototyping, and validating innovations in real networks for dynamic experience management, user behavior analytics, in-band user plane analytics, multipath content delivery, application awareness, and flow optimization. As a V2X chief architect, he created machine learning-based solutions for connected vehicles, including driver behavior analysis, situational awareness, real-time network communication optimization, and more. His recent works include research and standardization of intent-based networking concepts in 5G/6G for service and network management automation, applying AI for diverse datasets to develop domain-specific language models and semantic representation of software systems.

Péter has coauthored 70 patents and more than 30 publications in book chapters, journals, and conferences. He received the Nokia Technology Excellence Award (2015) and various recognitions as a leading inventor.

Nurit Sprecher is an ETSI Fellow, Head of Network Automation and Exposure at Nokia Standards, Distinguished Member of the Nokia Technical Staff.

A seasoned technology strategist and visionary leader with 30 years of global telecommunications industry experience, specializing in carrier-grade network and service architectures and innovative strategies. Recognized for driving paradigm shifts, adopting transformative technologies, and delivering end-to-end solutions that create societal value and new market opportunities. Regarded as a technology leader in areas such as open RAN, zero-touch network and service/slicing automation, cloudification, edge computing, network exposure, Network as a Platform, packet optical networks, fixed access, mobile backhauling, and technology policy and regulation, serving as a trusted source of knowledge.

Nurit is an author of numerous publications and a key contributor to projects within O-RAN ALLIANCE, ETSI, GSMA, 5G-ACIA, IETF, ITU-T, IEEE, and BBF. Actively engaged in core discussions on next-generation networks and services with Tier-1 carriers and various governments. She is a recipient of multiple industry awards, widely recognized and respected for her expertise and leadership.

Exemplified strong leadership in global standardization bodies as the founding chair of ETSI ISG MEC and vice chair of ETSI ISG ZSM for three consecutive terms. She has driven industry harmonization efforts and established impactful collaborations.

For Product Safety Concerns and Information please contact our
EU representative GPSR@taylorandfrancis.com Taylor & Francis
Verlag GmbH, Kaufingerstraße 24, 80331 München, Germany